AMERICA'S GREAT GUNMAKERS

by
Wayne van Zwoll

STOEGER PUBLISHING COMPANY

Published by Stoeger Publishing Company
55 Ruta Court
South Hackensack, New Jersey 07606

Library of Congress Catalog Card No.: 91-67407

International Standard Book No.: 0-88317-162-7

Manufactured in the United States of America

Distributed to the book trade and to the sporting goods trade by Stoeger Publishing Co., 55 Ruta Court, South Hackensack, New Jersey 07606

In Canada, distributed to the book trade and to the sporting goods trade by Stoeger Canada Ltd., Unit 16/1801 Wentworth St. P.O. Box 445, Whitby, Ontario, L1N 5S4, Canada

FOREWORD

No matter what its product, a manufacturing firm isn't merely a cluster of buildings huddled together inside a fenced perimeter and filled with humming machinery. It is, first and foremost, *people*. It's the men and women each company hires and trains who manage it, who conceive and design its products, who operate and maintain its machinery. People put their unmistakable stamp on a company. They alone determine how it's run, how the quality of its products is kept up and improved, and how they are marketed. The people who work for a company can, quite simply, make or break its reputation.

Armsmakers are no exceptions to this rule. The story of America's gun industry is really the stirring account of the men and women who invented, produced, decorated and promoted the rifles, shotguns and handguns that helped Americans past and present, down their game, win their wars, and fill in the empty spaces that once dominated this great land of ours.

The trouble with writing about people—especially interesting people—is knowing where to draw the line. How much biographical data should be included, which personal details and anecdotes should be retained and which ones excluded? These questions highlight one of the ironies of writing a book like Wayne van Zwoll's. At first, most authors wonder if they'll be able to dig up enough facts to make their book interesting. It isn't long, however, before they realize there is too much material—and then the tailoring process begins. That's one of the most painful chores any writer must face. Once he has created that magical phrase, that ringing sentence, that memorable paragraph, and then whipped them all into shape, the prospect of revamping, shortening or, worst of all, eliminating a section entirely can make even the strongest writer among us inconsolable.

And that's why editors were invented. Being cold-blooded by nature and training, they exhibit no qualms whatsoever about butchering the fruit of somebody else's labors in order to make the author's words fit a given amount of space, or simply agree with the editor's personal tastes. Wayne van Zwoll should know, since his suitably checkered past includes the editing of outdoor magazines—a strange calling for someone who began his adult career armed with a bachelor's degree in agronomy, of all things, and a master's degree in range and wildlife management.

So equipped, he has turned his hand at various professions, including teaching and newspaper reporting. He has also been a range conservationist with the Bureau of Land Management, a wildlife agent with the Washington (State) Department of Game, a contract photographer with the Forest Service, and a field director for the Rocky Mountain Elk Foundation. Now a full-time writer, he works on the staff of *Rifle* magazine and writes articles that appear regularly in *Field & Stream* and other leading outdoor magazines. In between writing assignments, he has hunted in 12 states and several Canadian provinces, plus two memorable African safaris.

In spite of his fairly broad experience afield with rifle and bow, I suspect Wayne would prefer to spend his hunting seasons prowling the high country, alone and on foot, looking for the granddaddy of all mule deer. His first book, *Mastering Mule Deer*, was published by the North American Hunting Club and has done well, I'm told. That comes as no surprise, since Wayne is about as professional a writer as anyone around—and a far better photographer than most. Best of all, as anyone who knows him will attest, he's a genuinely nice guy. That's no small compliment these days.

Al Miller

INTRODUCTION

A gun is a tool, like a rake or a hammer. It's built to do something for you that you can't do as well without it. But when you learn where the gun came from, how it was designed, and the story behind the men who built the company that produced it, you often find hidden treasures. Guns have an allure matched by few other tools (sports cars come to mind). Indeed, the history of armsmaking in America mirrors the history of this great nation. Guns helped men accomplish good things as well as bad. They enabled a few poorly acclimated immigrants to subdue hardy natives and impose on them a foreign culture. With guns, men at once pillaged and pioneered. Guns also helped establish and maintain democracies, win and sustain freedoms.

Some of the men who used those guns have become famous: Davy Crockett, Bill Cody, and Eddie Rickenbacker. Others, including Jesse James and John Dillinger, are infamous. Not all shooters have been men: Annie Oakley and "Plinky" Topperwein performed incredible feats for audiences who applauded fine marksmanship. Those audiences have now been replaced largely by people who don't understand guns, and don't want to. Their goal is to dispose of all guns, on the premise that in order to improve a society one must first disarm it and, through government edicts, protect society from itself.

The entrepreneurs who founded America's gun industry held different views. They were aggressive men, motivated variously by profit, invention, and that peculiar attachment to firearms no one has yet properly explained. They had the spirit, intellect and drive to succeed. Some are still at it. This is their story.

I soon learned that no book can treat with any depth all the gunmakers who have hung a shingle over American soil. Paring the list to the most important few was a strain. Obviously, Colt had to stay, along with Winchester and several other names everybody knows. Their contributions to American history command for them a place. Some old and famous companies were not included—Hawken, for example, which was dropped mainly because it had little lasting impact on the firearms industry. Figuring heavily in the gun design of an era wasn't enough to ensure a berth.

Company longevity and production totals had little to do with my decisions. Newton guns stayed only a short time, but the ideas Charles Newton fostered are with us still. Older companies, some with current telephone listings, have contributed less. Several makers were chosen because they reflected important movements in firearms manufacture; others survived the cut by contributing a significant product or design. Some stayed because their history was colorful, complete with a cast of impetuous characters no work of fiction could equal.

Pulling this material together has been a grueling but stimulating job. I hope you find this book a multi-paned window into the past, each chapter with a view and all chapters together affording a grand picture of America's arms industry. The men and their ideas, their guns and factories, their hardships and fortunes, all have comprised the fiber of a growing United States.

Wayne van Zwoll
Bridgeport WA

ACKNOWLEDGMENTS

A book is a group effort. The author is led by authors who have gone before, and behind him come an editor and publisher to ensure he'll be worth following someday by someone else.

A project like this includes the work of many able authors. In thanking them, I encourage every gun enthusiast to read their books.

Barnes (D.): *A History of Winchester Firearms 1866–1980*. Winchester Press (New Century Publishers, NJ). 1980. 3d ed.

Barnes (F.): *Cartridges of the World*. DBI Books, IL. 1985. 5th ed.

Brdlik (D.): *Standard Catalog of Firearms*. Krause Publications, WI. 1991.

Brophy (W.): *Marlin Firearms*. Stackpole Books, PA. 1989.

Browning (J.) and Gentry (C.): *John M. Browning, American Gunmaker*. Self-published, 1988. 8th ed.

Elliott (B.) and Cobb (J.): *Lefever: Guns of Lasting Fame*. Elliott Pub., TX. 1986.

Fadala (S.): *Great Shooters of the World*. Stoeger Publishing, NJ. 1990.

Grant (E.): *The Colt Armory*. Mowbray Co., RI. 1982.

Greener (W.W.): *The Gun and Its Development*. Bonanza Books, NY. 9th ed. (reproduction of 1910 ed.).

Hatch (A.): *Remington Arms in American History*. Remington Arms Co., NY. 1972 (2d ed.).

Jennings (B.): *Charles Newton, Father of High Velocity*. Self-published (Sheridan, WY). 1985.

Jinks (R.): *History of Smith & Wesson*. Reinfeld Publishing, CA. 9th ed. Also available from Roy Jinks, Willowbrook Enterprises, P.O. Box 2763, Springfield MA.

Johnson (P.H.): *Parker, America's Finest Shotgun*. Bonanza Books, NY. 1961.

Kirkland (K.D.): *Browning*. Brompton Books Corp. (Exeter Books, NY). 1989.

Murray (D.): *The Ninety-Nine* (Savage). Self-published (Westbury NY). 1980.

Sellers (F.): *Sharps Firearms*. Self-published (Alstead NH). 1988. 3d ed.

Williamson (H.): *Winchester, The Gun that Won the West*. A.S. Barnes and Co. NY. 1967. 6th ed.

Wilson (R.L.): *Colt, An American Legend*. Abbeyville Press, NY.

I also thank the gracious people at the various arms companies who supplied me with literature, allowed me to rifle their files, arranged factory tours, and put up with my cameras in the workplace:

Tony Aeschliman (Marlin)
Don and Norma Allen (Dakota)
Eric Brooker and Tim Pancurak (Thompson/Center)
Chet and Mark Brown (Brown Precision)
Linda DeProfio and Martha Woodruff (Ruger)
Dick Dietz (Remington)
Chris Dolnack (Smith & Wesson)
Nolan Jackson (Wichita Arms)
Kenny Jarrett (Jarrett Rifles)
Lynn Johnson (Savage)

Nick Maravell (Winchester)
John Nassif (Colt)
Betty Noonan (Weatherby)
Paul Thompson (Browning)

This project actually began three years ago, when Al Miller, then editor of RIFLE magazine (Wolfe Publishing, Prescott, AZ) accepted my idea for a column on America's armsmakers. The column became successful, prompting Bob Weise of Stoeger to suggest a book. Many long nights later, Bill Jarrett got the job of editing a 150,000-word manuscript while I sorted stacks of photos. I appreciate the work and encouragment of these men. Special thanks go to Bruce Jennings, Bob Elliott and Frank Sellers for permission to supplement my photos with prints from their books.

My wife, Alice, helped with the mechanics of this project. Besides tolerating my foul mood brought on by protracted research, she has steadied me, inspired me, and at times humbled me. *America's Great Gunmakers* is better for her influence.

Wayne van Zwoll
Bridgeport WA

CONTENTS

PART I

TAMING THE FIRE, DIRECTING THE BALL

AN INTRODUCTORY NOTE

Chipping a piece of rock to make a sharp arrowhead is tedious, tiring work. It is also delicate work, because as the implement becomes smaller and more like its planned shape, it becomes more fragile. For a long time, no better tools for hunting and fighting existed, so man went on making arrowheads.

Guns suddenly changed the hunt and battle alike, but the invention of gunpowder did not cause a quick revolution in either. Designing a gun that would fire dependably took many years; and making it portable took years longer. The refinement of powder manufacture and the skillful engineering of effective bullets consumed more than four centuries. Repeating guns that shoot accurately are recent inventions indeed; like an obsidian arrowhead, they are the products of much labor. Gunmaking in America came late in the world history of firearms and by necessity borrowed many ideas from European inventors. In a see-saw fashion, military and sporting markets influenced the direction of American gun development, each benefitting, one from the other.

The first bang from confined powder was like the eruption of a tiny spring high on a mountain. Like a rivulet made mighty by other rivulets, and by the acceleration of its own mass, armsmaking became a giant industry. Part I—"Taming the Fire, Directing the Ball"—is an overview of this evolution.

CHAPTER 1

THE STORY BEHIND THE BANG

Before men thought of making bows with which to launch arrows, they first had to develop the arrow. So it was with the gun, which only initiates and directs a shot. It does not generate energy or inflict damage on a target. Thus, when gunpowder appeared, according to the 13th-century writings of Arab Abd Allah, it wasn't called "gunpowder," because there were as yet no guns. A substance known as "Chinese snow" was used in Roman candles for a couple of centuries before Roger Bacon, an English friar and philosopher, described its composition in 1249. Soon afterward, Berthold Schwarz used this same violent substance to propel things, and by 1314 the first guns were being produced in England. A few years later, in 1327, Edward II put these guns to military use during his invasion of Scotland.

Bacon's gunpowder contained 41.2 percent saltpeter and 29.4 percent each of charcoal and sulphur. French chemists improved the mix in 1338, with corresponding proportions of 50, 25 and 25. Not to be outdone, the English soon revised their formula, and from then on gunpowder varied in content according to use. In 1871, English chemists settled on 75 percent saltpeter, 15 percent charcoal and 10 percent sulphur, a mix that remained the standard for black powder until the development of guncotton in 1846.

Before they established any gun factories, the American colonists built powder mills. The first was at Milton, Massachusetts, a few miles outside Boston. By the beginning of the Revolutionary War, the colonists had manufactured or captured some 40 tons of black powder. Half was promptly sent to Cambridge, where it was wasted before Washington assumed command; and by the end of 1775

it was all gone. At one time, Washington's men maintained a 13-mile perimeter within rifle shot of the British troops, and yet none of these brave Americans had any powder!

During the first few years of the war, the colonists manufactured nearly 50 tons of gunpowder; and by war's end more than 1,000 tons had been procured. Soon after the turn of the century, American mills were producing 750 tons of black powder a year. The step from fireworks to firearms was a long time coming, mostly because igniting powder in a container and then controlling its force proved difficult.

The first guns were heavy pipes of various names and dimensions. Swiss culverins (a type of early musket) required two men to fire them. The culveriner held the iron tube while his assistant, called a gougat, applied the priming charge, then lit it with the smoldering end of a stick or rope. Though awkward, undependable and inaccurate, these culverins became so popular that in 1476, at the battle of Morat, the Swiss mustered 6,000 culveriners. The forerunners of matchlocks, these weapons were eventually lightened so that one man could operate them. But ignition remained a problem. Some barrels were fitted with ax heads, in case the wick or match went out, or the priming failed, or the main charge failed to ignite.

The first trigger mechanism was a crude lever by which a smoldering rope end was lowered into a touchhole in the barrel. This first true lock was equipped with a serpentin (or cock) used for holding the match. Later matchlocks employed a second, stationary wick that was kept burning atop the barrel. The serpentin was eased onto the burning match, then lifted up once its cord caught fire. Mov-

This Italian portable cannon dates from the 14th century. The first recorded gun of this type came from Germany in 1381.

ing the mechanism to one side, the shooter then lowered the glowing match into the touchhole. Eventually, a spring was added to hold the primary match away from the touchhole, and a release mechanism (derived from the crossbow) was applied to the trigger. The result was the 16th-century Spanish arquebus.

The most advanced of all matchlocks to date, the arquebus retained that capricious smoldering wick. To keep the essential fire available, arquebusiers carried slow fuses in perforated metal boxes on their girdles. Even then ignition proved a nuisance, and the rate of fire was much too slow. In the battle of Kuisyingen in 1636, unpracticed soldiers managed as few as seven shots in eight hours! Two years later, at Wittenmergen, musketeers fired only seven times in a battle that lasted four hours.

Early in the 16th century, German inventors devised a new way to make fire. They equipped a gun barrel with a spring-loaded jaw that held a piece of flint. The flint, in turn, rested on a serrated bar, which was movable along the axis of the bore. To fire this "monk's gun," as it was called, the shooter grasped a ring at the rear of the bar and pulled it across the pyrite. As in the matchlock, ignition was carried to the main charge by a fine powder mix that lay in a pan next to the touchhole.

An improvement to this system was made in 1515, when the wheel lock mechanism was developed in Nuremberg. It featured a spring-loaded wheel wound with a spanner wrench and latched under tension by the trigger. Pulling the trigger sent the wheel spinning. Its serrated edge bore against

a spring-loaded pyrite in front of the wheel, showering sparks into the priming pan.

Wheel locks, although comparatively expensive, had several advantages over matchlocks. They were lighter, less affected by weather, less cumbersome to prime, quicker to ready, and easier to aim. Wheel locks were the first firearms to be widely used on horseback, and the first found suited to the use of lead bullets.

Early in the 17th century a new lock was developed, whether in Spain or the Netherlands no one knows. It was called the *Lock a la Miquelet*, named for a Spanish regiment of *miquelitos* (marauders) in the Pyrenees. This mechanism used friction similar to the wheel lock, but reversed the role of steel and pyrite. The Miquelet—or, as it later became known, the flintlock—featured a spring-loaded cock that held in its jaws a chip of flint. When released by the trigger, the cock swung in an arc, striking its flint against a steel pan cover or hammer. The hammer, knocked backward by the blow, exposed a pan primed to receive the sparks. This hammer later became known as the frizzen, and the cock a hammer. Though early flintlocks

The 15th-century petronel held by the soldier (above) was a hand-fired cannon. It was ignited by a wick and steadied with a forked stick.

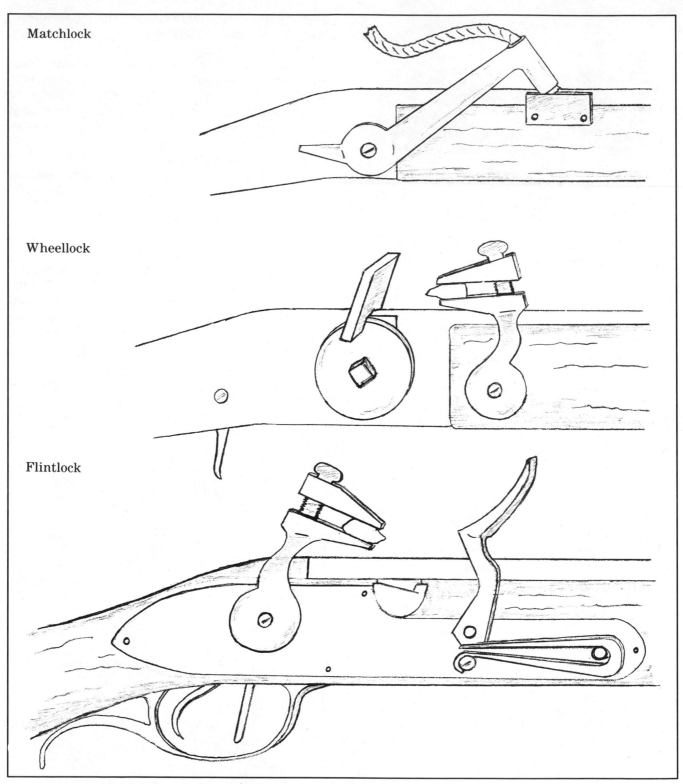

Matchlock

Wheellock

Flintlock

These illustrations represent the three basic firing mechanisms used by early armsmakers: matchlock (top), wheellock (center), and flintlock (bottom).

were crude indeed, those made in colonial America were reliable. At the peak of their development, they became the forerunners of sleek, accurate rifles and svelte, double-barrel shotguns.

The Discovery of Fulminates

The matchlock, wheel lock and flintlock shared one major weakness: in each, the priming mixture was exposed. Furthermore, the source of fire could fail easily. The matchlock's wick could be snuffed out, and a weak or errant shower of sparks in the wheel lock or flintlock might not be enough to ignite the priming. Even if the spark was properly transferred, the priming could still fail to deliver its fire to the main charge in the barrel, causing a "flash in the pan." The only thing that promised sure ignition was a spark generated within the gun. No doubt someone had thought of this while fumbling for his spanner wrench in battle; but not until chemists discovered fulminates would there be such an internal primer.

Fulminates, which are shock-sensitive salts of fulminic acid, or $CNOH$ (an isomer of cyanic acid), were first explored in the early 1700's. While black powder and some nitro compounds can be ignited by percussion between metal surfaces, the resulting explosions are neither as predictable nor as violent as those involving fulminates. Whereas black powder is harder to ignite and leaks its energy slowly, a fulminate ignites readily when struck and immediately releases its stored energy.

In 1774, the chief physician to Louis XV became the first to report on the explosive properties of fulminate of mercury; but no one applied his findings to firearms. Following the work of Antoine Fourcroy in 1785 and Nicolas Louis Vauquelin in 1787, the French chemist Claude Louis Berthollet substituted chlorate of potash for saltpeter in gunpowder. The new mixture was so unstable that it caused two big explosions, almost bringing Berthollet's work to a halt.

In 1799, an Englishman named E. C. Howard combined fulminates of mercury and saltpeter to create a sensitive but manageable substance, called "Howard's powder." Seven years later, a Scotch clergyman, Alexander John Forsythe, used fulminates to create a spark within the combustion chamber of a gun for the first time. And in 1808 Johannes Pauly, a Swiss gunmaker, developed a breech-loading percussion gun using a cartridge with a paper cap affixed to its base. By pulling the trigger, a needle was released, piercing the cap and

detonating the fulminate, which then fired the main charge. The Lefaucheux needle gun derived from Pauly's work.

Over the next several years, inventors rushed to build new ignition devices for guns. Some used loose fulminate, while others wrapped it in paper caps. In 1821, the English firm of Westley Richards developed a percussion gun that could use almost any fulminate primer. The pan cover was forced open by the falling hammer, exposing a cup of priming. The hammer's pointed nose drove into the cup, igniting the fulminate and sending sparks into the touchhole at the cup's base.

Joseph Manton's tube gun, developed three years earlier, employed a tiny cylinder of fulminate held tightly against the touchhole by a spring-loaded catch. When the hammer hit the side of this tube, the fulminate detonated. Breech pressure blew the tube off to the side on firing. Manton's design was also used in the Merrill gun, 14,500 of which were brought by the British government. As percussion ignition gained favor, touchholes were shortened and moved from the side of the barrel to its top. In 1823, an American physician, Dr. Samuel Guthrie, found a way to make pellets of fulminate. More reliable and convenient, these primer pills were used as late as 1851 in Samuel Porter's wheel-chambered repeating rifles and revolvers.

Lots of people have claimed credit for the copper percussion cap. One of the first to use it was Joshua Shaw of Philadelphia, who in 1814 developed a reusable steel cap to hold his priming mixture. Because he was British-born and hadn't yet lived in the United States long enough (two years), Shaw was denied a patent. The next year, he designed a disposable cap of pewter, followed shortly by one made of copper. This led to the hollow nipple, a pivotal development which eventually became a standard feature on percussion muzzleloaders. A few years later, in 1822, Shaw patented a lock to use with his caps.

Between 1812 and 1825, a total of 72 U.S. patents was granted to American inventors for various primers. Many of the percussion caps were weak, causing heavy loads to build up enough breech pressure to fragment them, endangering the shooter. But the more efficient caps prevented the escape of gas through the touchhole and produced much faster ignition than was possible with flintlocks. Indeed, the first fulminates were so quickly consumed they sometimes failed to ignite the main charge; either that, or they started the ball down the bore before the powder could generate any thrust.

A solution to this problem predated the metallic percussion cap. In 1787, when guns were made to accept loose fulminate, an Englishman named Nock designed an antechamber perpendicular to and directly behind the gun's main chamber. The touchhole led to this antechamber. When the fulminate detonated, powder in the antechamber caught fire. It could not be blown forward, because the priming blast was at right angles to the bore. As the powder burned, its flame ignited the main charge through a short passage.

The potential of this early example of percussion ignition went unrecognized by shooters who were well satisfied with the elegant flintlocks of the early 19th century, as well as governments wary of new things simply because they were new. Percussion guns, it was said, kicked harder than flintlocks. That was true enough; but when flintlock shooters claimed the percussion guns wouldn't reach as far or hit as hard, they were wrong.

Even the most learned of gun people resisted the changeover to percussion ignition. Colonel P. Hawker, an English authority on arms during the mid-1800's, wrote: "For killing single shots at wildfowl rapidly flying, and particularly by night, there is not a question in favour of the detonating system, as its trifling inferiority to the flint gun is tenfold repaid by the wonderful accuracy it gives in so readily obeying the eye. But in firing a heavy charge among a large flock of birds the flint has the decided advantage."

William Greener, a British inventor, later noted that the breech-loading gun ". . . cannot be made sufficiently durable to yield any reasonable return for the extra expense and trouble attending their fabrication." A generation later, fulminate primers and breech-loading guns would dominate field and battlefront alike.

Part of the suspicion surrounding caplock firearms had a legitimate basis. Early priming mixtures were so unstable as to be dangerous. They depended on chemical action, not on the visible mechanical strike of flint on steel. Chemistry was still a mystery to most people in 1800, and even the leading chemists of the day could not explain the workings of priming compounds.

Joshua Shaw, the U.S. sea captain (1776–1860), who designed one of the first copper percussion caps, found potassium chlorate too sensitive a priming mix. He later settled on a combination of potassium chlorate, fulminate of mercury, and powdered glass. At age 70, Shaw was given a

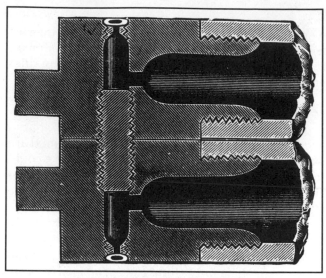

Nock's patent breech featured an antechamber, which prevented the priming blast from starting the ball and impeding ignition of the main charge.

Congressional honorarium for his work. His contemporary, British munitions engineer Charles Eley, did not live to savor the success of his now famous firm. He was blown up while handling priming compound at his factory in 1828.

Loading from the Breech

With the discovery of nitroglycerin in 1846—the same year Shaw received his honorarium—came a pivotal change in propellants, much the same as fulminates had changed firearms ignition. Long before the advent of smokeless powder and the self-contained cartridge, inventors had been thinking about new ways to load guns. Stuffing powder and ball into the barrel from the front end was a logical choice and made gun manufacture relatively easy. But it was a slow, awkward process, difficult to accomplish while lying on one's stomach trying to avoid the enemy. It required lots of movement, too, which spooked game that might otherwise have stayed motionless for a second shot. Loading from the breech was an early dream indeed.

An arquebus found in the Tower of London features a hinged breech block bearing the initials "H.R." and a date of 1537. Presumably owned by King Henry VIII, the gun is thought to be of French manufacture. A German gun of the same era, discovered elsewhere, has a similar mechanism. In each, a removable thimble was filled with the powder charge, then inserted into the breech and held there with a cotter pin (which also secured the stock).

A French gun made in the 17th century had a cylindrical breech plug that dropped when the trigger guard was turned. A charge was loaded into the barrel and the plug raised again for firing. Unfortunately, friction generated by the moving block sometimes ignited the charge prematurely. Wheel locks were fashioned this way, too. In many guns of this type, the chamber was located in the breech plug.

Hinges that allowed the barrel to drop, exposing the bore, came along as early as the 16th century. While a few wheel locks featured hinged breeches, most were developed later for flintlock guns. Some hinges allowed the barrel to move sideways, others vertically. Usually the hinge pin was placed well forward of the hammer mechanism and touchhole, so the breech was loaded from the front instead of the barrel from the rear. Removable thimbles made the loading of loose powder much easier.

In 1776, British Major Patrick Ferguson designed a fixed-barrel carbine with a threaded cylindrical breech plug that one could lower simply by turning the trigger guard. A charge placed in the barrel through the open top of the breech plug hole was sealed by screwing the plug back into place. Ferguson's flintlock rifle was the first breechloader used by regular British troops.

In 1804, a German inventor named Theiss developed a breechloader with a vertically sliding breech block. A button in front of the trigger guard raised the block until it was aligned with the gun's bore. After a charge was inserted, the block was lowered. This mechanism—also a flintlock—leaked lots of gas. Captain John Harris Hall of Maine invented one of the first successful American breechloaders. Its hammer, pan and frizzen rode on a movable breech block, much like the later Martini's, except it opened up instead of down.

During the 19th century, European inventors, including Robert, Pauly, Potet and Lepage, were among the first to design breech-loading guns for cartridges. In 1831, Demondion patented a breechloading gun with a top lever that raised the block, permitting insertion of a paper cartridge and at the same time depressing the mainspring until it caught on the trigger. Lowering the lever put the block behind the cartridge and on top of a primer tube protruding from the cartridge base. Pulling the trigger allowed the mainspring to snap upward against the block, crushing the tube and firing the charge.

Paper cartridges had been used as early as 1586, but there was no priming compound then, and the guns were all loaded from the muzzle. A shooter had to bite or rip off the cartridge base before loading in order to expose the charge to an external spark. As a result, the case was consumed on firing. When percussion caps replaced pyrite as an ignition source, the strong blast from the cap pierced the thin (or perforated) paper, so that loose powder no longer had to be exposed.

In 1835, a needle gun invented earlier by Johann Nikolaus von Dreyse was redesigned as a breechloader. A long striker was used to pierce a paper cartridge and its charge, then crush a fulminate primer at the base of the bullet. With all its faults, this mechanism was superior to other designs of the day. Dreyse was lauded for his work, and some 300,000 of these breechloaders were manufactured for Prussian military service over the next 30 years.

Less successful was Gilbert Smith's hinged-barrel rifle, designed in America but submitted to British ordnance people for testing in 1838. The chamber, which was part of the barrel, accepted a cartridge with a rubber case and perforated cardboard base. A chambered cartridge protruded slightly, but the rubber case was flexible enough to allow the gun to close. A percussion cap on the breech shot sparks through the touchhole and perforated cartridge base. Despite the gasket-like design of this cartridge, it still leaked gas and was abandoned.

During the mid-1800s, several ingenious mechanisms were devised to seal breeches and speed loading. It was hard to do both, given the external ignition and paper cartridges of that time, and the failures were many. Among the few practical designs was the Westley-Richards capping breechloader, adopted by the British as a cavalry arm in 1861 and used in South Africa until the turn of the century. This gun featured a fixed barrel. The top of the standing breech pivoted up to allow access to the chamber. A paper cartridge pushed into the barrel was locked securely by lowering the top, which wedged a "bolt" between breech and barrel face. The capping breechloader was easily converted to a muzzleloader by inserting a metal plug and a couple of wads.

Improving the Cartridge

By this time, inventors were trying hard to develop internal ignition. Lepage's attempt in 1840 to marry a metallic primer to a combustible case failed because the primer and a thick wad used in his process were difficult to remove from the cham-

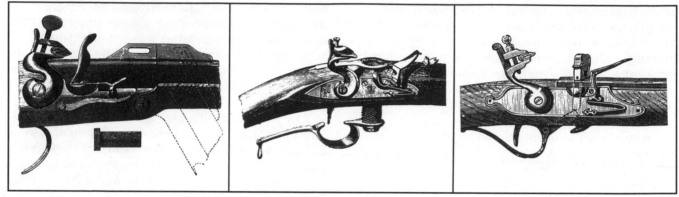

The first breechloaders, all flintlocks, included an Italian gun by Fresca de Borgia in 1694 (above, left); Patrick Fergusson's 1776 design (center); and the Theiss breechloader from Germany in 1804 (above, right).

ber after firing. Another Parisian named Houllier had a better idea. Instead of putting the primer outside the case, he placed a pellet inside. A pin projected up and at right angles to the bore, extending from the priming pellet through the base of the case. When the hammer came down on this pin, it crushed the primer and ignited the charge. Because the case did not have to admit spark from the outside, it could be made of metal. Upon firing, the metal pressed against the sides of the chamber, thereby sealing off any gas leaks. Patented in 1847, Houllier's pin-fire cartridge was soon adapted to M. Lefaucheux's hinged-barrel gun.

The Lefaucheux, developed in the early 1830s as an improvement on the Pauly and Smith mechanisms, was a crude and weak design. The double-barrel model of 1836 had a hinged breech with no ejectors; one simply pulled the cases out by the pins. Lepage's pinfire model featured a sliding breech that wasn't much better. Freed from external ignition, inventors now had to find ways to seal and support movable breech blocks. Breeches that opened were inherently weak. Metal cases helped seal gas but did not materially strengthen lockup; even the relatively mild charges of the day could not be contained.

Thereafter, European guns were built with barrels that pivoted on an axis, to the side, and even on eccentric hinge pins that moved the barrels forward before they dropped. In each case, the aim was to simplify operation and increase action strength. Meanwhile, on America's frontier, the Sharps rifle used linen cartridges and Maynard tape primers that advanced on a roll of paper to an external nipple. Distinctly un-British, the dropping-block Sharps was strong, winning enough royal favor that, by 1855, some 6,500 52-caliber tape-

primed rifles had been sent to England under government contract. [Note: Maynard had introduced in 1851 a cylindrical brass cartridge case with a wide, flat base soldered to one end. The base had a hole in the middle and was designed for use with a tape primer. Maynard tapes were available for only four years, but the principle was later resurrected for use on millions of toy pistols.]

Attempts to develop a self-contained cartridge led inventors to hollow bullets with no cartridge case. In 1847, Stephen Taylor patented a hollow-base bullet with internal powder charge and a perforated end cap that admitted sparks from an outside primer. A year later, Walter Hunt, an inventor from New York, completed work on a similar bullet. His cap was made of cork, and its perforations were covered by paper that could be pierced by the sparks of the external primer. A lever-operated, pill-lock mechanism advanced the primers. A new rifle was designed for Hunt's "rocket ball" ammunition a few years later, spawning the famous Henry repeater, forebear of Winchester's lever-action rifles.

In 1854, Horace Smith and Daniel Baird Wesson, founders of the famed company that still bears their names, designed a metallic case for the Hunt bullet. It looked somewhat like a rimfire case, though the head was flared, not folded. Priming mix was smeared across its entire inside surface. A metal disc inside the case acted as an anvil, so a strike anywhere on the head would ignite the priming. The cartridge proved difficult to make, so Smith, Wesson and B. Tyler Henry redesigned the original rocket ball, incorporating a fulminate-of-mercury primer placed in a glass cup located inside the bullet's hollow base. The cup rested on an iron anvil. A cork base wad contained the propellant, consisting first of fulminate and later of 6½ grains of black powder, and also helped seal the breech upon firing. In repeaters designed by Walter Hunt, the wad (or its residue) was left in the barrel to be expelled by succeeding rounds. Smith and his crew saw that the cork debris caused malfunctions; moreover, primers often misfired because the cork cushioned the striker. Their solution: a copper base cap, which was later changed to brass.

The most promising cartridge design of the 1850's, however, was the .22 Short rimfire introduced by Smith & Wesson in 1858. Its case was manufactured then much as it is now. A disc punched from a sheet of thin metal was drawn into a tube with one closed end. Next, a rim was "bumped" onto that end and the fold filled from inside with fulminate of mercury, which exploded when the striker or hammer smashed the rim against the chamber mouth.

A less successful design came from Major Ambrose Burnside of Civil War fame. His breech-loading rifle was fed by inserting a cartridge in the front of the chamber, back end first. The base of this drawn brass case was smaller than its mouth, to which a conical bullet was attached. A percussion cap fired the round.

The first centerfire cartridge recognized in America was the work of E.H. Martin at the Springfield (Massachusetts) Armory in 1866. This 50-caliber round had a bar anvil—a tinned, iron strut with priming compound at its center that was forced into the case from the mouth and crimped into position just above its head. The striker or hammer would dent the metallic case head, crushing the priming compound against the bar.

About this time in England, the Snider "coiled" cartridge appeared. It had a base made of brass and steel with a body of layered brass foil and paper. In the manufacturing process, these layers were wound about a mandrel, then shellacked and glued to form a cylinder. The inside was coated with shellac to shield it from the corrosive effects of black powder; and a metallic cup primer was placed in the middle of the case head. The Snider was among the first centerfire cartridges developed overseas. Adopted by British Ordnance in 1867, it was replaced in 1871 by the .577/450 Martini-Henry cartridge, which featured thin, pliable brass wrapped around a mandrel, much like the foil of its predecessor.

The coiled case got a poor reception in the U.S. Drawn brass was used as soon as it became available, around 1860. E.H. Martin's stab at centerfire design in 1866 resulted three years later in a patent covering a folded rim. Unlike the Smith and Wesson rimfire case, Martin's had no room for peripheral priming. In 1870, he took out another patent for a double fold. From this came the folded- or balloon-head case with a center pocket for a metallic primer. Cases were later drawn with no seams or folds, yielding first the semi-balloon, then the modern solid-head case. In either case, the base and rim are not crimped. Solid-head cases proved strongest because the web between primer pocket and extractor groove was thicker than in the semi-balloon design.

Priming the Primers

The first folded-head cartridges eliminated the need for an anvil inside the case. Instead, the central primer cup provided its own anvil. An orifice at the base of the primer pocket conducted sparks from primer to powder. Throughout the 1880's, primers based on Shaw's copper cap (but with internal anvils) were used to ignite black powder in metallic cartridges. The evolution of this design resulted in the Boxer primer now commonly used in American centerfire cartridges. It's available in two sizes for rifles and two for handguns. The large and small rifle primers are the same in depth and diameter as the large and small pistol primers, but the amount of priming compound differs. A large rifle primer weighs about 5.4 grains, with a priming charge of .6 grain; a small rifle primer scales 4.0 grains.

At the close of the 19th century, when solid-head cases and smokeless powder were giving cartridges more muscle, European ammunition makers chose to incorporate the anvil in the case. They designed it into the bottom of the primer pocket, instead of putting it in the primer cup. This required two flash holes, one on either side of the anvil, as opposed to the single hole in the flat bottom of a Boxer-primed case. The Berdan primer was superior in at least two ways: without an anvil, the cup had more space for more priming compound; secondly, the flame traveled in a straight path through the twin ports to the powder. Conversely, a Boxer primer, with its anvil placed over the flash hole, channeled the flame *around* the anvil. The Boxer had one great advantage, however; it could be easily punched out by the decapping pin in a reloading press, whereas Berdan primers must be removed by hydraulic pressure or a special hook. Most U.S. military and sporting ammunition is now Boxer-primed, but many foreign governments still use Berdan primers. Curiously, Edward Boxer was an

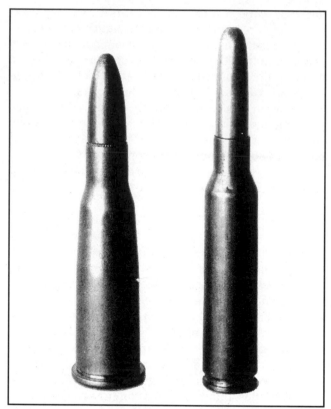

The French 8x50R cartridge (left) dates to 1886. It was the first smallbore smokeless military cartridge. Others, like the 6.5x52 Mannlicher-Carcano (right) followed quickly.

Englishman, and Hiram Berdan was an American. Both were military officers.

While the self-contained cartridge brought great excitement to the gun industry, new problems came with it. The first Boxer primers gave plenty of spark to ignite black powder, but misfires began to occur with the advent of smokeless powder. Consequently, more fulminate was added to the priming mix. When cases cracked as a result, smokeless powder got the blame. The real culprit was found in 1896 to be mercury contained in the primers. No damage occurred with black powder charges because the residue from fouled cases absorbed the harmful mercury. Smokeless powder, which burned at higher temperatures and left little residue, encouraged the mercury to attack the zinc in the case, causing brittleness.

The first successful smokeless powder primer was Government H-48, developed in 1898 for the .30-40 Krag. Non-mercuric, it used potassium chlorate as detonating material. The new primers had no harmful affect on cases and boasted a longer shelf life than mercuric primers. Like mercury ful-

minate, potassium chlorate had corrosive salts that attacked the gun's bore. But to shooters of the day, bore cleaning was considered a common, everyday chore that included swabbing the bore thoroughly with boiling water to dissolve the salts. Adding ammonia speeded up the removal of salt, while the water's own heat dried the bore. After that, a light coating of oil kept moisture off the steel. This ritual no doubt seemed a small price to pay for the luxury of positive ignition in metal cases—at least, to these turn-of-the-century shooters.

Then, in 1901, the German firm of Rheinische-Westphalische Sprengstoff (RWS) found a better way. RWS began manufacturing primers with barium nitrate and picric acid instead of potassium chlorate, because it found these compounds did not cause rust. A decade later, in 1911, the Swiss also developed a noncorrosive primer; and that same year, German rimfire ammunition began featuring "Rostfrei" (rust-free) priming. Rostfrei dispensed with both potassium chlorate and ground glass, the most common substance used to generate friction in primers. Ironically, barrel erosion caused by glass scouring was replaced by erosion from another source. During combustion, the barium peroxide in the mixture changed to barium oxide, which combined with carbon dioxide to form barium carbonate, an equally gritty compound.

By the time World War I began, America's H-48 primer had been replaced by FH-42, which contained no glass. While it was easier on cases than European mercuric primers, it was highly corrosive. By 1917, the accelerated pace of wartime production had pointed up another fault. During primer manufacture the drying houses got overloaded, creating humidity that caused sulfuric acid to form in the priming mix. The problem was spotted only after a rash of misfires. Meanwhile, U.S. Ordnance adopted the Winchester 35-NF primer, later known as the "FA (for Frankfort Arsenal) No. 70." Though it still included more than 50 percent potassium chlorate, this primer remained in service through World War II, after noncorrosive primers had been developed and refined.

The first successful noncorrosive primer marketed by an American firm was Remington's "Kleanbore," developed by chemist J.E. Burns in 1927. Winchester followed with "Staynless" and Peters with "Rustless." Like the early European compounds, these all contained mercury fulminate. That problem was quickly solved when two German chemists, Rathburg and Von Hersz, found a way to eliminate both potassium chlorate and mercury fulminate in primers. Remington was the first U.S. firm to produce non-mercuric, noncorrosive primers, of which lead tri-nitro-resorcinate (or lead styphnate) was a main ingredient. Then comprising up to 45 percent of the priming mix, this compound remains a primary component of rimfire and centerfire small arms primers.

The early problems with mercuric and potassium chlorate primer compounds also plagued shotshells. The shotshell primer has a deep battery cup containing the anvil, and a smaller cup filled with priming. As with rifle primers, a foil cover protects the mixture. The battery cup fits into a hole in the shell head, which, unlike the primer pocket of a rifle case, has no bottom and consequently no flash hole. The flash hole is located in the battery cup. Shotshell heads are made of thin, folded brass, much like the old balloon-head rifle cases. The head is reinforced with a dense paper base wad or by a thickening of the plastic shell body to form a heavy web inside the brass. Battery cups are long enough to seal the deep hole in the base wad. Every American battery cup for shotshells is now the same size; and all American shotshells now feature non-mercuric, noncorrosive priming.

In the late 1940's, Roy Weatherby and other experimenters designed sporting rifle cases to drive relatively small bullets with great charges of slow-burning powders. The powders proved hard to ignite in the required quantities, especially at low temperatures. Putting more priming compound in the caps would have increased the violence of the spark, but that might also have led to shattered powder grains in front of the flash hole and erratic, even dangerous pressures. The solution arrived in the early 1950's, thanks to the Speer Cartridge Works. Rejecting hot primers, Dick Speer and his chief chemist, Victor Jasaitis, looked instead for compounds that would burn *longer* and thereby provide more heat without increased disturbance to the powder. Their work resulted in the first magnum primer, with boron and aluminum added to the basic lead styphnate mixture. So successful was this innovation that it helped spawn a new Speer enterprise—Cascade Cartridge Industries, now known as CCI.

Primer manufacture is essentially the same now as it was 50 years ago, though new machines make the job easier. Most equipment is developed in-house and primers are made in huge batches. The cups are punched out of sheet metal, then drawn to form. Washed thoroughly, they're next poured in heaps on perforated sheets that index them, open end up, to receive the priming mixture. Meanwhile, another perforated plate is smeared with wet, dough-like priming compound and laid atop the first plate, their holes lined up so the mixture can be punched into the cups. A thin disc of foil or shellacked paper follows, covering each pellet. Anvils punched from sheet metal are then shaped, cleaned and aligned on another perforated plate and mated with the charged primers before being pressed into place. The completed primers are sent to a drying room and later tested and packaged.

New Muscle with Nitroglycerin

While late 19th-century priming developments dramatically altered gun design, so did progress in propellants. More potent powders meant higher pressures. The mechanical fit and structural strength of each part had to accommodate the added stress. The biggest changes began in 1846 with the discovery of nitroglycerin, a colorless liquid comprising nitric and sulfuric acids and glycerin. Unlike gunpowder, "nitro" is not a mix of fuels and oxidizers. It is instead an unstable, oxygen-rich chemical compound that can quickly rearrange itself into more stable, gaseous compounds. Any shock will start this rearranging process. Once started, it moves so fast and with such a violent release of gas that an explosion results.

Though nitroglycerin is now found in many explosives, it was viewed suspiciously by 19th-century miners who were used to blasting rock with black powder only. One salesman fared so poorly on the dusty streets of an early western mining town that he ran out of money. He left as room payment his suitcase with several unsold vials of nitroglycerin. The hotel keeper was no more impressed with this oily fluid than were the miners. He kept the suitcase in an upstairs hallway, where a bootblack used it as a footrest for his customers. One day, as red fumes curled out of the suitcase, the uneasy proprietor opened a window and threw the suitcase out. The decomposing nitroglycerin detonated, blowing the back out of the hotel and making believers out of skeptics.

Because nitroglycerin was so sensitive to shock and leaked readily, Swedish chemist Emmanuel Nobel and his son Alfred (who later instituted the famed Nobel Prizes) devised a way in 1863 to put nitro in cans. This eliminated some of the mess but none of the danger. Several shipments blew up, and so did Nobel's German factory. Alfred later found that soaking a porous earth, *Kieselguhr*, with nitroglycerin stabilized the explosive. From his discovery came Dynamite. It worked well as a blasting agent and was patented in 1875. Dynamite in its early form is rarely used now and has become a generic term for safer, more efficient explosives.

In the mid-1840's, while Ascanio Subrero of Italy was developing nitroglycerin, Christian Schoenbein discovered in his Swiss laboratory that sulfuric and nitric acids applied to cotton (or any cellulose-base material) form a compound that burns so fast that flames can consume a treated cotton patch without igniting a mound of black powder lying on top. Schoenbein sold his procedure to Austria and then obtained an English patent for it. Soon thereafter, John Hall and Sons built a guncotton plant in Faversham, England. The plant promptly blew up, along with most of the other guncotton plants that blossomed in mid-19th-century Europe. The compound had little appeal as a propellant; moreover, it was hazardous to load and burned too quickly. A gun was apt to explode before the ball had a chance to start moving up the bore. Despite these problems, adventurous people kept producing guncotton. In 1872, England's Waltham Abbey plant made 250 tons of it, mostly for mines, torpedoes and other products designed to come apart.

Chemical compounds like guncotton and nitroglycerin are high explosives; that is, upon detonation they can release gas in a wave action as fast as 21,000 feet per second. Black powder and other fuels must *burn* to release their gases. Their pressure curve isn't as steep, which gives them greater utility as propellants. Chemical compounds can also be burned; throwing dynamite on a fire, for example, may only cause it to flare brightly.

Less Smoke, More Fire

Munitions shortages during the Civil War prompted the use of "white powder," developed in the 1850's by J.J. Pohl. It was comprised of 49 percent potassium chlorate, 28 percent yellow prussiate of potash, and 23 percent sulfur. Inferior as a propellant and quite corrosive, it nonetheless proved useful when black powder was not available. Chlorate powders were pioneered by Berthollet in the 1780s; but when a French powder works plant at Essons blew up in 1788, Berthollet abandoned potassium chlorate as being too sensitive for use in firearms.

Following the Civil War, backyard mills in the U.S. made powder containing potassium chlorate and various household ingredients. Some powder

formulas were hawked through the mail by con artists who adjusted prices to suit the customer. One recipe called for 256 parts sugar, 16 parts coffee and 1 part alum in 320 parts water. To this brew was added 320 parts potassium chlorate, 8 parts alcohol and 1 part sulfur. Then, in 1869, a German immigrant named Carl Dittmar built a small factory in the U.S. to make "Dualin," which was merely sawdust treated with nitroglycerin. As a technical engineer back in Prussia, Dittmar had tried to make smokeless powder from nitrated wood. He later joined Johann Schultz, formerly of the Prussian Artillery, to further this work. The two men were long on talent but short on money and were forced to dissolve their partnership. A year later, in 1870, Dittmar announced his "New Sporting Powder," made of wood pulp boiled in alkaline solution, ground in starch and pelleted. The pellets were then treated with sulfuric acid and nitrated twice between dryings. Given enough money in 1878 to start up a mill in Binghamton, New York, Dittmar began making the new powder (along with Dualin). Unfortunately, the plant blew up a few years later, nearly demolishing Binghamton.

In failing health, Dittmar sold his company. One of his foremen, Milton Lindsey, went to work for the new concern, then joined the King Powder Company in 1895. With the firm's president, G.M. Peters, he developed "King's Semi-Smokeless Powder." Patented in 1899, it contained 20 percent wood cellulose, 60 percent saltpeter, 12 percent charcoal and 8 percent sulfur. DuPont's "Lesmoke," which came on the market later, had roughly the same composition. It was one of several semi-smokeless powders developed during the transition from black to smokeless powder. Most commonly used in .22 rimfire rounds, it proved exceptionally accurate. It fouled bores, but the fouling didn't cake or harden as was the case with black powder. While smokeless burned cleaner, it lacked the bulk needed to carry away residue from corrosive primers. When non-corrosive priming came along, the potassium salts in Lesmoke's black powder component made it more corrosive by comparison. Lesmoke was also considered too dangerous to produce and was abandoned around 1947.

While Dittmar and Schultz were nitrating wood chips, Austrian chemist Frederick Volkmann was patenting some new cellulose-based powders. His work went unrecognized for some time because Austrian patents then were not published. To make things even more difficult, the Austrian government started enforcing its monopoly on domestic powder supply in 1875, just after Volkmann had built up his production capacity. The plant was closed, and its industrious chief slipped from view, never to resurface. But some of the claims Volkmann made for his propellants in 1871 were eerily prescient. These included transparent smoke, less noise and barrel residue (but more energy than black powder), and safe manufacture, handling and storage. Further, Volkmann claimed that by varying molding pressure on his compounds, he could manipulate their gas production.

The development of smokeless powder is generally credited to Paul Vielle, a French engineer. In 1885, his "Poudre B" comprised ethyl alcohol and the ordinary pyroxylin known as celluloid. Poudre B was a single-base powder; that is, it contained no nitroglycerin.

Alfred Nobel found in 1887 that by increasing the percentage of nitrocellulose in his blasting gelatin he could tame it for use as a propellant. A year later, he patented "Ballistite," a mixture of 100 parts nitroglycerin, 200 parts soluble nitrocellulose, 200 to 400 parts amyl acetate, and 10 to 25 parts camphor (camphor was later deleted and a stabilizer added). Nobel started making Ballistite in Scotland in 1889 and was granted an American patent in 1891. Because it contained both nitrocellulose and nitroglycerin, Ballistite was a double-base powder.

Nobel's work paralleled that of Hiram Maxim, who in 1889 patented his own smokeless powder. About this time, the British War Office appointed a committee to find a better military powder. The committee came up with "Cordite," a modification of the formula Nobel had derived, with the addition of Maxim's acetone product. The resulting paste could be squeezed through a die to form cord-like strands. Original Cordite powder contained 37 percent gun-cotton, 58 percent nitroglycerin and 5 percent vaseline. Later the formula was changed to 65 percent guncotton, 30 percent nitroglycerin and 5 percent mineral jelly with acetone. Subsequently, Nobel and Maxim sued the British government for patent infringement, but without success.

The first smokeless powders contained lumps of varied shapes and sizes. The nitrated lignin of Johann Schultz's bulk powder made it look fuzzy. Bulk powder was so named because it could be substituted, bulk for bulk, for black powder. "Dense," or gelatinized propellants, generated much more pressure per load volume. Early shotgun charges typically weighed 3 drams (82 grains); but the powder was loaded by measure. So a measure of bulk powder gave roughly the same effect as a measure of black. When smokeless powders arrived, "drams" became "drams equivalent," as less of the dense, high-energy powder was needed to achieve the performance level of black powder.

The first military rifle designed for smokeless powder was the French 8mm Lebel, which appeared in 1886. Other nations quickly developed their own. The new propellant not only increased bullet velocities by a third, it kept smoke so low a rifleman could fire repeatedly without revealing his position or obstructing his sight picture. The only hitch was pressure. Smokeless generated double the pressures of black powder, causing guns not built for smokeless to come apart under the strain.

While stronger rifles were being designed, new powder formulas proliferated. In 1890, Samuel Rodgers, an English physician practicing in San Francisco, formed the United States Powder Company to produce an ammonium nitrate powder he had recently developed. Later that same year, his company merged with the Giant Powder Company. By 1894, Rodgers' "Gold Dust Powder" comprised 55 percent ammonium picrate, 25 percent sodium or potassium nitrate, and 20 percent ammonium bichromate. A foul-smelling propellant intended mostly for shotguns, it was also marketed to shooters who were accustomed to bulk measure. Consequently, careless loaders were apt to blow up their

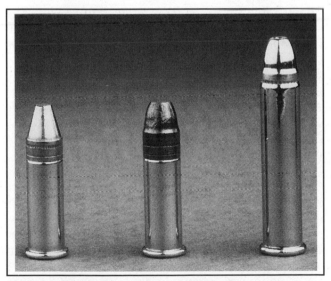

Modern .22 rimfire cartridges include (from left): Speer's Mini-Mag, .22 LR SGB (small game bullet), and .22 Magnum.

This carbine, made by the American inventor John Hall, was one of the last flint-sparking breechloaders.

guns. The Giant Powder Company plant was destroyed by an explosion in 1898 and was never rebuilt.

During the 1890s, the California Powder Works made "Peyton Powder" under contract with the U.S. government for use in .30-40 Krag cartridges. It combined a small amount of ammonium picrate with nitrocellulose and nitroglycerin. "Velox", produced by the Economic Smokeless Powder Company of Illinois, contained equal parts of ammonium picrate and barium nitrate, plus 15 parts picric acid.

Most of the powder companies formed in the 1890's to manufacture smokeless either went out of business shortly or were bought by bigger companies. The Robin Hood Powder Company of Vermont later became the Robin Hood Ammunition Company, and in 1915 it sold out to the Union Metallic Cartridge Company. The American E.C. & Schultz Powder Company went to DuPont in 1903, then to Hercules after DuPont was split by court order in 1912. Because powder production called for specialized machinery, plants were seldom idle. If a company went under, its equipment was usually acquired or operated—and sometimes moved to another site—by a more solvent firm.

The Leonard Smokeless Powder Company of Tennessee marketed "Ruby N" and "Ruby J" double-base powders. A company pamphlet in 1893 claimed that American sportsmen burned powder at the rate of ". . . not less than three million pounds per annum [and that] Leonard Powder will be sold at a profit at a price which will be relatively less than that of black powder, since one pound of Leonard Smokeless is equal in ballistic value to three of black."

For all its optimism, the Leonard Powder Company failed in 1894. It was succeeded by the American Smokeless Powder Company, which subsequently produced powder under government contract at Pompton Lakes, New Jersey. This company was taken over in 1898 by a creditor, Laflin & Rand, which five years earlier had negotiated for the American rights to Ballistite. Nobel's demand of $300,000 plus a royalty had seemed too steep. Later, under the control of DuPont, Ballistite was manufactured by Laflin & Rand, which developed the famous Sharpshooter, Lightning, Unique and L. & R. Smokeless powders.

Single-base powders had drawn the interest of Naval Ordnance people since 1897, when DuPont and the California Powder Works first started filling government orders. Their processes consisted of dissolving guncotton in a bath of ether and alcohol to form a colloid, which was squeezed into thin tubes. The tubes were then cut into short pieces. Among the first such powders was "Government Pyro," used in military ammunition for 1906 Springfield rifles. DuPont's 1147 and 1185 powders later fueled the .30-06 M1 cartridge, while IMR 4895 was used in the M2 round. Early double-base powders included the "W-A" (Whistler-Aspinwall) for the .30-40 Krag. Named for its developers at Laflin & Rand, it contained 30 percent nitroglycerin and proved erosive. Modern double-base powders still burn hotter than single-base, but most have less than 20 percent nitroglycerin and therefore do not harm barrels.

In 1906, Congress granted the War Department the sum of $165,000 to build its own powder plant near Wharton, New Jersey. This became the Picatinny Arsenal, with a daily production capacity of 10,000 pounds. Picatinny eventually handled all government chemical tests of powders. Frankfort Arsenal, in Philadelphia, conducted small arms and ammunition tests, and Maryland's Aberdeen Proving Grounds were reserved for proofing of artillery powders.

When World War I erupted in Europe, U.S. Ordnance contracted with DuPont, which by then had become the dominant force in the powder industry, to build two plants—at Old Hickory, Tennessee, and Nitro, West Virginia—with a combined capacity of 1.5 million pounds per day. After the war, DuPont bought the entire town of Old Hickory and established there a facility for making rayon. The powder equipment at both mills was dismantled. In August, 1924, a fire started in a solvent recovery building near the Old Hickory powder magazine and quickly destroyed 106 buildings and 50 million pounds of powder.

By this time, Hercules Powder Company was making nitrocellulose in its own facility at Parlin, New Jersey. Freed from the DuPont trust in 1912, it had manufactured dynamite—and up to 2,000 pounds of small arms powder a day—at its main Kenville (NJ) plant. The new facility produced Hercules E.C. powder, one of a line that included Bullseye, Infallible, W.A. .30-caliber, Sharpshooter, Lightning, HiVel, Unique, Bear and Stag.

During World War I, Hercules secured huge contracts for the production of Cordite and was at one time making 12,000 pounds a day for the British government. By war's end, it had shipped some 46 million pounds of the powder. The firm also manufactured nearly three million pounds of small arms powder and 54 million pounds of Pyro powder for field artillery use. Before hostilities began, Hercules had never made cannon powders and was only a year into producing propellants for sportsmen; indeed, fewer than a dozen members of its technical staff had even worked with smokeless powder.

Artillery ammunition of that day consistently fouled bores with copper residue. To combat this, French munitions people added tinfoil to the powder charges. Subsequently, DuPont added 4 percent tin to its No. 17 rifle powder, renaming it 17½ (DuPont No. 15 powder later received the same treatment). Tin reduced metal fouling, but rifles using National Match ammunition charged with No. 17½ powder began to reveal dark rings near their muzzles. These were caused by tin that had vaporized on firing, then collected on the cool muzzles. Though this residue was easily removed, DuPont subsequently kept tin levels below 2 percent.

The Modern Approach to Smokeless Powder

The materials and processes used in modern powder manufacture are much the same as those employed at the turn of the century. Equipment is more sophisticated, and, because of its special applications, is often custom-built. In producing black powder today, for example, sulfur, charcoal and saltpeter are first ground very fine and mixed at 3 percent moisture. An edge roller mill, comprising two huge cylinders on a circular plate, incorporates the mixture and ensures uniformity throughout. The powder mass is then broken into lumps, or powder meal, which is pressed into compact cakes. The cakes are fed through a granulating machine,

where toothed cylinders chop them into bits. After a screening process has segregated them by size, the granules are polished in revolving wooden barrels.

As a rule, big granules (or grains) of black powder burn slower than small ones. Extremely fine powder is used for priming charges, whereas coarse powder propels objects—the heavier the object, the coarser the powder. Black powder for small arms is designated (in decreasing order of coarseness) as follows: A-1, Fg, FFg, FFFg, FFFFg, and FFFFFg.

All smokeless powders begin as nitrocellulose—i.e., vegetable fiber soaked in nitric and sulfuric acids. Powder plants that do their own nitrating have elaborate recovery procedures for the acids. Most nitrocellulose used in gunpowder has about 12.6 percent nitrogen and is 95 percent soluble in a mixture of 2 parts ether, 1 part ethyl alcohol. Its industry name—"Pyrocellulose"—was applied to artillery powders during World War I. Guncotton, with 13.2 percent nitrogen, forms a particular kind of nitrocellulose that is less soluble in the ether-alcohol solution.

Nitrocellulose used in powder production derives from short crude-cotton fibers, or "linters", which are boiled in caustic soda before nitrating to remove oils. Water formed by the nitric acid is absorbed by the sulfuric acid, preventing decomposition by hydrolysis. A centrifugal wringer strips acid from the fibers, which are immediately rinsed in water, then boiled 48 hours to remove every trace of acid. If the nitrated fibers are not washed promptly, spontaneous combustion will result. The cotton is then beaten to a pulp and boiled again in wooden tubs, where agitators fluff it to remove any remaining acids. This process is repeated half a dozen times, each session lasting five hours. Afterward, the pulp is pronounced usable for making any smokeless powder.

Bulk powder originates in a "still," where nitrocellulose is agitated in a solution of barium and potassium nitrates. A solvent (usually a mixture of amyl acetate, benzol and paraffin) forms tiny globules, each one dissolving a calculated amount of nitrocellulose. The agitators keep the solvent evenly dispersed, and after a given time heat is applied to evaporate the solvent. Only hard grains of nitrocellulose now remain in the water. [Note: single- and double-base powders can also begin as wet nitrocellulose. Alcohol is forced through the fibers, displacing the water, and is then removed by hydraulic pressure. This process is much safer than the old air-drying method, which often resulted in spontaneous combustion.]

The cake of nitrocellulose, which retains some of the alcohol, is next dumped into a mixer with an ether solvent (single-base powders) or acetone (double-base powders) to dissolve the fibers. Nitroglycerin is then added to form double-base powders, at which point the "soup" becomes as unstable as it will ever be. After more mixing, it turns plastic and is squeezed into a cake-like form before being fed through dies by a hydraulic press. The dies determine the diameter and wall thickness of the powder, which emerges in spaghetti-like tubes that are gently coiled for feeding into the next machine. Special rollers ease these long noodles through a plate, where a whirling knife shears off measured sections. At this stage, single-base powders still contain a lot of ether, so they are sent to a warm solvent-recovery room where the ether can evaporate. Not all the ether is removed this way, however; the granules have to be "water-dried"—i.e., soaked in warm water for at least two weeks.

Wet single-base and freshly-cut double-base granules are air-dried and sieved, then polished in rotating drums containing powdered graphite. This tumbling process smooths rough edges, while the graphite coating reduces friction and changes powder color from yellow to charcoal. Batches are then mixed to ensure uniformity.

The tubelike shape of many smokeless powders is no accident. Perforations in the center of each grain increase its surface area and mitigate the "burn-down" effect of solids ignited on the outside. Perforated grains burn from two directions; while outside area decreases, inside area increases, generating more gas from an enlarged surface. The burning rate of powder is partly determined by the ratio of inside diameter (of each tubular grain) to outside diameter.

Ball powder grains become round about midway through their manufacture. By then, nitrocellulose has been powdered fine in a hammer mill and blended with water to produce a slurry. Pumped into a still, the slurry combines with chalk that has been added to counteract the nitric acids present in both newly-nitrated cellulose and old powder. Next, dipherylamine is introduced (to stabilize the powder) and ethyl acetate is piped in, dissolving the nitrocellulose and forming a lacquer. As the still is heated, large paddles stir the lacquer and break it into small particles. Once these particles have become the proper roundness and size, the ethyl acetate is distilled off, leaving hard grains of powder. In most modern facilities, the lacquer is now extruded through orifices in plates, instead of being broken up by paddles. The resulting strands are chopped into bits by a whirling knife, swept turbulently through a long pipe, and finally heated in stages to reduce viscosity. Round grains are the end product.

Sodium sulfate (salt) is added next to draw out retained water. Fresh water replaces the salt water, and the slurry of dried powder is piped through screens, where the grains are sized and batched. After being pumped to a heated "coating still," the grains are then immersed in an emulsion of nitroglycerin (to increase the powder's potency). Following this treatment, the powder is coated with deterrent in the same heated still to slow surface burning. Otherwise, untreated grains would burn too quickly on ignition, generating short, sharp pressure curves.

When all solvents have been sucked away, the powder is pumped in a water slurry to a centrifuge, where the water is removed. The grains are then tumbled in powdered graphite to prevent the buildup of static electricity in the sizing process, which follows. To make a finished product, ball sizes are often blended, each batch being carefully metered to ensure the desired burning properties. Fine ball powders have traditionally been more popular with shooters than coarser, slow-burning sizes.

CHAPTER 2

BULLETS, BARRELS AND BIRD GUNS

Early shooters were handicapped by crude projectiles that were unable to use powder gas efficiently. For example, in a hand cannon dating to 1388, a third of an ounce of powder was required to propel a feathered iron arrow weighing half a pound. Italian bombards of about the same vintage used tapered bores to accommodate projectiles (mostly stones) of various sizes. After arrows and stones, iron balls became popular, followed by cannon shot the size of walnuts. These wrought such devastation that German states outlawed their use.

Most of these muzzleloading arms, which were seldom fired more than once during a battle, featured chambers that measured only a third the diameter of the bore. When a fresh stone or bag of iron marbles couldn't be found, miscellaneous hard objects were used instead. Accuracy was unimportant. A gun's report, its smoke and the slap of projectiles striking near the enemy proved so demoralizing that actual killing was unnecessary. In short, war machines were more colorful than lethal. Two-ton bronze culverins wheeled about the battlefront by 17-horse teams may have looked impressive, but it was mostly hand-to-hand combat that drew the blood.

Lead projectiles soon supplanted iron and stone. Lead melted at low temperatures and could be molded readily into shot of various sizes or snug-fitting, bore-size balls. It was soft as well, ensuring obturation on firing and sealing the powder gas, while at the same time yielding to the barrel wall without boosting pressure. Lead was also dense, thus ensuring great range. As early as 1498 (in Leipzig, Germany) and 1504 (in Zurich, Switzerland), special target matches were held for rifle shooters. The bullets they used were presumably made of lead, because only soft material like lead conforms easily to lands and grooves. Lead accompanied our Pilgrims as they came ashore in New England, carrying their six-foot, 75-caliber "musket bores." They guarded their supplies of lead with great care, for later this commodity became a valuable barter item with the Indians.

By 1700, the French-style flintlock had become the most popular shoulder arm in Europe. From it evolved the *jaeger* (hunter) rifle that spawned America's own Kentucky rifle. An 18th-century jaeger typically featured a 24- to 30-inch barrel of 60 to 77 caliber, with seven to nine deep, slow-twist grooves. Its stock was almost modern in design, with a broad, flat butt, round grip and rectangular patch box. Most jaegers had double-set triggers. Practiced marksmen could hit 3½-foot targets, offhand, at 250 yards.

American colonists liked jaeger rifles, and during the Revolutionary War they soon learned to respect the King's elite Jaeger units as well. In building their own rifles, however, the frontiersmen tried to be more efficient. To save precious lead, they reduced bore size to .50, .45 and .40 (a pound of lead yields 70 or more 40-caliber balls, but only 15 of the 70-caliber size). Lengthening the barrel extracted more energy from the burning powder and increased sight radius. Hinged patchbox covers replaced the sliding lids of the jaegers. And American stocks, carved from walnut and maple, were more slender than their European counterparts.

One historian notes that, in battle, American colonists often defeated the crack Jaeger troops. Americans got an edge by using slightly undersize balls in a greased patch, while the Jaegers loaded their tight-fitting balls directly. The patched balls were easier to load and less noisy. Hammering bare lead down a rifled bore gave away a marksman's position. This leaves one wondering why the Jaegers rejected the patch. It had, after all, been used in Europe for over two centuries.

When the first Kentucky rifles were built by Pennsylvania gunsmiths, patches were linen or thin, tanned animal hide greased with saliva or animal fat. Today's commercial lubricants in paste and liquid form do a better job of cleaning the bore and sealing powder gas. Patch lube does not replace bore solvent, however. Black powder and Hodgdon's clean-burning substitute, "Pyrodex", are both hygroscopic and corrosive, which means barrels still need frequent cleaning.

Most lead balls for muzzleloaders are pure "soft" lead. While harder lead alloy works best for cast-bullet shooting with breechloaders, it doesn't allow adequate upset in a black powder bore that's charged from the front. After only a few shots fouling makes loading with bore-size balls difficult; so on the hunt, when fast loading is sometimes necessary, undersize balls are a good idea. A 50-caliber rifle may shoot most accurately with .498 or .500 balls; but after a few shots it can't be reloaded because of bore residue. A .490 ball, patched to fit tightly, loads more easily and will often shoot with equal accuracy. Because Pyrodex leaves less residue, it allows more shots between cleanings than black powder; moreover, it enables the shooter to use slightly bigger balls.

By 1835, percussion ignition had begun to replace flint, and hunters probing the plains demanded rifles of varying dimensions. The graceful Kentucky rifle was gradually nudged out of favor by a gun that looked more like the jaeger (from which the Kentucky itself had sprung). Plains rifles were shorter, for ease in carrying on horseback, and their stocks were thicker for added strength. Almost all of them featured percussion locks. And in order to handle the big balls necessary for elk, bears and bison, their bores averaged half an inch in diameter.

Meanwhile, target shooters were also experimenting with new equipment. The picket ball they'd been using wasn't a ball, but a blunt conical bullet tapered from base to tip. Loading proved difficult, and unless it was loaded perfectly the new bullet shot poorly. Around 1840, Alvin Clark invented the false muzzle, which enabled a shooter to start each bullet squarely. Soon after, the parallel-sided, paper-patched bullet supplanted all others at target matches. Groups that had been fired with patched

ball and picket ball at 20 rods (110 yards) could now be duplicated at 40. After a few years of refinements in rifles and ammunition, black powder muzzleloading rifles with paper-patched bullets were firing extraordinary groups at ranges up to 200 rods.

By the mid 1800's, the advantages of rifling were already well documented, but hunters and soldiers of that era didn't like the way rifled bores fouled. After all, fouling made loading slow and limited the charge. Smoothbores remained popular because they were quicker to load and delivered more punch at close range where most of the shooting was done and where accuracy was of secondary value.

Spinning the Bullet

The early development of conical bullets is closely tied to bore design. Making a bullet that flew far and true was the goal. Distance is gained by driving a dense bullet fast—just as a golf ball travels farther than a tennis ball. But density is only one requisite; the bullet must also stay point-on or it will not attain its maximum range or accuracy. Streamlining a bullet does no good if the bullet tumbles in the air. That's where rifling helps, because a spinning bullet is not apt to tumble.

The main problem with muzzleloading rifles was seating the bullet. Forcing groove-size bullets down long bores was hard, noisy work that took a long time and got more difficult with each shot. In 1826, Henri Gustave Delvigne of France tried to correct this fault through improved chamber design. The Delvigne chamber had sharp shoulders that arrested and upset the ball as it was rammed home. Undersize balls were thus expanded to fit the bore; but these deformed balls turned in poor accuracy. Another Frenchman, M. Thouvenin, put a central peg in the chamber to expand the ball, but it gave similar results.

Nine years later, Captain Berner of the British Brunswickers borrowed an idea presented originally by a Spanish officer back in 1725. He first built a rifle with two narrow, spiraling grooves in the bore, then made a ball with a belt, much like one of Saturn's rings. The belt fit the rifle's spiraling grooves. Though the shooter had to orient the ball before starting it down the bore, ramming it home was easy.

That same year, in 1835, English gunmaker William Greener developed an oval ball with one flat end and a tapered hole bored from the flat to the center of the ball. A metal peg was inserted into the hole and became part of the projectile. Its round head conformed to the watermelon shape of the ball, so that either end could be placed first in the bore. Upon firing, the peg was driven into the tapered seat, expanding the ball to fit the bore. Though accurate, Greener's ball was rejected by the British government because it comprised two pieces.

About this time, some British gunmakers were experimenting with unrifled bores made out-of-round, but spiraled. The Lancaster oval bore imparted spin without engraving its oval bullet. Loading was easy, but the bullet had to be properly oriented, and the mold had to match the rifle bore exactly. In battle, such oval and elliptical bores required too much attention in loading. Mass production proved difficult as well, because all bullets had to be cast out of round.

Delvigne recognized the potential of a hollow-based conical bullet and developed his own around 1841. He was the first to point out that firing expanded the skirts of this bullet, pushing them out against the rifling. At the same time, an innovative British colonel named Brunswick soldered a metal skirt to a ball, thus creating his own hollow-based conical bullet. Brunswick's design appeared the same year as Delvigne's. Meanwhile, French artillery people were experimenting with sabots to hold the ball and engage the lands. The sabots released their ball or bullet in flight and dropped away like the spent first stage of a rocket. Wooden sabots gave good performance, but metal sabots proved inaccurate.

By 1846, shooters were disenchanted with the tendency of hollow-based conical bullets to tip in flight. To eliminate this problem, British General John Jacobs developed a four-groove rifle and conical bullet with matching fins. When it was rejected by the Indian government, Jacobs persisted with his experiments, designing a heavy conical bullet that proved reasonably accurate to over 600 yards. Later, he invented a double-barrel, 32-bore rifle that fired an explosive bullet. Its nose held a copper cup with a charge of priming powder that detonated on impact. The rifle's four deep grooves were pitched one turn in 30 inches. Sights could be elevated to 2,000 yards.

African explorer and elephant hunter Sir Samuel Baker was looking for a big gun like this, but he wanted one with standard rifling. A British gunmaker named Gibbs built Baker a 21-pound, 4-bore rifle designed to launch 3-ounce balls or 4-ounce conical bullets with 16 drams of powder. Gibbs' 36-inch barrel had two grooves, pitched one turn in 36 inches. Like most rifles of that time, its grooves were made broad to facilitate loading. A barrel bored for patched balls had narrow grooves, its broad lands lending better support for the undersize ball.

In 1847, French Captain Claude-Etienne Minie developed a cylindrical bullet with an iron cup in its hollow base. Driven forward and outward by the powder gas, this cup jammed the bullet's skirt into the rifling. It expanded so readily, however, that some bullets were cut in two, leaving a ring of lead in the bore to be pushed out by the next bullet. A patch groove was cast into the base of the first Minie bullets but was later deleted. To shift weight forward, the nose was flattened and various grooves added to the base.

Minie's improved bullet was then tested against balls from smoothbore muskets at 100 yards. The musketeers scored 149 hits of 200 rounds on a target measuring 6 feet high and 20 feet broad, but riflemen using the new Minie bullet got 189 hits. At 400 yards, the differences were even more pronounced: 9 hits for the musketeers, 105 for the riflemen. The Minie shooters hit more targets at 200 yards than their counterparts did at 100, and twice as many at 300 yards as the smoothbore shooters did at 200. At 400 yards, the riflemen hit three times as often as the musketeers did at 300.

A few years later, Minie used the idea of a tapered cavity to design a new conical bullet. Much to William Greener's chagrin, Minie sold this bullet to the British military establishment for 20,000 pounds. Upon protest, Greener was later awarded 1,000 pounds for "the first public suggestion of the principle of expansion. . . ."

Rifling The Bore

To find out why military rifles shot inconsistently and varied one from another with respect to accuracy, British Ordnance Chief Viscount Hardinage consulted Joseph Whitworth, a bright English technician, in 1854. Whitworth thought unpredictable accuracy less a function of manufacturing methods than of rifle design. Elementary in retrospect, this view was a radical deviation from the then common belief that shop tolerances needed tightening. With government backing, Whitworth built an elaborate 500-yard enclosed range with movable targets and every appurtenance available. Soon after completion, the range was destroyed by a great storm.

The following year, another facility was built and Whitworth began his tests. Convinced that bullets could be made to fly predictably with the correct spin, he tried various rates of twist, from the standard one turn in 78 inches used for musket balls to an experimental one turn in 5. Later, he even tested a bore in which the bullet spun on its axis once for each inch of forward travel. In the end, a twist of one in 20 proved about right for the short bullets used in the test. Whitworth's choice of rifling design was the hexagonal bore, which he'd patented (though not invented) a year before. Bullets that fit comfortably between the flats, he discovered, would expand to fill the corners upon firing, thus enabling a shooter to load fast while at the same time achieving good accuracy.

Skeptics, questioning the sharp twist, wanted to know if it retarded the bullet. Whitworth tested his rifle against an issue Enfield, using a hexagonal bullet he had developed against the standard ball load. With identical powder charges, the Whitworth bullet penetrated 15 inches of elm, the Enfield ball only 6.

In 1857, Whitworth submitted his rifle for Ordnance testing at Hythe, England. His bullets flew so flat and accurately that even the most critical examiner acknowledged "the relative superiority of his small-bore rifle. . . ." Whitworth's targets showed a mean deviation of 4½ inches at 500 yards. The best anyone could muster previously was 27 inches. Still, British Ordnance personnel faulted the ignition on Whitworth's rifle, claiming the bullets wore the bore too fast and couldn't be produced in sufficient quantity. Rejected as a candidate for military service, the rifle later inspired other designers.

Meanwhile, William Greener experimented with "small-bore" guns of 40 to 52 caliber, rifled one turn in 30 inches. This relatively quick twist stabilized bullets to ranges of 2,000 yards. Despite the narrow lands, lead stripping apparently posed no problem. James Purdey built two of these rifles in 1856, one bored .40, the other .50. He called them "Express Train" rifles, for their great power. The word "Express" stuck and was later applied to many big British rounds.

By 1860, it was clear that guns of all types would eventually be loaded from the rear, thereby changing the future course of bullet design. If a bullet didn't have to be forced down the bore, it could be produced harder and longer and made to fit the grooves more tightly. Hard bullets could be stabilized with shallower grooves and driven faster. Rifling could be made with wider lands and a sharper twist and could even vary in depth and pitch from breech to muzzle.

Among the first to exploit the rifling potential of breechloaders was William Ellis Metford, a Britisher who favored the wide, shallow grooves still in use today. His were uniformly .004 inch deep, but of steepening pitch from chamber to muzzle. A slow initial rate of twist allowed the bullet a quick start without boosting chamber pressure. By the time it exited, the bullet was spinning smartly at one turn every 17 inches. Metford's gain twist was gradual: in a 34-inch barrel, the bullet turned little more than one full revolution. Ever the experi-

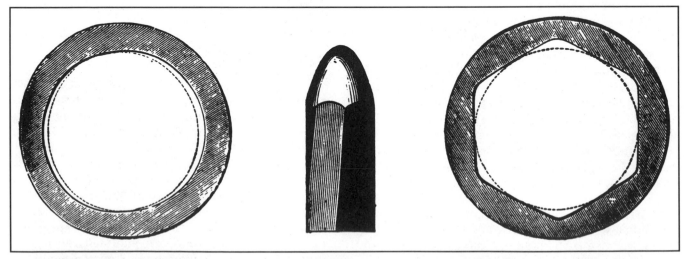

Joseph Whitworth, who thought gun design (not manufacturing problems) caused inaccuracy, patented the hex bore (right) in 1854, but bullets proved hard to make. The Lancaster oval bore (left) descended from Captain Bernier's elliptical bore.

menter, Metford went on to develop segmented rifling, with rounded grooves and lands.

Progressive grooving was also tried in early breechloaders. England's famed Enfield model had three grooves .010 inch deep at the breech, tapering to a depth of .005 inch at the muzzle. The Martini-Henry rifle featured seven grooves graded from .009 to .007 in depth, with the twist increasing from one turn in 72 inches to one in 22. Meanwhile, shooters debated the effect progressive grooving and gain twist had on bullets. According to Greener, the combination of hard bullet material and shallow rifling at the muzzle prevented any significant deformation. Bullets still had to be lubricated with wax or grease.

By the late 19th century, variations in groove depth and rate of twist within a bore had been judged unnecessary. Fine accuracy was obtainable with Metford's wide, shallow groove design in a bore with uniform rifling dimensions. Still, experimenters kept new ideas coming. Charles Newton, the brilliant U.S. inventor, reasoned that since a bullet bears on only one shoulder of each land, the other is unnecessary. He sloped his lands to the off side of the spin, making the bore look like a ratchet housing. This arrangement had been tried previously in England, but Newton's work during World War I proved its utility. Ratchet rifling, like most other forms, is no longer employed on mass-produced rifles. The Metford-inspired Enfield rifling has been almost universally adopted, with groove bottoms the same radius as the bullet. Land shoulders are square and land tops flat. Neither groove number nor depth determines rifling type—only the cross-sectional configuration.

While rifling form has changed little since World War I, the manufacture of rifled bores has changed a great deal. A single cutter guided by a rod running in a spiral groove remained the most common rifling method until the 1940s. After each pass the barrel was indexed for the next groove. When all the grooves had been shallowly etched, the hook was adjusted to cut a few ten-thousandths of an inch deeper and the passes were repeated.

Shortly after World War II, engineers devised a way to "iron" rifling into a bore. It was even simpler than the hook method: just push a carbide die through the bore with the rifling in reverse. The die, or button, has proved so efficient and precise that leading barrel makers like Shilen, Douglas and McMillan all button-rifle their best barrels.

An even newer method is hammer forging, in which a hard mandrel with the rifling machined in reverse serves as the core. Around this core a barrel blank is hammered (or kneaded) until the mandrel and the blank are fast together. The mandrel is then removed from the blank, leaving its impression in the bore. This technique, which originated in Germany, leaves a fine finish. Because the barrel is formed around a stationary mandrel, hammer forging accommodates innumerable options, including gain twist, progressive grooving, and polygonal or oval bores.

The rate of spin needed to stabilize a bullet depends on the speed and dimensions of the bullet. Long bullets require a sharper rifling twist than short ones, and slow bullets must spin quicker than fast ones. Even round balls benefit from rifling, which tends to prevent precession, or the rolling of a ball down the bore. A ball that doesn't spin is like a baseball pitcher's knuckleball that doesn't rotate: eventually the ball will yaw because its flight axis lacks a stabilizing force. A spinning top remains upright because its rotation counteracts the tug of gravity on its sides. In effect, it changes sides so fast it can't lean one way or another long enough to fall down. At some point, the rotation becomes so slow that the top wobbles and then crashes.

In 1879, a British ballistician, Sir Alfred George Greenhill, devised a formula to determine the proper rate of spin for all bullets with a specific gravity of 10.9. Since pure lead has a specific gravity of 11.4, most jacketed bullets qualify. Greenhill published his formula in the "British Textbook of Small Arms, 1929," as follows: *Required twist in all calibers equals 150 divided by the length of the bullet in calibers.*

To validate Greenhill's formula, take Speer's 100-grain .257 bullet as an example. Its length is one inch, or 4 calibers, so the proper twist should be 150 divided by 4 = 37.5. Multiplying 37.5 by .257 equals 9.64. Most .257 Roberts and .25-06 rifles have a 1–in–10 twist, which squares with Greenhill's formula; i.e., to be properly stabilized, a 25-caliber bullet should turn once every 10 inches of travel.

Walter Hunt's "Rocket Ball"

At the start of the Civil War, round balls were still standard, but soldiers were quick to see the advantages of "Minie" balls (pronounced me-NAY, after the French inventor Captain Claude Minie). Before they were loaded in the Union Army's Enfield rifles, these hollow-base conical slugs were lubricated with mutton tallow and beeswax. At first, a wooden plug was placed in the bullet skirt to aid expansion, but it was later discarded. Bullet and powder were carried in a paper pouch, with the powder kept in a second paper pouch atop the bullet. To load, a soldier tore off the folded tail of the outside bag with his teeth. This opened both pouches, which had been crimped together on closure. After emptying the powder into the bore, he inserted the bullet, using the pouch paper as patching.

Several other rifles used conical bullets, including the Lindsay, a unique muzzleloader that accommodated two loads, one behind the other. One trigger operated two hammers, each with its own vent. The right hammer was designed to trip first, sparking into the front vent, which entered the chamber just forward of the rear bullet, and firing the forward charge. A second tug on the trigger fired the rear charge. If the left hammer alone was cocked, the rear charge safely launched both bullets. This ability to fire more than one shot without reloading had limited utility, however. Each charge still had to be loaded from the front. Repeat shots could not be guaranteed in rifles of practical weight. Still, the technique of breech loading cleared the path for the repeating rifle. The idea of a gun with one chamber and barrel but a magazine holding ready ammunition prompted inventors to work on new actions. Only a few early ones functioned reliably. Locking mechanisms and steels of that period lacked the strength to bottle high pressures. The large cartridges used in single-shot rifles did not fit repeating actions, either. Big game hunters stuck with the more powerful single-shots until the late 1870's.

The most noteworthy first-generation repeating rifle was designed by New York inventor Walter Hunt, whose credits also included the safety pin, fountain pen and typewriter. In 1848, Hunt patented a conical bullet containing a powder charge in its hollow base. The cap, made of cork, had a hole in its center that was sealed by paper. Hunt's bullet, which he called his "rocket ball," was mated in 1849 to a 54-caliber rifle. It featured a spring-loaded tubular magazine under the barrel and a pill-lock mechanism that fed primers as each cartridge was being chambered. Despite several inherent weaknesses, Hunt's rifle demonstrated several worthwhile principles and was later refined by Lewis Jennings, an accomplished gunsmith. In 1858, Oliver Winchester commissioned Benjamin Tyler Henry to develop a metal-cased cartridge for the rifle, which by that time had undergone many

changes and was called the "Volcanic." From Henry's work and Winchester's business acumen evolved the lever-action line of Winchester rifles.

In Europe, the door-lock principle developed by the German inventor Paul Mauser was hailed for its simplicity and strength. During the late 1800's, Mauser dominated the market for military rifles. Model 1871 was a single-shot chambered for the German 11.15×60R. Its 386-grain lead bullet at 1,400 fps matched the performance of its contemporaries, among them: Turkey's 9.5×60R and Serbia's 10.15×63R; the Swiss 10.4×38R; Italian 10.4×47R; Austrian 11.15×58R; and the French 11×59R. Great Britain's .577/450 Martini-Henry pushed a 480-grain bullet at 1,350 fps; and the U.S. .45-70 drove its 405-grain bullet at 1,320.

For these holdovers from black powder days, paper-patched lead bullets worked fine. But soon smokeless powder would exact higher velocities from smaller bores. The first small-bore smokeless round adopted by a military power was the French 8mm Lebel, in 1886. England followed in 1888 with its .303 British and Switzerland joined in 1889 with the 7.5×55 Schmidt-Rubin. By the mid-1890's, virtually all armies used small-bore bolt rifles firing smokeless cartridges.

As black powder, straight cases and big bores lost favor in the last years of the 19th century, shooters found that old bullet designs didn't fit the new bottle-neck rounds fueled with smokeless powder. Blunt bullets quickly lost velocity downrange; moreover, any lead bullet sent zipping through a barrel at 2,000 fps would strip, losing its accuracy and fouling the bore.

While long, pointed bullets improved downrange performance, encasing bullets in metal jackets promised to reduce leading. The first commercial bullet jackets, developed in the early 1890s, were made of steel and coated with cupro-nickel. They performed well enough in the .30-40 Krag, but any .30-06 rifle shooting the same bullet developed rough spots in the bore near the muzzle. The problem—metal fouling—was caused by the higher velocity of the .30-06 bullet. Once metal fouling started, it accelerated quickly. Tiny lumps of bullet jacket adhered to the relatively cool steel at the muzzle, compounding the problem by tearing the jackets of succeeding bullets.

Shooters found a cure for this malady in "ammonia dope," a brew of 1/2 ounce ammonia bicarbonate, 1 ounce ammonia sulfate, 6 ounces 28-percent ammonia water, and 4 ounces tap water. The mixture was poured into a barrel plugged at the muzzle, then left to work for 20 minutes. Great care was taken not to spill the dope on other gun parts, because if the mixture contacted metal to air, pitting resulted.

After Army tests prior to World War I proved that bullet lubricant reduced metal fouling, "Mobilubricant" was issued for this purpose. Subsequently, Colonel Townsend Whelen found that lubricated bullets boosted pressures in the .30-06 from 51,000 to 58,000 psi—and coating the entire cartridge jacked them up over 70,000 psi. By 1921, the Army had outlawed the use of grease on small arms ammunition.

About this time, ordnance people began testing tin in rifle bullets. During World War I, the French had added strips of tinfoil in artillery powders to reduce metal fouling. The tin, having apparently formed an alloy with the copper, prevented copper's adhesion to the bore. By 1921, .30-06 National Match ammunition included cores that were 30 parts lead and 1 part tin; at the same time, jackets were electrically plated with tin, adding .0006 inch to bullet diameter. These bullets performed well, but later tests showed neck tension increased with age because the tin "cold-soldered" to the case. Despite this bonding, chamber pressures stayed within reason—but only until a cartridge was greased. The combination of a lubricated round with a tinned bullet set firmly in its neck spelled

trouble. The lube kept the neck from moving outward to release the bullet and increased back thrust on the bolt. One bullet recovered at a firing range still wore the case neck! Tin plating was soon abandoned by the Army.

A better idea was to incorporate tin in the bullet jacket. The cupro-nickel encasing the steel-jacketed Krag bullet in 1893 was 60 percent copper, 40 percent nickel. In 1902, cupro-nickel replaced steel in the jackets. Gilding metal—90 percent copper and 10 percent zinc—was also tried, but it was considered too soft for the high-velocity 150-grain .30-06 service bullet. When tin plating failed, the Western Cartridge Company came up with a new jacket material, called Lubaloy. It comprised 90 percent copper, 8 percent zinc and 2 percent tin. Lubaloy produced none of the fouling caused by cupro-nickel. It worked so well that in 1922 Western was chosen to provide Palma Match ammunition loaded with 180-grain Lubaloy bullets. That same year, the Frankfort Arsenal began loading bullets with gilding metal jackets without the tin. The company discovered that gilding metal could be made to stand the stress of high velocity. Now most rifle and handgun bullets are jacketed with gilding metal. Tin is no longer a specified component of any brand-name jacketed bullet.

Bullet Manufacture Today

Jacket composition varies by make, but most bullet firms now use a 95-5 alloy instead of the original 90-10 copper-zinc material. An exception was the 90-10 jacket for Nosler Partition bullets made on screw machines before 1970. Since Nosler (Bend, Oregon) adopted the impact extrusion process for making jackets, it has used 95-5 stock for both rifle bullets and its cup-and-draw-formed handgun bullets. Barnes (American Fork, Utah) manufactures its thick jackets of "pure" copper tubing. The extra ductility helps curb fragmenting.

Most bullet jackets began life as a thin strip of gilding metal that's fed into a press. Like a big cookie cutter, the press stamps out little discs that are then formed or drawn into cups by a series of dies. After being trimmed to length and stuffed with a lead slug, the jackets are shaped and finished off at the nose.

Impact extrusion forms jackets from metal rods chopped into short segments and annealed. The billets, after being fed into a punch press with 60 tons psi, emerge looking like a cup drawn from a metal sheet. Nosler claims impact extrusion ensures greater concentricity and uniformity. Its Partition

As new powders and bullets and stronger actions boosted ballistic efficiency, U.S. military cartridges grew smaller and more effective. From left: .45-70 (1873), .30-40 Krag (1892), .30-06 Springfield (1906), .30 Carbine (1941), 7.62 NATO or .308 Winchester (1954), and 5.56 Ball M193 or .223 Remington (1964).

bullets, featuring lead cavities fore and aft, are run into the punch twice.

Nosler used machine tubing for its first Partition bullet jackets, and Barnes still does. Nosler claims the old bronze-tinted bullets from their screw machines can't match the new impact-extruded Partitions for accuracy. Section an old Partition bullet longitudinally down the middle, and you'll find a tiny hole in the gilding metal divider, revealing the concentricity of the tubing and jacket. Rarely is the hole perfectly centered.

Cores for big game and military bullets are mostly lead, with some antimony for extra hardness. A common ratio is 97 1/2 percent lead, 2 1/2 percent antimony. A little antimony makes a big difference; cores with 3 percent antimony are much harder than those with half a percent less. Six percent is about the limit in commercial bullets. Sierra (Santa Fe Springs, California) uses three alloys for rifle bullets, with antimony proportions of 1½, 3 and 6 percent, respectively. Bullets designed to open quickly or at low velocity perform best without antimony, so most makers use "pure" lead for pistol and varmint-class rifle bullets. Barnes makes all its bullets without antimony, regulating expansion by varying the thickness of its heavy, ductile copper jackets. Unalloyed bullet lead has traces of copper, zinc, nickel, arsenic and aluminum. As little as .1 percent copper can cause hard spots in a bullet.

Cores are joined to jackets in several ways. Most are inserted cold into the gilding metal cup, which is then formed around the core in a die. A cannelure enables the jacket to grip its core, though cannelures are used mostly as crimping grooves that help the case grasp the bullet. Most big game bullets for handloading now lack cannelures, though Hornady, Winchester and a few other companies have retained them. Some firms offer cannelures only on bullets that are commonly crimped. Big bullets for powerful cartridges, such as the .458 Winchester Magnum, are generally cannelured because crimping helps prevent bullet creep in the magazine under recoil. Pistol bullets wear cannelures because crimping helps offset the weak case grip caused by shallow bullet seating. Ammunition factories still use cannelured bullets because they routinely crimp their bullets. Many shooters say crimping compromises accuracy, though tests of carefully loaded hunting ammunition have failed to verify that. Most cannelures are rolled on, but Nosler cuts the crimp in its 210-grain .338 bullet for loading in Federal's Premium ammunition (Federal Cartridge Company, Anoka, Minnesota).

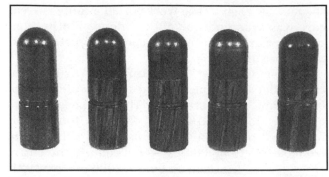

These one-piece bullets used for big game are not meant to expand. Only the one at far left is unfired—the rest were recovered from game or test media and can be used again.

Mating a lead core to a gilding metal jacket is not difficult; but eliminating variances in the finished bond and jacket is. So is devising bonds that regulate bullet expansion in game. Everyone wants an accurate bullet, and most shooters are hunters concerned with what a bullet does inside an animal. Target bullets need no internal mechanism for expansion, but outside tolerances are critical. Sierra, for example, allows only .0003-inch variations in jacket thickness on its target bullets, and it limits weight differences to 0.3 grain. A test lot of 168-grain .308 match bullets must shoot into .250 inch at 100 yards to pass muster at Sierra. If it doesn't, that production run is rejected. Such stringent standards increase costs, but they also ensure fine accuracy.

Most match bullets have tapered heels (boattails) and long, pointed noses that slide easily through the air. Their hollow points help shift the center of gravity rearward, further enhancing accuracy. Incorporating these features in a hunting bullet makes it perform better, too—that is, until it strikes flesh. Then, different standards prevail, and different designs work better. Expected bullet velocity and shot distance influence bullet design, as does the intended game. A 200-grain bullet built for launch by a .30 Magnum at 2,900 fps will not reach its potential if fired in a .308 Winchester at 2,500 fps. An elk offers more resistance than a whitetail deer, so a 90-grain .243 bullet designed to open properly on whitetails will likely fragment on the shoulder of an elk. High bullet velocity, close shooting and substantial target resistance tend to tear a bullet apart. Low speed, long range and soft targets act to impede expansion. A great variety of sporting bullets have been developed to accommodate most hunting situations.

This modern 124-grain 9mm pistol bullet (left) has a big hollow point for quick expansion at relatively low velocity. Shot into clay (right), it makes a huge wake.

Introducing the Shotshell

Most early shotgun development took place in England, where "proper" bird shooting demanded the best of tools. By 1880, British shotguns had set a formidable standard for sophistication. Meanwhile, American gunmakers had been concentrating primarily on rifle design. Yankee guns of any description were, after all, made to be shot, not fondled. While most functioned well, they lacked the smooth, finished feel and delightful balance of England's best.

In those days, waterfowlers on both continents endured paper-hulled cartridges that swelled when wet and would not chamber. Soaked shells began to disintegrate, and eventually the powder was affected. The answer was a metal shotshell, like those used for rifles and the huge smoothbores carried by explorers in the tropics. These 10-, 8- and even 4-bore shotguns had versatility and great power. They were heavy, but someone else generally carried them for the shooter. The drawn brass cases then in use became known as "solids." Frightfully expensive, they were almost fail-proof and worth the cost when dangerous animals were the game.

Expensive ammunition was a liability for grouse guns, however. The ensuing demand for af-

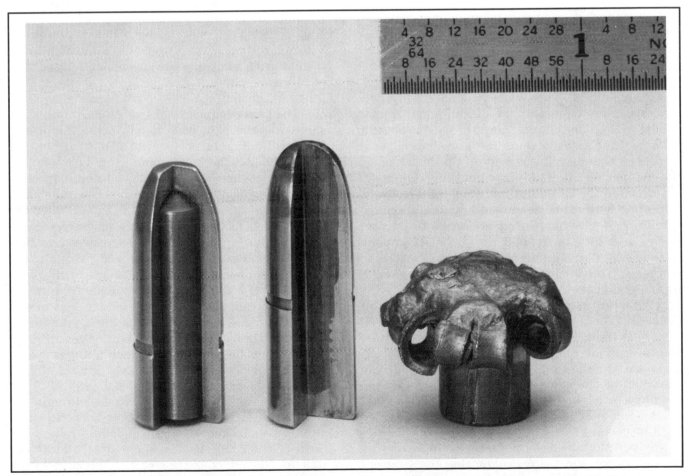

Speer's "African Grand Slam" bullets come in solid (left) and soft-nose (center) form. The expanded bullet mushroomed perfectly (right).

fordable waterproof cases led to the development of the "Perfect" or "Thin Brass" hull. In its production, a tube of drawn brass was affixed to a standard shotshell head, forming a waterproof case at less than the cost of fully drawn cases. The main problem with the Perfect hull was its small diameter. Because the tubes were so thin, their internal dimensions exceeded those of paper shells. That meant different wads had to be used, with shot and powder charges altered as well. A 12-bore Perfect cartridge might have the same charge weights and ballistic properties as a 10-bore paper round. Special chambers and barrels were made for Perfect shotshells, which were crimped just enough to hold a top wad. Shellac held the wad in position and helped waterproof the mouth of the case. While these cartridges worked well, the escalating price of copper and zinc in Europe just before World War II drove them off the market. They've not been revived.

A similar case, featuring a thin tube of zinc on a brass head, was developed in Belgium in 1935. It was given a full crimp in the manner of military blank rifle cartridges, with no over-shot wad. Because the crimp took up more of the case than the partial crimp on Perfect shells, loaded zinc cartridges had to be made shorter, with overall length less than 2 inches. Thin walls made internal capacity about the same as that of full-length paper shells, so the same charges could be used in shorter columns. Zinc's most serious flaw as a shotshell case was its malleability. Cases made of this metal sealed the chamber on firing properly, but they were easily deformed in the cartridge bag. Steel hulls tested at that time held up better afield but didn't expand enough under normal firing pressures to prevent gas leakage. Finally, in 1938, the Rottweil Company in Germany designed an aluminum case drawn in one piece. Tough as steel, it was malleable enough to seal chambers.

War interrupted commercial production of metal shotshells in Europe until, in 1947, Imperial Chemical Industries Limited made a large experimental run of one-piece, drawn-brass .410 cartridges with full crimp. The Italians tried a 12-bore shotshell of the same type but with a roll crimp holding a celluloid over-shot wad. Each product was successful, but the climbing price of brass scuttled both projects.

Paper shotshells, now largely supplanted by plastic, were for many years the shotgunner's standard ammunition. And they are still widely available. The shell body traditionally produced in Great Britain comprised layers of paper that were treated to repel water, glued together, and rolled into tubes of the proper size. Packed in cages, the tubes were first dried at 100 degrees F., then sent to a conditioning room where 9 percent moisture was added. Sizing machines produced uniform hulls only when the moisture content did not vary from one shell to the next.

The tubes, which were three to five times the finished cartridge length, were then chopped into the proper length, polished inside and out, checked for size, and fitted into cartridge heads. These had been cupped from circular sheets of brass, annealed, tempered, drawn, trimmed, and re-annealed. Early paper shells featured an iron reinforcing cup, also drawn to shape, that was fitted to the inside of the head. "Gas-Tight" cases had a tubular lining made of varnished metal that coiled around the powder, protecting the paper and reducing the risk of cut-offs. Cut-offs are case separations, usually induced by moisture that weakens the shell directly in front of the metal. Instead of opening the crimp, firing pulls the front part of the paper tube free and pushes it down the barrel with the shot, thereby boosting the pressure. Cut-shells, made by scoring the hull with a knife, were once popular in the Midwest, where hunters used the scored shells as slugs for deer hunting.

The final component of traditional paper shotshells was the base wad. It reinforced the primer cup, positioning the powder ahead of it, and braced and cushioned the head upon firing. Following its insertion, a shell could be primed and inspected. The loading of powder, wads and shot came next; and finally, the cartridge was crimped. Over the years, wads have undergone as much change as shotshell hulls. The first shot cartridges had four wads: an over-powder card, felt wad, over-felt card and over-shot card. The main purpose of the over-powder card was to protect the powder from grease in the felt wad, whose mission, in turn, was to seal powder gas and cushion the shot during the thrust of firing. The best felt wads had fine texture and were light-colored, whereas cheap felt was coarse and dark. Grease was commonly applied to felt wads to lubricate and help seal the bore.

For years, shooters had searched in vain for an inexpensive substitute for felt. Cork, an early alternative, lacked strength and uniformity; but then, in the early 1930's, a pneumatic cork wad was introduced, consisting of a simple disc with a hole in its middle. Under the compression of firing, air in the hole expanded the wad and cushioned the shot charge. This cork wad worked as long as pressures were kept in check and the central hole was made small enough. A large hole allowed powder gas to rupture the over-powder card, zipping through the wad and muscling into the rear of the shot column, leaving fragments of wad in the barrel.

In 1936, Imperial Chemical Industries of Great Britain introduced the Air-Cushion wad, consisting of a stout paper tube crimped on both ends, with a thin card wad in its center. If the rear crimp did not hold, gas would simply drive the card forward instead of blasting through the top crimp. To ease the strain on the rear of this wad, a thicker, 1/8-inch over-powder card was recommended. The pneumatic action of the Air-Cushion apparently did what it was supposed to, but the design never caught on in the U.S.

The over-felt card, like the over-powder card, was a $1/12$-inch disc. Its purpose was to prevent the shot from sticking to the felt wad and tearing it apart under the force of firing. Over-shot wads held the shot in the shell before full crimps were developed. Because they preceded the shot charge in flight, many shooters felt they disrupted patterns. In 1926 and 1927, Major Gerald Burrard, a British gun authority, set up a screen with a 6-inch hole 6 feet from the muzzle of a shotgun and fired at the hole 200 times. In every instance, the over-shot wad was found on the near side of the screen, and in only a handful of cases did any shot mark the periphery of the hole.

Until plastic came into use in the early 1960's, wad column components evolved slowly in this century. The first plastic parts were thin over-powder cups, replacing the card behind the felt or fiber wad. Alcan's Plastic Gas Seal and others like it sealed off the powder chamber and, following obturation, filled the bore behind the wad, increasing shotshell efficiency by 10 percent. By the mid-1960's, one-piece plastic wads were supplanting fiber wads, and soon plastic shot collars became available as well. They improved patterns by eliminating the friction that flattened peripheral pellets as they skidded down the bore. Fewer fliers meant more holes in the middle of the target.

The logical sequel was a one-piece shot cup incorporating a shot collar as the leading edge of a wad. Straps within the wad would flex under the thrust of firing, reducing the violence of set-back within the shot column. Slits in the collar would allow it to open like a parachute after exit, braking it as the shot charge carried on.

By then, compression-formed plastic hulls had

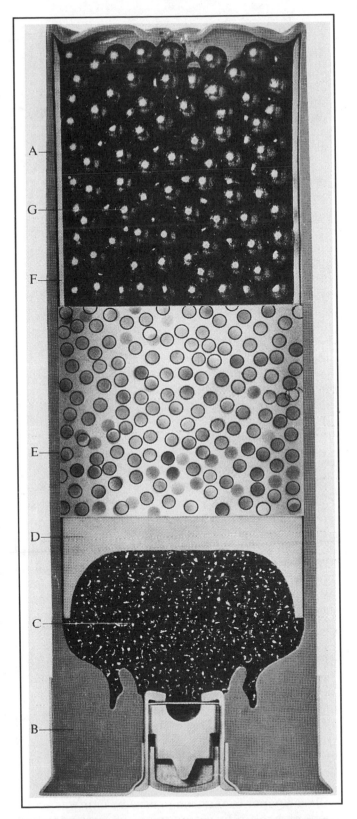

The basic components of a modern shotshell: A. Hull B. Integral base wad C. Powder D. Over-powder wad E. Fiber wad column F. Shot collar G. Shot

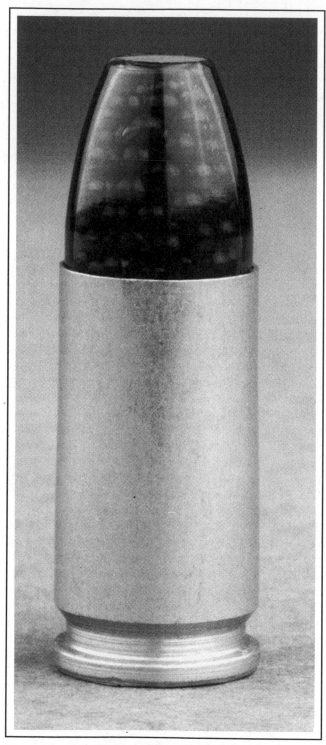

Plastic shot capsules, such as this 9mm CCI shotshell, have given new utility to handgun cartridges.

reinforcement. Tough and resilient, it could be loaded many more times than paper. It sealed the chamber tightly upon firing and didn't leak gas internally. It also yielded higher velocities at lower pressures, cost less than paper, and was waterproof.

Eventually, a Puerto Rican company—ACTIV (which is now located in West Virginia)—improved on the plastic shotshell by eliminating its brass head. This had been tried before, but with mediocre results. ACTIV's shotshell, however, functioned flawlessly. A thin metal disc, inserted before the rim was molded, strengthened the head, which was fastened to an extruded plastic tube by injection molding.

Lead Shot, Steel Shot, Slugs

A rifleman in the 1920's had comparatively few cartridges to shoot, and few bullet choices for any given round. Shotgunners, though, could select from more than 4,000 loads. Rifle rounds and their components have increased in number since, providing handloaders with more options. In contrast, fewer options remain for the shotgunner. Shotshells have become so much better than they were 70 years ago that selection need not be as great. Still, ammunition firms offer more choices in shotshells now than most shooters can use.

Today's shot pellets are only roughly similar to the first shot chipped from sheets of lead. By the turn of the century, ammunition companies were making shot by pouring molten lead through a sieve atop a high tower. The size of the hole in the sieve determined the shot size, and the free fall formed the pellet into its round shape. Shot towers are still in use, including Remington's, which has a huge cauldron on top that is kept within 15 degrees of 750 degrees F. at all times. The lead soup, laced with measured amounts of arsenic and antimony, leaves this cauldron in pipes that feed two colander pans. Holes in the colanders size the shot, which then falls 133 feet into 6 feet of water. Bucket belts dredge the cooled shot from this tank and carry it to a polishing machine. From there the pellets are piped to the tops of several sloping plates and released. As they tumble down, the round pellets pick up speed, causing them to bounce when they hit bottom. Good pellets will bounce high enough to clear gutters placed strategically at the bottom; misshapen shot lands in the gutters and is removed. Remington's plant can make 1.2 billion of these pellets a day.

replaced paper for almost all uses. Plastic was scuff-proof and self-lubricating to ensure better feeding and extraction. Its one-piece design was strong, incorporating a base wad that needed no additional

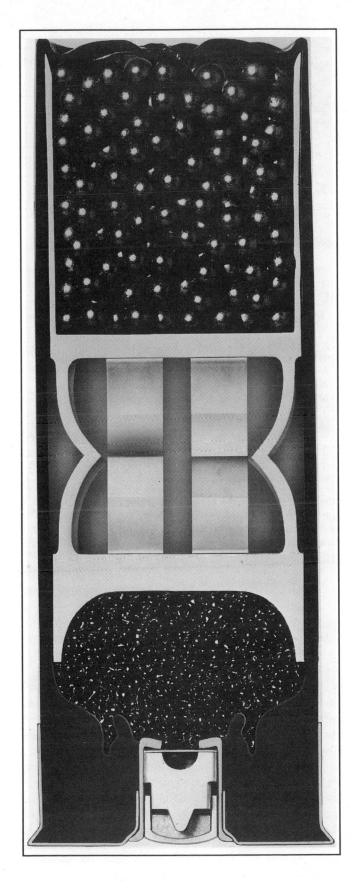

While towers work well for birdshot, most manufacturers mold buckshot. Steel shot is made the same way as ball bearings (though ball bearings are three times as hard as steel shot and cannot safely be used in shotshells). Steel wire is first cut into short pieces, which are then placed between two massive plates. The plates roll the chunks into spherical pellets. Shot size is determined by wire diameter, the length of cut sections, and the spacing of the plates.

The first birdshot made in the U.S. was almost pure lead, with a touch of arsenic to make it spherical as it fell from the shot tower. The result was a soft pellet too easily deformed by setback on firing. Chamber pressures as low as 7,000 psi could maim such shot before it left the shell. Patterns indicated that full-choke guns left half their pellets outside a 30-inch circle at 40 yards. Some inexpensive loads still contain soft shot and are poor performers. Some hunters have claimed that soft shot is more deadly than hard pellets because it deforms on impact, but that is not the case. Round pellets retain more energy in flight, and while one flattened pellet may make a nasty wound, each round pellet has a greater likelihood of hitting the bird.

"Chilled" shot arrived in the late 1940's. Its name has nothing to do with the way it is made but refers to pellets that contain antimony as a hardener. Not much antimony is needed—only 1 percent in big shot, 2 or 3 percent in small shot—to boost pattern percentages as much as 10 percent.

Magnum shot has more antimony than chilled shot—from 2 percent in BB and #2 sizes to 6 percent in #7½ and #8. Patterns fired with magnum shot can be 20 percent thicker than those fired with chilled shot because fewer pellets are deformed and lost as fliers. Plating shot makes it even more durable. Patented in England in 1878, plated shot wasn't marketed successfully in the U.S. until the 1950's. Now most premium loads feature it.

Though smooth bores have limited utility with single projectiles, modern shotgun slugs boast more than twice the range of buckshot designed for deer hunting. Many single-barrel repeaters will put slugs in a 6-inch group at 80 yards, and shotguns with rifled barrels can do even better. The development

The plastic one-piece wad in this shotshell has an integral collar to protect the shot in its travel down the bore. Its basal section flexes to absorb the shock of firing, preventing the pellets from thrusting violently against each other.

of slugs and slug guns has accelerated because many populous states now require them for deer hunting. Rifles, some people fear, throw bullets dangerously far, whereas a spent slug comes to earth much sooner.

Slugs replaced so-called "pumpkin balls," which were lead spheres cast to give versatility to the shotguns of 19th-century farmers, pioneers and adventurers. Pumpkin balls flew erratically because they had to be cast slightly undersize. European farmers used them to keep the wild pigs out of their potatoes. Their double shotguns had one choked barrel and another featuring a short section of rifling near the muzzle. Accuracy with that rifled tube was not bad. The English Paradox guns, with their shotgun chambers and heavy barrels, also shot well. Some had rifled muzzle sections, some full-length rifling, and still others had oval bores. The Paradox was popular with explorers because it was so versatile.

The first successful shotgun slug was developed by the great German inventor, Wilhelm Brenneke. His innovation featured a pointed nose and parallel sides cast with offset ribs. These ribs contracted to ease passage through the choke and thus impart spin to the slug. A wad "sandwich," consisting of two card wads with a thick felt disc between them, was screwed to its base. The Brenneke flew straight mainly because it was nose-heavy, like a shuttlecock. It was modified in 1931 for use in Paradox guns, and four years later it became available with an optional steel tip for deeper penetration. The current Brennekes sport a plastic base wad.

In the 1930's, Karl Foster, an American researcher in ballistics, designed a one-piece slug with a round nose and hollow base. It had shallow offset ribs and operated on the nose-heavy, nose-first principle Brenneke had pioneered. The hollow skirt compressed easily in chokes and was said to expand sufficiently to seal the bore on firing (expansion depends on gas, however, and in this case gas is blocked by the shotshell's wad column).

The most recent and ballistically efficient slugs are called "sabots"—projectiles shaped like an hour glass and weighing about the same as the Foster (one ounce in the standard 12-gauge loading). Sabots are smaller in diameter, though, and are secured by a thick, plastic, bore-size cocoon that falls away upon leaving the muzzle. The plastic marries comfortably with new rifled barrels and does not lead them, as Brenneke and Foster slugs do. Sabot slugs shoot as accurately as many hunting rifle bullets to 100 yards. Slugs in general do not harm

Restrictions on rifles for deer hunting in settled areas have prompted the development of special big game shotguns and more effective rifled slug and buckshot loads. The slug (above) is a nose-heavy Foster-style, developed in the 1930's. The buckshot (below) are cradled in plastic crumbs to curb pellet deformation.

chokes, although the best slug performance usually comes from guns with little or no choke.

Shotgun Chokes

While the British pioneered shotgun and shotshell development in the early 1800's, Fred Kemble of the U.S. has been credited with one of the most important smoothbore developments ever: the choked barrel. Kemble's first attempt to constrict a shotgun's muzzle produced such disheartening results that he reamed the barrel out again. But apparently he didn't get all the choke, because his patterns jumped to nearly 100 percent at 40 yards. A Midwest market hunter, Kemble subsequently used choked barrels to kill embarrassing numbers of waterfowl—including, in one day, 57 bluebills with 57 shots. This happened in 1870, four years after William Pape, an Englishman, reportedly experimented with choke. Kemble made the benefits of the choke widely known, however, and may or may not have known of Pape's work.

Chokes can be swaged or reamed into a barrel. Most American chokes are reamed from a thickened section of barrel 2 or 3 inches back from the muzzle and tapered to it. Some extend farther back to permit a short length of parallel bore at the muzzle. A long taper, though it may seem less severe than a short one, actually creates greater friction among the pellets, because pressure is exerted over a longer period of time. Though shot deformation by barrel friction is all but eliminated by plastic collars, the jostling of pellets within the charge scars their surfaces, pulling the pellets away from bore axis on exit much like a pitcher's curve ball. Short chokes need less total constriction to work. They don't elevate pressures as quickly or sustain them as long as extended bore tapers. Barrels that have been cut can have jug or recessed chokes reamed in just back from the muzzle. Most muzzles are thick enough to accommodated screw-in choke tubes for added versatility.

The English measure choke in points, or thousandths of an inch. A 12-gauge bore miking .730 inch and given 40 points of choke measures .690 inch at its most constricted place. That is full choke by U.S. standards, designed to put roughly 70 percent of a shot charge inside a 30-inch circle at 40 yards. In the U.S., three-quarter choke means 30 points of constriction or improved modified; half choke is 20 points, for a modified choke that patterns about 60 percent; and quarter choke is improved cylinder, which normally throws 50 percent patterns. Cylinder bores have no choke at all. Extra full is an American invention. Skeet #1 and #2 correspond to cylinder and improved cylinder. Once common terms, they have lost favor because chokes on skeet guns show a lot of variation. Trap guns are bored full or extra full.

PART II

THE GUNMAKERS WHO SHAPED AN INDUSTRY

AN INTRODUCTORY NOTE

Immediately before and after the American Civil War, an avalanche of activity in gun development gave rise to the most famous names of that industry—Colt, Smith & Wesson, Winchester, and Sharps, with Browning and Marlin close on their heels. Only Remington predates the mid-1800's, when gun and ammunition design changed so fast that mechanisms became obsolete in five years.

All the armsmakers included in Part II got their start during the black powder days, when mass production of steel parts was just becoming practical. While cotton gins were fashioned of interchangeable parts well before the Civil War, metals and machining tolerances weren't up to the task of mass-producing guns. An ill-fitting part on a farm implement might still work, but on a gun it could cause a malfunction or even a breech failure. By the time metallic cartridges came along, mass production had been adapted to gunmaking. Sharps offered the first truly powerful rifle built with assembly-line parts.

Of the seven companies featured here, only Sharps is now defunct, while others have scaled back production sharply. Accommodating great, sometimes abrupt, swings in demand for products requires great flexibility from an armsmaker—especially given the huge overhead in tooling necessary for gun production. Six of these seven companies have managed to do that for more than a century, all the while engineering better guns in a highly competitive industry. All seven have proven themselves pivotal to the success of American gunmaking.

CHAPTER 3

REMINGTON: AMERICA'S OLDEST GUNMAKER

The year was 1816. Jethro Wood of Cayuga County, New York, had not yet invented the first all-metal plow, and Eliphalet ("Lite") Remington II was going on 23. Lite and his wife Abigail lived in his father's stone house on Staley Creek in Litchfield, New York, four miles from the German Flatts and the Mohawk River. A wooden flume carried creek water to a big paddlewheel, powering the elder Remington's forge where Lite fashioned his first gun from iron scrap and home-sawn walnut.

Certainly no American gun company operating today has deeper roots than Remington. According to some genealogists, they reach back to an English clergyman named Richard Remington, born in 1500. His son, Richard, came along in 1535, and a third Richard Remington followed in 1570. The last Richard became an archdeacon and Rector of Lockington, Yorkshire (England). The Rector, in a fit of originality, named his son John, who further broke with tradition by sailing with his wife and two young sons to America in 1637.

This lineage is contested by some Remington family members who claim that John was the son of Sir Thomas Remington of Lockridge Abbey. But whatever his ancestry, John joined other Yorkshiremen in founding the settlement of Rowley, near Salem, Massachusetts. Apparently he'd been indentured—perhaps to pay his passage—because in March of 1639 he became a freeman. A year later he showed his military bent by offering to "drill the militia company at Rowley." In 1645, John became sergeant of the militia, and in 1647 its leader.

John's progeny became reasonably prosperous, marrying English girls and fathering mostly sons. Jonathan Remington, born in 1677, became Professor of Law at Harvard, then probate judge in Bos-

ton, and finally a Massachusetts appellate court judge. John's grandson Thomas moved to Suffield, in Litchfield County, Connecticut, in the late 1670s, siring a family that remained there for a full century. In 1745, Remington twins, John and Josiah, were born. John married Patience Mason in 1767, and the young couple became parents on October 13, 1768. They christened the boy Eliphalet. John died a year later.

Raised with strict Methodist principles and trained as a carpenter, Eliphalet proved an enterprising young man. By the time he married Elizabeth Kilbourn at age 23, he'd become well established in Litchfield. His first son, Eliphalet Remington II, was born October 28, 1793, a year after daughter Elizabeth.

By that time, adventurous New Englanders were heading west in substantial numbers. The Revolutionary War had reined back the drift of settlers beyond settlements, but when the fighting stopped, pioneers struck out for the richer soil rumored to be "just up the Mohawk." Virgin soil, it was, with no rocks to dig.

Eliphalet's Uncle Josiah joined other adventurers and bought 680 acres of forest in Glen's Purchase north of Little Falls and south of the Mohawk. The Purchase was part of a plateau with deep, fertile ground that needed only logging and planting. Josiah wrote back home enthusiastically of his new farm, and of the opportunities for young men with a trade. Eliphalet eagerly read the letters and, in 1799, decided to look at his uncle's paradise firsthand.

The 180-mile trip from Suffield to Fort Dayton (what is now Herkimer) took six days. Eliphalet traveled partly by foot, partly by stage, and partly

Eliphalet Remington II founded a company because other shooters liked the rifle he built for himself on his father's forge.

the land. They finally persuaded him to join them in this new township, which they named Litchfield after the county they'd left behind in Connecticut.

Before Eliphalet Remington returned to Suffield, he'd paid James Smith $275 for the 50 acres he'd marked above the Gulph. It was a steep price, but forest land commanded a premium then, and Eliphalet knew what he wanted. Besides, taxes were lower in New York. Cultivated land required that you pay only one sixth of one acre's produce for each hundred acres. Forest land was taxed at 12 cents per hundred acres.

Despite the rigors of an oxcart move to a wilderness property, Elizabeth Remington was game. The Remington's hastily built cabin didn't match a clapboard house for comfort, but her industrious husband worked hard to make it appealing. His frugality had left him enough money to pay laborers $7.50 an acre for cutting timber, bucking it into 14-foot lengths and piling the brush for burning. Sub-

by wagon. Upon reaching the palisades at Little Falls, the gateway to new opportunity seemed truly to beckon. A canal, built by the Inland Lock Company, enabled boats to continue upriver. Young Remington passed farms where, during the War, Tory Rangers under Walter and David Butler, along with Seneca and Mohawk Indians led by Chief Joseph Brant, had murdered families of settlers and raced north to sell their scalps to the British at eight dollars apiece. But now the farms were prospering again.

Beyond Fort Dayton, Eliphalet had himself rowed across the Mohawk to the fortress church of Herkimer, then walked on through the German Flatts to the tiny settlement of London. Turning south, he climbed up through a glacier cut in the hills, known as the Gulph. A plateau with beech, walnut and chestnut trees carried the road then, till it fell away into Staley's Creek. This seemed an ideal place for a cabin, with creek water to run a mill and trees for lumber, and deep earth to grow a garden. That night Eliphalet Remington slept with friends from Litchfield near Crane's Corners. He stayed several days, helping them build and farm

The original Remington homestead in Ilion, New York, was built by Eliphalet Remington in 1799.

sequently, Eliphalet raised good crops of hay and grain, but they depended largely on his carpentry for a steady income.

The Remingtons schooled their children at home and raised them strictly but lovingly. Because there was initially no church in the area, Methodism came with the circuit rider or was taught in the evenings by candlelight. By 1807, Eliphalet was prospering. He bought an adjoining 195-acre parcel for $585 that year and later added 71 acres more. In 1809, he began building a more substantial house for his family, quarrying rock from the Gulph.

The War of 1812 had little effect on the Mohawk settlers, though American troops cut the new river road to ribbons with their supply wagons. By this time, Eliphalet II, or "Lite", had become a young man. While he shared his father's business sense, he was also poetic and precocious. Lite become enamored of Abigail Paddock, who had moved to Litchfield Township in 1809. After a five-year courtship, they were married in the church that had been built at Crane's Corners. The newlyweds spent their first two years living in the Remington house. Eliphalet senior had just built a forge on Staley Creek and found it so profitable that he constructed a dam and installed a furnace for smelting ore. It was in this forge that Lite began his career as a gunmaker in August of 1816.

Lite's Frontier Enterprise

Building a firearm in that day entailed more than merely assembling parts—you also had to *make* the parts. Pumping the bellows, Lite first heated the rod he'd chosen for his barrel to a bright glow, hammered it until it was half an inch square in cross section, then wound it around an iron mandrel. The mandrel was not quite as big in diameter as the finished bore—in this case, 45 caliber. Next, he heated the barrel until it was white hot, sprinkled it with Borax and sand and, holding one end in his tongs, pounded the other vigorously on the stone floor to seat the coils. When the tube had cooled, Lite checked it for straightness and hammered out the curves. Finally, he ground eight flats, because most barrels in that day were octagonal.

After several days' work, Lite's barrel still was not rifled. For that, he traveled to Utica, a growing town of 1,200. Some say that Morgan James cut the grooves there for Lite, but at least one historian argues that James, albeit well known for his barrel work, did not operate a shop at the time and that Remington's rifling job was done by someone else. The price—four double reales (a dollar in country

currency)—was considered fair for two days' work at a time when most mill hands made about $200 a year.

Back at the home forge, young Remington bored a touchhole and forged a breech plug and lock parts, finishing them with a file. He brazed the priming pan to the lockplate and finished all metal parts with hazel-brown, a preservative of uric acid and iron oxide. The walnut stock, shaped with draw-knife and chisel, was smoothed with sandstone and sealed with beeswax. Lite put together his new rifle with hand-wrought screws and pins. Not long after that, he took his gun to a local shooting match and placed second. Other shooters were impressed; in fact, even the winner of the match wanted a Remington rifle. How much would it cost, he asked, and when could he have it?

"Ten dollars," Lite said, "and you'll have it in ten days."

Remington rifles soon became known throughout New York. Their success was due largely to a need for finished rifles on the frontier. While the Honorable Hugh Orr had produced the nation's first "factory" guns at his Bridgewater, Massachusetts, foundry in 1748, only government arsenals at Springfield and Harper's Ferry were mass-producing muskets in 1816. Most of the riflemakers on the frontier furnished a few gun parts and locks to complement barrels that were imported, often at great cost, from England and Belgium.

During the summer of 1817, Lite and Abigail and their young son Philo shared their new home on Staley Creek with gun customers, many of whom stayed for a time to help build their own rifles and save a little money. Remington scoured the countryside for scrap iron—including pots, plowshares, horseshoes, anything that could be smelted down and fashioned into gun parts. Soon he was offering rifled or smoothbore barrels as well as finished guns.

During his fourth year in business, Lite sold more than 200 barrels and complete rifles. At that time, plain iron barrels cost $3 and steel barrels $6, while "Stubbs twist" (Damascus) sold for $7.50. Although barrels comprised a large part of his business, Remington developed a model industry by building rifles he later sold in wholesale quantities. Soon his Staley Creek foundry was unable to stay abreast of demand.

When the Erie Canal was completed on October 26, 1825, the cost of moving a ton of goods from New York to Buffalo dropped from $100 to $12. It made good economic sense for Lite to build a new facility closer to port, but he was reluctant to leave

Eliphalet Remington II (above, left) started his work at this old forge (above, right) in 1816 in an area called Litchfield (NY).

the peaceful religious community of his youth. He managed to delay the move until January of 1828, when he purchased 100 acres on the Mohawk from John Clapsaddle. Remington Arms still occupies the ground, which included most of what is now Ilion's business district, purchased 160 years ago by its founder for $28 an acre.

While the new foundry was being built, Lite's father erected a second house for his son, so Lite could live close to his work. The elder Remington hauled timber from the Gulph, where many years earlier he'd climbed afoot to survey the land that became his home. Tragically, on June 22, 1828, Eliphalet Remington was thrown from a loaded wagon on a steep grade. Despite the frantic efforts of his driver, a huge iron wheel rolled over Eliphalet's chest. Five days later, he died.

That summer, the grieving Lite moved his family into the new house at Morgan's Landing; and that fall, Abigail delivered her third son. At the time, the Remingtons comprised 20 percent of the village population, but they contributed in much greater proportion. In summer, the foundry employed 20 machinists; and in winter, when ice froze the water-powered equipment, nearly as many workers assembled guns full time. As long as the Canal stayed open, the guns were easy to ship. Wrapped in bundles, they were carted to a nearby bridge, from which they were tossed on the cabin roofs of passing freighters.

When Remington's first factory building was completed in 1832, production capacity doubled. Lite then took to the road in an attempt to broaden his marketing territory. Pulled by relays of horses that were changed every 10 miles, Canal packets offered a 300-mile trip, Albany to Buffalo, for $14.33—meals included. But the packets were slow, so Remington often traveled by rail coach. When the Schenectady and Utica Railroad opened, with eight-hour service to Albany, canal ice no longer impaired winter travel.

In 1839, Lite became a partner in a smelting

Remington's plant in Ilion, New York, as it appeared in 1828.

and remodeled the old forge. Later, a new millrace was installed and another factory added. Known as Armory No. 1, it remained in use until World War I.

Ever on the prowl for machinery to boost his production, Remington encountered the N.P. Ames Company at Chicopee Falls, Massachusetts. The Ames Company, renowned for its cutlery, had failed on an experimental breech-loading carbine designed by William Jenks under contract with the Navy. Remington acquired the Ames gun business for a small down payment and $3,871.50 in installments, a price that included the services of Jenks.

Remington's top gunsmith, Riley Rogers, then helped Jenks redesign his carbine. In 1847, the Navy contract was filled—with guns featuring the first drilled-steel barrels sold to the government. The lock, developed by Edward Maynard, used percussion caps on a paper tape. With their barrels tinned for protection from salt spray, the first carbines went to Admiral Perry's fleet at Veracruz (Mexico).

Jenks, a Welshman, by now accustomed to the Army's bureaucratic bullheadedness, kept on plugging his rifles for military service. In one 1,500-round test session, a nipple broke on shot number 1,400 and his rifle was disqualified. Fed up, Jenks turned to England and France, where his designs were welcomed. The U.S. government, finally coming to its senses, begged him to return, which he did, submitting a new carbine in 1858. The lock was modified to feed cardboard cartridges coated with beeswax and tallow. After being immersed in water for one minute and set aside a full day, the gun was fired and passed muster. A year later, William Jenks toppled from a hay wagon on his farm near Washington, D.C., and died from the injuries.

Eventually, Remington sold rifles that incorporated Jenks' new lock, but most of the company's business came from barrels and traditional rifles made for western pioneers. In the 1850s, cast steel Remington barrels sold for $3, but you could buy an iron barrel for $2. Damascus barrels cost $4, and a match pair of cast steel tubes for double guns went for $6.50. The company sold 588 barrels per month in 1850, 672 in 1851, and 835 in 1852. A high count of 1,475 barrels was shipped in August, 1852. About that time, the company name was changed to E. Remington & Sons, Philo and Sam becoming partners with their father.

A new Remington foundry, completed in 1856, made gun parts and tooling for the armory, which was soon expanded to meet increasing demand. In

plant upstream from his factory where farm and sawmill equipment, as well as gun parts, were produced. His son Philo soon became part of the business and contributed several ideas that helped it succeed. Instead of straightening barrels with a plumb line, the accepted method of the time, Philo used the shadow of a window bar in the bore. The principle is still used by experienced barrelmakers. He also installed steel facings on trip hammers, to ensure closer manufacturing tolerances. The Remingtons used a scaled-down cannon drill to bore small-caliber holes through four feet of bar stock, a technique that enabled barrels to be made without seams.

On August 12, 1841, Abigail and her daughter Maria hitched a spirited horse to the carriage for a drive up through the Gulph to their old house. On the same road that had taken Lite's father, Maria decided to open her parasol. It popped like a pistol shot, frightening the horse and sending it galloping out of control across a stream. The carriage was smashed to splinters against a great oak and Abigail was instantly killed.

Growth, War, and a Poem to Maria

Though Abigail's death profoundly affected Lite Remington, his company continued to prosper. Impending war with Mexico in 1845 prompted the government to contract with the John Griffiths Company of Cincinnati, Ohio, to produce 5,000 percussion Harper's Ferry rifled muskets. When production lagged, Remington bought the contract. He called his son Sam in from the West to manage it

Remington's Model 78 centerfire rifle embodies what Remington is famous for—a functional mechanism, an accurate barrel, a stock that's comfortable to shoot, and all at an affordable price.

those days before the start of Civil War, Remington also manufactured locks, safes, vaults, telescopes, kaleidoscopes, and the newly invented Sayre cultivator tooth.

The Remingtons took an active civic role in their town, which grew quite literally around their business. Still, as late as 1843 the town had no name. Called London, Steele's Creek and Morgan's Landing by locals, it became known after 1830 as Remingtons' Corners. To provide adequate postal service, an area meeting was held to determine a name. More than 30 possibilities were submitted, one of the most popular being Remington, a suggestion that Lite graciously squelched. By vote, the winning name was Fountain, and so read the postal petition delivered to Congressman Charlie Benton of Mohawk. Benton didn't like the name, though, and changed it to Remington. Angered by such blatant presumption, Lite refused to list his return ad-

dress as Remington. Piles of business letters to "German Flatts" created big problems for the postal service, so Postmaster David Defoe asked Lite about naming the town after ancient Troy, as befitting a neighbor of Rome, Syracuse and Utica. Remington consented, and thus in 1852 the town became "Ilion" (the Greek word for Troy).

Philo, Samuel and Eliphalet III lived in modest frame houses on the same street as their father. Instead of spending his money on family comforts, Lite invested in the town. He founded the Bank of Ilion, of which he became the first president. His concern for other people extended to his employees, who never struck. He enabled his skilled workman to become contractors, producing parts as efficiently as they could and getting reimbursed by the piece. The Remingtons' integrity apparently was beyond reproach and generated strong loyalty among the workforce. Later, when the company came on hard times, contractors and employees alike dug in their own pockets to help.

Remington entered the handgun market briefly in 1849 with an improved version of the Beals revolver. Several models of various finishes and barrel lengths were manufactured in 31, 36 and 44 calibers. Shortly afterward, Joseph Rider, who later helped develop the rolling block rifle, came to Remington with a curious revolver design. Remington paid Rider 12 braces of revolvers and 400 acres in Ohio for partial rights to his gun. Rider built the first double-action revolver mechanism in 1859, meanwhile experimenting with ladies (or "muff") guns as short as 2 inches; the latter fired single BB shot powered by a percussion cap. Remington offered more formidable protection in its .41 Derringer designed by William Elliott, who also introduced a four-barrel, zig-zag pistol in which the firing mechanism jumped from one barrel to the other in turn. In 1858, John Thomas, a Remington mechanic, also designed an unusual "cane" gun, but none of these Remington pistols seriously challenged the Colt or Smith & Wesson revolvers of their day.

When Civil War erupted in 1861, the North was faced with a serious shortage of rifles. Eliphalet Remington II immediately expanded his Ilion plant to accommodate what would amount to nearly $30 million in gun orders from the Army and Navy. By this time, he'd installed a 500-horsepower Corliss steam engine (which remained in use until 1935). In nearby Utica, he converted the Hamilton Hotel into a factory producing 200 pistols a day. He also built some 18,000 Maynard percussion locks and installed them on old 1842 flintlock muskets. Bayonets were drop-forged at Remington's plant and fitted to Harpers Ferry rifles. By war's end, the company was producing almost 1,000 rifles a day, and its ammunition production totaled almost 10 million cartridges, plus great quantities of reloading tools and other accessories.

At first, many Northerners thought the war would be brief, but even the most optimistic were sobered when Stonewall Jackson's brigade routed the Union Army at Bull Run on July 2, 1861. Two nights later, Confederate troops were camped just outside Washington. A month after that Lite Remington was bedridden with what his doctors called "inflammation of the bowels." It might have been appendicitis; certainly it had something to do with the strain of wartime production at the Remington plant, where Lite had driven himself hard for a man nearing 70. On what proved to be his death bed, he dictated to his daughter Maria a poem that had nothing to do with the gun industry:

In manhood's strong and vigorous prime
I planted a young linden tree
Near to my dwelling, which in time
Has spread its branches wide and free.

Oft have I viewed its healthful growth
With something like a parent's pride
Who sees the offspring of his youth
Grow to strong manhood by his side.

But now, old age had damped the flame
That glowed within me at that day
Energy and strength desert my frame
And I am sinking in decay.

But thanks! I've lived and long have shared
Health and vigor like this tree
And when I'm gone let it be spared
A mute remembrance of me.

New Leadership and a New Rifle

Eliphalet Remington II died on August 12, 1861. The Remington factory closed down for Lite's funeral and burial in Ilion's cemetary, where his wife Abigail already lay. It resumed full-throttle production under Philo, Samuel and Eliphalet III. Samuel, a lively, outgoing man, was Remington's top salesman, his genial manner and natural charm contrasting with the subdued, almost shy personality of Eliphalet III, who managed the accounts. Philo had inherited his father's organizational skills and mechanical aptitude, so he took charge of the armory. One of his first projects was to invite gun designer Leonard Geiger to join the company.

Orders for more military weapons came thick and fast. One Ordnance Department contract called for 20,000 Geiger carbines, which Remington subcontracted to Savage Arms of Middletown, Connecticut. By 1864, the need to increase ammunition production prompted Remington to erect five new buildings and install more machinery. Before these new facilities reached capacity, however, the war ended. In April 1865, amid endless parades, the boys at Ilion sat by silent, heavily-mortgaged machinery and pondered the future. Fortunately, the company had become somewhat diversified. In 1864, the foundry located across the Erie Canal from the armory had been equipped to produce industrial machinery, and the following year a separate joint stock company, called The Agricultural Works, was formed, with Philo Remington as President, Sam as vice-president, and Eliphalet III as

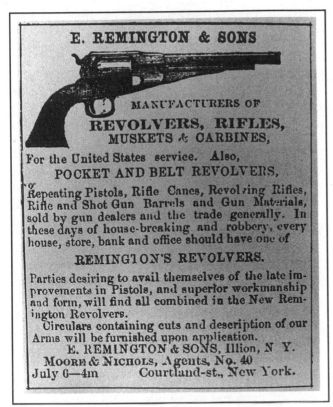
This 1866 ad features a single-action revolver, patented in 1858. Remington has made about 40 models of handguns but currently markets only one.

secretary-treasurer. Aware that agricultural tools had a brighter future than guns in the post-war era, Remington capitalized this new venture with $1 million, creating an asset value of $1.5 million.

Instead of letting their arms company go into bankruptcy, the Remington brothers mitigated the effect of abruptly-cancelled government arms and ammunition contracts with a new breech-loading rifle designed for sportsmen. Because Joseph Rider's improvements on Leonard Geiger's split-breech mechanism had been rushed, the gun fared poorly in the 1865 Army trials against such contemporaries as the Henry, Peabody and Sharps rifles. But by early 1866, Rider had corrected the flaws, and the company introduced its famous Rolling Block Rifle.

A strong, simple gun, the Rolling Block used a rotating breech block to seal a cartridge in the chamber. The hammer hit a striker in this block, firing the round. Breech block and hammer were of high-tensile steel (.69-inch thick) and interlocked at the moment of firing to give increased resistance to higher pressure. Easy to maintain and almost foolproof in operation, this mechanism was so quick to load that a practiced shooter could fire 17 rounds a minute. It was strong, too. In one test, a 50-caliber Rolling Block was loaded with 40 balls and 750 grains of powder, the charge filling 36.31 inches of a 40-inch barrel. Upon firing, it was reported that "nothing extraordinary occurred."

The new rifle got its first combat test in 1866 when a band of 30 cowboys led by Nelson Story drove some 3,000 cattle through Wyoming's Sioux country. Story had just bought new Remington Rolling Blocks at Fort Leavenworth and with them he and his men were able to repulse an Indian attack near Fort Laramie. Forbidden to proceed beyond Fort Kearney, Story waited two weeks while camped three miles outside the fort. Finally tired of the delay, he quietly slipped his herd onto the trail again and, on October 22, 1866, headed north.

Hostile Sioux were waiting for him. Led by Red Cloud and Crazy Horse, they swooped out of the hills to attack. Grossly outnumbered, the cowboys fired carefully but urgently, their guns becoming so hot they had to pour water on the barrels to cool them. The circling Sioux anticipated a pause in the deadly volleys, but none came. After retreating, they stopped to look back, discovering to their dismay that the Remingtons not only reloaded quickly but reached much farther than most other rifles they'd encountered.

Twice more on the drive, Story and his cowboys repulsed hostile Indians. By the time they reached Montana, the cowpunchers had used a lot of ammunition—but only one man was lost. A few weeks after Story left, Captain J.W. Fetterman led a mixed group of infantry and cavalry out of Fort Kearney. They were ambushed by Sioux and every man was killed. The next year, Fort Kearney was resupplied with fresh troops armed with breech-loading rifles.

In 1866, Samuel Remington replaced Philo as company president. A glut of surplus military rifles having crippled the post-war market for hunting guns, Sam, a super salesman, was obviously the man best suited to woo foreign buyers. He traveled to Europe, courting military and civilian markets there. Establishing a headquarters in Paris, Sam lived in high style. He found that most tradesmen were not permitted audience with the aristocracy. But the favorite pastime for many heads of state was hunting, so gunmakers enjoyed warmer welcomes. Sam had great success selling his Rolling Block Rifle, except in Prussia. There, amid great pomp, the king was invited to shoot. Unfortunately, the Rolling Block's firing pin fell on a dud cartridge and the king, soon to become Kaiser Wilhelm I of Germany, rode angrily from the field.

Sam's luck improved when Ismael Pasha, an Egyptian leader, asked to see a demonstration of the Remington breechloader. Sam got along so well with the statesman that he was given an expensive parcel of land in Cairo. Because it would have been rude to leave it barren, Sam built there a small but expensive marble palace. After his death, it was sold to the British government and used until 1952 as a place to entertain dignitaries.

Prosperity, Invention, and Failure

By 1870, the Remington Arms plant covered 15 acres of floor space. At the rolling machines, four men produced 350 rough barrels a day; and 400 milling machines were required to finish the guns. The monthly payroll had reached $140,000, an impressive sum at a time when dinner at a good restaurant cost 25 cents. To meet the deadline on one French contract, production peaked at 1,530 rifles a day.

Remington's growth brought prosperity to Ilion, which doubled in size between 1860 and 1876, reaching 4,000 in population. A grand opera house, built in 1870 thanks to a $20,000 grant from Hamlin Maben, a local physician, brought famous performers to town. At the same time, Philo Remington moved into his new house on Armory Hill. Though he maintained that his old one was adequate, others insisted that it had no quarters for guests and was too scruffy for the new Remington image. The finished residence must have appalled Philo, who'd been raised a straightlaced conservative. Built of pink and gray sandstone in the form of a castle, it featured turrets and towers and terraced gardens outside, with walnut panels, satin draperies and domed ceilings inside. Philo reportedly kept to his puritanical principles by entertaining royalty with hearty toasts of lemonade.

While Remington offered several sporting guns in the early 1870's (one listing for only $8), the Rolling Block remained a top seller. Its strongest competition came from Winchester's lever-action Model 1873, which (in .44-40) proved a reliable repeater and offered more power than its predecessor, Model 1866 (.44 Henry). Still, Winchester's short, relatively weak mechanism would not accommodate truly potent big game rounds like the .45-70. The Rolling Block did, and with greater accuracy. Following a hunting expedition in 1873, George Armstrong Custer wrote: "With your rifle I killed far more game than any other single party . . . at longer range." And at the Battle of Little Big Horn in 1876, Custer's doomed troops were armed only with converted Springfields, while the attacking Sioux carried rifles made by Sharps, Winchester and Remington.

The Rolling Block was also a favorite tool of buffalo hunters. Buffalo hides in the late 1800's sold for up to $50, and good hunters could earn $10,000 a year. One sharpshooter, Brazos Bob McRae, claimed 54 buffalo with as many shots at a single stand with his .44-90-400 Remington and Malcolm scope. The days of buffalo hunting were short and shameful. The supply of game was soon exhausted, and without their buffalo the starving Indians could offer little resistance.

In 1874, L.L. Hepburn, a Remington engineer, began work on a target rifle for long-range matches, similar to those used by the Irish in their recent victory at Wimbledon. The Irish challenged "any American team" through an ad in the New York Herald. Each team would comprise six men, shooting three rounds (at 800, 900 and 1000 yards) of 15 shots per round. A newly formed National Rifle Association, along with the cities of New York and Brooklyn, each put up $5,000 to construct a range for the match on Long Island's Creed's Farm. The State of New York helped by providing land for the facility called Creedmoor.

Remington's new target rifle, a .44-90 shooting 550-grain conical bullets, came off the line in March of 1874. In September, a favored Irish team shooting muzzleloaders bowed to the Americans and their Remington and Sharps breechloaders. The score was 934 to 931, with one Irish crossfire. Subsequent matches held in 1875 and 1876 were won more decisively by the U.S. team, with Remington's "Creedmore" rifles posting the highest scores.

Meanwhile, as new Midwest firms competed with lower shipping costs, Remington's Agricultural Works lost much of its profitability. A few items, including the Crawford reversible mower and the Scattergood cotton gin, failed. One of the company's more productive ventures included a horse-drawn fire engine with a pumper powered by the team of horses pulling it. Remington also made dynamos and iron bridges, a steam trolley car, and heavy equipment. Some of these products were financed with profits from the armory; none of them proved profitable in the long run.

T.J. Jones, formerly of the Singer Sewing Machine Company, convinced the Remingtons to enter the sewing machine market. They incorporated Jones's ideas into a fine machine, but marketing manager W.H. Hooper spent too lavishly to promote and establish offices for the new Remington Sewing Machine Company of North America. As a result, before the machine could gain a reputation the company's entire marketing capital was exhausted. Philo and Eliphalet III assumed the debt themselves, paying a million dollars to creditors.

The Remington typewriter came from an original design by C.L. Sholes, a Milwaukee newspaperman who coined the name "Type Writer" and later sold royalty rights to his marvelous machine to a partner for $12,000. "I have been trying all my life to escape being a millionaire," Sholes said later, "and I seem to have succeeded admirably." Sholes started inventing in 1867 and patented his first typewriter in 1868. Five years later, he had produced 25 different models, the last and best of which had all the basic features of a modern typewriter, including the universal keyboard.

In February of 1872, a bright young Remington executive, Henry Benedict, saw a typed letter sent to Philo by Sholes' partner, James Densmore. When Philo asked Benedict his opinion of the product, he cried, "This is a wonderful invention! Don't let it get away!" Philo took Benedict's advice and contracted with Densmore for manufacturing rights to the machine. Perfected by William Jenne and introduced in September 1873, the Remington typewriter worked well but sold poorly. Its $125 price tag was partly to blame; and surprisingly, many people considered printed letters an affront to their intelligence. Moreover, typed letters were considered poor form among elite social circles.

The business continued to flounder until a young Remington employee, Clarence Seamens, was given the top selling job. During his first year, Seamens sold 1,200 typewriters, and in 1882 he formed a partnership with William Wyckoff and Henry Benedict. The three men opened offices in New York and Paris, convinced an avalanche of demand was imminent.

It was, but it didn't move in time for the financially squeezed Remingtons. In 1886, Philo informed Benedict that he would have to relinquish the typewriter business to preserve the armory. "Then sell it to me," urged Benedict. That same afternoon, Remington sold its typewriter business, which eventually earned untold millions, to employee Henry Benedict for $186,000.

During its slide toward bankruptcy in the 1870's, E. Remington and Sons, as it was now known, engaged James P. Lee to engineer a bolt-action repeating rifle, called the Remington-Lee. A structural weakness in the breech caused some early rifles to eject their bolts rearward on firing, but this problem was soon corrected. Among the rifle's best features was its box magazine, patented in 1876. Initially, Remington made rifles for the Lee Arms Company, with James Lee as the selling agent. But in 1884 Lee let Remington make and market the guns on a royalty contract. Later, when Remington went into receivership, Lee got back his manufacturing rights, and shortly thereafter the British adopted Lee's design in their Lee-Enfield rifle. The SMLE (Short-Magazine Lee-Enfield) subsequently became the most famous of all British infantry rifles.

In 1877, Samuel Remington returned home to handle company sales programs from his house in New York City and an estate in Cazenovia. Five years later, he died. His brothers were unable to stop the steady erosion of profits in the arms plant, though much of their personal wealth had already been used to control the hemmorhaging. Ever selfless in prosperity or hardship, they continued to loan money to friends and gave freely to charity. Eliphalet III donated $500,000 to help found Syracuse University.

By 1886, Remington was reduced to paying its contractors (many of whom had grown rich) with script redeemable in goods at Ilion stores. Employees and contractors helped as much as they could to keep the company afloat, but later that year creditors forced bankruptcy proceedings. The money from the sale of the typewriter business had not lasted a month.

Remington assets at this time totaled over $1.7 million, while liabilities came to less than $1.3 million, leaving a surplus of $456,000. But most of that was tied up in specialized machinery that a nation at peace could not use. Finally, in March of 1888, Marcellus Hartley, founder of Union Metallic Cartridge Company, joined Thomas Bennett, son-in-law of Connecticut Governor Oliver Winchester, in a buyout. They paid $200,000 for Remington's property, production facilities, stock and reputation.

What had been most recently E. Remington and Sons became, with this deal, Remington Arms Company. Marcellus Hartley was its president and Thomas Bennett its vice-president. W.W. Reynolds, a salesman at U.M.C., was elected treasurer, and Wilfred Hartley took the secretary's post. In short order, Hartley and Graham (a firm largely under Marcellus Hartley's control) bought Bennett out. So Remington became essentially a Hartley enterprise. While Marcellus Hartley still owned Union Metallic

Cartridge and two other firms, he kept his companies separate. The only merger involved the sales departments of U.M.C. and Remington.

Marcellus Hartley Takes Command

Like Eliphalet Remington II, Marcellus Hartley had descended from Scotch clergy. The Reverend David Hartley was Vicar of Armley in York in 1705. His son, Dr. David Hartley, became a well-respected voice in medicine, philosophy and metaphysics. The next David Hartley earned a seat in Parliament and became the first member of that body to introduce a bill abolishing the slave trade. He also sided with the Americans in their Revolutionary War and was appointed by Lord North to sign the treaty acknowledging America's independence.

Marcellus Hartley's grandfather, Isaac, was not so distinguished. A schoolboy chum of William Wordsworth, he ventured to America in 1797 and,

two years later, sent for his wife and four children. Robert Hartley was only three when his family settled in the Mohawk Valley near Schenectady, New York, where he grew up. He moved to New York City while still a young man, starting up his own business in 1822. Using his business acumen to benefit other people, Robert Hartley founded the Association for Improving the Condition of the Poor and helped establish the Hospital for the Ruptured and Crippled. His first son, Marcellus, was born in 1827. Schooled in both private and public institutions as a lad, Marcellus knew both Latin and Greek by the time he finished his formal education at age 17. He tried working in his father's business for a time but fretted until, in 1847, he sought a job with a hardware and gun distributor: Francis Tomes and Sons. Within six months, Marcellus was placed in charge of the gun department and soon proved a capable, energetic salesman.

Schuyler, Hartley & Graham, a large sporting goods firm in New York City, was the training ground for Marcellus Hartley, who later became Remington's president.

In 1854, Hartley joined with J. Rutsen Schuyler and Malcolm Graham to form Schuyler, Hartley and Graham, Importers and Manufacturers of Guns, Pistols and Fancy Goods. The order of names in the business derived from the amount of money each man contributed. Three days after launching their enterprise, Schuyler and Hartley were on a ship bound for Europe to negotiate for merchandise. Hartley contracted with such great English gunmakers as Purdey and Westley Richards, then traveled to the Continent to acquire Lefaucheux's breech-loading shotguns. Meanwhile, Schuyler went after other products, and soon shiploads of material were packed and sent back to New York. Between calls, Hartley had time to pen letters to his favorite girl, Frances White, and a year later they were married.

Hartley's subsequent trips brought copies of Renaissance paintings and coral jewelry from Italy, both of which fared very well on the American market. Returning from a tour in 1857, he found the country in a financial panic. Eighteen New York banks had failed, and nobody wanted what he had to sell. But the partners had sound financing and were already well established. They rode out the storm, taking quick advantage of the recovery. For the next few years, Hartley remained stateside. He built a business relationship with E. Remington and Sons, and by 1860 his firm was the biggest sporting goods distributer in the country.

During the Civil War, Marcellus Hartley was asked by President Lincoln to procure guns for the Union Army from the Island of Nassau. Hartley argued that the guns there were already consigned to the South, delivered by British makers in league with British banks with heavy investments in U.S. cotton. "I'd go to England instead," Hartley offered, and Lincoln agreed.

Armed with 80,000 pounds credit from the U.S. government, Hartley went first to Birmingham, England's industrial center. In one week, he bought 30,000 guns and was already out of money. "Please send another 100,000 pounds," he wrote back. Bucking Southern sympathizers in European banks, gun factories and shipping firms alike, Hartley managed to acquire more guns from England and the Continent than he'd hoped, undercutting Confederate offers and scuttling contracts to the South. By war's end, Hartley, now 37, was looking for new challenges.

He decided there was opportunity in the self-contained rimfire cartridges made for the Spencer rifle by the Crittenden and Tribbals Manufacturing Company of South Coventry, Connecticut. He bought the plant, along with a similar one in Springfield, Massachusetts, and moved all cartridge operations to Bridgeport, Connecticut. In August, 1867, he incorporated the Union Metallic Cartridge Company with Schuyler, Graham, and two other men: Charles H. Pond and Robert J. White.

At first, U.M.C. lost lots of money. But then A.C. Hobbs came along. Hobbs was a gifted mechanic who once accepted a challenge from the British Government to open a lock devised especially for the Bank of England. After 51 hours of continuous work, Hobbs succeeded and won a $1,000 reward for his efforts. Hartley put Hobbs in charge of the manufacturing plant, where his mechanical genius and attention to detail soon made the operation more profitable and safer as well.

Shortly after Hobbs began what became a 20-year tenure with U.M.C., an Armenian named Azerian approached Hartley. "I'm from Turkey," he said, "and my government needs 10 million rounds of ammunition." Though he lacked the facilities for such an order, Hartley quickly closed the deal, then farmed some of the work out to Winchester Arms, which was also new to the ammunition business.

Another huge break came when Colonel Hiram Berdan of Berdan Sharpshooter fame called Hartley with an idea for stronger cartridges. Instead of blowing priming compound into a folded rim, Berdan advised placing it in a percussion cap that fit into a pocket in the center of the case head. The solid brass rim would have great strength. Two flash holes on either side of a fixed anvil in the pocket would guide the spark into the case. This became the first practical centerfire design, superior in some ways to the Boxer cartridge developed in England at about the same time.

Hobbs worked furiously to build machinery to make the new cases, and only a few months after consummating a deal with Berdan, Hartley and company offered ammunition so far superior to any other that it quickly established U.M.C. as an industry leader. In 1867, the firm had one small plant operated by 30 employees. Four years later, its buildings and personnel were producing over 400,000 cartridges a day.

In 1868, U.M.C. entertained the chief inspector for ammunition of the Russian Army, General Gorloff. His order was for two million cartridges, and during their testing 22,720 were fired with no failures. One of the Russian shipments went via the bark Forya, which was dismasted in a gale and abandoned. Five weeks later she was found, barely afloat, and salvaged. Samples of the 10,450 cartridges were retrieved from their soaked paper boxes and fired perfectly. Twenty years later, more of the salvaged ammo was tested without a misfire. The battleship Maine also gave new meaning to the word "waterproof." Thirteen years after she was blown up and sunk in Havana Harbor in 1898, naval engineers brought her up. U.M.C. cartridges found in her hull were sent to Bridgeport for testing, and not one failed!

Among the largest orders received by U.M.C. was from the French Army, which was desperate following its defeats by the Germans at Metz and Sedan in 1870. Under a new republican government and Premier Leon Gambetta, France defended its beloved Paris, now besieged by German troops. Despite the Prussian needle-gun's crudeness, it had more going for it than the pathetic French Chassepot (a bolt action rifle firing a paper cartridge). The defenders' only hope was to acquire American rifles and ammunition.

Gambetta approached William Reynolds, Paris representative for Schuyler, Hartley and Graham, who had stayed on despite the danger. "We need a hundred thousand rifles and eighteen million rounds of ammunition," Gambetta pleaded. "Here's a draft on Lloyd's for the money."

Reynolds, always a practical man, asked: "How do I get out of Paris? The Germans have surrounded the city." Without blinking an eye, Gambetta replied: "Get a balloon."

In a balloon made of silk gowns sewn together by French women and paid for with $1,250 in gold, Reynolds prepared to leave. But before he could take off, Gambetta commandeered the balloon for an emergency trip to the front, forcing Reynolds to wait for another. He finally lifted off on a freshening wind one morning and, ducking the snap of bullets from the German lines below, passed serenely over the countryside. The daring salesman landed in a field near Ville Roy, his order intact.

U.M.C. made cartridges for all kinds of hand-held guns, and by 1900, when diversity was fashionable, it offered 15,000 different loads, from BB caps to 10-gauge shotshells and big-bore rifle cartridges. Hartley managed to meet the flood-and-drought needs of the military without compromising production for sportsmen, who comprised a more stable market. His shop philosophy paralleled that of the Remingtons: "Insist on top quality in the product and hard work from your people; treat employees fairly and never lose your integrity." As a result, Hartley had no significant labor problems.

Loading ammunition in those early years was a hazardous business, but the biggest explosion in the Bridgeport (CT) plant didn't come from the primer room or charging machines. One afternoon, a local boy on his way home from a hunt with his Remington-Lee sporting rifle took a shortcut through the U.M.C. grounds. To check his sights, he fastened a piece of paper to the wooden door of a curious-looking beehive structure in a fenced field. When he pulled the trigger, the whole town shook to its roots. After waking up in the hospital, the lad was chided for using powder magazines as a backstop. After that costly incident, U.M.C. bought a powder park of 361 acres and secured it against intrusion. All powder magazines are now bullet-proof and surrounded by boy-proof fencing.

In addition to his many other interests, Marcellus Hartley organized the Bridgeport Gun Implement Company to make accessories for firearms, breaking up the monopolies of one-man shops that offered one-of-a-kind items to shooters and reloaders. It proved so successful that soon the Company was marketing all sorts of sporting goods. Hartley also wanted a piece of the future of electricity in the U.S. and hired a young American inventor named Hiram Maxim, who would later design the Maxim gun and disenchant his supporters with the notion that he could build a flying machine. Maxim's radical idea of using alternating instead of direct current appealed to Hartley, who gave the young man laboratory space in Bridgeport and bought patents for his dynamos and incandescent lights. Hartley then founded the United States Electric Company, financing it with a stake of $1.5 million.

The gas companies, threatened by this new source of energy, ganged up on U.S. Electric. The corporate brawl almost destroyed Hartley's firm, but a friend, George Westinghouse, stepped in to suggest that he and Hartley merge their companies. Hartley agreed and became vice-president at Westinghouse. Alternating current now has far more applications than direct current.

When Remington Arms Company came under his control, Marcellus Hartley continued the Remington tradition of bringing bright young inventors to Ilion. In 1892, Arthur Savage came there to work on a hammerless lever-action gun with a spool magazine. Savage later built a thriving company around his Model 99 rifle.

During the 1890's, Remington's typewriter division produced 100 typewriters a day in a new brick building where the old Remington Agricultural Works had been headquartered. The company also built bicycles, reflecting Marcellus Hartley's concern for broadening Remington markets. Hartley was a businessman, not a gunsmith. His canny advice put him on the boards of railroads, banks and insurance companies. He founded the International Banking Corporation and in 1896 engineered the sale of a floundering *New York Times* to a publisher from Chattanooga by the name of Adolph Ochs. Ochs came to New York to woo people from the Equitable Life Insurance Company, which then had a large interest in the *Times*. Marcellus Hartley was a member of Equitable's powerful Finance Committee at the time and finally agreed to see Ochs, who impressed him. After other interviews, Ochs got Equitable's backing along with a personal loan for $100,000 from Hartley.

In January of 1902, Marcellus Hartley visited his doctor, complaining of indigestion. After the doctor declared him "sound as a dollar," Hartley went immediately to a board meeting of the American Surety Company. There, midway through the meeting, he collapsed forward on the table and, at age 75, was pronounced dead. A year later, his grandson, Marcellus Hartley Dodge, became president of M. Hartley and Company, successor to Schuyler, Hartley and Graham.

The Browning Connection

The day Marcellus Hartley died, two men came to his office with an invention. When they learned of the executive's death, they decided to take their invention overseas, to Belgium. Thus did Matthew and John Browning walk out the Remington door. Their autoloading shotgun had received a cold shoulder at Winchester, and now, with its helm suddenly vacated, Remington was in no position to deal.

The Brownings' subsequent arms contract with Fabrique Nationale de Guerre at Liege permitted that company worldwide license to sell Browning products. However, tariff restrictions in the U.S. soon made Belgian imports unprofitable. Thereafter, the Brownings were allowed to approach domestic firms that could more effectively distribute in the U.S. Once more they called at Remington, and this time they found an interested audience. Marcy Dodge, U.M.C. President William Bruff, and Remington President George Jenkins awarded John Browning a contract worth $1 million over the next 10 years. Browning was then sent to Ilion to oversee production of the first autoloading sporting arms made in America.

Before their association with armsmakers in

Marcellus Hartley Dodge (above) as he appeared in 1963, shortly before his death. He took the corporate reins at Remington in 1903, a year after the death of his grandfather, Marcellus Hartley. He then forged a deal with John Browning for the manufacture of his new auto-loading shotgun, which became the Remington Model 11.

the Northeast, John Browning and his brothers had run a small gun shop in Ogden, Utah. Winchester's President, Thomas Bennett, had visited there in 1883 to investigate the origin of a single-shot rifle picked up by one of his salesmen. He recognized a rare genius in John Browning and hired him to develop the company's 1886 and 1895 lever-action rifles. Eager to design autoloading guns, Browning went to work for Colt in 1889. His Colt air-cooled machine gun employed the first successful gas-operated mechanism and proved better than the Gatling and Maxim guns. In 1895, Browning developed Colt's first autoloading pistol, which became the Model 1911. Ten years later, at Remington, he produced the country's first autoloading shotgun, followed by an autoloading rifle in 1906.

No more prolific inventor than John Moses

Browning ever worked on guns. At the turn of the century, a company's willingness to adopt Browning's ideas was, in part at least, a measure of its ability to compete in the next decades. Marcy Dodge, with his grandfather's business intuition, knew no price was too high for the hump-backed shotgun he'd been offered. Since then, Remington has stayed ahead of its competitors in autoloading shotgun sales.

In 1907, J.D. Pedersen, a Danish contemporary of Browning, developed Remington's first slide-action shotgun, the Model 10. The Model 12 .22 rimfire arrived in 1909 and a centerfire Model 14 followed in 1912. While these guns sold well, U.M.C. was having difficulty with its shotshell ammunition. The market was solid, but the price of raw shot was rising. The C.N. Marshall Lead Works at Granite City, Illinois, from which U.M.C. had historically bought its shot, had been gobbled by Thomas Fortune Ryan's National Lead Company in 1905. Soon the profit margin on shotshells was all but eliminated by the high cost of pellets. And nobody wanted to hike the price of shells.

Harry H. Pinney had a better idea. Pinney, whom Marcy Dodge had hired from the Pratt and Whitney Machine Tool Company, was one of U.M.C.'s most gifted mechanics, commanding a salary of $10,000 a year. He'd already revamped the armory, enlarged the powder park to 400 acres, and built new magazines. He'd bought three tiny steam locomotives from the City of New York to haul powder to charging machines and eliminate excess powder storage on the loading floor. To reduce the risk of primer compound exploding during handling, Pinney had installed vacuum dryers. Now he suggested that Remington build its own shot tower. The project was approved, and work started in July, 1908. The 190-foot tower was completed in seven months and has served Remington well ever since, producing over one billion shot pellets daily.

Soon after the shot tower began operations, Marcy Dodge realized that Winchester had a marketing advantage over Remington and U.M.C. simply because Winchester ammunition was bought by people who also owned Winchester guns—a kind of brand loyalty. While U.M.C. was highly regarded, Remington shooters saw no connection in the two names. Changing the company name to include both titles was not popular with the old guard at U.M.C. After all, with $15 million annual gross sales, it was generating 30 times the revenue of Remington's plant. But Dodge went ahead anyway. In 1912, at age 30, Marcy Dodge bought the last of the family stock and became the sole owner of Remington Arms-Union Metallic Cartridge Company.

Remington-UMC helped sponsor Annie Oakley's trick-shooting exhibitions (Oakley's husband, Frank Butler, later became a Remington salesman) along with several shooting teams. The firm designed its Model 24 .22 autoloader for an Italian General named Pisano, who could hit rimfire cases tossed in the air.

Remington Prepares for War

Then suddenly, in 1914, the carefree days of glass balls and applause were cut short at Sarajevo (Yugoslavia), when an assassin's bullet killed Archduke Ferdinand. As tensions spiraled in Europe, Marcy Dodge and Remington President Sam Pryor prepared. Remington's first war assignment was to make a few thousand Lebel rifles for France. Great Britain was next in line, with bigger demands. The improved British Enfield, with a caliber change from .276 to .303, had never been manufactured in quantity. Suddenly, England needed a million rifles, with delivery to begin on January 1, 1916.

Quadrupling production to 2,000 rifles a day, Remington had the first Enfields ready for test-firing in October of 1915, one year after the contract had been signed. Ilion's payroll jumped from 1,400 employees in 1914 to 15,000 three years later. At peak production in March, 1917, Remington shipped 61,000 Enfields a month. To make these rifles on time, the plant needed 3,895 machines, 5,905 fixtures, 7,000 tools and 3,415 gauges. Remington's plant quickly expanded down Bridgeport's Main Street (the old River Road), with overhead bridges connecting one building to another.

To boost production further, Dodge and Pryor, with other industrial magnates, formed the separate Remington Company of Delaware. They also leased an unfinished locomotive factory at Eddystone, Pennsylvania, staffing it by replacing every other skilled workman at Ilion with a trainee. The Eddystone plant eventually produced 450,000 Enfields.

The last military power to order from Remington was Russia, which requested one million rifles and 100 million cartridges. By then, Ilion was tied up with British contract work, and Bridgeport's best yield was estimated at only 50,000 7.62mm rounds a day. To build new facilities, Marcy Dodge borrowed $15 million by selling company bonds. He raised another $15 million against his own stock and secured $13 million more in personal loans. Implementing early plans to move military arms production to Bridgeport, he ordered 13 new five-story buildings, 12 service buildings, five forges and a huge power plant at U.M.C. In one year, new construction gave Remington more than a million feet of additional floor space and a production capacity of 5,000 rifles a day. Cartridge capacity doubled with the addition of 160 new buildings and 24 acres of floor space; but still it could not handle the Russian order on top of demands for .303 and 8mm Lebel ammo.

Marcy Dodge next recalled Harry Pinney from the Chalmers Motor Company to help. "With a year's time and two million dollars, I'll have a plant turning out two million cartridges a day," Pinney promised. Ten months later, a factory rented from the Hoboken Land and Improvement Company was producing 2.5 million Russian rounds daily. Between it and the main Bridgeport plant, U.M.C. spewed out 28 million cartridges a week for the war effort.

Rifle manufacture didn't proceed as smoothly, mostly because the Russian contract called for hand-fitting of gun parts and gauge components. When Pinney checked the first runs, he found production at only 125 units per day. Abruptly, he told the engineers to change their style: "I don't care about Russian blueprints. I want rifles!" By early 1917, 5,000 rifles were being crated each day.

While Remington juggled to keep its payments on schedule and production lines at capacity, Tsar Nicholas II lost his government. The new republic immediately canceled all arms contracts. Remington's Russian production lines stopped, as did those of other armsmakers supplying U.S. allies in Europe. Then Germany declared unlimited submarine warfare, and soon 600,000 tons of Allied shipping were being sunk each month. Finally, on April 2, 1917, President Woodrow Wilson asked Congress for a declaration of war.

By this time, broken contracts had placed Remington-U.M.C. and its compatriots in a tight financial bind. The government helped at Ilion by buying 600,000 of the 750,000 Russian rifles already produced, cutting Remington's losses from $10 million to about $300,000 (the rifles were later sent to the Russian White Army).

Strengthened by Russia's collapse, Germany turned all its might on France. French troops, demoralized by the loss of two million comrades, called on the U.S. for arms. At that time, only 700,000 Springfields were stocked in American arsenals, and manufacturing capacity stood at only 350,000 a year. And yet, requests for rifles totaled

four million! To make use of current tooling and to speed production, Remington engineers, having just filled the Enfield contracts, suggested the adoption of an Enfield modified for the .30-06 cartridge. Remington started building the new rifles in December, 1917, and production peaked at 4,000 rifles a day. Over the course of the war, the Ilion and Eddystone plants turned out more than 1.6 million of the 1917 Enfields. After the war, a million of these rifles were placed in storage, to be shipped to England after the disaster at Dunkirk in 1940.

In all, Remington built 69 percent of the rifles shipped to American forces in World War I. In addition, half of all Allied ammunition was made by Remington, including rounds for the Colt, Browning, Vickers, Lewis and France's Chauchat machine guns. All the ammunition used by Belgium's troops came from the Bridgeport plant, which at one point was boxing 40 million rounds a week.

Surviving the Depression

At war's end, Remington-U.M.C. closed three plants, but capacity was still far above peacetime needs. Deleting U.M.C. from its name, Remington delved into cutlery, cash registers and other enterprises. The cutlery division made money until World War II, but cash register sales were poor (that section was eventually sold to NCR). Predictably, sporting arms and ammunition sales grew. During one day in 1922, 51 carloads of shotshells and rifle cartridges—more than 27 million rounds—were shipped from Bridgeport.

Remington introduced its Model 30 and 30S bolt-action rifles in 1921 and later developed the "Hi-Speed" .30-06 sporting cartridges for them. In 1926, the company offered the first non-corrosive priming made in the U.S. This new compound contained no potassium chlorate, lead styphnate replacing this corrosive element. Developed by Jim Burns, who had worked for the United States Cartridge Company, this priming compound did not promote rust, even in bores left uncleaned in humid places. Remington awarded prizes to W.A. Robins of Jonesboro, Louisiana, and Nelson Starr of Goshen, Indiana, for independently suggesting "Kleanbore" as the appropriate market name for its new priming.

When the stock market fell in 1929, Remington was badly shaken. That year, sales exceeded $21 million; but by 1932 they'd fallen to $8 million, suffering an annual loss of $1 million. To rescue the company, Marcy Dodge offered controlling interest in Remington to E.I. DuPont de Nemours & Com-

C.K. Davis, pictured above, was Remington's president from 1933 to 1954.

pany, a firm that had long supplied Remington with powder. DuPont had been established in 1802, enjoyed a firm financial base, and had wisely diversified to strengthen its position as one of America's most powerful companies. DuPont leadership voted to approve the acquisition in the spring of 1933. Remington remained a separate company, however, with Marcy Dodge as board chairman.

In June, 1933, the board of Remington Arms named Charles Davis as president. Remaking Remington in "Roosevelt's Recovery" amid the Great Depression of the 1930's, Davis managed to eke out a profit for the company; but a severe accounting policy by DuPont wiped all the black ink off the pages during the early years of Davis' tenure. Remington's equipment was old, and some of its assets overvalued. In 1934, a bank loan raised funds to buy out bondholders, and new preferred and common stocks were issued. To boost employee morale, which had been devastated by the Depression, Davis raised wages 10 percent and decreed a 40-

hour work week. Bonuses, pension plans, job incentives and better insurance followed, making "C.K." Davis a popular boss indeed with his people.

In 1936, Remington sales stood at nearly double the Depression low, and while dividends had been paid on preferred stock during the 1920's, this was the first year Remington paid dividends on its common stock. During the Depression, Remington also bought the Peters Cartridge Company, a rival firm founded in 1887 by Baptist preacher Gersham Peters. Soon after that, the Parker Gun Company was also acquired. Charles Parker had started his business in 1832 to make coffee grinders, but during the Civil War he'd retooled to make Springfield rifles. Later, his three sons reorganized the company, introducing their first double-barrel shotgun in 1868. Remington manufactured Parkers until the 1940's.

In 1933, Remington bought the Chamberlain Trap and Target Company, maker of "Blue Rock" targets and Leggitt "Ideal" traps. The conservation movement, in which C.K. Davis and other Remington officials took an active role, had reduced wing-shooting opportunities and made trap and skeet increasingly popular. Chamberlain, which had been hit hard by the Depression, benefitted greatly from Remington's purchase.

Prompted by a slowly recovering economy in the late 1930's, Remington designed several new sporting guns. These included the slide-action 141 centerfire and autoloading 241 rimfire (1935); the autoloading 81 centerfire and slide-action 121 rimfire (1936); and the 37 rimfire target rifle (1937). The 500 series of bolt-action .22s arrived in 1939, and in 1940 the box-fed 511, tube-fed 512 and 513 target models made their debuts. The 550 series appeared in 1941, becoming the only .22 autoloader able to digest mixed loads of Short, Long and Long Rifle rounds.

Europe Rescued, Remington Reborn

Now, 25 years after The Great War had inflamed Europe, another conflict was smoldering. Nine months after Germany's invasion of Poland, European nations had still not committed to making defensive armament. America's neutral stance allowed Hitler to draw supplies from Russia, but prevented U.S. Allies from getting American guns. In fact, when Englishman H.E. "Ted" Clive visited Bridgeport in 1939 to observe military ammunition being produced, he was denied a pass. Great Britain eventually ordered ammunition from Remington, only to cancel. France showed the same indecision. When Nazi troops claimed Holland and Belgium in

The Remington Model 700 BDL Varmint shown here is widely considered one of the most accurate mass-produced rifles.

at Ilion's plants rose from 900 to 9,000, with up to 3,000 rifles being completed each day.

The pace of ammunition manufacture was even more hectic. In June, 1940, the British had confirmed their need for 30-caliber rifle ammunition and 50 caliber machine gun rounds. England's Teddy Clive now worked closely with Remington engineers to boost production capacity for the .30's by 600 percent and the .50's by 2,000 percent. British ordnance engineers had also designed (but not produced) an incendiary machine gun bullet for Spitfires. Remington adapted it for mass manufacture and supplied the British from the company's Bridgeport plant.

Beginning in August of 1940, Remington engineered the construction of ammunition plants for the war effort. The Frankfort Arsenal was expanded and a factory at Lake City (MO) was designed from scratch. Comprised of six units in all, the latter facility produced 30 caliber and 50 caliber cartridges. Each unit was capable of producing finished ammunition from raw material. Lake City was, in fact, the first munitions plant with a closed-cycle, continuous-feed design. A total of 21,000 workers was eventually recruited to man the plant, which produced its first ammunition in October of 1941, just 10 months after construction had started. Lake City's 3,800 acres included 25 miles of road,

the spring of 1940, then shredded the Union Jack at Dunkirk, the British found themselves with only a few light tanks, 100 field pieces, enough rifles to arm only two divisions, and fewer than a million cartridges.

Winston Churchill wanted the U.S. to supply England with Enfields, but the official U.S. battle rifle was now the Garand. A conversion of American machinery to produce Enfields would take months. Besides, retooling would leave the U.S. without the machinery necessary to produce parts for its own Springfield rifle, which was still used by many U.S. soldiers. C.K. Davis strongly urged that the machinery, most of which lay in storage at Rock Island Arsenal, not be changed. Finally, in January of 1941, the British said Springfields would do, and 37 days later the machinery was running. To mass-produce its new "O3A3" model, Remington eliminated 12 of the Springfield's original 91 parts, leaving only 24 unchanged. Meanwhile, the work force

Remington's automated cutting operation takes place inside the completely enclosed T-10 machine center, part of the company's Flexible Manufacturing System (FMS). In this operation (see above), a constant spray serves as a cooling, lubricating and removing agent for metal chips.

236 major buildings, 11 miles of railroad, a hospital, its own fire and police departments, and parking for 5,000. At full throttle the factory could produce 8.9 million cartridges a day.

Remington also started a new facility near Denver, Colorado. Seven months after the groundbreaking in March, 1941, the first 30-caliber cartridges came off the line, reaching a total capacity of 10 million rounds a day. Another Remington factory became active at Salt Lake City, Utah, only six months after construction began. Its plant manager, Maxwell Warden, later succeeded C.K. Davis as company president.

Remington's Bridgeport plant was overhauled several times during the war. Its 14,000 workers produced 30- and 50-caliber rifle and machine gun rounds, .22 Rimfire training cartridges, .45 ACP shot cartridges for South Pacific airmen, frangible bullets for use on U.S. training planes, and 20mm cannon shells. Remington engineers developed super-speed artillery rounds, electrically fired machine gun primers, a grenade launcher for the Garand, and a 12 gauge shell to activate torpedo gyroscopes.

In 1942, a shortage of copper prompted Remington to refurbish a cotton mill in Lowell, Massachusetts, to make steel cases. Eventually, this plant produced 3.5 *billion* rounds of steel-cased ammunition. Meanwhile, at Peters' Kings Mills plant, Remington was producing up to two million .30 Carbine cartridges daily, plus 125 million shotshells for use in training aerial gunners. In short, Remington took charge of all domestic small-arms ammunition production. Under the Lend-Lease Act, the company procured 27,300 machines worth $200 million. "Perishable" tools in the munitions plants—cutters, dies and punches—wore out at the rate of 30,000 a day. Bicycle and jewelry shops helped furnish precision tooling. All told, Remington expanded its operations by 2,000 percent during

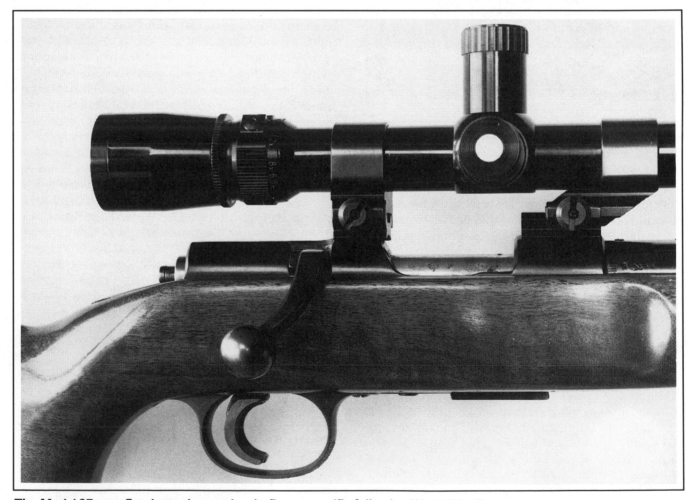

The Model 37 was Remington's premier rimfire target rifle following World War II.

the war. In 1939, it had employed barely 4,000 people; four years later, 82,500 workers were on the payroll. Remington turned out more than a million rifles for the government and 16 billion rounds of ammunition. And yet, with all the urgency of wartime production, there was only one serious accident: under emergency orders to boost ammunition production, a crew handling primers set one off in a tray, triggering a blast that killed seven people.

War's end brought with it a predictable glut of cartridges for military rifles, even though cutbacks in production had started as early as the summer of 1943. The Lake City plant was shut down five months before D-Day, and operations at the Denver facility stopped in July, 1944. Immediately, Remington began to expand its sporting-gun line, designing new models to take advantage of modern materials and manufacturing techniques. The company's "Family of Guns" marketing concept, hatched in the 1950's, called for the use of common receivers, trigger assemblies and other parts in guns of different design. Where common components were not practical, the same raw materials and rough shaping were engineered into different guns, while expensive machining operations were deleted. Clever designs and attention to fit and finish made the resulting guns as attractive—often more so—than older models that were more expensive to produce. This move positioned Remington well for the competitive post-war business of gun manufacture. Its Model 870 pump shotgun, for example, is in its various forms the country's perennial top-selling pump. Before the war, Winchester's Model 12 set the standard; but now that model has become too expensive to make and sell at a profit to hunters on a budget. Remington's 870 is every bit as reliable; and it handles as well, if not better.

With its strong ties to DuPont, Remington has predictably ranked among the top companies using synthetic stocks. Its "Nylon 66" .22 rifles and "Zytel"-stocked XP-100 pistol have been followed by a number of bolt rifles with stocks of various materials. It has pioneered ammunition, too, most recently the 6mm and 7mm BR, 8mm and .416 Rem-

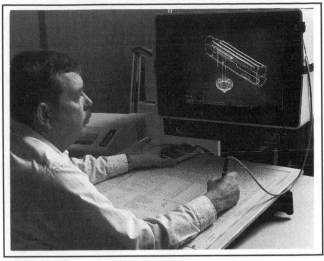

A Remington research designer uses a computer-aided design system (CAD) to detail a receiver for the SP-10 Magnum 10-gauge shotgun.

ington Magnums, plus factory loads for the .35 Whelen. Older credits include (with "Remington" suffixes): the 6mm, .25-06, .280, 7mm-08, and one of the most popular centerfire rifle rounds ever, the 7mm Magnum. The company has been almost as active, and remains very competitive, in the shotshell and rimfire market. Like other companies, it has had its losers as well—the 5mm rimfire and .350 Magnum, for example. But the number of bloopers from Ilion and Bridgeport has been amazingly small.

Now Remington is diversifying, adding its name to outdoor clothes and accessories. It must adapt to a public that did not grow up on a frontier and, in large measure, sees little use for firearms of any kind. The guns will continue to sell as long as there are sportsmen, however. America's oldest gunmaker retains the reputation provided by its founder, and there remains a little of Marcellus Hartley in the company, too. Still tenacious and innovative, Remington Arms is meeting marketing challenges now as it has for more than 150 years: with accurate, reliable firearms that practically sell themselves.

CHAPTER 4

SAMUEL COLT: GUNS THAT BUILT AN EMPIRE

When Sam Colt's mother died in 1820, he was only six. But thanks to his father, Christopher Colt, who owned a silk mill in Ware, Massachusetts, Sam and his five surviving brothers and sisters fared quite well. Later, young Sam entered the equivalent of prep school, then continued his education at the prestigious Amherst Academy. The upbringing he'd received at his father's mill had taught the boy something about chemistry; so when in 1829, at the age of 15, he contrived an underwater mine, the device detonated as planned. The crude raft he'd assembled as a target had floated away from the mine, however, causing an eruption of mud and water that drenched the onlookers.

One of those spectators was an up-and-coming engineer named E.K. Root. He and Colt shared an interest in munitions and quickly became friends. Eventually, Root would become superintendent at Colt's Hartford plant, and a revolver would bear his name.

In 1830, Sam Colt went to sea aboard the *Corvo*. Watching the ship's wheel spin and lock as it steered, he conceived the idea of a firearm with chambers that revolved in a cylinder, locking, each in turn, behind the barrel. Back home, Sam, who was still only 16, showed a model of his invention to his father and a family friend, Henry L. Ellsworth. Both thought the idea a sound one. Ellsworth, then Commissioner of the U.S. Patent Office, helped Sam file a caveat, or intent to patent. Anson Chase, a local gunsmith, made Colt's first working firearms.

From 1832 to 1836, gunsmiths in Albany, Hartford and Baltimore hand-built from Colt's drawings prototypes of 16 pistols, 9 rifles and a shotgun. Colt financed the work by lecturing on laughing gas (ni-trous oxide), whose anaesthetic properties had been discovered by Sir Humphrey Davy in 1800. "Dr. Coult of Calcutta," as he dubbed himself, toured the U.S. and Canada, honing the marketing skills that would later prove so valuable in selling firearms.

Colt had little to do with the initial manufacture of his guns. The first Colt repeater, a pistol, blew up. The first rifle fared better, although it shared with the pistol a fatal flaw. Every prototype made in those first four years featured a flash plate in front of the cylinder, causing sparks from the fired chamber to ricochet off the plate into the other loaded chambers. After a few guns had been ruined this way, the plate was deleted and no production guns carried it.

Samuel Colt owed a great deal of his early success to John Pearson, a Baltimore gunsmith. Pearson not only translated sketches into blued steel, he improved the design along the way. He also tolerated Colt's habitual tardiness in paying bills. His patience must have been remarkable, as this letter from Pearson to Colt suggests:

"I am getting on with the work as well as I can but it has been such cold weather and this shop so cold that I had like to be frose. But I hope it will be milder soon. I have got our pistol to work very well and am getting it ready for stocking and part of the others but I am out of money and the rent is due today and I want some more wood for fire so you must send some money immediately or I shall be lost. Please to write as soon as you get the goods and let me know that you get them but Dont Forget the Money."

Colt's voyages on the *Corvo* in 1830 and 1831 no doubt introduced him to earlier arms with re-

This statue of Samuel Colt near Armsmear depicts the young sailor fashioning a revolver cylinder of wood.

volving cylinders. James Puckle's revolving machine gun, patented in 1718, was on exhibit at the Tower of London, while other examples were displayed at The Armouries and even some English gun shops. Collier revolving flintlocks were common in India, where Colt visited; in fact, Collier's design borrowed heavily from that of Artemus Wheeler, who in 1818 had patented a revolving mechanism in the United States.

When Colt wrote a history of repeating arms in 1851, he claimed his first encounter with other revolvers was in 1835, when he secured his first patents. His publisher, The Institution of Civil Engineers in London, felt that to reveal earlier exposure to revolving mechanisms would open Colt to patent litigation.

The development of percussion ignition gave Sam Colt a huge advantage over his predecessors. More compact and reliable, percussion guns could also be made lighter. Wisely following Ellsworth's advice to seek patents only after building working models, Colt had some percussion revolvers in hand when he traveled to England in 1835 for his first patent (he needed the British registry because England did not recognize patents issued in her former colonies). The patent was granted on October 22, 1835, whereupon Colt returned to the U.S. and got a U.S. patent in February, 1836. A couple of months later, he went to France for still another patent. Those first patents guaranteed Colt a virtual monopoly on the manufacture of revolvers until 1857. The following applications were covered by Colt's patents:

1. Caps at the end of the cylinder
2. Partitions between caps
3. A shield over the caps to guard against moisture and to keep smoke from fouling the lock
4. A rotating and locking cylinder
5. A connecting rod between hammer and trigger
6. A shackle to connect cylinder and ratchet
7. An arbor running from recoil shield to barrel extension to unite the barrel and cylinder
8. An adopter and lever for pistols

Paterson: The Factory, The Gun

On August 29, 1839, Colt was awarded his second patent, covering internal improvements and the addition of an attached loading lever and several accessories. These innovations were made for the Paterson, a handgun named after the New Jersey industrial town where Colt moved in 1836 to set up his new Patent Arms Manufacturing Company. The Paterson revolver would become one of the most collectible of American firearms. A year after Colt started his business, several New York banks faltered, triggering the "Panic of 1837" and seven subsequent years of economic depression. Cotton and textile mills that had proliferated on the banks of the Passaic suffered along with Colt's young gun firm.

The incorporation papers for Colt's company, which were drawn up on May 5, 1836, authorized $300,000 in capitalization, but only about $230,000 was initially subscribed. The corporation was described as "manufacturing firearms, machinery and cutlery." Colt established a showroom and sales office in New York at 155 Broadway, where he acted as salesman, consultant, designer, engineer and demonstrator. He was paid a percentage of sales plus $1,000 a month for the first six months. After that, he depended almost entirely on sales, his fixed fee dropping to $1,000 a year.

Colt's first stock offering came through the "Publick House" of Truman Anderson in Jersey City (New Jersey). It called for $5 on each $100 share, due up front, with another five percent payable by May 8, 1836. The first board of directors included Daniel Holsman, Elias Ogden, Elias Vanarsdale, Jr., Daniel Allen and Thomas Emmet, who also served as chairman. The board-appointed treasurer was Colt's cousin, Dudley Selden, who bought 240 shares of stock (and fumed over the expensive entertainment Colt lavished on prospective customers).

Before building his Paterson plant, Colt traveled to Springfield, Massachusetts, to inspect the Springfield Armory. While there, he hired Pliny Lawton as his shop foreman, and together they visited other factories to learn about mass manufacturing. Soon after that, Colt returned to Paterson and erected a four-story building, capped by a weathervane in the shape of a rifle. The building and its machinery cost about $55,000.

A year and a half elapsed before the first Colt rifles appeared, with pistols following a few months later. *The New York Evening Star* and *New York Chronicle and Enquirer* each carried the first Colt advertisements on December 18, 1837.

About 200 of Colt's First Model Ring Lever Rifles comprised the initial production run. Barreled in calibers 34, 36, 38, 40 and 44, the guns came standard with eight-shot cylinders (a few 10-round rifles have also appeared). Pulling a ring in front of the trigger cocked the firing mechanism and indexed the cylinder. Colt took his rifle to the U.S.

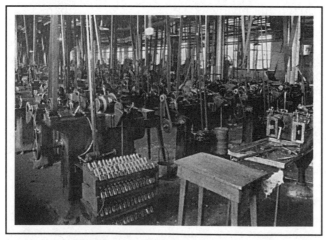

Early Colt machine shops were powered by belts that hung from ceiling shafts turned by steam (above).

Military Academy at West Point in June for military trials, but it fared poorly. Officers in charge criticized the gun's "complicated character, its liability to accidents . . ." and concluded, "This arm is entirely unsuited to the general purposes of the service."

About that time, Colonel William S. Harney helped engineer the sale of 50 Ring Lever Rifles, at $125 each, to General Thomas Jessup's troops, who were busy chasing truculent Seminoles in Florida. Ironically, on his way home from the Everglades, Colt lost the government's $6,250 check when his boat capsized. Its replacement took months.

In 1837, both the Pocket Model and Belt Model Paterson revolvers made their debuts, each bearing a serial number starting with "1". About 500 of the 28-caliber Pocket Models—or "Baby Patersons"—were built before Colt dropped them from the line in 1838. About 850 Belt Models in 31 caliber, with either straight or flared grips, were made between 1837 and 1840. Colt called the Pocket Model "No. 1," and the two variations of the Belt Model were designated Nos. 2 and 3.

The No. 4 Paterson Revolver was introduced in 1838. A heavy 36-caliber arm, it became known as the "Texas Paterson," after Texas Ranger Jack Hayes and his men used it successfully in the famous Pedernales fight in 1844. In that battle, 15 Texas Rangers trounced 70 attacking Comanches. Oddly enough, the big Paterson had by that time been out of production for four years (only a thousand were shipped in all). While building the pistol, Colt also turned out 500 44-caliber Second Model Ring Lever Rifles, but in 1841 that gun too was dropped.

The most trouble-free of Colt Patersons was the Model 1839 Six-Shot Carbine, a .525 smoothbore with an external hammer instead of the ring-cocking mechanism. It sold well—950 were shipped between 1838 and 1841. During the same period, Colt manufactured its last Paterson, the Model 1839 Shotgun. It's been called a 16-gauge, but the bore was actually .62, not .662 as is standard for most modern 16-bores. The shotgun's 3½-inch cylinder was an inch longer than that of the carbine, but the two guns operated alike. Each had six chambers. Demand for the shotgun apparently was much softer, with only 225 copies produced.

In 1840, Colt's penny-pinching Dudley Selden was succeeded as the firm's treasurer by John Ehlers, another major shareholder. A year later, Colt's Patent Arms Manufacturing Company folded. The court settled Ehlers' claims first, as he was the firm's

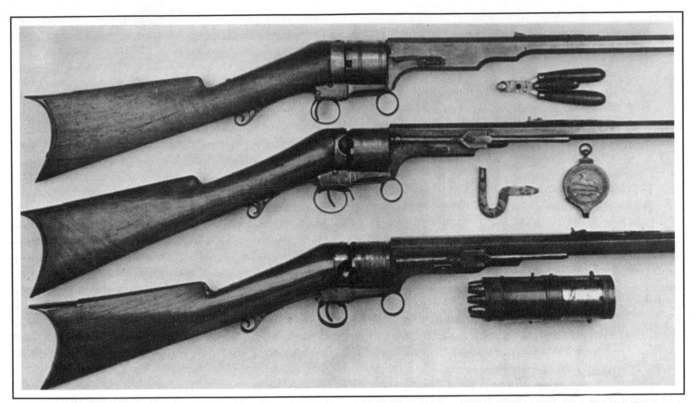

This trio of No. 2 Ring Lever rifles are examples of the variations produced by Colt at his Paterson plant in New Jersey. They were produced from 1838 until 1841, when the operation folded.

biggest creditor, awarding him 820 completed pistols and long guns, as well as parts for 500 more, mostly handguns. Ehlers was entitled to sell all of them. Pistols assembled from parts during 1842 and 1843 can be distinguished from earlier Colts by their slightly shorter cylinders and different barrel markings. The Ehlers guns also had attached loading levers; however, Colt started using attached levers in 1839 and retrofitted some earlier guns with them as well. Baby Patersons marketed by Ehler are called Fourth Model Ehlers, while Belt Model Patersons became known as Fifth Model Ehlers.

Ehlers was still selling guns in 1847, advertising them as "Colt's Repeating Fire Arms . . . with the latest improvements of 1844, 1845 and 1846." In 1845, he'd managed to negotiate a Navy contract for part of his inventory. All told, Ehlers probably realized more profit from the Paterson enterprise than did Colt, who wrote that "nearly 30,000 pounds was expended without any beneficial result, except in gaining experience, both in the arms themselves and in the machinery required for their manufacture."

Colt's four years on the Passaic River gave him a turbulent start—but a start nonetheless. Including the Ehlers, 2,850 handguns and 1,912 long guns rolled out of the Paterson plant. These comprised 19 kinds of pistols and 10 of long arms, not counting the many variations in barrel length.

The Walker and First Model Dragoon

Discouraged but hardly despairing, Sam Colt traveled to New York after the collapse of his company. At New York University, he met Samuel F.B. Morse, a professor of painting. Colt helped Morse market his new invention, the telegraph. Then the two men began running tests on underwater explosives. In short order, Colt wangled a huge grant of $50,000 from the government to experiment with the electrical detonation of mines. He continued to work on various explosives projects until 1846, when Captain Samuel H. Walker of the new state of Texas came calling.

While on a visit to Washington, D.C., Walker had written Colt to ask for some revolvers. The Texas Paterson had established a stellar reputation for Colt in the Southwest, as expressed in Walker's own words:

"The pistols which you made for the Texas Navy have been in use by the Rangers for three years. . . . [Their] confidence in them is unbounded, so much so that they are willing to engage four times their number. . . . With improvements I think they can be rendered the most perfect weapon in the world for light mounted troops. . . .''

With no place to build any pistols, the ever ambitious Colt quoted prices on quantities of one to 5,000 revolvers. Within a week, the Ordnance Department agreed to buy 1,000 44-caliber pistols, with Walker and Colt collaborating on the design and the New York City gunshop of Blunt & Syms producing the prototype. Colt contracted with Eli Whitney, Jr. to build his new guns. An additional 100 were ordered for public sale.

The Walker was a huge revolver, sporting a 9-inch barrel and weighing 4 pounds 9 ounces. Serial numbers started anew for each Texas Ranger company—A through E—chosen to receive the guns. Each unit received 220, except Company E, which got 120. The 100 civilian guns were parcelled out on the open market or embellished for presentations. In any event, the Walker proved a runaway success, and Colt busied himself with plans to build his own factory in Hartford, Connecticut. Back in Texas, during the Battle of Juamantla in October of 1847, a Mexican soldier ran his lance through Captain Sam Walker, killing him. One of the two Colt pistols he was wearing at the time went back to Colt's personal collection, as Walker had specified.

By the end of 1847, Colt had a new pistol on the market. It came to be called the "Transition Walker" or "Whitneyville-Hartford "Dragoon." ["Dragoon" is what horse soldiers were called before the Civil War. After that, dragoons became known as cavalry.] Smaller than the original Walker design, this gun boasted several refinements but retained the .44 bore. Only about 240 were built, of which roughly 20 have survived. The following year, Colt again announced a new revolver, the First Model Dragoon, which he marketed to both soldiers and civilians. Later came the Fluck Model, Second Model, Third Model and Hartford-English Model, all built between 1847 and 1861. Each gun weighed 4 pounds 2 ounces and carried a 7 1/2-inch barrel. The roll-engraved cylinders held six 44-caliber balls. Of the 22,000 Dragoons produced, 9,380 went to fill government contracts. These big Colts, usually issued in pairs, were not carried on the soldier's belt, but in two fully-enclosed holsters slung from the pommel of his saddle.

Colt's critics claimed the Dragoons were weak and easily put out of commission by rust and dirt. They also said the cylinder gap leaked gas. Colt countered with accolades sent him by famous fighting men, such as General Zachary Taylor, the future president, who wrote: "I have been much pleased with an examination of your new modelled repeating pistols, and feel satisfied that, under all circumstances, they may be safely relied on."

The Ordnance Department's George Talcott strongly opposed the adoption of Colts as military arms. Faced with overwhelming pressure to approve them, he suggested to the government that it manufacture Dragoons under a licensing arrangement. Sam Colt was too shrewd to bite on that. He knew he had a monopoly, and he'd carefully guarded it by stamping deep patent markings on all his percussion revolvers. His clever marketing campaigns warned buyers of imitations. A few Liege (Belgium) firms were authorized to make guns under Colt patents. Most copies were not lawful, however, and Sam Colt vigorously denounced them as unsafe, threatening to prosecute dealers who sold them.

In 1848, Colt introduced a miniature of the Dragoon, a 31-caliber, five-shot pocket pistol, with barrel lengths of 3, 4, 5 and 6 inches. The Baby Dragoon became an instant success and within a year was followed by an improved version: the Pocket Model of 1849. Colt's production run for the original Baby Dragoon totalled 15,000, and for its successor, 325,000. About 200 variations of these guns, some of which held six shots, have been identified. The 1849 Pocket Model became the best-selling Colt of its century.

Sam Colt's original 1836 patent was due to expire in 1849, but by claiming he'd not received a reasonable return from it, he was able to obtain an eight-year extension. Challenges mounted, but Colt's able and well-paid attorney, Edward Dickerson, turned them back. His victory in the case of Colt vs. Massachusetts Arms Company protected the company from serious rivals until 1857.

Meanwhile, Colt was beefing up his production staff, wooing Elisha King Root away from the Collins Company with a salary claimed to be the highest paid to any New England plant superintendent. The initial "T" stamped on Colts from 1847 into the 1850's signified the approval of chief inspector William Tuller, who maintained a high level of quality control. Colt's only regret in assembling a first-rate stable of managers was the hiring of his own brother, James B. Colt, who was eventually fired.

Two Union cavalry soldiers pose with their sidearms—Colt 1860 Army revolvers—tucked in their belts. A 44-caliber six-shooter, the 1860 Army was popular with Civil War troops because of its reliability and relatively light weight (1 ½ pounds less than a Colt Dragoon).

The 1849 Pocket Model, with its 7 1/2-inch barrel and six-shot cylinder, actually made its debut in 1850, along with Colt's Model 1851 Navy. The Navy model had been designed three years earlier, but hectic production schedules for existing guns kept it off the market. Between 1850 and 1873, 215,348 of these 36-caliber pistols were shipped from the Hartford plant, and 42,000 from Colt's facility in London. The rolled motif on each cylinder (which varied by model in early Colts) depicted an 1843 naval battle in which Colt-armed Texans defeated a Mexican foe. The Model 1851 Navy weighed 42 ounces, compared to the Model 1849's 27 ounces. Four basic variants of the Navy were made, including one with a special grip that accommodated a shoulder stock patented in 1859. The popularity of Colt's Navy revolver prompted plant engineers to retain its basic look and proportions in designing the Single Action Army Model in 1873.

While the size and weight of the 1851 Navy proved useful for military and domestic confrontations, it lacked the punch of a Dragoon. In his book, "Thirty Years of Army Life on the Border," Colonel R.B. Marcy described how, after missing a grizzly bear with his rifle, he decided to haze it toward a group of troopers coming up behind him. "Several mounted men, armed with the navy revolvers, set off in pursuit. They approached within a few paces and discharged ten or twelve shots, the most of which entered the animal, but he still kept on, and his progress did not seem materially impeded by the wounds. After these men had exhausted their charges, another man rode up armed with the army revolver, and fired two shots, which

Colt shipped guns by steamboat from this company dock on the Connecticut River.

brought the stalwart beast to the ground. Upon skinning him and making an examination of the wounds, it was discovered that none of the balls from the small pistols had, after passing through his thick and tough hide, penetrated deeper than about an inch into the flesh, but that the two balls from the large pistol [a .44 Dragoon] had gone into the vitals and killed him."

Sam Colt had displayed 450 of his guns at London's Great Exhibition of 1851, strategically presenting engraved revolvers to people in high office. The next year, he started building a plant on London's Thames River. Colt staffed it with people from his Hartford operation, but many did not like England and left their jobs. Hiring British gunmakers proved even more troublesome; they were not used to American methods of mass production and persisted in the traditional work habits of England. At wit's end, Colt gathered together several unskilled laborers from the English streets and countryside. He paid them two shillings a day to start and was surprised at their industry and willingness to learn. Many became skilled machinists, prompting Colt to exclaim thereafter; "Do not bring me a man that knows anything if you want me to teach him anything."

A New Plant, Marriage, Armsmear, Civil War

The end of the Crimean War in 1856, coupled with competition from English gunmakers and Colt's Hartford plant, brought an end to the London facility. It was shut down in 1857, and all parts were eventually transferred to Hartford.

Colt's Patent Fire Arms Manufacturing Company was incorporated in 1855. All but four of 10,000 shares, each with a par value of $100, belonged to him. His H-shaped factory on Hartford's South Meadows was 500 feet on a side and three stories high. A star-studded blue dome with a gilded, rampant colt capped the structure, which rested on a floodplain of the Connecticut River. Colt spent $125,000 to build dikes to protect his factory, planting them in willow trees to prevent erosion.

Colt expected his employees to work 10 hours a day and consistently promoted good men, some of whom became famous in other arenas. For example, Rollin White's patents helped Smith and Wesson build a business; and Francis Pratt and

The U.S. Army immediately adopted the Colt Single Action Army after it was introduced in 1873. Here an 1880's cavalryman poses field-ready with his service-issue Colt pistol.

The original Colt plant in Hartford is readily distinguished by its blue dome.

Amos Whitney founded the company that now makes many of our jet aircraft engines.

Colt also built Charter Oak Hall as a social center for factory personnel, and he even organized an Armory Band. Mark Twain's classic work, "A Connecticut Yankee in King Arthur's Court," is said to have been inspired by Samuel Colt (Twain having spent 16 years in Hartford).

The first new gun produced at Colt's stunning Hartford complex was the Sidehammer, featuring a solid frame with the barrel screwed in instead of being fixed in place by a wedge, as with earlier models. The cylinder could be removed by pulling its axis pin from the rear of the frame. Both pistols and rifles were made with this action, also known as "the Root," after its designer. Seven variations of the Root pistols included barrel lengths of 3½ and 4½ inches, and in calibers of 28 and 31. About 40,000 of these five-shot guns were produced between 1855 and 1870. Colt Model 1849 Pocket revolvers offered stiff competition, and once Colt's patent protection expired in 1856, other gunmakers bombarded the marketplace.

The Sidehammer models lasted only until 1864, after some shooters complained that the rifle spit burning powder and bits of lead onto their left arm. A gasket on the back of the frame could be adjusted to force the cylinder against the barrel, but powder fouling soon tied up the mechanism. About 18,300 Root rifles left Colt's plant, most of them 56 caliber (some .44's and a few .36's were made as well). Many variations have been identified, with barrels of 15 to 37½ inches.

In June, 1856, Sam Colt married Elizabeth Jarvis, who was the sister of his company vice president, Richard Jarvis. After a European honeymoon that lasted six months, the Colts returned to Hartford and moved into a mansion that was built during their absence. Called "Armsmear," it reflected Colt's insistence on doing everything first-class. Comprising elements of English, Italian and Oriental architecture, the residence featured a magnificent ballroom and tower.

Of Sam and Elizabeth's five children, a son and two daughters died as infants. A third daughter was stillborn shortly after Colt's death. The other son, born in 1842, was named Samuel Caldwell ("Collie") Colt. He was alleged to be illegitimate, and Sam Colt always referred to him as his nephew. Collie led a wild life filled with loose women. Indeed, he was shot dead by an angry husband in 1894 while climbing out a bedroom window in Florida. Elizabeth Colt established a parish house for the

The Colt mansion, Armsmear, which Sam Colt called his "shanty," was among the most elegant in all of New England, comprising a huge lawn with a lake, greenhouses, an orchard and an oriental conservatory.

Church of the Good Shepherd in Collie's memory; she even kept his yacht, "Dauntless," in fine repair until it sank in a storm after the turn of the century.

The imposing figure of Samuel Colt, the industrialist, stands in a park near Armsmear.

Samuel Caldwell Colt (above) was the only child of five fathered by Samuel Colt to live past infancy. Noted for throwing wild parties aboard his racing yacht, "Collie" Colt met his end in a Florida bedroom at the hands of a jealous husband.

With the onset of the Civil War, Colt's 1860 Army, 1861 Navy and 1862 Police and Pocket Navy revolvers were added to the Colt line. Thanks to the U.S. Ordnance adoption of the 44-caliber 1860 Army, more than 200,000 of this model were produced prior to 1873, at least 80,000 going to the government. A six-shot repeater with an 8-inch barrel, the Army revolver featured a new "silver steel" that was so strong it could be machined down to smaller proportions than earlier Colts. The first Model 1860 Army's were built by paring metal from the obsolete Dragoon frame; but soon it proved more efficient to alter the Model 1851 Navy frame, making that gun bigger. The result was a gun that weighed 2 pounds 10 ounces—a full pound and a half less than a Dragoon!

Unlike earlier Colts that were rarely altered for shoulder stocks, most Model 1860 Army guns were so fitted. Those without cuts on the butt and recoil shield, but with the four frame screws, command higher prices today. Few variations of the 1860 Army were produced, mainly because the pistol as designed got such good reviews. Each copy bore a serial number, starting with "1."

Colt's Model 1861 Navy revolver was a 36-caliber gun with a 7½-inch barrel. Like the 1860 Army, this revolver came standard with an unfluted cylinder, though some fluted guns were made. Only a few were adapted for shoulder stocks. A factory fire in 1864, plus competition from the 1851 Navy and some new cartridge firearms, limited the production of Colt's new Navy's to 38,843.

In 1861, Colt also began making Model 1862 Police and Pocket Pistols (or the New Model Police Pistol and Model 1862 Pocket Pistol of Navy Caliber). Of some 47,000 produced through 1873, 28,000 were of the Police variety. Both had five-shot cylinders and 36-caliber barrels in lengths from 4½ to 6½ inches. The Trapper's Model, with 3½-inch barrel, is among the rarest of Colt revolvers.

During this period, Colt continued his habit of presenting specially engraved and accoutred guns to people in high places. Many survive, unused, in their original cases. Most engraving came from Gustav Young, whose pupils included the Ulrich brothers of Winchester fame. Young was under contract with Colt from 1852 to sometime in the 1860's. In 1869, he went to work for Smith and Wesson. Cuno Helfricht, who began a 50-year stint as Colt's main engraver in 1871, learned his trade at S&W from Gustav Young.

The Civil War only accelerated the rapid growth of Colt's Patent Fire Arms. Sam Colt, astute businessman that he was, had sensed the rumblings well in advance of John Brown's raid. He'd geared up for arms orders and, in 1860, ordered his crew to run the armory, "Night and day with double sets of hands until we get 5,000 or 10,000 ahead of each kind. . . . Make hay while the sun shines." Thus, when war demanded more guns, Colt's warehouses were full and his production lines in top form. The company also built 58-caliber, single-shot percussion rifles for the Army. After the war 50,000 went to Europe, where they were converted to *flintlocks* and sent on to Africa.

The success of his business rewarded Sam Colt handsomely. By 1861, his annual personal income exceeded a million dollars. While he enjoyed hobnobbing with the wealthy and powerful, he apparently never lost his common touch, nor did he ever lack enthusiasm for work. His father-in-law once observed: "He must love work for its own sake . . .

and it really seems that the more he has to do, the more he enjoys himself.''

The frantic pace finally caught up with Colt just after New Year's Day of 1862. For the next week, he was in and out of delirium. On January 8, Samuel Colt bade his wife and children a loving goodbye, and two days later he died. As Colt had planned, his old friend and able chief E.K. Root assumed leadership in the company, which trundled on through the war.

On February 4 and 5, 1864, a fire, thought to be set by a Confederate saboteur, reduced to rubble most of the factory Colt had built in 1855. Over half the work stations were demolished, forcing the company to occupy an adjacent tobacco warehouse. Less than $400,000 of insurance money came in to cover the $1.2 million in losses. Elizabeth Colt, who now controlled the $15 million estate, ordered the facility rebuilt. Slackening demand for guns at war's end delayed completion of the new Colt plant for three years.

Elisha K. Root, a capable gun designer, worked as Colt's superintendent and became company president at Samuel Colt's death in 1862 (he died three years later).

When Elisha Root died suddenly in 1865, Mrs. Colt named her brother, Richard Jarvis, as company president. He held that office longer than any president since, from 1865 to 1901. Elizabeth held the majority of Colt stock well into the 1890's.

Metallic Cartridges to Machine Guns

While Colt's marketing genius had left his wife an estate worth many millions, he failed to seize on the potential of the metallic cartridge. In 1849, Walter Hunt had designed a repeating rifle that fired what he called ''rocket balls''—hollow-based conical bullets containing a primer and light powder charge. The .44 slugs generated little energy, and the rifle needed many refinements, but the principle of self-contained ammunition proved workable.

As Sam Colt had made his fortune on the idea of a multi-chambered cylinder, Horace Smith and Daniel Wesson built an empire developing revolvers for metallic cartridges. For a time they worked on Hunt's recalcitrant rifle, which became the Volcanic

Elizabeth Colt, Samuel's wife, ordered the Colt armory rebuilt after the disastrous fire of February, 1864. She kept an active hand in the company until her own death in 1905.

This part of Colt's original Hartford facility now houses the production of semiautomatic rifles.

repeater. They left that project in 1856 to apply an 1855 patent to revolvers. The patent had been issued to Rollin White, a Colt employee. Legend has it that White once approached Sam Colt with his idea and got a cold response. Smith and Wesson paid White royalties in producing the first .22 rimfire cartridges; by the time Colt died, they'd built over 22,000 cartridge revolvers.

Subsequently, Colt management tried to shoulder in by negotiating a licensing agreement. Smith and Wesson asked for $600,000, and Rollin White demanded an additional $500,000 for all rights. It was too steep a price in 1866, especially for a patent that was due to expire in three years. Colt then tried to circumvent patent restrictions with a cartridge gun loaded from the front of the cylinder. Developed by Alexander Thuer, who also engineered its tapered rimfire ammunition, this design proved unsuccessful. Only about 5,000 Thuer guns—all of which held six shots—were produced between 1869 and 1872, most of them Model 1849 Pocket, 1860 Army, 1861 Navy, 1862 Police and Pocket Navy revolvers. A second Thuer patent in September, 1868, enabled his revolvers to fire either metallic or cap-and-ball loads, with only a quick change of cylinders. In 1870, this clever inventor patented one of the first cartridge loading tools.

Stymied by White's patent, the Colt firm made oblique runs at the cartridge revolver market with other conversions for its popular cap-and-ball guns. Models designed by Colt engineers C.B. Richards and William Mason, together with the 5,000 Thuer revolvers, accounted for 46,000 Colt revolvers in the late 1860's and early 1870's. They preceded the company's first cartridge firearm, the "Open Top .44," which made its debut in 1872. It featured the same three-piece construction as the Walker and Dragoon, with a wedge fastener that locked the 7½- or 8-inch barrel in place. Its ejector rod resembled that of the later Peacemaker Model. Only 7,000 Open Top .44s were shipped, all in 1872.

While revolvers comprised the focus of Colt engineering and the bulk of Colt sales, the company also held exclusive rights to the manufacture of Richard J. Gatling's crank-operated machine gun. Production ran from 1866 well into the 20th century. And in 1871, Colt introduced a top-break deringer, its first gun designed specifically for metallic cartridges. Henry Deringer had developed this tiny percussion pistol in the 1850's. All were single-shots, marketed in pairs. Colt was one of several companies that capitalized on Deringer's idea with single- and double-barrel versions, mostly in .41 rimfire. But in 1870 Colt decided not to design its own model, and instead bought out the National Arms Company of Brooklyn. The Brooklyn No. 1 and No. 2 Deringers enjoyed a fine reputation and provided the basis for Colt's first entries. Colt No. 1 was all iron in construction, while No. 2 had walnut grips. They were sold in pairs—a total of 6,500 No. 1's and 9,000 No. 2's.

Even the British were fond of Colt's deringers, mostly because of their "compact size, light weight and large bore." The most popular was the Third (and last) Model, designed by Alex Thuer. It was a side-pivoting .41, made from 1875 through 1912. Over 45,000 units were shipped, most with the standard 2½-inch barrel. [A reproduction of the Thuer deringer, in .22 rimfire, appeared in 1959. It was dropped in 1963, then reappeared briefly in 1970.]

The first revolver chambered by Colt for metallic cartridges was the "Cloverleaf House Pistol," so named for the cloverleaf cross-section of its four-shot cylinder. Manufacture began in 1870, and marketing commenced the following year. Later House Pistols held five shots and came to be known as "Jim Fisk" guns, after the flamboyant financier who'd been murdered with one. At the ensuing trial, the defendent waxed eloquent about the little weapon, describing it as "All silver-plated, everything white [with] an ivory handle."

Colt's 22-caliber "Open Top Pocket Pistol" also came out in 1870. The first seven-shot Colt, it featured the wedge fastener common to early revolvers but proved inferior to the Smith and Wesson .22's already available. Nonetheless, 110,000 were sold between 1871 and 1877.

In 1873, William Mason, who'd come to Colt from Remington 16 years earlier, designed the "New Line" of Colt revolvers. Five frame sizes accommodated the .22 and .30 rimfire, and the .32, .38 and .41 rimfire and centerfire. Barrels varied from 2¼ to 10 inches in length. Cylinders were fluted, with the cylinder pin doubling as an ejector rod. Late models of the New Line included the "New House Pistol" and "New Police" (alias "Cop" and "Thug") versions. Colt fought hard in the small pistol market to distinguish its guns from an increasing number of cheap imitations, which it called derisively "Suicide Specials." Rather than cut corners to lower the price, Colt stopped the manufacture of its spur-trigger revolvers—with the trigger set in a frame extension, or spur, instead of in a trigger guard.

By 1889, Colt had diversified its manufacturing to include a double rifle and double shotgun, a single-shot rifle, bolt-, pump- and lever-action rifles, and a double-action revolver. All the while, it kept turning out sewing machines, printing presses, ticket punches and various types of plant machinery. Sam Colt's wooden revolver had indeed sparked a manufacturing empire.

Colt's Legendary Single Action Army Revolver

Ironically, the most popular Colt gun of all was developed after Sam had died. The Single Action Army of 1873 followed quickly on the heels of the Open Top .44, which had been submitted to (and rejected by) U.S. Ordnance as a cavalry arm. The SAA had a solid frame, with a topstrap and 7½-inch screwed-in barrel. Its design is usually attributed to William Mason, though the best aspects of Sam Colt's ancient Walker Model were clearly evident in its construction.

The U.S. Army adopted the new revolver almost immediately. Representing the test board,

These Colt Single Action Army revolvers wear plastic sleeves to prevent fingerprints on the unblued barrels.

Captain John R. Edie commented: "I have no hesitation in declaring the Colt revolver superior in most respects and much better adapted to the wants of the Army than the Smith and Wesson." A Colt publication noted that, among "seven different military pistols experimented upon at Spandau during the past year by the Prussian Government, the firing of this pistol was the best in all respects." Over the next eight years, Colt produced 37,063 SAA's under government contracts, with total production exceeding 550,000. Dropped from Colt's line in 1940, the SAA was picked up again in 1956, then discontinued once more in the 1980's. It has been chambered for 30 cartridges, from .22 rimfire to .476 Eley, with barrel lengths (without ejectors) ranging from 2 to 7½ inches (4¾ to 16⅛ with ejectors). Serial numbers prior to World War II ran from 1 to 357,859. After the War, Colt introduced a new numbering system, beginning with 1SA. While government SAA's ("U.S. Martials") generally had blued barrels, case-hardened frames and walnut grips, dozens of different metal-finish and grip-material combinations were supplied. Bat Masterson, for example, wanted his guns "nickel-plated . . . easy on the trigger [with] the front sight a little higher and thicker than the ordinary pistol." He ordered eight of them in all. About 3,500 prewar Colt SAA's were factory-engraved on special order or as gifts for important people.

Sears' 1901 catalog offered a "fine handsome Colt Single Action Army Revolver, .45-caliber, 5½-inch barrel, beautifully hand-engraved in leaf and scroll design on the barrel, frame, cylinder, guard and butt; blued steel finish, inlaid gold lines around the muzzle and breech of the barrel, two gold stripes around the cylinder and inlaid gold lines around the frame under the cylinder and on the handle behind the hammer. Beautifully selected pearl handles, and a figure of Columbia in raised carving on the right stock similar to the figure shown on 1875 25-cent silver coin. . . . This revolver cost $60 to be finished in this way, and we offer it in a handsome purple plush and satin-lined case covered with drab color buff leather, making one of the nicest Cow Boy [sic] revolvers you ever saw. Our special cash price on this revolver, including case—$50.''

Another Colt favorite was the Buntline Special, which was introduced at the Philadelphia Centennial Exhibition in 1876. It featured a 10- to 16-inch barrel with a flattop frame grooved for adjustable sights and fashioned at the rear for a detachable shoulder stock. A long hammer screw and knurled nut tightened the nickel-plated brass stock to the gun. In the 1930's, the book, "Wyatt Earp, Frontier Marshal," made the Buntline famous. Ned Buntline—his real name was Edward Z.C. Judson—

supposedly gave one each of the long handguns to Wyatt Earp, Bat Masterson, Neal Brown, Charlie Bassett and Bill Tilghman, all lawmen in Dodge City, Kansas, but there's no evidence to support this. Only one run of Buntlines was produced, in the serial range 28800 to 28830.

More common were short-barreled (3- or 4-inch) Sheriff's or Storekeeper's SAA's. No ejectors were provided, which meant shooters had to poke the cases out with a stick, or pull the cylinder pins and remove the cylinders. Flattop Target Models, which were made only from 1880 to 1890, also came without ejectors, presumably for better balance. They were the only SAA revolvers that came standard with blued (not case-colored) frames. The Bisley, with its special humpbacked target grip, came along to replace the Flattops. The Bisleys, which featured a low hammer spur, curved trigger and oversize trigger guard, were chambered for 18 of the SAA's 30 cartridges.

Virtually every famous—or infamous—fron-

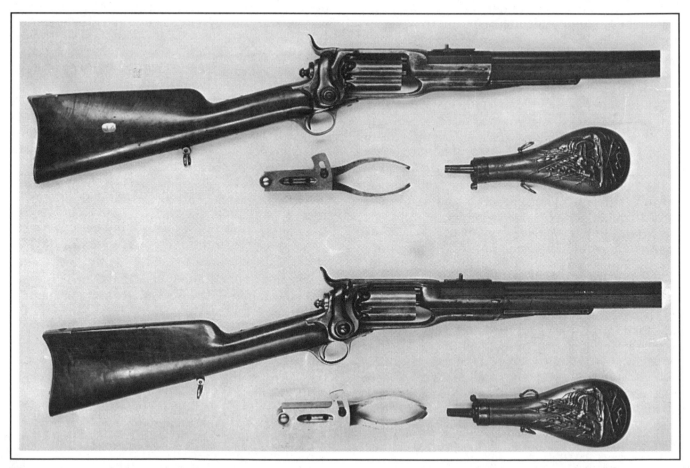

These sets of Colt Model 1855 Root sidehammer rifles were sent to Czar Alexander II of Russia. Colt became renown for presenting custom models to important figures of his day.

tier character in the last quarter of the 19th century used a Colt Single Action Army. Even Colt's London agency reported brisk sales. A classic gun in every sense, it became the most prized Colt to thousands of admirers. Hog-Leg, Thumb-Buster, Equalizer, Six-Shooter—these and other fond names made it legendary. The Colt factory, which stood as ready as Sam himself to take advantage of every marketing opportunity, added its own monikers to the line, including Peacemaker, Bisley and Frontier Six-Shooter. The most popular early chamberings included the .32-20, .38-40 and .44-40, the same ones that were listed for the enormously popular Winchester Model 1873 rifle. Carrying one kind of ammunition for both guns simplified life a great deal for the frontiersman.

Swing-Out Cylinders and Double-Actions

With the metallic cartridge came new interest in double-action revolvers. Featuring a trigger mechanism that rotated and locked the cylinder while the hammer was withdrawn, then tripped, a double-action did not require thumb cocking and made for fast repeat shots. It was not a new idea, however. Pistols of this design had been around since the 1830's, and the mechanical principle was considered public domain by the patent office. Sam Colt himself had built a double-action experimental gun on the Paterson frame in 1842, but the absence of a half- or full-cock hammer notch made double-actions unsafe in his mind. They were also inaccurate, he maintained, because the long, hard trigger pull inevitably moved the gun off target.

Fifteen years after Colt's death, his company announced the Model 1877 Lightning double-action revolver. Designed by Colt's prolific engineer, William Mason, the Lightning was available in 38 and 41 caliber (the "Thunderer"). Barrels without ejectors varied from 1½ to 6 inches in length (4½ to 10 inches (with ejectors). Checkered wood grips were standard on the first Lightnings, but many have been found since with ivory and mother-of-pearl grips—especially guns with a nickel finish. Hard rubber, made popular by the Single Action Army, was another grip option. Lightning grips featured a distinctive "bird's head" shape, with a rounded butt, and a forestrap with much the same curve as an SAA.

Sam Colt may not have approved of the Lightning, but it did have hammer stops that permitted safe handling and single-action operation. The gun

sold well and remained in Colt's line until 1909, with production totaling 166,849.

The company's next double-action revolver followed quickly. Called the "D.A. Frontier," it had a larger frame than the Lightning, thus accommodating cartridges like the .32-20, .38-40, .44-40 and .45 Colt (the first three of these rounds were later listed for the Lightning slide-action rifle, introduced by Colt in 1884). These pistols featured 3½- to 4-inch barrels without ejectors and 4¾, 5½ and 7½ inch barrels with ejectors. The D.A. Frontier also held six shots in a fluted cylinder and was serialed separately from other Colts, starting with number 1. Its many variations included an Alaskan Model, with an oversize trigger guard for gloved hands. Some D.A. Frontiers were made without hammer spurs, to prevent them from hanging up on one's clothes. Flattop versions and barrels of 2½ and 12 inches were made on special order. In all, 51,210 D.A. Frontiers left the Colt factory between 1878 and 1905.

The next logical step in revolver development involved a new and better way to clear and load a cylinder. Poking cases out one at a time, or pulling the axis pin to remove the cylinder, proved cumbersome and time-consuming. Oddly enough, the first gun company to explore a swing-out cylinder—Winchester—was so involved in making rifles around 1876 that it did not pursue the brilliant work of its engineers, S.W. Wood and Hugo Borchardt. By 1881, the ever alert William Mason had revived the idea at Colt and devised a swing-out mechanism of his own. He was granted five patents, with several others acquired by C.J. Ehbets and Horace Lord, who also worked for Colt.

During the eight-year hiatus between Mason's first swing-out cylinder and Colt's announcement of its Model 1889 New Navy revolver, Winchester reminded the company that its designers had, after all, been first with the idea. Probably Winchester had no interest in building revolvers, but at that time Colt was rumored to be experimenting with a lever-action repeating rifle, and the potential for costly competition in that field had alarmed the people at New Haven.

About 31,000 New Navy revolvers were made between 1889 and 1894, their square-shaped heels distinguishing them from Colt's two earlier double-action revolvers. The frames were different, too; a New Navy model looks much like a modern revolver. New Navy revolvers built on government contracts were chambered to .38 Long Colt and featured 6-inch barrels, blued finish and walnut grips.

Most bore a serial number under 5,000. The other standard chambering, .41 Long Colt, was available in guns for civilian sale only.

The New Army and Navy guns of 1892, 1894, 1895, 1896, 1901 and 1903 filled the company's government contracts. Each differed from the others, but often in obscure ways, such as grip thickness. Barrel lengths ran from 2 to 6 inches, with calibers in .32-20, .38 S&W, .38 and .41 Short and Long Colt. The series was phased out after 1908. Total production reached about 291,000, including the Officer's Model, which was introduced in 1904.

Colt's Army Special succeeded the New Army and Navy but was not serialed separately. It featured a removable sideplate, a round thumb latch, and the single column of cylinder stops common to modern Colts. Model 1889 New Navy, by the way, was the first Colt with stops located on the periphery of the cylinder; and, like the New Army and Navy guns, it had two rows of stops. In addition, the 1889 model featured a positive lock, which prevented accidental discharge when the hammer struck. This same feature was carried over into most versions of the Army Special. Chambered for the .32-20 and .38 and .41 Long Colt cartridges, the Army Special wore barrels of 4 or 6 inches. Standard grips were of hard rubber. Serial numbers ran from 291,000 to about 540,000 (but Colt's new Official Police jumped in at number 513,216 in 1927).

Colt's Official Police model differed only slightly from its predecessor, though several improvements were made over the next 50 years. A .22 rimfire was serialed separately. About 30,000 of these revolvers left the factory, many with special-order sights for target shooting. Gaps in the numbering sequence account for the 1-to-47,016 serial range. The centerfire models came in several calibers—up to .38-44 S&W—and in barrel lengths of 4, 5 and 6 inches. The blued steel frames wore checkered walnut grips. Variants included the short-barreled, parkerized Commando in .38 Special (produced during World War II) and the scarce Marshall, a gun similar to the Commando but with a rounded butt.

More Power, Less Weight

The Officer's Model DA included several special versions: the O.M. Target, O.M. Match, O.M. Special, and Mark III O.M. Match. All told, about 105,000 were manufactured, most of them in .22 rimfire and .38 Special, plus a few .32's. Barrels ran from 4 to 7½ inches, with checkered walnut grips and blue metal finish as standard features. The numbering

of Officer's Model Colts has confused even highly experienced collectors, with some guns falling into the serial range of the Army Special and Official Police. Later revolvers were even numbered (with a "J" prefix) among Colt's "Lawman" series. The 22-caliber Target variation, introduced in 1930, had its own serial range.

When in 1953 the Official Police model changed to a flat top, along with adjustable rear, ramp front sights and heavy barrel, it became known as the "Colt Trooper." Available in .22 rimfire and .38 Special, the Trooper served as Colt's standard police revolver until 1969, when the Mark III was introduced. About 15,000 Troopers, armed with wide hammer spurs and target grips, were chambered in .357 Magnum between 1953 and 1961. In 1955, the handsomely finished Python .357 appeared, and quickly became the company's premier handgun. It was followed 11 years later by its twin, the Diamondback, which was chambered in .22 rimfire and .38 Special.

More recent double-action developments include the Viper, a 4-inch, .38 Special with an alloy frame. It came along in 1978 but is no longer listed. The Anaconda, Colt's current entry in the .44 Magnum market, resembles the 6-inch Python (which is still available in 2½-, 4-, 6- and 8-inch barrels). The King Cobra, which made its debut in 1985, is similar but is made of stainless steel and has a rib.

During its move to more powerful belt guns, Colt also kept the market supplied with concealable revolvers. In 1893, it introduced the 32-caliber New Pocket, a six-shot, double-action model with barrels from 2½ to 6 inches in length. By 1905, about 30,000 New Pockets had been shipped; the model was then replaced by the Pocket Positive, with its new positive lock mechanism. About 130,000 Pocket Positives were made before the gun was dropped in 1943.

In 1896, the popular .32 Long Colt cartridge was considered entirely adequate for law enforcement, though by modern standards its 82-grain bullet at 790 fps is anemic at best. In the New Pocket revolver with its slender frame and barrel, the little .32 made sense. In a service revolver, though, it was inappropriate. Still, that is what Colt chambered in its New Police double-action three years after the New Pocket was announced. In the next 11 years, some 49,500 New Police revolvers left the Colt plant. These included standard guns with 2½-, 4- and 6-inch barrels, and a special 6-inch, flat-top target model. In 1907, Colt introduced its replacement: the Police Positive, which was very similar but incorporated the company's Positive Lock. About 199,000 were made, with serial numbers starting where the New Police numbers stopped. A few thousand second-quality Police Positives were sold outside the United States between 1933 and 1941. These came to be known as "pequanos" (Spanish for "little one").

By 1905, Colt, having recognized the utility of more powerful cartridges in service arms, announced the Police Positive .38, which it described as "larger in bore, with greater penetration, velocity and range. As a .38 caliber Pocket Revolver it has NO equal." With a 150-grain bullet at 770 fps, the .38 Long Colt was no dynamo, but it beat the .32. About 200,000 Police Positive revolvers were built for this round, some on .32 frames, the last one rolling off the line in 1943.

Colt's most widely used revolver was the Police Positive Special, introduced in 1908 on the heels of the P.P. .38. Chambered for the .38 Special cartridge, it was hailed as "the most compact and also the lightest revolver ever produced to take this powerful ammunition. . . . The most effective pocket and house arm on the market." By the mid-1970's, production totalled over 750,000, the longest continuous run for any Colt revolver. Barrel lengths varied from 1¼ to 6 inches. Many variations have been uncovered, among the rarest being the 4-inch Border Patrol made in 1952. Roughly 400 of these were produced.

Colt's Detective Special was a compact version of the Police Positive Special. It came out in 1927, a year before Colt announced its Banker's Special, an offshoot of the Police Positive .38. While about 400,000 Detective Specials have been made (most with 2-inch barrels, some with 3-inch), the Banker's Special in .22 rimfire, .38 Colt and .38 S&W sold only 35,000 copies before production stopped in 1943. The grip heel on this model was changed from square to round in 1934.

Colt's aluminum-frame Cobra appeared in 1950. It was a 15-ounce Detective Special, the company's lightest pocket gun ever. An 11-ounce variation, the Aircrewman, subsequently became the only revolver with both cylinder and frame made of aluminum alloy. About 1,189 Aircrewmen were built, but when government tests proved the cylinders were too weak for certain .38 Special loads, Colt issued a recall on those already sold and they were destroyed.

In 1962, Colt introduced the Agent, a Cobra with a 2-inch barrel and short grip. Its steel cylinder and aluminum frame ensured its acceptance, and

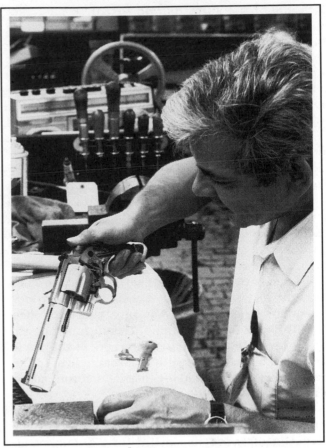

A Colt technician tunes the trigger on an Anaconda, Colt's exquisite .44 Magnum double-action revolver.

since its introduction more than 50,000 have been made. The Courier, in .22 rimfire and .32 Colt New Police, sported a 3-inch barrel but had the same grip as the Agent. Only about 3,000 Couriers were manufactured between 1953 and 1956.

Colt's big-bore double-actions began in 1898 as the New Service line. The guns were offered in 18 chamberings, from .38 Long Colt to .456 Eley, and eight barrel lengths, from 2 to 7½ inches. Production totalled over 356,000 by 1944, when Colt discontinued the line. About 40 percent of the run consisted of M1917 U.S. Army revolvers chambered for the .45 ACP. The rimless cartridges were loaded and held in the cylinder with half-moon clips. Each flat, spring-steel clip held three rounds, and a practiced shooter could reload very quickly. These service revolvers had plain walnut grips with lanyard swivels and 5½-inch barrels. Other well-known big-frame Colts of this era include the Old Model Target, Model 1909 U.S. Army, and U.S. Navy and Shooting Master.

Advent of the Autoloading Pistol

Back in the 1880's, European engineers had developed a new kind of gun, one that would extract, eject, cock, feed and lock by itself. The autoloaders of Mauser, Luger and Borchardt made little impression on U.S. gun buyers, who were quite pleased with their Colt and Smith & Wesson revolvers. Then, in 1897, Colt collaborated with gun genius John Moses Browning in exploring the potential of autoloading pistols. Three years later, Colt marketed the first successful autoloader produced by any domestic manufacturer. Undaunted by the negative reaction of government ordnance people to a .38 prototype, Colt brought the new gun into production.

Military tests of Model 1900 proved favorable, the examining board noting that, "The test to which this pistol was subjected was in every way more severe than that to which revolvers have been heretofore subjected, and the endurance of this pistol appears to be greater than that of the service revolver . . . this pistol is a suitable arm for use in the U.S. service, and it possess numerous advantages over the revolver."

Colt's first run of 3,500 Model 1900's was sold mostly on the open market. After approval by Ordnance, the government asked for 200 autoloaders for "actual trial in the field." During the next 70 years, more than 3,000,000 Colt autoloading pistols were sold to police and U.S. armed forces.

While Model 1900 was the first Colt made expressly for smokeless cartridges, its offspring—Model 1911—became the first Colt manufactured under license by other companies. Between these two model years, Colt developed autoloaders at a frantic pace, with new guns announced in 1902, 1903, 1905, 1907 and 1908. While the 1900 and 1911 models featured external hammers, other Colts of that era were hammerless (actually, they had internal hammers). Model 1900 had a 6-inch barrel and a 7-round magazine.

In 1903, Browning helped Colt design an improved version of the 1900: Model 1902 Sporting. About 7,500 were made, with serial numbers starting at 3500 (where Model 1900 stopped). A Model 1902 Military, equipped with a lanyard swivel, was numbered separately, from 15,001 to 15,200, then backward from 15,000 to 11,000, finishing in 1929 with a run from 30,200 to 47,100. The 1902 Military sold well, with roughly 18,000 copies shipped.

Colt's Model 1903 Pocket Hammer featured the same action as the 1902 Sporting autoloader, but with a shortened barrel and frame. About 15,000 were numbered consecutively, but serials from the last batch were mixed with those of the 1902 Military pistols. When production ceased in 1929, a total of 26,000 Model 1903 Pocket Hammer guns had been manufactured.

The 1903's hammerless version—in .32 ACP—gained the best sales record of any Colt pocket auto. It was an eight-shot gun with a 3¾- or 4-inch barrel. Like its forebears, its design came from John Browning (who also sold patent rights to armsmakers in Europe). The European guns gave Colt stiff competition, and eventually trade agreements were made restricting Fabrique Nationale at Liege (Belgium) to marketing in Europe. In return, Colt would sell only in the U.S. Its Model 1903 Hammerless was the first pistol produced under these arrangements. During its 42-year life, 572,215 rolled off the line.

As the 1903 continued to earn its way in the marketplace, Browning and W.M. Thomas (of Remington) were already engineering its successor. They started by designing a new cartridge, the .380 ACP. The gun they developed was a beefed-up version of the Model 1903 Hammerless. The .380 first appeared in 1908 and was separately numbered, then dropped in 1945 after 138,009 copies had been produced. Its 3¾-inch barrel was the result of the development of Model 1908, which also carried a 3¾-inch barrel only. Most of the Model 1908s and .380 ACPs were sold to the U.S. government, and some of the .380s were bought by the Shanghai Police Department.

Colt also produced a miniature Model 1908 in .25 ACP. Its 33-year sales figures totaled 409,061. And shortly after World War II, two exposed-hammer .25s were introduced: the Junior Colt and the Colt Automatic .25. Both were available with a .22 rimfire conversion kit. Astra of Spain produced these guns for Colt, and they are so marked. The Gun Control Act of 1968 stopped importation of these little Spanish Colts, but production of the outside-hammer .25 resumed at Hartford in 1970. The last of these guns were shipped in 1974.

The 1911: Browning's Brainchild, Colt's Crown Jewel

The early Colt autoloaders worked fine with small- and medium-bore cartridges, but big-bore power was still limited to revolvers. That changed in 1905, when Colt introduced what was to become the most widely respected autoloading pistol in the world. "In the new Model, caliber .45, we offer a weapon of tremendous effectiveness. . . . Loaded with smokeless powder only, the cartridge has a full metal cased bullet, giving a velocity of 900 ft. per second and a penetration in ⅞-inch pine boards of: 7 boards at 225 ft., 6 boards at 325 ft."

The U.S. Government initially ordered only 200 of Colt's new Model 1905, but in 1907 it contracted for 201 more—all for testing purposes. Production of the 1905's totalled 6,100, of which 500 were fitted with detachable shoulder stocks. The improved version of Colt's .45 Automatic began its long march in 1911. It proved deadly and reliable on the battlefield as well as the police beat. Gunsmiths made it shoot ever tighter groups on the target range, and its design was indisputably among the most brilliant of any firearm ever produced.

The War Department studied Colt's autoloading pistols for 12 years before adopting Model 1911. Its final report stated that, "the Service has secured the most powerful, accurate and rapid firing pistol that has yet been produced. It is a No. .45 caliber, eight-shot automatic pistol. Seven of the cartridges are in the magazine and one in the chamber when the pistol is ready to be fired. The rapidity with which it can be discharged is shown when it is known that one man fired 1,000 rounds in thirty-eight minutes. By the official test the revolver was fired 6,000 times without any damage. . . ."

While Savage also submitted an autoloader for testing, the ordnance people decided that the Colt was "more powerful, accurate and rapid than the Savage." They weighed almost the same—roughly 2½ pounds—but the Colt was quicker to take apart and put back together. Its apparent recoil was less, too.

Over 200 kinds of Model 1911 Colts have been identified, not counting those produced with different chamberings. Perhaps the best known of the small-bore 1911's is the Ace, a .22 rimfire version produced from 1931 to 1941 and separately serialed. It allowed shooters to practice with inexpensive, light-recoiling ammunition. Slightly less than 11,000 of these 10-shot autoloaders were shipped. Assembly of the final guns was delayed until 1947.

The Ace seemed like a good idea, but in practice the little .22 round sometimes failed to cycle the slide. In 1937, a clever ex-convict named David Williams patented a "floating chamber" that magnified the .22's recoil. The chamber, a free-moving part, accelerated to the rear just like a .45 case might on firing. Its weight and basal area ensured positive function. Williams, incidentally, became popularly known as "Carbine" Williams. While

serving out a murder sentence, he designed the M1 Carbine in a prison shop. In return for his work and good behavior, he was allowed to pursue firearms development in prison during his middle years. The U.S. military took good advantage of this.

Several target-grade 1911's have been built, from the first National Match gun to the Gold Cup. Variants include a pistol built in the 1950's for the special .38 AMU round. Parts were supplied to the military, which then assembled the guns on standard .45 or .38 Super frames.

In 1929, the 1911 .38 Super replaced 1902 Military and 1903 Pocket Hammer autoloaders. Although it looked just like a 1911 in .45, it had its own serial range. The .38 Super cartridge, featuring a 130-grain bullet at 1275 fps, generated 470 foot pounds of energy—100 more than the .45! During its 42 years in the Colt line, the .38 Super sold over 202,000 copies, including 5,000 "Super Match" guns between 1935 and 1941. It also proved popular in Mexico, where the use of .45 ammunition was prohibited.

In 1949 Colt introduced a new 1911—the Commander—with a 4¼-inch barrel. Chamberings were 9mm Luger, .38 Super and .45 ACP. The slide was made of steel (but shorter than on standard 1911's) and its alloy frame was developed jointly by Colt and Alcoa. The Commander weighed just over 26 ounces, compared to 40 for its steel cousins. Colt now makes a Combat Commander with a steel frame (as well as the original alloy-frame gun, which it calls the Lightweight).

More custom gunsmithing has been done on Colt Model 1911-style autoloaders (above) than on any other handgun.

Colt's Delta Elite, chambered for the potent 10mm automatic cartridge, is the company's latest gun based on the 1911 design. Like the target-grade .45 Gold Cup, it closely resembles its forebear. A much smaller version of the 1911 is Colt's .380 Automatic, with a 3¼-inch barrel and 7-round magazine. Even smaller are the Mustang .380 and Officer's Model .45, both available with an alloy frame or in blued or stainless steel.

Colt's first venture with a full-size .22 pistol—the Woodsman—became another classic in firearms design. The brainchild of John Browning, G.H. Tansley and F.C. Chandwick, the Woodsman made its debut in 1915. Until 1927, it was known as the "Colt Automatic Pistol, Target Model." Subsequent cosmetic changes produced the Target, Sport, Match Target, Challenger, Huntsman and Targetsman. The first serial range went from 1 to 187,000 (which occurred sometime during the middle of World War II). Originally, its barrels were 6 inches long, but a 4½-inch barrel was added in 1934. Walnut grips and a blued finish were standard.

Postwar Woodsman pistols had flat butts (earlier stocks angled down in the front), and its slide locks and safeties were different from prewar models. Slanted instead of vertical slide grooves, a ramp front sight and plastic grips were among other changes. Colt resumed production of the Match Target Woodsman in 1948. It had been introduced 10 years earlier, but dropped during the war effort after only 15,000 copies were made. The Match Target, or "Bullseye" model (so-called for the roller marking on its slide), remains one of the premier rimfire target pistols ever produced in the U.S. Colt's Second and Third Model variations followed, with the lighter, less expensive Challenger and even trimmer Huntsmen entering the line in the 1950's. The last Woodsman guns were produced in 1977.

Self-loading mechanisms had served Colt well ever since the company's association with Dr. R.J. Gatling in 1866. All Gatling guns produced in the U.S.— some 25 Models—were made by Colt. Later military contracts were signed for the Browning-designed Maxim and Vickers machine guns, the Model 1909 Benet-Mercie Machine Rifle, the Browning Automatic Rifle, The Model 1917 water-cooled Machine Gun, the 50-caliber M2, the 20mm Cannon and, in 1921, the first run of 15,000 Thompson Submachine Guns. Colt refused additional orders for the Thompson because it had quickly gained infamy as the "weapon of choice" for notorious gangsters of the time. This cost the company many millions of dollars, as more than 1,750,000 "tommy guns" were manufactured during World War II.

Colt Tries the Rifle Market

One of Sam Colt's objectives for his company had been a complete line of handguns and long arms. Due to the success of his early revolvers, fac-

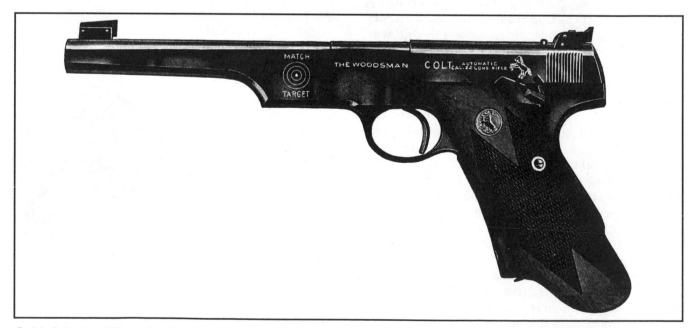

Colt's full-size .22 autoloading pistol was the Woodsman (above), which was introduced in 1915.

tory time and resources were not soon applied to the development of shoulder arms. The revolver's mechanism was best used with loads of moderate violence and in guns with short chambers. When the metallic cartridge made front loading obsolete, the Colt firm wisely used its energy to adapt its handguns to the new ammunition. Only then did it seek ways to break into the rifle market.

The first Colt rifle project was the conversion of Model 1861 Muskets to cartridge loading. Next came the application of Alexander Thuer's revolver conversion to the company's Model 1855 Sidehammer rifles. Neither effort produced a government contract. Colt then turned to Hiram Berdan, the well-known Civil War commander and inventor of the Berdan primer. [Berdan's elite rifle unit used Sharps rifles primarily, and he is credited with coining the term "Sharpshooter."] In 1866, Berdan patented a breechloading single-shot mechanism that interested the people at Colt. They contracted with Berdan to alter some muskets using his design, then build a new rifle around it. In the meantime, Colt got an order from the Russian government for 30,000 rifles in .42 Berdan centerfire. Between conversion work and the Russian contract, Colt was able to stay afloat in the lean years after the Civil War.

During that time, General W.B. Franklin influenced many gun projects at Colt. While his efforts in securing military contracts directly benefitted Colt, his one rifle project failed. Franklin used the Berdan mechanism as a starting point, then added a nine-shot magazine. It was gravity fed, however, a poor feature on any gun used for hunting or in battle. Franklin offered his .45-70 to the government, but tests showed it was inferior to the Remington-Keene and Winchester-Hotchkiss bolt-action rifles.

Colt's first successful post-Civil War long gun was the double-barrel 1878 Hammer Shotgun, considered among the very best of domestic, mass-produced doubles. It weighed 7½ pounds and featured rebounding locks, imported barrels, and Circassian walnut stocks. "In beauty of finish, quality of materials and accuracy of workmanship these guns are unexcelled . . .", claimed Colt. Model 1878's came in 10 and 12 gauge with damascus barrels 28, 30, and 32 inches long. They were followed by Model 1883 Hammerless Shotgun, a boxlock which Colt claimed was the equal of anything England had to sell. Weighing nearly 13 pounds, it offered the same gauge and barrel-length combinations as Colt's Model 1878, and the same finishes. Special

orders were readily accepted (President Grover Cleveland, an avid hunter, bought a pair of 8-gauge '83's with 34-inch barrels).

Colt also built a double rifle. Commonly accepted as Caldwell Colt's project, this brief venture never resulted in commercial sales. Only about 40 double rifles are thought to have been made—so few that the markings were engraved, not stamped. Most were chambered in .45-70. There's evidence that Model 1878 shotgun frames provided the foundation for at least some of these. The barrels were rifled in opposite directions. Like the exquisite Model 1883 Hammerless Shotgun, Colt's double rifle faced huge odds in the marketplace. Hunters didn't want an English-style rifle and were even less enthusiastic about paying for one. Cheap pump shotguns, lever- and bolt-action repeating rifles all robbed double rifles of a fighting chance on the frontier.

In 1882, Andrew Burgess, an inventor, approached Colt with the idea for a lever-action rifle that looked like (and would compete with) the successful Winchester Model 1873. It would even fire the same popular .44-40 ammunition. Colt agreed to the Burgess project and in 1883 started producing rifles. The production run lasted only two years, in which time 3,810 rifles and 2,593 carbines were shipped. The Burgess model did not threaten Winchester's '73 rifle, but apparently it did disturb some Winchester executives. Legend has it that Winchester sent Colt some experimental Winchester revolvers after Colt had presented the New Haven firm with a special Burgess, inscribed: "Hon. Wm. F. Cody July 26, 1883, with Compliments of Colts Co." Buffalo Bill had traditionally used Winchester rifles. The revolvers Colt received in return were reportedly shown at the same board meeting in which the company decided to pull out of the lever-action rifle market.

Dumping the Burgess project did not mean abandoning all rifle projects, however, and in 1884 Colt announced its new Lightning series of slide-action rifles. Over the next 20 years, 185,000 Lightnings left the plant, a company record for long guns until the advent of the AR-15 and M16. The Lightning came in three frame sizes and a great many chamberings, from .22 rimfire to .50-95 Express. Barrel lengths ranged from 20 to 28 inches, and magazine capacity from 8 to 15 rounds. The Lightning was the first commercially successful pump rifle made in the U.S., predating Winchester's Model 1890 and Remington's Model 12 rimfires.

Small-frame Lightnings with 24-inch barrels in

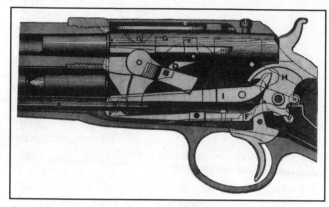

Colt's Lightning pump-action magazine rifle (above) was made in three frame sizes from 1884 to 1904. Total production came to 185,000.

.22 rimfire sold best and stayed in production longest, until 1904. Just under 90,000 copies were made, a few more than the total of all Colt medium-frame guns. The .44-40, .38-40 and .32-20, in that order, proved the most popular cartridges in the medium frame, which was discontinued in 1901. Only 6,496 of the big Lightnings were manufactured during a seven-year production run, with Winchester and Marlin lever rifles giving it bruising competition. Colt promoted the rifle's "simpler and more perfect" breech mechanism, and the gun's quick feeding. "By holding the trigger back, and using the reciprocating motion with the left hand, the Rifle can be fired with great rapidity and without further use of the trigger." No mention was made of the accuracy one might attain with this method of fire.

Colt did not get serious about rifles again until after World War II. In 1957 it introduced a center-fire rifle built on the FN Mauser action with a Sako trigger and contemporary-style sporting stock. Production of the 5,000 Model 57 rifles in calibers .243 and .30-06 fell to a subcontractor, the Jefferson Manufacturing Company of North Haven, Connecticut. The following year, Colt added two more chamberings and relabeled its bolt rifle the Coltsman. Production shuffled along beside sales until 1962, when the company replaced the Mauser action with Sako's. Kodiak, the successor to Jefferson Manufacturing, produced the standard model, while Sako built the deluxe version. Colt dropped its bolt rifle in 1965 after a total production of about 10,000.

During the 1960's, the company had a brief affair with an autoloading .22 rifle. Then, in 1970, it announced a new single-shot centerfire rifle built

on the dropping-block action of the famous Sharps. Available in several chamberings from .17 Remington to .375 H&H, the Colt-Sharps proved too expensive to manufacture for what was then a tepid single-shot market.

Recently, Colt again entered the rifle market with a bolt-action model built by Sauer in Germany. Noted for its very slick action, this expensive rifle could not pay its way and was eventually abandoned. Sauer also made some drillings for Colt. The bolt rifle was available in a wide choice of chamberings, and the drilling came in .243 and .30-06 under double 12-bore barrels. Also, between 1961 and 1966, Colt subcontracted with Jefferson for 2,000 pump shotguns, and with Franchi of Italy for about 4,500 autoloading shotguns.

The most important Colt long gun of all time is certainly the AR-15 autoloader, which became the selective-fire M16 used by U.S. ground forces in Vietnam. The M16 is still the official U.S. service rifle. Its origin was not at Colt, however, but at the

The author examines a polishing drum, or parts tumbler, at the Colt factory.

Armalite Division of the Fairchild Engine and Airplane Corporation, from whom Colt bought all rights in 1961. Two years later, following the astute politicking and dogged work necessary to procure Ordnance approval, Colt's AR-15 found a military home after Air Force General Curtis LeMay championed the gun at the Pentagon. Thereafter, the AR-15 became the M16, a lightweight (6½-pound), synthetic-stocked, .223-caliber autoloader, destined to replace the formidable but more cumbersome M14. Several variations of the M16 have since been produced for military applications. Colt built a new plant in West Hartford expressly to make this rifle, which is also produced under Colt license in Korea, the Philippines, and Indonesia.

The fortunes of Colt during the 20th century reflect some pivotal changes in our society—not just economic blips, but attitudes. Shortly after the turn of the century, the company was sold by Colt's widow to a group of New York investors. After World War I, business slowed, followed by a violent labor strike in 1935, which lasted several months and weakened Colt severely. The next year, a flood swamped the Hartford plant up to the second floor, forcing employees to come to work in rowboats. Damage to company records, machines and guns exceeded a million dollars.

World War II again brought prosperity. In Colt's three factories, more than 15,000 people in three shifts worked around the clock, every day. Just before the war's end, Graham Anthony succeeded Sam Stone as company president. Stone had steered Colt for 22 years, but wasteful practices during the recent war effort left Anthony with a financial mess. The postwar lull in demand prompted Colt to lay off some experienced foremen, thus preventing a quick rebound. For two years after the war ended, the Colt plants remained idle.

Eventually the company began boosting production and designing new guns—like alloy-frame revolvers, first built in 1949. A year later, the Korean War brought more gun orders from the military; but this infusion of money was not enough to keep Colt on its feet. In 1955, Colt joined the Pratt & Whitney Machine Tool Company and other firms as a subsidiary of the Penn-Texas Corporation, one of the nation's first conglomerates. And in 1957, Colt donated its collection of 2,000 guns and company memorabilia to the Connecticut State Library.

Two years later, with the acquistion of Chicago's Fairbanks Morse Company, Penn-Texas was renamed the Fairbanks Whitney Holding Company. In 1964 it became Colt Industries, establishing a

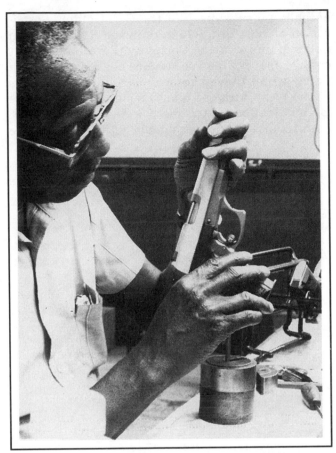

This Colt worker weighs the trigger on a Double Eagle autoloading pistol, available in 9mm, .38 Super, .45, and 10mm.

gun branch called Colt Firearms, which was split into military and small arms divisions in 1969. The Colt Custom Shop started up in 1976; three years later, Colt Industries was ranked number 162 in the Fortune 500 list of major manufacturers.

By the end of 1981, Colt's executive offices and most of its manufacturing had been moved from the old armory under the blue dome to a new West Hartford facility. An employee strike by members of the UAW Local 376 in 1986 threatened to paralyze the company, but production lines stayed open. Two years later, an even harder blow fell when Colt lost its M16 contract with the U.S. government, worth $112 million, to a Belgian firm. The lost requisition covered 267,00 rifles over a five-year period.

In 1989, annual Colt Industries sales were still at $1.6 billion, generated mostly by its aerospace, automotive and industrial services divisions. The following year, Colt Firearms was put up for sale, becoming a subsidiary of the C.F. Holding Corporation of Hartford, which renamed its acquisition Colt's Manufacturing Company. Fortunately, that change has not had a serious negative affect on Colt's production or personnel. New Colt products at the West Hartford plant include a Double Eagle .45 autoloading pistol and the Anaconda .44 Magnum revolver. Another double-action pistol, to be chambered in 9mm, .38 Super, .40 S&W and 10mm Auto, was under development in 1991.

Whatever its future, Samuel Colt's industrial empire has figured heavily in the development and preservation of these United States. Few accolades would have meant as much to that miller's son who began whittling on a sailing ship more than 160 years ago.

CHAPTER 5

CHRISTIAN SHARPS' SHORT, EXUBERANT LIFE

The first breechloading rifles, invented around 1400 A.D., had a lot in common with the first successful breechloaders manufactured in the mid-1800's. The only real difference was in tooling. Fifteenth-century technology couldn't guarantee uniformity in the structure or dimensions of a gun's parts. That meant each gun had to be built individually; it also meant that shooters had to trust not only the design of a breech-locking mechanism but the integrity and assembly of its parts. Most early shooters lacked that kind of faith.

In the late 1750's, the French national arsenals at Malherbe and Charlesville became proving grounds for a new method of manufacture, one that used patterns to ensure interchangeability among gun parts. The problem was, each part was still being made with hand tools; so workmen heavily influenced the product. In other words, two parts fashioned after the same pattern by two people produced different results. Thus the French project was scrapped after four years.

Near the end of the 18th century, however, two Americans—Eli Whitney and Simeon North—revived the French idea of making parts to a pattern. Working independently, they came to the same conclusions: guns of a uniform nature could be made from uniform parts—and the only way to make uniform parts was with machinery. Whitney and North both received government contracts for their guns in 1797. Sixteen years later North was given his first contract that called specifically for interchangeable parts.

Until this time, breechloading mechanisms had been of two basic types: Some incorporated a removable breech plug, while others had a removable chamber. With the evolution of mass production, removable chambers fell out of favor, and various kinds of dropping, sliding and rotating breechblocks were devised. To be practical, a plug had to be easy to make on a machine and, once installed, work effectively to seal gas. The mechanism had to operate with minimal effort, even under adverse field conditions.

Among the few rifles that came close to meeting these requisites was one by John Harris Hall, who was granted a patent for his breechloader on May 21, 1811. Two years later, this inventor from Maine asked that his rifle be considered for military service. Hall's request went unanswered until 1817, when the government finally ordered 100 rifles for evaluation. After the trials in March, 1819, Hall was commissioned to produce rifles for the government at the Harpers Ferry Arsenal, Virginia. Hall moved his family there at once and became superintendent of the project. His contract called for guns that were "interchangeable in all of their various parts."

A perfectionist and tough disciplinarian, Hall was a hard man to work with and for. Among the young filers who came to work at Harpers Ferry during Hall's watch was Christian Sharps. Apprenticed at the armory sometime during the early 1830's, he stayed at least through the government trials conducted there in 1837. These tests gauged the merits of muzzleloading rifles and muskets and breechloading rifles entered by Hall and others. The frontloaders and four of the breechloaders tested were American in origin. Baron Hackett of England submitted a French rifle, the "Fusil Robert," named after a gunsmith from Nancy, France, who developed several breechloading rifles in the late 1820's. One of these arrived at Harpers Ferry with Baron

Hackett. In 1831, M. Robert moved to Paris, to work with August Demondion, who had devised a cartridge for Robert's rifles.

Good Ideas, Poor Etiquette

While the American review board had some good things to say about the Robert gun, no contracts were approved, whereupon Baron Hackett packed up and headed back to England. Meanwhile, Christian Sharps decided to build a new rifle, incorporating the best of the Robert and Hall models, but eliminating their weaknesses.

A native of Washington, New Jersey, Christian Sharps was only 27 at this time. He and his three brothers were then affluent landowners in Warren County, but little is known about the early years. The courthouse containing Christian's birth record burned, and no family history appears to have been written. By the time young Christian began engineering his own gun in the 1840's he had become a proficient gunsmith. He left Harpers Ferry sometime after the 1837 trials to stay four years with his brother Caspar, a steam engineer in Cincinnati. Then he moved on to Washington, D.C., where, on September 12, 1848, he accepted his first patent.

Sharps's patent model was made from an 1841 Mississippi Rifle, its lock and breech cut off and replaced by the new mechanism. A sliding block operated vertically by an under-lever that formed the trigger guard. Dropping the block exposed the rear of the barrel, into which a paper cartridge was inserted. Closing the action sealed the breech. In describing his rifle, Sharps took pains to point out its tight breeching. He surely remembered that the chief weakness of John Hall's rifle was a loose joint between barrel and breechblock. Given Hall's design, a better fit would have rendered the action too hard to operate, so shooters were stuck with a breech that leaked gas excessively.

According to Sharps, "The moving part of the breech [on his gun] being but little exposed to the fire, it does not become tight by the heat of discharging; and, again, the moving part of the breech being performed by a lever of high power, is made to close the barrel perfectly tight, and no accident can occur by loading, as the cap does not reach the hammer of the lock until the breech is perfectly secure."

While Sharps' sliding vertical breechblock was a great improvement over most contemporary mechanisms, the young man failed miserably in his first efforts to market it. He needed someone to build

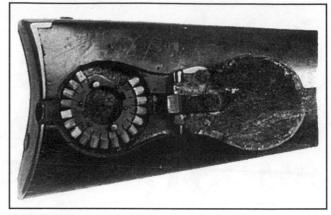

This "patchbox" on a Sharps Model 1849 Sporting Rifle is actually a recess for storing spare priming wheels.

his rifle and, recalling the blessings bestowed by government contracts at Harpers Ferry, decided to approach the government directly. Unfortunately, Sharps ignored protocol, going right to George W. Crawford, U.S. Secretary of War. Predictably, Chief of Ordnance George Talcott was cool toward Sharps when the brash engineer's request finally worked its way down to his level.

After spending three months in Washington, Sharps was almost broke. A loan of $500 from businessman Jonathan M. McCalla to "interest an established manufacturer" in making patent rifles helped, but most armsmakers still weren't interested in Sharps' rifle. Finally, in February of 1849, Sharps met Albert S. Nippes, a gunsmith who managed his father's gun shop in Mill Creek, Pennsylvania. Nippes contracted with Sharps in March to manufacture between 100 and 200 breech-loading rifles, with Nippes providing his shop and extra tooling at a cost "not to exceed six hundred dollars." Sharps and Nippes further agreed to pool their labor in the manufacture of the guns. When the run was completed, all equipment and material costs would be deducted from the sale price to pay Nippes. The remaining proceeds would be declared profit and split equally between the two men.

The contract further stated that Nippes had an exclusive right to manufacture the Sharps gun "so long as he is able to supply the demand and fill the orders for the same." If he declined to continue production after the first lot, half of the tooling would go to Christian Sharps. If he chose to make more guns, he would pay Sharps half the cost of the tooling. Other stipulations in this rather lengthy

The Model 1849 Sharps featured a priming wheel (above) that held 18 primers, advancing them as the action was cycled.

agreement included one that prevented Nippes from manufacturing Sharps rifles if he failed to produce enough to meet the demand and Sharps was able to open his own factory.

Nippes went right to work equipping his shop for this project. By late April, 1849, he'd completed his first rifle. Plain in appearance, it featured an octagon barrel in 36 and 44 caliber; a "wheel primer;" a cap-feeding mechanism; and a back-action lock that positioned the main-spring and hammer. Known as Model 1849, between 50 and 75 of these guns were built, mostly by Nippes.

The wheel-primer was an ingenious device that replaced a simpler but less reliable tube-feed system on the patent model. The wheel held 18 caps in a spoke-like arrangement. Spring tension forced the wheel to revolve, counterclockwise, whenever the breechblock was operated. A priming box stripped primers off the wheel and directed them into a channel where the primer furthest to the rear was picked up by a nipple on the rising breechblock. The "patchboxes" on this variety of Sharps rifle were actually designed to hold spare priming wheels.

For this first manufacturing run, Nippes got little help from Christian Sharps, who was experimenting with other gun designs. Apparently this didn't bother Nippes, because less than a year after the first contract had been signed he entered into another with Sharps. This one called for the formation of a company that would manufacture not only the rifle, but a new repeating pistol invented by Sharps. Under the new contract, Sharps was to

obtain permission to use Maynard primers should he fail to receive a patent for his own "priming hammer"; he must also acquire rights to an 1848 patent by George Leonard for his pistol. Under the agreement, Sharps was to receive $1,000, the loan of another $1,000, and royalties of $2.00 per rifle and $1.00 per pistol.

A lengthy supplement to this agreement provided for the disposition of guns should Nippes fail to establish a company for their continued manufacture by April 1, 1850. In that case, he'd be permitted to sell remaining stock to anyone as long as he paid Sharps the stated royalties. Sharps would be obliged, in turn, to extend a one-year mortgage for $1000 to Nippes on the patent rights to his mechanism (to cover a $1000 payment delivered to Sharps the day the contract was executed). Failure to make good on the mortgage would cost Sharps his patent rights, but in the meantime he'd be free to contract with other armsmakers for the manufacture of his guns. As it turned out, Nippes was unable to form a company by April 1, 1850, so he received the mortgage from Sharps (who also executed a $2,000 bond to repay Nippes and discharge other debts).

Later that summer, Nippes did manage to put together a company for the manufacture of Sharps rifles, paying 25¢ for each Maynard primer lock and 20¢ per 1,000 primers. A minimum annual royalty of $325, covering 500 locks and a million primers, would apply. Albert Nippes would continue to build the rifles, while his brother Daniel and Jesse Butterfield agreed to market them through an office in Philadelphia under the name, A.S. Nippes & Co.

By this time, George Leonard had sold his patent rights to Robbins & Lawrence of Windsor, Vermont, making them unavailable to Nippes and scuttling the pistol project. The company started making rifles almost immediately, however, calling them Model 1850 to distinguish them from guns produced under the earlier contract. Fewer than 100 of these rifles were finished before production ceased on June 4, 1851.

The rifles produced by Nippes in late 1850 and early 1851 were very similar to the Model 1849 Sharps. The only significant difference was a substitution of Maynard's tape primer for the standard percussion cap on the Sharps-designed wheel mechanism. Patchboxes on the Model 1850 were really patchboxes, a bit smaller than the wheel compartments on previous rifles. Iron hardware replaced brass, but otherwise only a few other minor changes were made.

The Problem with Peace; A Hartford Factory

After his 1849 contract with Nippes had elapsed, Christian Sharps formed his own gun company with Arba Maynard, who was to solicit government contracts and arrange for the production of Sharps-designed rifles. Maynard managed to get the Sharps breechloader included in U.S. Marine ordnance trials in October, 1850, and subsequently received a letter inviting him to submit rifles for a test on November 12 in Washington, D.C. The partners entered two muskets and two rifles against stiff competition. The judges voted in favor of Sharps rifles, declaring them, "Superior to any of the other arms loading at the breech."

Unfortunately, the kudos included no orders. Sharps was further miffed when, without consultation, his partner contracted with Courtlandt Palmer, a New York financier, for 1,500 guns. The partnership was dissolved. Meanwhile, even the crusty General Talcott conceded publicly that Christian Sharps' gun had military merit. Ordinarily, this would have given Sharps the pull he needed for a contract—if there'd been a need for rifles. But the doldrums of peace had settled on Washington.

Enter George H. Penfield, entrepreneur and promoter, who had dealt extensively in military goods and recognized the value of Sharps' rifle. In January, Penfield visited the Nippes offices and made Sharps an offer: if Sharps would give him 9/16 of his patent rights, he would pay Sharps $1,500 a year—"To assist in making models and making improvements"—plus 7/16 of the profits.

First, Penfield had to clear the patent mortgage held by Albert Nippes and resolve a claim against the patent filed by Arba Maynard. After some fast financial footwork, including help from a backer (coal dealer Merrick W. Chapin), Penfield freed Sharps of his obligations and sent him to Hartford, Connecticut, to look for a manufacturing site. Meanwhile, Penfield bought the remaining Sharps stock from Nippes & Butterfield for $16,000. Including a $4000 bonus to Christian Sharps, a payment of $1,000 to Arba Maynard, and the necessary legal and banking fees, Penfield paid a total of $22,853 for his patent rights.

Sharps found that the only Hartford plant big enough for his purposes was Colt's. Penfield joined him on a second trip, and the two men decided to build their own 10,000-square-foot factory. Temporary headquarters were installed on the second floor of a Pearl Street shop, and there Sharps en-listed 10 men to assemble and finish the rifles Penfield had bought from Nippes. These were patterned after, but not identical to, the Model 1850's made at Mill Creek. Only 67 rifles are known to have been built during this period, and in February, 1852, the upstairs shop was shut down. Sharps sold the remnant parts and tooling for $2,000 to William Robertson, who then finished assembling some Model 1850 rifles identical to those put together by Nippes and Sharps. The octagonal barrels were 30 to 34 inches long, with a brown finish (except for the shorter blued barrels fitted to carbines, only six of which were produced). The actions were case hardened, and the stocks were oiled or varnished walnut.

In August, 1851, contractor George King finished Penfield's factory. It was built in the shape of an L, with a short wing 70 feet long and two stories tall, and a long wing 130 feet in length and three stories tall. The site proved ill-chosen, however, because a flood soon inundated the lower levels. Penfield refused to move in, whereupon King agreed to build him another factory. But Penfield may have had other plans. In June, before he signed a second pact with King, he had contracted with Robbins & Lawrence for 5,000 Sharps rifles, a number large enough to meet projected demand.

By this time, the government had decided to order 200 Sharps carbines, featuring 32-bore (.54), 21-inch barrels and Maynard locks, and weighing 7¼ to 8 pounds. In a prompt reply to Captain William Manadier, acting Chief of Ordnance, Christian Sharps indicated on August 23, 1851, that his arrangement with Penfield was unsatisfactory and he would seek a new partner. This got the immediate

The last of these Sharps factory buildings in Hartford was torn down in the 1920's. The 17-acre tract is now part of Pratt & Whitney.

attention of Penfield, who paid Sharps the money owed him and wrote to returning Chief of Ordnance Colonel H.K. Craig that he was ready to build the rifles.

Robbins & Lawrence: Cradle of the Gun Industry

Even with this pending government contract, capitalization in the amount of $100,000 was hard to find, but by October he had made the necessary commitments. The Sharps Rifle Manufacturing Company was incorporated on October 8, with M.W. Chapin holding 800 shares and George Penfield 500. S.E. Robbins and Richard Lawrence received 250 shares each, and 11 other investors bought in at 200. This diverse group of shareholders included a grocer, banker, druggist, and an Episcopalian minister (who happened to be Sam Colt's father-in-law). A board of four directors was established at the first stockholders meeting on November 13, and five weeks later the company negotiated a settlement with Penfield. For all of his contracts with Sharps, Nippes, Maynard and Robbins & Lawrence—plus orders, tooling and stock on hand—Penfield got $25,000 in cash, exclusive rights to retail the Sharps rifle, and 5 percent of the gross on all sales. Penfield was required, however, to maintain a retail outlet in New York and to promote the company's products to the U.S. government.

When, on December 2, 1851, Colonel Craig

Richard S. Lawrence was first hired as a gunsmith for $100 a year by N. Kendall & Company. Later, he and Samuel E. Robbins formed a manufacturing firm that played a key role in the corporate beginnings of Sharps, Winchester and Smith & Wesson.

sought to nail down costs for the carbine contract, company president John C. Palmer quoted $35 per carbine. Craig countered with an offer of $25 and the parties settled on $30, with slight additional charges for accessories. The company then strengthened its bond to Robbins & Lawrence by drawing up a new contract for the production of these guns, to replace the agreement signed by Penfield.

The firm of Robbins & Lawrence had its origin in 1838 at the Windsor (Vermont) prison, where N. Kendall & Company made guns. Richard S. Lawrence, 21, was fresh from military service on Canada's frontier. He had stopped in Windsor to install a peep sight on a rifle belonging to a local resident who'd never seen one. So enthralled was he with the device that he persuaded Lawrence to show it to the Kendall crew at the prison. Kendall & Company promptly hired Lawrence for two years, at $100 a year plus board.

After this firm quit its gun operations, Lawrence went to work for the state as a foreman in the carriage department. He opened his own gun shop about a year later, and in 1844 met S.E. Robbins, who'd earlier suggested that Lawrence join him in bidding on a government rifle contract. Their bid of $10.90 per rifle, "appendages extra," beat out the competition by a dime, and shortly thereafter a contract for 10,000 rifles went to Robbins, Lawrence & Kendall. Ordnance officials were both surprised and pleased when the contract was filled in 18 months. The partners were promptly rewarded with another contract, this one for 15,000 rifles. They also agreed to produce 5,000 Jennings repeaters for New York financier Courtlandt Palmer, who had worked earlier with Horace Smith, Daniel Wesson and B. Tyler Henry on Walter Hunt's "rocket ball" gun. That rifle sired the Jennings repeater and later became known as the patriarch of Winchester's line of lever-action repeaters.

Samuel E. Robbins was an entrepreneur, not a gunsmith. He'd been educated in Boston, then amassed a great fortune in Maine's lumber business. He retired at 33 in South Windsor, Vermont, and plunged into gun manufacture, mainly because he saw its enormous potential. By 1849, Robbins and Lawrence had bought out Kendall and had built an arms factory that comprised nine buildings. It was the biggest private gun plant in the country, surpassed in size only by U.S. government arsenals at Harpers Ferry, Virginia, and Springfield, Massachusetts. The foundry was 80 by 50 feet. Next to it stood a 3½-story brick rifle factory and machine

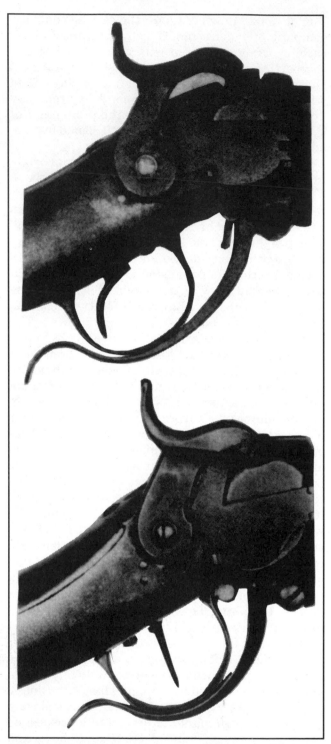

These Model 1850 prototypes were made by Sharps for Robbins & Lawrence. The bottom gun was built later and has a single set trigger.

shop, measuring 100 by 40 feet. Three blacksmith shops held 20 forges and five triphammers. A four-story boarding house nearby was made available for unmarried workers. Besides building guns for

various inventors, Robbins & Lawrence developed several machines specifically for the gun industry. Lawrence claimed to have fashioned the first bullet with grease grooves. The company even published a ''bell card,'' showing when bells rang in dormitories and factories (a forerunner of daylight savings schedules).

When in June of 1851, George Penfield asked Robbins & Lawrence to contract for the production of Sharps rifles, in June of 1851, he got a warm response. The Mexican War was over, and no new military contracts were pending. The last order for 15,000 was to be filled within a year, with the Jennings contract due for completion before that. Robbins & Lawrence agreed to Penfield's proposal and signed a contract in September, 1851. But when the Sharps Rifle Manufacturing Company purchased all contracts from Penfield the following month, that meant no rifles would be built in Windsor (Vermont) for Penfield.

The Sharps people wanted Robbins & Lawrence to manufacture the rifles specified, but with some changes. An addendum to the contract directed the Vermont firm ''to furnish the necessary funds and purchase a suitable site . . . and supply the same with the necessary power, shafting, machinery, and tools to constitute and equip an armory . . . [and] to manufacture ten thousand Sharps patent firearms per annum, in a good and workmanlike manner; the whole to be done and completed in or before the month of August, 1852, and sooner if practicable; which said lands, buildings, power, machinery and tools, shall be conveyed to said Sharps Rifle Manufacturing Company, and the legal title thereto remain in said corporation during the continuance of this contract. . . .'' In return, Robbins & Lawrence was to receive ''further sums.''

The Sharps Company changed rifle specifications, too, but these did not materially affect price or manufacture. Robbins & Lawrence suggested changes later on to make the gun more compatible with mass production. Christian Sharps and Lewis Lippold altered the design accordingly, but even this version proved difficult to manufacture. Instead of sending the blueprints back for a second revision, Richard Lawrence and company engineer William Jones adapted the gun themselves. Sharps was in Windsor at the time, but was not consulted. While these changes did not compromise the function of his rifle or significantly alter its looks, he was apparently irritated by the lack of communication. Sharps never again worked with Lawrence in a gun enterprise.

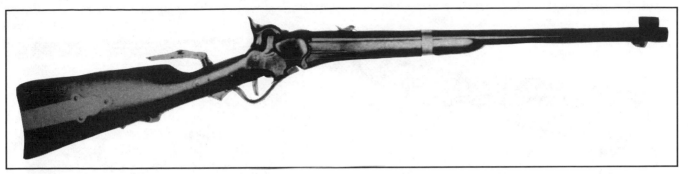

The Sharps Model 1851 Sporting Carbine (above), featuring a special globe front and folding tang rear sights, was made in 32, 60 and 90 bore between October, 1852, and April, 1855.

The gun produced at Robbins & Lawrence on the pattern provided by Lawrence and Jones was Model 1851. It differed in many details from the Model 1850, most strikingly in the placement of the hammer, which was now *inside* the lockplate. This innovation prompted the now familiar nickname, "boxlock." While both rifles and carbines were to be built, the latter comprised the entire production run for the first six months.

In February, 1852, Christian Sharps bought two rifles from Robbins & Lawrence for the purpose of perfecting a priming mechanism he'd been working on since 1849. Meanwhile, another inventor, Alonzo Perry, was claiming the right to patent this same device. Sharps was awarded the patent that October, a month after the U.S. Ordnance Department had ordered 50 carbines with Sharps' priming arrangement and learned it was being contested by Perry. Instead of fanning the government's interest with a personal demonstration of his priming hammer, Sharps simply sent in a couple of guns for inspection. Even though Ordnance officers approved the priming hammer (and chafed while Robbins & Lawrence adapted it to the Model 1851 rifle), the Sharps Rifle Manufacturing Company decided not to renew Christian Sharps' contract when it expired in October. This was due in part to the bad blood between Sharps and Lawrence, which had compromised the production and marketing of the rifles.

Meanwhile, Lawrence and Jones once again revamped the Sharps mechanism. It took them until March, 1853, to come up with a prototype that would accommodate the new primer hammer. By then, they had changed the gun in several ways. The bigger breechblock required a new receiver, which in turn called for stock alterations. The government's 50 carbines were finally delivered in the autumn of 1853. Called Model 1852, this was the first Sharps gun produced with a lever key retainer (in the forend) and the pellet priming mechanism found in all later percussion Sharps. This new mechanism consisted of a primer well that was fed from a tube containing the pellets. The tube was withdrawn after loading. After the hammer was thumbed back, a primer magazine spring pushed a new pellet into the feeder track. As the hammer fell, it forced the pellet feeder forward, freeing the pellet, which it smashed on the nipple.

By March of 1852, Robbins & Lawrence had contracted with Sam House and George Rust for a gun factory in Hartford to fulfill its contractual obligations to the Sharps people. The buildings, completed in November, included a two story "manufactory" with 16-inch brick walls, an engine shop, a forge, a boiler house, and a trip-hammer shop. Total cost: $25,000. Robbins & Lawrence spent five months equipping the plant with a 50-horsepower Corliss steam engine, two dozen milling machines, 14 drill presses, 13 lathes, 100 bench vises, various reamers, broaching and rifling machines, with other special-duty hardware. In all, the company invested $40,000 in tooling. By May, 1853, the 200-man factory was operable, but a shortage of workers relegated all but the barrel production and final assembly of Model 1852 rifles to the Windsor facility (Model 1851 Sharps was made entirely at Windsor). When Model 1853 made its debut, complete with its modified lever key retainer, the new Hartford factory geared up to make it. By July, 1854, both plants were operating at near capacity, building a surplus stock of guns to ship. This worried the Sharps people, who had expected more government orders, and in April, 1855, the Windsor facility stopped all production of Sharps rifles. So far, 2,050 Model 1851's and 5,133 Model 1852's had been assembled there.

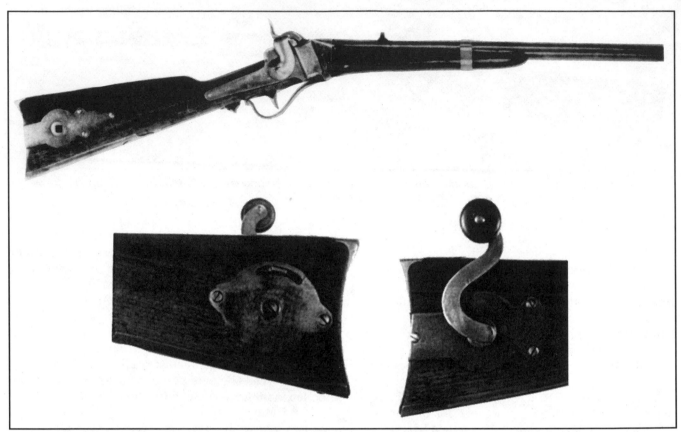

A few Sharps Model 1853 carbines (top photo) were made with coffee mills in the buttstock (see details in bottom photo) which the soldiers also used to grind grain.

The Final Varied Enterprises of Christian Sharps

After his break with the Sharps Rifle Manufacturing Company, Christian Sharps continued to receive substantial money in royalties. But he was itching to organize a new company to manufacture rifles, and building a factory took more money than he had. Upon asking the Commandant of Springfield Armory if there was any government-owned space for lease, he was told that some facilities were available for $750 a year. With tooling costs added, that was too much for Sharps, and so he remained in his shop at the Roberts Building in Hartford. There he was joined in December, 1852, by inventor William Robertson, who bought remnant Nippes parts and quickly assembled 50 Sharps rifles for resale. He then conferred with executives from the Sharps Rifle Manufacturing Company about the potential for a single-shot pistol designed by Christian Sharps for manufacture. At that time, Robbins & Lawrence was making all the Sharps rifles in addition to producing pistols on a patent by George

Leonard, so it was not interested in taking on another pistol. Robertson then assembled half a dozen prototypes and submitted a cost estimate for building the pistols himself, but the Sharps people decided not to pursue the project.

Meanwhile, Christian Sharps had voiced his dissatisfaction with the company to several people, claiming it had violated his patent rights. That animosity did him no good when he approached two wealthy industrialists, Sam Colt and Henry Beech, for help in starting his own company. They turned him down flat.

In May, 1853, Sharps went into partnership with Harvey Lull to make cartridges and pellet primers for the Sharps Rifle Manufacturing Company. But the new firm of Sharps & Lull was unable to fill even the first small contract and had to get help from Crittenden & Tibbals, a cartridge firm in South Coventry, Connecticut. Sharps and his partner lost money in this deal, forcing Sharps, who'd been unsuccessful in his bid to draw patent damages from the Sharps Rifle Manufacturing Company, to settle out of court. In a new contract dated April

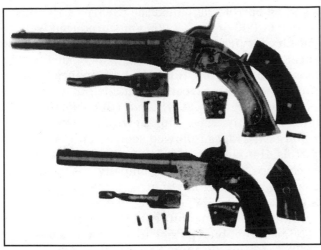

The Hartford Single Shot Pistol (top) is a survivor of only 20 experimental guns made in 1853. It featured a mainspring like that found on early Nippes rifles. The pistol at bottom is a commercial model Single Shot Pistol built at the C. Sharps & Company's Rifle Works in Philadelphia.

10, 1854, Sharps was to receive $1 from the sale of each gun and 25 cents for each primer mechanism sold. He'd also receive $4,000 and 400 new rifles to sell. With that, Sharps picked up his guns and departed for Philadelphia, where he opened a retail store. Unable to sell the guns, he offered them to the government at a discount—$25 each. But Colonel Craig, Chief of Ordnance, did not want to buy more Sharps rifles.

In November, 1854, Christian Sharps joined Ira Eddy in a partnership at Eddy's rifle factory located across the Schuylkill River from Fairmount Basin in West Philadelphia. There the Eddy and Sharps Company produced the single-shot pistols Sharps had designed at Hartford. Except for their cylindrical breechblocks, the actions looked identical to those found in Sharps rifles. Indeed, Sharps was infringing on his own patent when he built these pistols, for no patent had ever been issued for them.

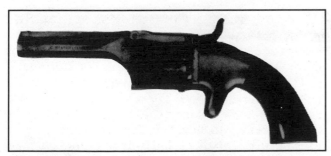

Sharps built 2,000 of these small 25-caliber percussion revolvers between 1857 and 1858.

At the same time, his attorney, R.D. Hubbard, continued efforts to pin patent violations on the Sharps Rifle Manufacturing Company. Since it was located in Connecticut, and not his home state of Pennsylvania, the suit would be a difficult and expensive battle. So Hubbard and his client devised a plan to move jurisdiction of the case to Philadelphia. It was a complex plan, rife with deception, but it worked. And when the case was finally decided in a U.S. District Court, Christian Sharps emerged with the tentative right to use his 1848 patents. But by then, he was no longer manufacturing pistols that required their use!

In mid-1855, the Wire Bridge factory in Philadelphia shifted from the production of small 31-caliber pistols to larger guns of 34 and 44 caliber. The company also made what it called the "pistol rifle"—a trim rifle weighing about six pounds. It featured a "mule-ear" cartridge, with a basal flap that the shooter grasped while extracting the case. Eddy & Sharps made 500 of these guns and entered their pistol rifle in ordnance trials. It functioned well but was rejected because of its small size. Eddy and Sharps also built a five-shot, 25-caliber revolver resembling the early Smith & Wessons. About 2,000 of these were manufactured during the first four years of the partnership—double the number of single-shot pistols.

While in Philadelphia, Christian Sharps received a patent for a revolver, but it was never made in quantity. He also invented a bolt action rifle that could be fired 10 times a minute. His rifle prototypes were fashioned from muzzleloaders, a conversion that Sharps claimed would cost the

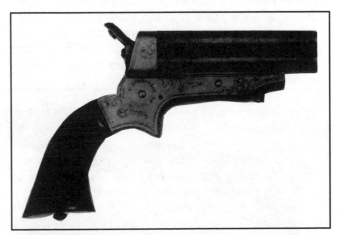

This Model 2A .30 rimfire 4-barrel pistol boasts the sparest engraving of any of its type. Along with similar models, it issued from a C. Sharps Patent of 1859.

government less than $3 per gun. While preliminary trials resulted in an order for 10 more prototypes, the Ordnance Department did not pursue a contract.

Between 1855 and 1859, Christian Sharps and his business interests proved hard to track. During the first two years of that period, it's known that "C. Sharps & Company" operated a retail store at 336 Franklin Road in Philadelphia, while at the same time "Ira Eddy & Company" was building Sharps guns at the Wire Bridge plant. Late in 1857, a man named Nathan Bolles joined the partners and the firm once again became C. Sharps & Company. Sharps lived in various places during this time, but always stayed close to his work. In 1860, William Hankins became part of the company; and he, along with Sharps, Bolles and Eddy, continued to live in the same four-story house.

On January 25, 1859, Christian Sharps was awarded two patents—one for a tipping-breech rifle (that was never manufactured), the other for a four-barrel repeating cartridge pistol derived from an early Sharps percussion design. The percussion gun had never been produced because of patent conflicts with the George Leonard pistols, and because it could not compete with the Colt revolver for durability or firepower. A relatively simple gun featuring a rotating striker, the cartridge pistol proved successful; in all, more than 100,000 of these four-barrel repeaters were manufactured in Philadelphia over the next 15 years. The most common chamberings were .22, .30 and .32 rimfire, but others were available. Two foreign manufacturers—Tipping & Lawden of England and L. Ghaye in Belgium—were licensed to produce copies; but only the British firm manufactured them in quantity.

By 1862, Ira Eddy and Nathan Bolles had left C. Sharps & Co., and William Hankins had become a partner with Christian Sharps, the firm name changing to "Sharps & Hankins." For five years, beginning in 1862, the company built and marketed a sliding-barrel rifle, called the "Sharps & Hankins." About 11,000 of the 13,000 guns produced went to military service—3,486 carbines to the Army, 6,986 carbines and 604 rifles to the Navy. Meanwhile, money supplied by Hankins had financed a new factory on 24th Street in Philadelphia, near the house on Green Street where the four partners had once lived. By 1864, this new plant was making rimfire cartridges followed soon after by rifles and pistols. Hankins left the firm in 1867 and it became once more "C. Sharps & Company". A year after that it was "Christian Sharps, Firearms." In 1870, Sharps moved to Vernon, Connecticut, where he continued to invent and refine gun mechanisms, receiving a revolver patent in 1871 and another in 1873 for a single-shot, Spencer-like rifle. Sharps died of tuberculosis in 1874, leaving his wife, a daughter and a son. After his death, the Sharps factories in Philadelphia were shut down.

The Sharps Rifle Manufacturing Company was still very much alive, however. Since its split with Christian Sharps in 1852, it had sought government contracts with varying degrees of success. The U.S. military establishment had no particular need for rifles in the mid-1850's, and while it did funnel a few orders to Sharps, they were of little consequence. The Maynard tape primer had so impressed Ordnance officers that company president Courtlandt Palmer ordered the Maynard feed mechanism adapted to the Model 1853 rifle. Frank Buckingham, who was then in charge of the Hartford factory, complied only after orders were delivered in writing. His objection: "If the Maynard primer is to be made it will require additional machinery to the amount of at least six thousand dollars." The 400 military carbines on order for the government would cost $16.60 each, which was roughly 20 percent less than the wholesale price listed for plain Model 1853's in October of 1854. Engraved guns cost $30, $40 and $50, depending on the coverage,

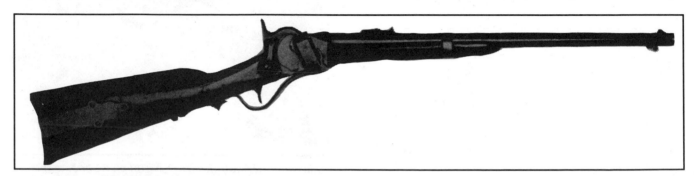

Most of the 6,796 Model 1855 Carbines produced in .54 caliber between 1856 and 1857 (see above) were for the British and U.S. governments.

and "Extra fine engraved" rifles were $60 and up. A carved or checkered stock boosted the price of any grade by $10.

In July, 1855, the Sharps Rifle Manufacturing Company was awarded a British contract for 1,000 carbines (later hiked to 6,000). But the British also wanted Maynard priming, which meant Sharps couldn't use its warehoused guns to fill the order. Nor could it quickly manufacture 6,000 of the Maynard mechanisms. And so, in November, the company contracted with Robbins & Lawrence for 6,500 Maynard-primed carbines, half with 18-inch barrels and half with 21-inch barrels, including 500 rifled with six grooves and the remainder with three.

Delays in completion of these carbines almost lost Sharps the entire contract by the time the Crimean War ended in 1856. The guns were no longer needed, so Palmer hurriedly renegotiated a second contract that gave Sharps more time to fill the order. Still, only 900 carbines met the deadline; the rest were sold at $20, not $25, reflecting the $5 penalty the British had imposed on late units in lieu of scuttling the contract altogether.

Berdan, Brown, Beecher—and War

Robbins & Lawrence went out of business in October, 1856, and the Sharps Rifle Manufacturing Company foreclosed on its mortgage. Sharps also took over operation of the Hartford plant, but no significant changes occurred in manufacturing. Up to this time, six Sharps guns had been produced—Models 1849, 1850, 1851, 1852, 1853 and 1855. The last four were "slant breech" types, so-called because the breechblock did not operate perpendicular to the bore; rather, it slid at an angle of 112 degrees (measured in an arc above the barrel) to the bore. The receiver walls plainly indicated this. Variations within each model resulted from differences in barrel length and configuration, priming, stock design, metal finish and boring. Some guns were equipped with double-set triggers, some with tang sights, and some with functional coffee mills in the butt, so troops could boil their own brew without packing an extra implement. While Sharps built mostly rifles, it also offered shotguns, and at least one "Sporting Rifle" was furnished with a left-handed lock. The bore size of a slant-breech Sharps was commonly expressed not in calibers, but in "bores," which are equivalent to shotgun gauges. The most popular bore diameters were 60- and 90-bore (.44 and .36), but 32-bore guns were also listed and other sizes could be ordered.

In 1858, Richard Lawrence revamped the Sharps breechblock, largely because the Conant gas ring then in use had proved unsatisfactory as a seal. In Lawrence's new "gas plate" design, the breechblock was moved forward, restoring its right-angle position in relation to the barrel. Lawrence patented his idea on December 20, 1859, but rifles featuring the new design, later known as Model 1859, were already in production beginning late in 1858.

By 1861 the Sharps factory had grown substantially. A 250-horsepower Corliss steam engine was installed in the basement of the main building. It had a single cylinder 26 inches in diameter and a 20-foot driving wheel. About 450 men were employed at the plant year round, producing 30,000 rifles annually. The guns underwent many changes, resulting in four new versions: Model 1859, New Model 1859, New Model 1863 and New Model 1865. All had beefier breech components than the earlier slant-breech Sharps.

An odd-looking Sharps of this period was an over/under rifle, with the top barrel a breechloader and the bottom a muzzleloader. In this model, a folding hammer extension fired a percussion cap on a nipple attached to one side of the lower barrel. The most common caliber among these vertical-breech rifles was 52 (standard for military arms), although available bore sizes ranged from .44 to .58.

Government business had so strengthened during this period that Sharps was building most of its guns for military service even before the Civil War. Both the Army and Navy tested Sharps guns, and both had sanctioned their use. When war began, the merits of various breechloading designs became

Colonel Hiram Berdan (left) poses with chief scout Joseph Milner, better known as "California Joe." The rifle is a New Model 1859 Sharps military rifle.

less important than the availability of finished guns. Between 1861 and 1865, Ordnance Department contracts called for 80,512 Sharps carbines and 9,141 Sharps rifles. Probably more than 100,000 Sharps guns were carried by soldiers during the war, with most of the carbines going to cavalry units, where the Sharps proved very popular.

The Sharps also became the issue arm for Colonel Hiram Berdan's famous "Sharpshooters." These two regiments, one under the command of a Colonel Post, accepted only the most skilled marksmen in their ranks. Each recruit was tested on the range, and competition grew keen. Initially, the Ordnance Department had furnished these men with Springfield muzzleloading rifles, but when this drew loud objections Chief of Ordnance General James Ripley decided to send the Sharpshooters his over-supply of Colt revolving rifles already warehoused. Berdan complained bitterly, however, and his troops were so disgusted they threatened to mutiny if better rifles weren't forthcoming. By February, 1862, the government had placed an order for 2,000 Sharps rifles and 200,000 cartridges. Always pushing for more, Berdan specified directly to the company that the guns be equipped with double-set triggers; but Ripley found out and countermanded the order. Nevertheless, the New Model 1859 rifles with their 30-inch barrels pleased the troops and may have played a decisive role at Gettysburg, where only 100 men from the 1st Regiment of Sharpshooters shared Little Round Top with 200 soldiers from the 3rd Maine Infantry. Facing 30,000 Confederate troops, Berdan's men fired nearly 10,000 rounds in 20 minutes, holding the gray advance until General Meade could bring up Union reinforcements.

In 1864, squabbles over pricing strained the relationship between the Sharps Rifle Manufacturing Company, which hadn't substantially hiked prices since 1850, and the government, which was just beginning to comprehend the enormous cost of the war. The two parties broke off negotiations in January, 1865, with a difference of $2.50 per rifle hanging in the balance. The war ended soon thereafter. Had it not, the increasingly popular Spencer carbine would certainly have provided stiff competition for the Sharps among U.S. cavalry units.

During the war, Samuel C. Robinson, owner of the Belvidere Planing Mills in Richmond, Virginia, contracted with the State of Virginia to produce carbines for the Confederacy. They were to be of the Sharps pattern, with Sharps priming. While crudely finished, Virginia's carbines did indeed resemble Sharps guns. About 5,700 were produced—a substantial number, considering wartime demands on factories and the conscription of workers. The latter threatened even to strangle Sharps' Hartford plant; but conscription was not enforced at Hartford once company executives pointed out the disastrous effect this would have on arms production.

The Robinson guns immediately got a bad reputation when in March, 1863, green Virginia recruits fired their new carbines for the first time and "seven of the nine burst." Improper loading and reloading procedures were no doubt at fault, but

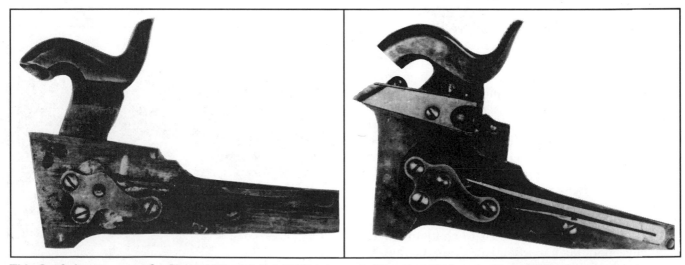

This Confederate copy of a Sharps New Model 1863 (above, left) was made late in the Civil War and contrasts sharply with the crisp New Model 1863 commercial lock (above, right). Sharps rifles were the first in America to use interchangeable parts, made possible by improvements in steels and closer manufacturing tolerances.

the stigma remained and no further efforts were made to train raw recruits to use these guns.

Sharps rifles were known to the Southern cause long before the war. They had been shipped to Kansas "Free Staters" by eastern Abolitionists in the hope that people there would be encouraged to defeat slavery by vote under the Kansas-Nebraska Act of 1856. One shipment of a hundred 52-caliber Sharps carbines, sent aboard the river steamer *Arabia*, was stolen in Lexington, Missouri, by pro-slavery bandits. But the breechblocks had been removed and sent on a different route! Another shipment of 200, which came to be known as the "John Brown Sharps," were sent by the Massachusetts Kansas Aid Society in September, 1856, but never made it to their destination. After being held up in Tabor, Iowa, and stored there while an uneasy peace hovered over Kansas, the carbines were later turned over to John Brown at his request. He and his men took them east and stashed them at the Kennedy farm in Maryland, near Harpers Ferry. There, on the night of October 16, 1859, Brown and 21 other insurrectionists took control of the Harpers Ferry armory. The group was routed out and captured by U.S. Marines under Colonel Robert E. Lee. The cache of Sharps carbines at the Kennedy farm was soon discovered, but only 102 of the original 200 rifles were recovered.

The Kansas "Border Wars" earned for the Sharps the nickname of "Beecher's Bible," after a news article revealed Abolitionist preacher Henry Ward Beecher's belief in the rifle as "a truly moral agency . . . [and that] You might as well read the Bible to buffaloes as to those fellows who follow Atchison and Stringfellow; but they have a supreme respect for the logic [of] Sharps rifles."

Sharps Conversions and the Freund Enterprise

After the Civil War, the U.S. Ordnance Department still had in storage or active service about half of the 100,000 or so Sharps rifle it had purchased beginning in 1851. The advent of metallic cartridges had made percussion guns obsolete, so the Sharps Rifle Manufacturing Company was asked if the surplus guns could be converted to this new ammunition. The slant-breech models did not lend themselves to conversion; but in October, 1867, the government signed a contract authorizing the company to proceed with a vertical breech conversion it had already submitted for testing. Under the agreement, the rifles were proof-fired with 200,000 50-caliber rounds supplied by Springfield Armory.

Many of the surplus rifles had oversize bores, so Ordnance officials decided to have all those over .5225 inch in diameter relined at Springfield Armory, at a unit cost of $1.58. Some of the guns were given full-length liners, some chamber liners. John Palmer, president of Sharps, suggested to Chief of Ordnance General Dyer that the firing pin return spring on these converted guns be replaced by a cam, and that a safety notch be added to the half-cock and full-cock notches on the hammer. Dyer approved Palmer's first idea but not the second. As a result, most of the 32,000-odd postwar conversions, known as Sharps Model 1868s, contained relined bores and cam-operated firing pins. The Model 1867 conversion, with its spring-retracted firing pin, was applied to only 1,900 carbines.

These converted Sharps worked fine, but they showed hard use and the soldiers didn't like them. The Ordnance Department had not improved their appearance when the guns were shipped to the Sharps Rifle Manufacturing Company for conversion. They'd been piled in heaps in boxcars, with no padding.

In 1871, the Sharps company and Springfield Armory collaborated on the conversion of 1,300 more rifle-muskets and 250 carbines. The remaining percussion guns held by the government were sold to Schuyler, Hartley & Graham, a huge sporting goods distributer that also dealt in military arms. A year earlier, this firm had purchased approximately 9,000 Sharps rifles and carbines (linen- and metallic-cartridge versions) and sold them all to the French government. After the Franco-Prussian War, many were marketed by Herman Boker & Company of New York City.

Because the percussion lock was obsolete by this time, Boker approached the Sharps Rifle Manufacturing Company and inquired about converting the old guns. With its government contracts finished, Sharps was now prepared to work with commercial firms it had not been willing to accommodate before. Boker's contract called for the conversion of 7,500 guns at around $4.25 each. As in the case with its previous government contracts, Sharps discovered later that it had cut the price too fine. Complying with the terms of the contract nonetheless, Sharps finished work on September 28, 1877; but when Boker asked about additional conversions, the Sharps people told him a new, higher price must apply. Apparently, the price was too high for Boker, for he did not purchase any more percussion guns.

Sharps converted about 4,000 rifles for other

firms, however, among them E.C. Meacham of St. Louis, where frontier gunsmiths had altered about 1,250 Sharps percussion rifles to take metallic cartridges. The results were satisfactory, but the methods and materials varied. Total postwar conversions, including those completed for the Ordnance Department and arms dealers like Boker and Meacham, came to 44,000. Few conversions were done after 1880.

In February, 1877, a German immigrant named F.W. Freund wrote to the Sharps Rifle Manufacturing Company from Cheyenne, Wyoming, where he operated a gunshop. Freund, who'd served with Union forces during the Civil War, had an idea for a different kind of conversion and sent Sharps a modified action. Sharps did not reply, so Freund wrote again in March. Meanwhile, an important distributor of Sharps rifles—F.C. Zimmerman of Dodge City, Kansas—sent the company a hearty recommendation of Freund and his invention. Although further correspondence failed to produce a contract, Freund did eventually receive a quote from Sharps for getting his conversions done in quantity. But the price was very high. Sharps executives were evidently irritated by the persistence and what they perceived as the arrogance of this frontier gunsmith. "Mr. Freund won't live long enough to hurt the reputation of the old gun," they maintained. "The so-called Freund improvement is simply a device for forcing the cartridges into the rifle & extracting the shells. The rifle is no better with the 'improvement' than without it, and no worse." Undaunted, Freund tooled up to convert and upgrade Sharps rifles in his Cheyenne shop. About 300 Freund guns were built, some of them completed after the German gunsmith had moved to Jersey City, New Jersey.

Converting old guns to accept new cartridges was not enough to sustain the Sharps Rifle Manufacturing Company. Since the mid-1850's, Richard Lawrence had urged the firm to diversify, to make items that would sell as well in peacetime as rifles did in war. But company executives did not agree, and while other armsmakers spread their risk with ventures into such things as farm implements, typewriters and bicycles, Sharps plodded on with only its single-shot guns. The end of the Civil War brought an expected halt to new government contracts, and commercial sales slumped in a soft economy. Many soldiers turned civilian simply bought their service rifles from the government, as was the custom of the time.

Cartridge Rifles Doom the Buffalo

In 1869, the company decided to court sportsmen with its New Model 1869 metallic cartridge rifle. It was the first commercially-manufactured Sharps with no provision for outside priming, and no plugged holes. Chambered in .40/50, .40/70, .44/77, .45/70 and .50/70, it preceded by a few months Model 1874, which was introduced in late 1870. Only about 650 New Model 1869s were made, but the production of Model 1874 spanned nearly 12 years. These fine guns, available in many configurations, became extremely popular; indeed, they're what most people now envision when they hear the name "Sharps."

Still, the new guns could not compensate for the loss of fat wartime ordnance contracts. Accordingly, early in 1871, the Sharps Rifle Manufacturing Company sold its factory to the Weed Sewing Machine Company of Hartford. Weed, which had been supplying the armsmaker with lock parts since 1865, then rented part of the building back to Sharps for $200 a month. Gun sales improved, and in 1872, after Sharps rifles had helped an inexperienced U.S. shooting team beat the heretofore unbeatable Irish at the first Creedmoor match on Long Island, the company prospered once again.

By that time, the short, bloody era of the buf-

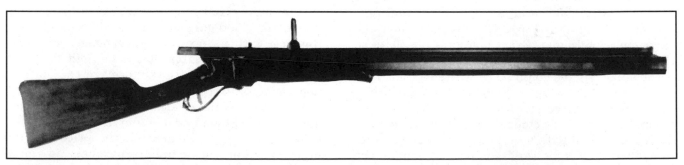

This 22-pound .44/90 Sharps Model 1874 target rifle has a factory-installed scope with spirit level. It was custom-made in 1875 and sold for $118.00.

falo hunter had come booming onto the plains. Buffalo hunters praised the Sharps rifle for its durability and Sharps cartridges for their power and range. In a story that appeared in the Kansas City Star in 1930, George Reighard, who had "worked" the central plains, explained how he hunted buffalo:

"In 1872 I organized my own outfit and went south from Fort Dodge to shoot buffaloes for their hides. I furnished the team and wagon and did the killing. [My partners] furnished the supplies and the skinning, stretching and cooking. They got half the hides and I got the other half. I had two big .50 Sharps rifles with telescopic sights . . . Those guns would kill a buffalo as far away as you could see it, if the bullet hit the right spot.

"We had flour, coffee, sugar, salt, blankets, four 10-gallon kegs for water, a dutch oven, two frying pans, a big tin coffee pot, a camp kettle bread pan, tin cups and plates, but no table knives, forks or spoons. We used our skinning and ripping knives . . . Our diet was mostly buffalo meat, fried, stewed or raw. . . .

"We kept moving the camp as the herd moved, often staying a week in a camp. Each morning I

Jesse Hendricks, a Kansas buffalo hunter, carries a Sharps rifle to work in the early 1870's.

would either ride out or walk, depending on how far away the herd was. Usually I went to the top of some rise to spy out the herd [then] sneak up to within good ranges. Between 200 and 350 yards was all right, the closer the better. I would choose my spot, behind some natural screen, a soapweed, cactus, sagebrush, or the like, would lie flat on my stomach, get my guns ready, spread a lot of cartridges out on the ground, adjust the gun sights, and be ready to shoot. Usually I carried a gun rest made from a tree crotch, which I would stick into the ground to rest the gun barrel upon.

". . . The leader was the oldest cow in the group, so [I would first] drop her. If aimed true the bullet would pierce her lungs [and she] would wobble, weakly, then stagger forward and fall.

"Meanwhile I would have jammed another shell in the breech and, watching the herd carefully, I would note any movement on the part of any buffalo to take fright and start off, and that one would be my next victim. . . . The whole idea was to keep the herd milling, round and round, in one restricted spot. . . .

"The time I made my biggest kill I lay on a slight ridge, behind a tuft of weeds 100 yards from a bunch of a thousand buffaloes that had come a long distance to a creek, had drunk their fill and then strolled out upon the prairie to rest, some to lie down. I followed the tactics I have described. After I had killed about twenty-five my gun barrel became hot and began to expand. A bullet from an overheated gun does not go straight, it wobbles, so I put that gun aside and took the other. By the time that became hot the other had cooled, but then the powder smoke in front of me was so thick I could not see through it; there was not a breath of wind to carry it away, and I had to crawl backward, dragging my two guns, and work around to another position on the ridge, from which I killed fifty-four more. In one and one-half hours I had fired ninety-one shots, as a count of the empty shells showed afterwards, and had killed seventy-nine buffaloes, and we figured that they all lay within an area of about two acres of ground. My right hand and arm were so sore from working the gun that I was not sorry to see the remaining buffaloes start off on a brisk run that soon put them beyond range. . . . On that trip I killed a few more than 3,000 buffaloes in one month, which was an average of about 100 a day."

Nelson King and the Creedmoor Sharps

In 1874, the Sharps Rifle Manufacturing Company reorganized for financial reasons. Incorporated in July, 1875, the new Sharps Rifle Company was capitalized with a thousand shares of stock at $100 each. E.G. Westcott, who'd purchased 934 shares, assumed the patent rights of the old firm and then sold them back to the new business for $1. W.L. Hubbell and S.J.B. Dibble were the other shareholders, with Westcott assuming the presidency and Hubbell taking over as secretary. Westcott promptly began advertising Sharps rifles in a host of magazines and newspapers, some as distant as Central and South America. Sharps products, he observed, had hardly been advertised at all, and it was about time to start. Eventually, the company concentrated its ads in outdoor publications like *Forest and Stream* and the *Army & Navy Journal*, both popular weeklies in the 1870's.

The new company needed a plant superintendent, so Nelson King, who'd been working for Winchester and had been in large part responsible for the development of Winchester's Model 66, was picked. Westcott's suggested salary of $2,500 a year did not suit King, who asked for double that amount, plus a $5,000 block of stock. Westcott acceded.

During 1875, the company strove to increase production efficiency by paring special-order options, limiting the number of rifle styles within models, and standardizing as many parts as possible. It investigated (but did not manufacture) shotgun and repeating rifle mechanisms. Though sales were reasonably strong, the company had trouble accumulating capital for expansion or diversification.

About that time, the company announced it was looking for a new Connecticut location. Several cities responded with attractive offers, but the decision went to Bridgeport, where the famous showman, P.T. Barnum, served as mayor. The city provided a factory site to Sharps (for $1), where Sharps subsequently built a 4½-story, 90,000-square-foot plant. Dissatisfied with the parts it had acquired recently from outside contractors, the company turned to inside contracting, a popular arrangement in other gun factories. The contractors were on the company payroll and they employed company people to do the jobs for which they (the contractors) were paid. Expenses were deducted from the agreed-upon price of the item or job, and the contractor kept the profit. Efficient, industrious people got substantial rewards this way, and the company benefited by increased production and tighter cost accounting.

In June, 1876, Nelson King was dismissed as superintendent, because he'd had chamber gauges enlarged without alerting company executives. Perhaps he'd done this to help standardize the manufacture of barrels; but its immediate result

This Sharps Model 1875 prototype, with its Scheutzen-style stock by A.O. Zischang, was made entirely by hand.

was to cause cartridges to rupture. A rash of such burst cases prompted an investigation. It was only when cases from the Union Metallic Cartridge Company were found to be faultless that King's change was discovered.

When King left, Hugo Borchardt, who'd already worked for Sharps in another capacity, took over as superintendent. By this time, Sharps' new Model 1875 rifle had been announced. Developed during 1875 by Nelson King, Richard Lawrence, Charles E. Overbaugh and A.O. Zischang, this gun was essentially a refined version of Model 1874. The patent was issued to King on May 23, 1876, just prior to his departure. Part of the mechanism—one that cocked the hammer when the lever closed—derived from a design patented by Rollin White back in 1855. Self-cocking Sharps prototypes were made, but no guns with this feature had ever been manufactured commercially. Model 1875 was introduced at the Philadelphia Centennial Exposition in April, 1876; but when pressed for details about the gun, company president Westcott declared that these would "not be made at present." Nelson King's dismissal no doubt had something to do with E.G. Westcott's cool response; after all, the rifle incorporated King's patent. Westcott may also have anticipated a new rifle constructed on a Borchardt action, which was then under development. Only two Model 1875's were made: a Military Rifle and

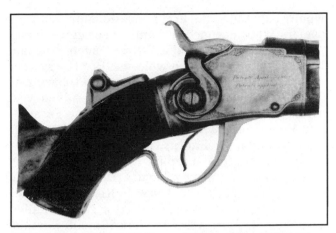

This Model 1875 Long Range Rifle sold for $300.00 following its exhibition at the Philadelphia Centennial. It is the only known example of the model, which never reached commercial production.

a Long-Range Rifle. The Long-Range (Creedmoor) model was sold to a Colonel John Bodine after the Philadelphia Exposition for $300. It survives today in a private collection, but only the action of the Military Rifle has been located.

Charles Overbaugh, one of the designers who worked on Model 1875, was a senior salesman and exhibition shooter for Sharps. Another was A.O. Zischang, a gunsmith of great renown among target shooters. Their influence was evident in the next rifle to come from the Sharps plant: Model 1877. Like Model 1875, it had a strong resemblance to the 1874 Sharps, which by this time had been offered in several forms at $20 and up. Overbaugh, in search of a better target gun than the Model 1874 Creedmoor, redesigned that gun by trimming weight from the action and adding it to the barrel. That way, the rifle could take stiffer loads but still meet the 10-pound Creedmoor weight limit. The leaner, rounder action became Sharps' Model 1877. Its locks were imported from P. Webley & Sons in England, and so were the barrel blanks. Three grades of the Model 1877 Long-Range Rifle were listed—at $75, $100 and $125. Apparently only the top two grades were sold. A remnant lot of Model 1877's, assembled by C.E. Overbaugh at his New York shop, were sold for $45 each to a local dealer, Homer Fisher, early in 1879. Overbaugh made a total of 73 Scheutzen-style rifles on the 1877 action, because the company lacked the manpower to fashion these rifles in-house. In 1880, the Sharps catalog described a "special Model 1874" that was really an 1877. About 75 of these were available, and apparently all went to Denver dealer J.P. Lower. They've been dubbed the "Lower Sharps."

Fewer than 300 Model 1877's were built. Because they were intended for serious shooters and produced in limited quantities, these rifles generally showed better workmanship than their Model 1874 forebears.

The first Creedmoor match sparked a relatively short-lived interest in long-range shooting. Between 1874 and 1882, Sharps and Remington supplied rifles specially adapted to the task, and each company claimed its products were superior. Both were, in fact, good rifles. The Sharps was a safer gun, because the sensitive primers of that era were less likely to be accidentally detonated by the closing of a Sharps breech. Remington's block came down *on* the cartridge instead of coming to battery *across* it. What those first matches clearly showed was the superiority of breechloaders over muzzleloaders. American shooters won consistently with their Sharps and Remington cartridge rifles, the English and Irish finally conceding that their front-loaders were outclassed.

The three targets commonly used at a long-range match in the 1870's included a short-range (300-yard) bulls-eye 8 inches across, a mid-range (600-yard) bulls-eye 24 inches across, and a long-range (1,000-yard) bulls-eye 36 inches across. The targets—measuring 2 feet, 4 feet and 6 feet across, respectively—had "centers," or surrounding areas, that also scored. The early bulls-eyes and centers were square, but in 1875 all were made round. The ranges specified at each shoot did not necessarily match the furthest distance specified for each target. Remington's Diamond Badge Match, for example, was fired at 500, 800 and 1,000 yards. By the mid-1880's, long-range shooting had been supplanted by offhand or "Scheutzen" competition at ranges up to 200 yards. The great Creedmoor range was closed down in the early 1890's. Sharps retained its reputation as a premier maker of long-range target rifles, however, and in 1900 William DeV. Foulke won the 1,000-yard National Rifle Association match with his Model 1878 Sharps firing 100 grains of FG powder to push a 550-grain bullet.

Borchardt's Hammerless Rifle, a Sharps Shotgun

During the days of the buffalo hunters, domestic military contracts were as scarce as friendly Sioux. An important contract for Sharps came from the Chinese government, which ordered 300 of a new type of rifle patented by Hugo Borchardt on December 26, 1876. The guns were completed (with considerable trouble and unexpected expense) in

The Model 1878, shown here with Nimschke engraving, was Sharps' first hammerless rifle.

September, 1877, and were the first to be built on the Borchardt patent. The mechanism—for which the inventor was paid a flat fee of $1,855 in January, 1878—later spawned a hammerless commercial rifle, called the Sharps Model 1878.

Though originally intended only for military use, the Model 1878 action worked fine in sporting rifles. Sharps recognized this soon after production commenced and developed several styles, priced from $18 to $125. As in Model 1874, the barrels were drilled from soft steel billets. Pratt & Whitney rifling machines cut six grooves with a right-hand twist of one turn in 20 inches. The grooves were wide, with flat bottoms and square shoulders, and averaged .005 inch deep in hunting rifles (.003 inch deep in target barrels). All barrels except those intended for military use were lapped. Primarily for the sake of economy, most Model 1878's came standard with round barrels. Like its predecessor, Model 1877, this Borchardt-designed rifle boasted a better finish than the 1874 Sharps, which upstaged it in popularity.

During late 1876 and early 1877, a salesman and trick shooter named Frank Hyde toured the southern states to drum up business for the Sharps Rifle Company. His reports were dismal—no demand for sporting rifles, and the dealers wouldn't buy unless they had a customer's order in hand. There was sporadic interest in military weapons, depending on how people perceived their enemies. But the need, when it came, was urgent; sales floundered when Sharps couldn't make or ship orders quickly. Discounting to individuals, warned Hyde,

would sabotage the firm's relationship with its dealers, who depended on a uniform pricing scheme.

Almost anything that stirred such stagnant waters would have been welcome. But the cyclone came from within, not from the marketplace. And it further jeopardized the company's solvency. It began with John Tracy, president of the Farmer's and Mechanic's Bank of Hartford, who'd been a financial pillar for Sharps. In March, 1877, Tracy went bankrupt, and in its scramble to recover Sharps obtained money from Arthur Winchester, who in turn struck a deal with B. Kittredge & Company of Cincinnati, a major sporting goods retailer. The Kittredge firm agreed to buy $30,000 worth of Sharps products over the next year in return for substantial discounts.

Among the guns considered by Kittredge in this deal was the Sharps double-barrel shotgun, a new item to be built in England by Philip Webley & Son, but marked "Old Reliable Sharps Rifle Co." As early as 1875, the Sharps Rifle Company had pursued the production of a shotgun, negotiating then with George Fox for the purchase of patents, models and tooling that would enable Sharps to manufacture his shotgun. But the asking price of $25,000 was too high. When Edwin Westcott's offer of $15,000 was turned down, he decided to look elsewhere for a shotgun (Fox's gun and equipment were later sold to the American Arms Company).

Early in 1877, Charles Pond of Sharps wrote to Webley proposing a cooperative venture, which resulted in a prototype, developed by Webley, of an exposed-hammer gun with laminated steel barrels and a side-mounted opening lever (Sharps later specified a top lever). E.G. Westcott then met with Webley officials in the summer of 1877 to work out an agreement for the manufacture of shotguns. The largest order, received in May, 1878, was for only 80 guns, with 50 more to follow in October. Delivery was slow—the first batch didn't arrive until the following summer—and Sharps apparently lost interest in the venture. On June 4, 1880, the company explained to a customer in the West: "We never completed our shotgun. The demand for our rifle kept us so busy that we could not without much inconvenience bring out the shotgun."

Westcott's main reason for sailing to Europe in 1877 was to land some foreign military contracts. He didn't get any; but back in the U.S., the market for sporting guns looked encouraging. In fact, 1878 proved a boom year for the Sharps Rifle Company. This was the first year Model 1878's were made available in a full range of styles, and sales for

Model 1874 were strong. Military contracts from Michigan and Louisiana gave an additional boost to production. Sharps even imported some English shotguns and began experimenting with a magazine rifle developed by James P. Lee at Winchester.

Failed Foreign Contracts, A Repeating Rifle

The idea of a repeating rifle had long appealed to people at Sharps. As early as 1875, they'd solicited inventors to obtain a practical action for commercial production. Bethel Burton was among the first to respond, but his royalty demands were high, and the condition that he act as sole marketing agent was unacceptable to the Sharps board of directors. Several other designs were examined later. Even the Russians participated. They didn't submit a design; rather, the Russian government asked Sharps to build a repeating rifle out of its single-shot Berdan service arm. After considerable effort and expense, Sharps was informed by the Russian ordnance people that the project was called off.

Late in 1877, Sharps began developing a magazine rifle built around the Swiss Vetterli action. By the time a prototype was finished, the gun did not look much like a Vetterli; its cartridge feeding mechanism resembled more closely that of the Ward-Burton. Sharps entered the gun in ordnance trials at Springfield Arsenal in the spring of 1878, but it malfunctioned. Further tests proved it was incapable of handling gas from ruptured cases properly. Rust on the bolt made it inoperable; sometimes a round jammed in feeding, or the extractor often failed. Finally, the Vetterli project was dropped.

Meanwhile, Sharps' E.G. Westcott had begun a

Frank Freund, a prolific inventor and talented gunsmith, modified Sharps actions and others at his Cheyenne (WY) shop in the late 1870's. This Freund "Wyoming Saddle Gun" was built from scratch, however.

correspondence with James Lee, who was now working at Remington. Initially, Lee told Westcott he had nothing of interest for Sharps, but in January, 1878, he described a new repeating mechanism that might be of interest. The design was not far enough along for the construction of a prototype in time for the April ordnance trials at Springfield, but Sharps and Lee pursued a contract. A year went by before papers were signed forming the "Lee Arms Company", headquartered at the Sharps Rifle Company factory at Bridgeport. In April, 1879, Lee wrote to the Secretary of War, offering to convert Springfield single shot rifles into Lee magazine rifles for $10.37 each, with parts furnished by the government coming to $7.31. This proposal made Lee's rifles as affordable as "trap door" conversions, Still the Army rejected it. Lee then offered a better deal to the Navy and was again turned down.

Lee and Sharps next evaluated the market for sporting guns, asking dealers what they'd like to stock. A patent was issued for the Lee rifle in November, 1879, and the following spring Frank Hyde of Sharps submitted a Lee prototype for Navy ordnance tests. Subsequently, Hyde and Charles Pond traveled to Europe to ferret out military contracts. By this time, Sharps was suffering major financial ills, and designer Hugo Borchardt had threatened to resign. Borchardt had a lot to do with the Lee project, and his resignation would have seriously jeopardized the venture. Though nearly 300 rifles were in some stage of completion, the tooling had not been finished, and design problems remained.

Borchardt stayed on, but the rapid deterioration of the Sharps Rifle Company after 1879 prompted Lee to sign an agreement with Remington Arms for the production of his gun. A total of 47 Lee rifles were recorded as being built at the Sharps plant, of which only six have survived. The military rifles were made in .45/70 (U.S.), .450 Gatling (England), .43 Spanish and .42 Swedish. Sporting rifles and carbines were also manufactured.

An Unsuccessful Fight for Solvency

Problems with the development of a magazine rifle failed to dampen the enthusiasm at Sharps for its hammerless Model 1878 single-shot. Company directors and newly elected president Arthur S. Winchester (who was not connected with the Winchester Company) decided to promote this rifle at the expense of their Model 1874. Winchester showed his faith in the program by providing an additional loan of $10,000 for operating capital. But shooters apparently preferred the Model 1874. Some pointed out that an outside hammer was almost a requisite for the western market, while others complained of the 1878's rough trigger. At odds with its customers, Sharps was dealt another blow when a major barrel supplier, R.H. Wolff & Company of New York, failed to deliver 1,500 barrels as scheduled in October. Timely shipments of rifles had proven a problem for the company earlier, and this debacle once again put the production line on a catch-up schedule.

To hold down costs, Sharps tried to consolidate orders and make more of fewer types of guns, further limiting the special-order options and dropping styles that didn't sell well. Dealer and customer discounts, which had been handed out with abandon (and inequitably) in the mid 1870's, were either discontinued or dispensed on an advertised schedule. A glut of sporting guns on the market forced the company to drop its prices overall, and that in turn forced dealers who were holding stock bought at higher prices to adjust. Starved for cash and with no respite in sight, Sharps was holding out for a miracle when it sent Charles Pond to Europe for one last go at military contracts.

Pond—formerly of Cooper & Pond and the first president of the Union Metallic Cartridge Company—had come to Sharps in May of 1876. He served as board member and company secretary, and among his many talents was the ability to sell guns. He and Hugo Borchardt sailed on May 10, 1879, bound for England, Austria and Russia. They planned to demonstrate the Lee rifle to these governments, ask the British about overdue payments (for some Long-Range rifles ordered the previous year), and check on the production of double shotguns to be exported from England.

The trip was largely fruitless. In August, A.S. Winchester wrote Westcott: ". . . as things look now we shall have some tall kiting and triangulation to do next week. I am very sorry to be in such shape at bank & feel exceedingly sheepish when I go near the factory, feeling that I have exhausted all my ingenuity in standing off payments. . . ."

In September, Charles Pond wrote back from Europe concerning a reduction in force that would preclude further development or promotion of Model 1878, implying that all factory energy be shifted to the production of Lee repeaters. During the final months of 1879 and most of 1880, the Sharps factory produced few new rifles, though it revamped many in-stock guns. Some target models were rebarreled to lighten them and make them more attractive to the general public. These guns sold at steep discounts to dealers. Schuyler, Hartley & Graham sent the company 218 rifles for rebarreling, primarily to replace odd-caliber barrels with those bored for the popular .45/70, which had become the official U.S. service round in 1873.

Strangely, Sharps accepted a relatively large number of custom orders in 1880, perhaps to reduce its stock of special-order parts. Its reasons for taking and refusing orders were often obscure and sometimes contradictory, such as: "We have not the necessary parts & it would not pay us to fit up the machinery to make so small a lot." Persistent dealers and customers usually got what they wanted— but only if the cash was on the table. Sharps even over-shipped to its best dealers. Carlos Gove & Son of Denver asked for 210 Model 1874's and got 270. The price was right—$15 to $17 each—but there was desperation in these deals. By April, 1880, all hope for a successful turn-around had vanished.

The last large order completed by the Sharps Rifle Company was for Joseph Frazier, who in July, 1880, sent to the plant 1,500 percussion carbines and muskets for conversion to metallic cartridges. The money from this project lasted only until October, when the Sharps plant stopped making guns. On October 8, only 19 employees recorded any work time, and nobody reported work hours after that date. The only operation that continued was the shipping of parts and guns as orders came in. The last of these sales took place in the summer of 1882.

Later that year, J.W. Coffin of the Davenport Arms Company prepared a prospectus for investors, sending one to Arthur Winchester, who still owned 1,025 shares of Sharps Rifle Company stock. Coffin proposed a recapitalization of Sharps, in

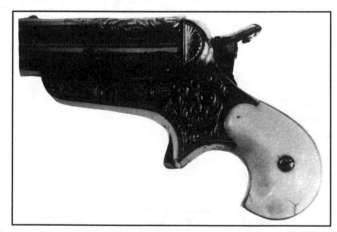

This Model 4B .32 rimfire 4-barrel gun has ivory grips and Nimschke engraving.

which he'd provide $25,000 of the necessary $100,000, with the rest to be acquired through stock sold at par. The effort failed. Machinery and tooling in the Sharps plant was subsequently sold and the factory leased to R.H. Wolff & Company, which had supplied barrel blanks to Sharps and also made springs.

For 12 years after the Sharps plant fell silent, the board of directors continued to hold regular meetings, with Arthur Winchester continuing as president and E.G. Westcott as secretary. The business now was all in real estate, though the company name had not been changed. Westcott died in 1897, but Winchester remained a part of the firm until 1902 or later. Efforts to sell the factory failed, and the Sharps Rifle Company last appeared in Connecticut records in 1904.

Sharps Ammunition: Linen, Paper and Metal

During its short life, this important American armsmaker also cataloged ammunition. The first Sharps cartridges had paper bodies, because they were designed for the early rifles with external priming. Sharps & Lull of Hartford contracted to make the first of these cartridges in 1853. The company may not even have begun production, as no boxes with that stamp have been located. In 1859, the Boston firm of A.G. Fay, Potter & Tolman started manufacturing ammunition for Sharps. Fay and company operated several New England powder mills under various names, and many of the Sharps cartridges produced by Fay in the last days of the Civil War do not carry the Fay stamp. The company made rifle cartridges in 44, 50, 52, 54, 56 and 58 caliber and a 56-caliber shotgun round. In Frank Sellers' fine book on the Sharps, A.G. Fay, Potter & Tolman is said to have produced 28 distinct box labels for the 52-caliber rounds alone.

Other firms supplying percussion cartridges for Sharps included Crittenden & Tibbals, Johnston & Dow, C.D. Leet, William Lawrence (Troy, New York), William Mason, Benicia Arsenal, Richmond Arsenal, Washington Arsenal, and Watervliet Arsenal. While most of these used linen, Christian Sharps made paper cartridges in Philadelphia for the guns he built there—primarily 31- and 36-caliber pistols. The Philadelphia plants also supplied the government with 54,600 pinfire and two million rimfire rounds.

Springfield Arsenal provided the space and Martin the tooling for Sharps' production of metallic cartridges (folded-head and bar-primed). Later, the Union Metallic Cartridge Company fur-

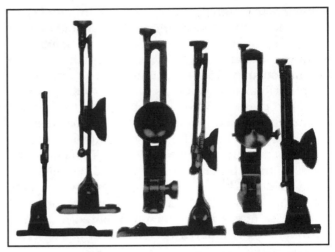

These tang sights were available on Sharps Model 1874 rifles—Sporting, Business and Hunter models. From left: Mid-Range, German Pattern, and early Creedmoor sights (side and rear views).

nished cases for both the Sharps Rifle Manufacturing Company and the Sharps Rifle Company that followed. All folded-head brass was Berdan-primed, with 14 cases and more than 50 bullets cataloged to yield a wide assortment of loads. The only solid-head Sharps cases were made in 1877 by the U.S. Cartridge Company of Lowell, Massachusetts, for rifles built that year for the Chinese.

Sharps bullets were swaged from cold lead and sized after casting. The company recommended that handloaders buy patched bullets rather than trying to patch them at home. Sharps spoke out against the use of thick "Everlasting" shells, stating in its 1879 catalog that ". . . experiments have proved ordinary shells to outlast the 'Everlasting' which cost four times as much. . . . We are prepared to chamber any of our arms for these heavy shells to order, but do not recommend them to our customers, believing that they cannot be made to average well for durability." Sharps did, however, nickel-plate cases for about $2.50 extra per 100.

In 1879, Sharps offered hardened steel shells with a small powder chamber capped with a ball. Available in .40/65 2½-inch and .45/70, these shells were intended for gallery shooting and became reasonably popular. The company also listed loading tools between 1874 and 1880. Because factory ammunition was expensive and often hard to find, many hunters "rolled their own" Sharps cartridges. And to accommodate buffalo hunters during the mid-1870's, some gun and ammunition dealers actually followed the hide wagons.

Winchester and Remington also loaded ammunition for Sharps rifles, and it's impossible to tell the Remington ammunition from that loaded by Sharps using the same U.M.C. brass bought by Remington. Later, boxer-primed Winchester and Remington ammunition became easy to spot. Sharps ammunition did not sell as well as that produced by these two big companies, because it could not be manufactured as cheaply or, consequently, priced as low. Until Hugo Borchardt developed a patching machine that could wrap 2,500 bullets an hour, Sharps bullets were all hand-patched and hand-loaded. They were also all roughly the same shape, no matter the caliber. Grooved bullets had a flat base and a more sharply tapered nose than plain bullets, which featured a hollow basal cavity for the patch.

Metallic cartridges marketed by the Sharps Rifle Company included six 40-calibers, three .44's, four .45's and three .50's, all distinguished within groups by their case length. The longest cartridge made by Sharps had a 2⅞-inch straight .45 case. The "Big 50," the most powerful of the lot and the one favored mostly by buffalo hunters, had a 2½-inch case. It used a standard load of 100 grains powder behind a 473-grain, paper-patched bullet. A more popular choice was the .45 2¼-inch or .45/70. Bullet weights ranged from 293 to 550 grains, the standard load being 70 grains powder pushing a 420-grain, paper-patched bullet. The Indians doubtless favored Sharps rifles chambered for this cartridge, because functional ammunition could be found anywhere. The warrior who captured a Sharps of some other chambering could use it only as long as the ammunition he took with it lasted. Consequently, many Sharps rifles were found, smashed to bits, near the bodies of hapless hunters and pioneers, whereas Winchesters and Springfields would have been grabbed up by the marauding Indians no matter what their chamberings.

In Sum. . . .

Even though Christian Sharps and the companies that developed and marketed his rifles disappeared before the automobile supplanted horses, they influenced a major shift in the U.S. gun industry. Sharps proved that powerful guns could be mass-produced, tested the merits of metallic cartridges and obliterated lingering doubts about breechloaders. Henry's rifle had demonstrated great speed of fire, but it could not deliver the pile-driving, first-round thump of a stout muzzleloader.

Sharps guns had greater range than riflemen of that era had ever seen, and better accuracy than the most sophisticated European muzzleloaders. The Sharps was a sure killer—perhaps too sure—at what we consider normal, open-country hunting ranges for modern smokeless rounds today. Men with forked sticks and Sharps rifles swept the Great Plains of bison, leaving a fly-blown moonscape of stinking carcasses that would yield to human scavengers more than three million tons of bones.

The Sharps was a rifleman's dream at a time when riflemen shaped the lusty new land west of the Mississippi. Like the bison, it was big and powerful—and, in just two decades, it became a part of the past. When the bison were gone, there was little use for the Sharps or the men who carried them. They'd all played their roles furiously in perhaps the shortest, most shameful hunt in history. And each had marked an important turning point in America's adolescence.

CHAPTER 6

SMITH & WESSON'S REVOLVER DYNASTY

To many shooters, the name "Smith & Wesson" translates into double-action revolvers, but ironically the firm's greatest accomplishment predates its first gun. That's when Horace Smith and Daniel Baird Wesson, the company founders, mechanics and entrepreneurs alike, developed the rimfire cartridge, an invention that changed the gun industry.

Horace Smith was born October 28, 1808, in Cheshire, Massachusetts. The family moved to Springfield when Horace was four, his father, Silas, having found work as a carpenter at Watershop, which was then part of the Springfield Armory. Twelve years later, Horace began his apprenticeship at the armory, forging bayonets. He became an apprentice toolmaker in 1828, later earning journeyman status and inventing several machines for the manufacture of gun parts, one of which was used to checker hammers.

In 1842, after 18 years at the Armory, Smith moved to Newtown, Connecticut, then on to New Haven, where he made tools for Eli Whitney. Fifteen months later, he took a job with Allen & Thurber of Norwich (Ct.), a manufacturer of percussion pepperbox pistols, and a few years after that opened his own gunshop in Norwich. There he made whaling guns and is said to have developed the exploding bullet used to kill whales. In 1852, Horace left Norwich for Worcester, Massachusetts, where he worked for Allen, Brown & Luther, a toolmaking firm. Smith also worked at the Robbins & Lawrence company in Windsor, Vermont, before moving to Worcester. Robbins & Lawrence made machine tools and guns on contract and later figured heavily in Smith's career.

The first repeating firearms Smith worked on were probably Allen & Thurber's pepperboxes. By 1850, he was manufacturing (in Norwich) a unique magazine pistol invented by Orville B. Percival and Asa Smith. The gun had a normal looking percussion lock mechanism; but in front of the hammer, where the nipple would be, two drums protruded from the top of a collar that rotated around the barrel. The front drum, or magazine, held the lead balls, while the rear one held powder and primers. With the drums upright, the shooter dispensed a ball from the forward magazine; simultaneously, powder and a primer dropped into place behind it. The collar was then rotated 180 degrees, putting the drums down in front of the trigger guard and offering the hammer, with its nipple-like extension, access to the seated primer. This gun proved impractical, but it no doubt fanned Horace Smith's interest in repeating mechanisms. He'd soon meet a man with similar ambitions. His name was Daniel Baird Wesson.

From Brother's Helper To Shop Superintendent

Born May 18, 1825, Wesson grew up on his father's farm near Worcester, Massachusetts. Daniel's older brother, Edwin, opened a gunshop in Grafton in 1835 and soon earned a reputation for the manufacture of fine target rifles. As a teenager, Daniel spent more time tinkering with guns than he did using them. In 1842, his father, Rufus Wesson, Sr., agreed to indenture Daniel to Edwin so the young man could learn the profession. Edwin agreed to pay his father $250 over three and a half years for Daniel's services; he would also give his younger

Daniel Wesson's older brother, Edwin, who started his own gun shop in 1835, built this percussion rifle in the 1840's.

Walker around New England. Colt had written Edwin to say he'd visit, but in later correspondence he expressed regret at not having met the elder Wesson. He may have done business with Daniel, however. Colt left a prototype Walker revolver so the Wessons could supply a quote on 1,000 barrels for the gun. In February, 1847, Colt wrote to request from the Northboro shop several moulds for the conical bullets Edwin had predicted would shoot best in the Walker. He also asked that some "cherries" be sent so Colt could manufacture the moulds itself.

Captain Walker must have liked what he saw of the Wesson products, because in January, 1847, he ordered an 8-pound, 44-caliber rifle and further implied he'd like to see his regiment equipped with Wesson guns. The following month, Walker promised the shop an order for 1,000 rifles, but a contract was never drawn up.

In March, 1848, Edwin Wesson moved his operation to Hartford, Connecticut, and formed a partnership there with Daniel and a gun mechanic from Harpers Ferry (Virginia) named Thomas Smith (apparently no relation to Horace Smith). The firm was known as Wesson & Smith. Its first order of business was to build 1,000 rifles; however, no production run of that size has been recorded, for Captain Walker or anyone else. Edwin's shop never manufactured more than 150 rifles a year.

During the summer of 1848, Edwin started making a new cavalry (dragoon) revolver designed and patented by an inventor named Daniel Leavitt. He still hoped his shop would secure a government contract for rifles. On November 22, he acknowledged the completion of Daniel's apprenticeship by signing a release. Daniel continued to work for his brother, until, on January 29, 1849, Edwin Wesson died suddenly.

Edwin had borrowed heavily to expand his enterprise, and the 16 businessmen who held notes now met to discuss the company's future. Selling it would mean absorbing a heavy loss, so they agreed to contract with Thomas Warner to produce, at Wesson's shop, 400 rifles within one year and 600 the year following. The bondholders then formed a stock group, called the Wesson Rifle Company. Subsequently Daniel, as an heir, sold his interest in Edwin's yet unissued patent for a new pistol to Benjamin F. Warner (Thomas's brother) for $1,000. The patent was granted four months later.

In August, 1849, the Wesson Rifle Company's creditors attached all of Edwin's property. Left with no tools, Daniel sold his brother's estate to get

brother suitable room, board and clothing. In addition, Daniel was to receive three months of regular schooling and all the shop instruction necessary to make him a master gunsmith by age 21. In return, Daniel agreed to apply himself faithfully to any jobs Edwin gave him.

When Daniel started working for his brother, the Wesson shop was in Northboro, Massachusetts. Within two years, the precocious lad had proven himself so capable that Edwin was able to leave him in charge during his absence. One of Edwin's infrequent trips away from Northboro came about because another gunsmith had infringed on the patent rights that had been awarded to him for a false muzzle. Thus did Daniel learn about the importance of protecting inventions and how patent rights were obtained and guarded.

Exposure to other people in the gun industry also helped prepare Daniel for his later work. He met Samuel Colt late in 1846 or early in 1847, while the Hartford industrialist was showing Captain

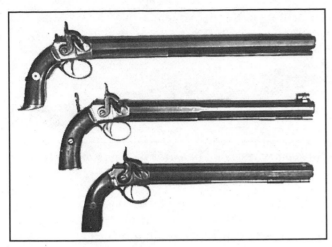

In the 1840's, Edwin Wesson turned out these percussion pistols during his brother Dan's apprenticeship.

them back. But a Hartford judge ruled that the Wesson Rifle Company and the rights to Edwin's patented muzzle must be sold at public auction. On November 22, exactly one year after Daniel had completed his apprenticeship, Edwin's company was auctioned off to a group of Chicopee Falls (Massachusetts) businessmen, who formed the Massachusetts Arms Company. Thomas Warner became superintendent of the new gun firm, whose stockholders included Daniel Leavitt, Benjamin Warner, Joshua Stevens, William Miller, Daniel Wesson and Horace Smith. Massachusetts Arms was incorporated on March 5, 1850, for the purpose of making Edwin Wesson's revolver.

After the dissolution of the Wesson Rifle Company, Daniel, together with his brothers, Franklin and Martin, continued to build percussion rifles and pistols in the Hartford shop. In October, 1850, after a year of disappointing returns, the brothers left to seek other employment. Daniel, now married, moved back to his home town of Worcester and found work as shop superintendent at the Leonard Pistol Works there. This company marketed pepperbox guns made under contract by Robbins & Lawrence of Windsor, Vermont. It's quite likely that Daniel Wesson first met Horace Smith at Robbins & Lawrence.

The Hunt-Jennings Repeater

In 1850, the Vermont firm had agreed to build the most revolutionary of firearms: the Hunt repeater. Born in 1796, Walter Hunt had learned the machinist's trade in his home town of Martinsburg, New York. He moved to New York City in 1826 and

lived there until his death in 1859. An inventor of broad interests and great talent, Hunt had no mind for business; he even failed to patent the lock-stitch needle that would one day fuel the development of the sewing machine.

On August 10, 1848, Hunt was granted U.S. patent 5701 for his design of a conical bullet with a hollow base. The base held propellant ignited by an external primer that shot sparks through a hole in a cork base cap. The next logical step was to design a gun to fire these "rocket balls," as Hunt called them.

A year later, Hunt was awarded patent 6663 for a repeating rifle with a brilliantly designed tubular magazine but a complex and trouble-prone firing mechanism. He named it his "Volitional" repeater. Lacking money to promote or even improve his gun, Hunt assigned patent rights to fellow New Yorker George A. Arrowsmith, a model maker and machinist. At that time Arrowsmith had on his payroll Lewis Jennings, a skilled gun mechanic. Working in their shop on Manhattan's Gold Street, the two men soon found serious flaws in the Hunt mechanism, and Jennings set about to correct them. His improvements were patented in December, 1849, the rights being assigned to Arrowsmith, his employer.

At this point, Arrowsmith wanted to sell the rifle. He found a buyer in Courtlandt C. Palmer, past president of the Stonington & Providence Railroad and a leading New York hardware merchant. Palmer paid $100,000 for all the rights and patents pertaining to the modified Hunt rifle. He immediately looked around for someone to make 5,000 of the rifles so he could recoup his investment. Since Robbins & Lawrence was an established firm employing several first-rank gunsmiths, Palmer decided to contract the work there.

The new Jennings repeaters were to be of 54 caliber, with an automatic primer feed. Problems in the manufacture of these rifles in 1850 prompted Palmer to engage Horace Smith to improve the mechanism. Smith, who was working at Robbins & Lawrence, bettered the design of the breech pin and lifter, an effort that earned him a patent on August 26, 1851. Although it was issued to Smith, the patent was assigned to Palmer, who by then was keenly disappointed in the rifle. A businessman, not a mechanic, Palmer wanted to see dollars instead of patents.

The last of the 5,000 contracted rifles—some of them with Smith's improvements—were manufactured in 1851. Because of problems with the

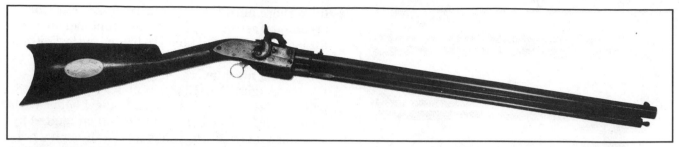

Lewis Jennings and Horace Smith combined their talents to produce this repeater, patented by Smith in 1851.

feeding mechanism, many were altered slightly to function as single-shots. Sales were so slow that Palmer decided not to produce more. By this time, Dan Wesson, who'd been working at the Leonard Pistol Works, expressed interest in the Jennings gun—presumably through his association with Robbins & Lawrence. A year later, in 1852, Smith and Wesson both found themselves working at the Allen, Brown & Luther plant in Worcester. No doubt they discussed the Jennings repeater, especially its most serious faults. Bullets for the Jennings were limited in their performance by the size of the basal cavities that held the powder charge; in addition, the primer-feeding mechanism malfunctioned often. Wesson, in particular, was probably the first to consider the use of different ammunition to solve both problems. During his tenure with the Leonard company, he'd studied the French Flobert pistol; it was a single-shot "saloon" or target gun of relatively low power that chambered a ball seated on the mouth of a percussion cap. Wesson purchased the caps and buckshot needed to duplicate such cartridges from Crittenden & Tibbals and reportedly even built some single-shot pistols to fire them. He probably reasoned: "If a self-contained cartridge could be married to the Jennings action, the primer feed could be eliminated altogether, and bullet performance could be enhanced simply by making the cartridge case bigger to hold more propellant."

Smith, Wesson and Palmer Build a Pistol

And so it was in 1852 that Daniel Wesson began working with Horace Smith to explore these ideas, with Courtlandt Palmer financing their efforts. On May 10, 1853, Smith and Wesson filed for a patent covering a new feature for metallic cartridges. It did not protect the cartridge, because Flobert already had two French patents, issued in 1846 and 1849, to protect the design used by Smith and Wesson in their work. The patent applied to the insertion of a disc atop the priming compound in the case head. This disc kept the compound evenly spread and served as an anvil for the striker.

Two weeks after that filing, Smith and Wesson went after another patent, this one to cover hammer operation in the Jennings repeater. Instead of requiring a separate cocking motion after chambering a cartridge, the new action featured a hammer that was cocked by the bolt during its rearward movement. It also incorporated an extractor for the Flobert-style case, to which Smith and Wesson adapted the Jennings mechanism. That patent was issued on August 8, 1854.

By May of 1853, the partners had decided their new firearm should be a pistol. Perhaps they despaired of the poor market image already shadowing the Jennings repeater. Certainly they realized Flobert-type cartridges were best suited to short-range guns. Compared to plains rifles of the day—either muzzleloaders or the Sharps single-shot breechloaders with their combustible cartridges—any long gun that shot a Flobert-style cartridge appeared anemic at best.

To build their pistol, Smith and Wesson went to nearby Norwich, where Horace Smith apparently still owned some property. Parts for about 250 large-frame pistols were produced there in late 1853 and early 1854, before the pistol patent was granted on February 14. The guns must not have worked properly, as none survive, but the partners managed to salvage some by adapting them to a modified rocket ball. This 115-grain bullet incorporated a copper cup that held the cork base cap. In the middle of the cap, fulminate was kept in place by a metal disc located on the cork's inner face. While this design did not solve the problem of a small propellant chamber, it did offer internal ignition. Smith and Wesson were granted a patent for it on January 22, 1856.

Had it not been for Courtlandt Palmer, Smith and Wesson could not have continued their work. The Jennings gun had intrigued them but, like a

Horace W. Smith (above, left) and Daniel B. Wesson (above, right) worked together on several firearms projects, including the Hunt rifle (which fathered the Jennings, and later the Henry). Their work with double-action revolvers followed their first major achievement—a modern rimfire cartridge, the .22 Short—in 1857.

flirt, would not submit to them. There was still no profit in the venture, only potential. Despite the setbacks, Palmer persevered. On June 20, 1854, he joined with Smith and Wesson in a limited partnership and put up $10,000 for new tooling. The company would be known as Smith & Wesson.

Subsequently, the partners built two pistols with essentially the same mechanism: a seven-shot 31-caliber gun on a small frame and a 10-shot 41-caliber on a large frame. In loading either gun, the magazine follower slid toward the muzzle, compressing the spring and unlatching a spring-loaded catch from its recess in the barrel. This allowed the shooter to rotate the front of the magazine tube, exposing the empty rear portion for charging. Once loaded, the gun would chamber a round and cock the hammer with each forward-and-back motion of the finger lever. Early advertising claimed that "Thirty charges can be loaded and discharged in fifty seconds." The gun became known as the "Volcanic" pistol, although the origin of that name is uncertain. Popular theory is that it came from a magazine review of the gun by the Scientific American in 1854, its speed of fire no doubt conjuring up images of the fiery eruptions of a volcano.

The first Volcanics were almost surely 41-calibers, because they lack the patent date of February 14, 1854 (almost all .31 Volcanics carry this marking). Variations among the pistols produced were common because the guns were manufactured individually, not on an assembly line. The large-frame pistols were numbered separately from those with small frames. Serial numbers ran from 1 to 100, then started over again with a letter prefix, which in turn changed after another 100 guns. After the "F" prefix, the system was altered to allow numbers to continue beyond 100; however, the prefixes were retained, with a new one added at numbers 100, 200, 300, and so on. In 1854, Smith and Wesson modified the .41 pistol slightly and offered it with a new 16-inch barrel and detachable carbine stock. Probably fewer than 500 large-frame pistols and 1,200 small-frame pistols with Jennings-inspired actions and magazines were built by Smith & Wesson.

While the company's modified rocket ball ammunition proved superior to Flobert-style cartridges, it was hardly perfect. If the chamber of a gun was too deep, or the bullet a bit undersized, the hammer blow would simply push the bullet for-

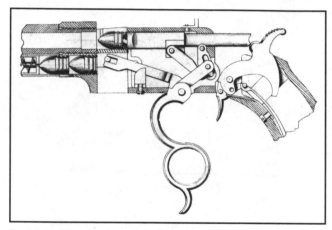

Smith & Wesson's magazine pistol (above) became known as the "Volcanic" pistol, probably because its speed of fire evoked images of an active volcano.

ward without detonating the primer. Extraction was difficult then because the base of the rocket ball was out of reach of the extractor hook.

By October of 1854, Smith & Wesson was suffering for lack of product sales. About that time, J.W. Post, a cutlery dealer from New Haven, Connecticut, approached the partners to ask about obtaining their guns to sell through his firm. Horace Smith then discussed with Post the possibility of a joint stock venture to raise $15,000 additional operating capital. As a result, a group of about 40 businessmen from New York and New Haven bought Smith & Wesson, incorporating it as the Volcanic Repeating Arms Company. Capitalized at $150,000 with 6,000 shares of common stock at $25 a share, Volcanic procured from Smith & Wesson all rights to manufacture, improve and sell firearms as described by the various patents transferred in the sale. Smith and Wesson together received $65,000 in three cash payments, plus 2,800 shares of stock and additional money for the machinery at their Norwich plant. Daniel Wesson was made plant superintendent; but Horace Smith left the company to return to Springfield, Massachusetts, where he worked for a time with his brother-in-law.

Meanwhile, Wesson continued to experiment at Volcanic with other guns as well as the Flobert-type cartridge. In August of 1856, he completed a wooden model of a revolver designed to fire a 22-caliber cartridge. Wesson knew that Colt's original revolver patents had expired in February of that year and thus anticipated no trouble in producing the gun. But he soon discovered that Rollin White, who had worked at Colt, held a current patent for a revolver cylinder bored end to end. That meant Wesson could not market his pistol without White's permission. Upon requesting that permission, Wesson was invited to call on White at his office in New York.

The two men met on November 17, 1856, and signed an agreement that gave Wesson—actually, Smith & Wesson—exclusive license to make a revolver with a bored-through cylinder. White would get 25 cents for every gun manufactured under his patent until the patent expired in 1872. Oddly, White also agreed to relinquish his right to manufacture under the patent and to pay for any extension or defense that might be necessary. This last concession was pushed hard by Wesson, who remembered the trouble his brother had experienced while defending Alvan Clark's false muzzle. Rollin White's decision would cost him dearly once other inventors discovered the revolver's potential.

Although Wesson negotiated with Rollin White alone, the signed agreement listed "Smith & Wesson" as the participant. Daniel Wesson may have forged a legal bond with Smith that required this gesture, or perhaps he included his longtime partner because he knew Smith would contribute to any revolver project he had in mind. Possibly he felt a debt to Smith, for whom he had no doubt developed a great affection as well. At any rate, with the White agreement in hand, Wesson left the Volcanic Arms Company to join Horace Smith in Springfield. There the partners formed the Smith & Wesson Revolver Factory. Daniel Wesson had a little over $2,000 to contribute, and Horace Smith added about $1,650. A few months later, at a cost of $46.64, Smith and Wesson produced a metal prototype of the wooden model that had prompted Wesson's visit to White. In April of 1857, Daniel Wesson sold his New Haven home and moved to Springfield, where he and Hor-

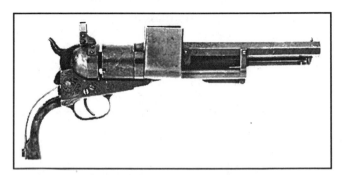

This view of Rollin White's patented revolving cylinder gun shows the right-side compartment into which linen cartridges were fed to the cylinder by an underbarrel loading lever.

ace Smith rented a tiny shop at 5 Market Street. The remainder of 1857 was spent mostly on tooling up for the new revolver. In fact, by year's end Rollin White had received just $1 in royalties from the sale of four revolvers! But better times were coming.

Little Cartridges and Revolvers Make Big News

The new firm of Smith & Wesson grew rapidly, with ammunition receipts rivaling those from the revolver business. In March, 1860, a new factory on Stockbridge Street was completed to afford the company more space. In 1862, Smith & Wesson turned out 6.4 million rimfire cartridges—roughly three million each of .22 and .32 revolver cartridges and just over 400,000 of the .44 rimfire rounds (manufactured for the "Frank Wesson Rifle," named apparently after Daniel's brother, Franklin). Production reached 7.7 million rounds in 1863, with the company selling enough .22 cartridges to supply every owner of a Smith & Wesson .22 with 115 rounds.

The first Smith & Wesson revolvers—called "seven shooters" after their cartridge capacity—were hinged-frame, spur-trigger guns. Called tip-ups, because the barrels were hinged at the front of the topstrap, they were chambered for Smith & Wesson's .22 rimfire, which came to be called the "Number 1" cartridge. To load, the cylinder was removed and each chamber was cleared by sliding it down over the fixed ejector rod located beneath the barrel. After inserting cartridges and swinging the barrel back into place, the hammer was cocked the same as any single-action gun. This trim revolver, which became officially known as Model 1, weighed only 10 ounces.

Model 1 worked satisfactorily, but it was a difficult gun to make because of the oval brass frame that required hand filing. Moreover, the round sideplate that allowed access to internal parts was only half an inch in diameter. Smith and Wesson changed these features in the spring of 1860, when it redesigned this gun for more efficient factory production. A flat brass frame replaced the oval one, and a much bigger, irregularly shaped sideplate was installed. The two-piece hammer on the original pistol gave way to a one-piece design. Called "Model 1 Second Issue," this revolver was first manufactured in the new Stockbridge Street plant in Springfield. Its production run of 115,400 ended in 1868.

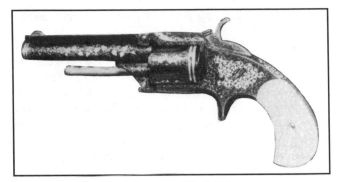

This ornate Smith & Wesson Model 1, a spur-trigger revolver dating to 1858, held seven .22 rimfire cartridges.

Both styles of the Model 1 generally came with silver-plated frames. The cylinders and $3\frac{3}{16}$-inch barrels were blued. As with many guns of that period, variations were common; in fact, two specimens are recorded as having solid silver frames. The standard Model 1 Second Issue sold to dealers for $10.50, but Smith & Wesson also offered "Second Quality" revolvers at a $2 discount. These were functional guns with minor imperfections in the finish. The demand for guns of all types increased so dramatically at the start of the Civil War that the company found discounting its seconds much more profitable than remaking them. More than 4,400 of these revolvers were marketed.

The last of the Model 1's, called the "Third Issue," made its debut in 1868. It featured a cast iron frame, fluted cylinder, "birds-head" grips, and round barrel (earlier barrels were flat-sided). A shorter, $2\frac{11}{16}$-inch barrel was also available, along with several finish combinations. The basic gun cost dealers $9.50.

By 1870, annual production of these pistols exceeded 20,000, and the firm had begun marketing them aggressively overseas. Smith & Wesson displayed its products at the Paris Exposition of 1867, signing sales agreements with J.H. Crane of London and C.W. May of Paris. These and other contacts helped the company increase its worldwide sales through 1872. Rollin White's patent expired that year, however, and now other manufacturers jumped in to grab the booty. Foreign receipts dropped markedly. The last of Smith & Wesson's tip-up revolvers, the Model 1 Third Issue, was discontinued in 1882 along with its cartridge. Oddly enough, the .22 rimfire round that had brought early success to Smith and Wesson lay dormant for a full decade.

Clever Engineering Boosts Power and Sales

Before they'd sold their first Model 1, Smith and Wesson knew it could not compete with the cap-and-ball revolvers of the day. Like the Jennings rifle, it had great potential but a weak punch. The partners wanted to build a large-frame pistol for a bigger cartridge, but they also anticipated serious problems. The thin copper base of a .22 cartridge expanded on firing and seized the cylinder by grabbing the recoil shield. That problem was solved (in the Model 1) by engineering a recoil shield that turned with the cylinder. Smith and Wesson figured that if a .22 could bind up a gun, so could the swelling in big-bore cases. Probably the bulge would be even more severe; moreover, a rotating recoil shield wasn't practical on a large revolver.

The partners attacked this problem by thickening the shield located directly behind the chamber to be fired. In other words, the rest of the shield was recessed. This ensured proper headspacing for the round under the hammer, while allowing the cylinder to turn freely once it was rotated a notch. The design was patented on July 5, 1859, and Smith and Wesson started work immediately on a larger gun. Chambered for Smith & Wesson's Number 2 cartridge, or .32 Long Rim Fire, the new iron-frame Model 2 looked exactly like a big, long-barreled Model 1. Its announcement in June of 1861 corresponded with the onset of the Civil War. Union soldiers promptly flooded the company with orders, and in 1862 Smith & Wesson had more than it could fill for the next three years. As a result, it was forced to refuse orders. At that time, it was the only U.S. firm that could build cartridge revolvers legally.

The six-shot Model 2 was well engineered and underwent few changes in its 12-year life. Standard in blued finish with 5- and 6-inch barrels, Model 2 was offered with a 4-inch barrel in 1864. Few were sold. One of the rarest Smith & Wesson revolvers of all is a Model 2 with an 8-inch barrel, extended grips and target sights. Known as the company's first target pistol, probably fewer than 10 of these were produced in a model run of 77,155.

While Model 2 served admirably as a belt gun, requests soon came in for a pocket-size revolver that shot big bullets. Smith & Wesson responded in 1865 with its Model 1½, a small-frame gun designed for the company's .32 Rim Fire Short cartridge. The five-shot cylinder would, however, accept the Number 2 (.32 Long) rounds as well.

Because Smith & Wesson was operating at full throttle, it had no space or machinery left for production of the Model 1½. So the firm of Savage and King (Middletown, Connecticut) was contracted to make most of the parts. These were sent to Smith & Wesson for assembly.

Smith & Wesson's first mid-size revolver, Model 1½, came standard with a 3½-inch barrel and three finishes (blue, nickel, and a combination of blue and nickel). The First Issue was produced up to 1868, with production totaling 26,300. A 4-inch barrel was offered in 1868 but again proved unpopular. The New Model 1½ made its debut that year, continuing the serial range. Because the war had ended and demand for its guns had subsided somewhat, Smith & Wesson was able to produce the New Model in its own plant, although some parts came from Savage and King's factory. The New Model proved a popular arm—the French government even bought a few—and remained in production until 1875. Total production came to 100,800.

During the early years of the Civil War, the Stockbridge Street plant served Smith & Wesson well, but by 1863 the company had outgrown it. Horace Smith and Daniel Wesson decided then to build another factory where only ammunition would be manufactured, leaving the Stockbridge Street facility for gun-building. The new plant, on Mill Street in Springfield, was run by Dexter Smith, Horace's son, along with Charles Farmer and company bookkeeper Joe Hall. The new enterprise was called Smith, Hall & Farmer. About the same time, Smith & Wesson further expanded its ammunition business by licensing C.D. Leet of Springfield, and Crittenden and Tibbals of South Coventry, Connecticut, to produce rimfire cartridges, with a three-percent royalty on sales payable to Smith & Wesson. The newly-formed Union Metallic Cartridge Com-

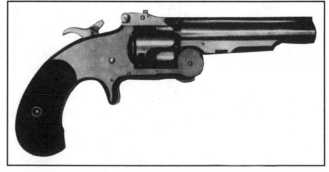

Smith & Wesson's first mid-size revolver, Model 1½ (above), came standard with a 3½-inch barrel.

pany was granted a similar license in 1866. Royalty payments ended in 1868, when the cartridge patents expired. That prompted Horace Smith and Daniel Wesson to sell their cartridge plant the following year.

During their first years in business, the partners had built a few rifles chambered in .44 rimfire ("Frank Wesson" rifles). But the firm's main product was still revolvers. On May 27, 1867, Daniel Wesson organized the Wesson Firearms Company to produce a shotgun of his own design. Horace Smith, Cyrus Buckland (the new plant superintendent), and J.W. Storrs served as directors, with Wesson as president. The shotgun, a double-barrel 12-gauge built at the Stockbridge Street plant, was released in 1869. Intended to compete with expensive imported English guns, it cost almost as much: $225. That was more than most hunters would pay for a shotgun, and the sportsmen who could afford it continued to buy imports. In 1871, after a production run of fewer than 250 shotguns, Daniel Wesson dissolved the Wesson Firearms Company, buying the stock and assets himself.

Sewing Machines and Solid Frames

That same year, Horace Smith, now 65, sold his interest in Smith & Wesson to his partner, whose three sons were already active in the company. The eldest, Walter H. Wesson, had majored in business at Williston Seminary in Easthampton, Massachusetts, and became the firm's bookkeeper in 1871. His brother, Frank, having worked in the publishing field for a time, returned to Springfield in 1881 to serve as assistant plant superintendent at Smith & Wesson. Daniel's youngest son, Joseph, had studied engineering at Worcester Polytechnic Institute and joined the company in 1880. A year later, he was issued his first patent.

By this time, Smith & Wesson employed about 500 people and was producing 400 revolvers a day. In 1882, Walter Wesson became a partner in the business, followed by Joseph in 1887 (shortly after Frank's death). While sharing responsibility, Daniel still held the company reins. Because his attempts at building long guns had failed, he devoted the firm's resources almost entirely to the production of revolvers. The exception was a short plunge into the manufacture of sewing machines in 1880. With Walter serving as president of the Wesson Sewing Machine Company, the venture lasted less than a month.

During the 1860's and '70's, Smith & Wesson established itself as a leading handgun manufac-

turer, not only in the U.S., but abroad. One of its most significant developments was a .44 rimfire revolver developed to meet the demand for a big military sidearm. Patterned after the 32-caliber Number 2 Army gun, this .44 was on the drawing board as early as 1862 and was designed to use the same .44/100 cartridges already in production for the Frank Wesson rifle. Wartime manufacture of other guns delayed the production of .44 revolvers; but in 1864, after responding to a request from gun dealer Cooper & Pond for 3,000 of these pistols, Smith & Wesson contracted with New Haven's Whitney Armory to make them.

Rollin White objected, maintaining that his agreement with Daniel Wesson did not allow Smith & Wesson to use outside contractors for the manufacture of revolvers. The company backed off, postponing production until it could handle the job itself. In January of 1865, it declined a proposal by J.W. Preston of the Rollin White Arms Company to build a big-bore revolver designed by White. When the war ended, Smith & Wesson accelerated the development of its .44.

While tip-up revolvers had sold very well as pocket guns and .32 belt models, they promised trouble when mated to cartridges with significantly more power. In tests, the .44 prototypes sometimes opened on firing, flinging the barrel up and back and damaging the hinge. Smith & Wesson redesigned the pistol, giving it a solid frame and calling it Model 3. Cartridges were loaded through a gate in the recoil shield. An ejector rod under the barrel was secured with a spring-loaded latch. To punch out the cases, the rod was removed. A short chain connected the rod to the frame to prevent loss.

Despite its stout design, the pistol did not receive the Army's blessing. One reason was its size: It measured 13¾ inches in length and weighed half an ounce shy of three pounds. The company scrapped this gun and developed instead a four-shot, .41 rimfire revolver on a lighter frame. Ironically, heavy solid-frame .44's later became hugely successful items in Smith & Wesson's product line.

The new .41 rimfire was introduced at the Paris Exposition of 1867. Because no .44's had been released, the "Model 3" designation was transferred to the .41. This gun was not successful, mostly because its four-shot capacity and barrel-locking system brought sharp criticism. Only 38 are known to have been made.

Frustrated with its lack of progress in developing a big-bore handgun, Smith & Wesson approached Remington about converting its popular

During its 34 years of production, beginning in 1878, the single-action new Model No. 3 (above) was offered in 8 barrel lengths and 14 chamberings.

New Model .44 Percussion Revolver to a .46 rimfire round. Remington agreed, and by April of 1861 Smith & Wesson had converted 4,575 guns, the first large-caliber cartridge revolvers to be produced in quantity under Rollin White's patent. Smith & Wesson inspected and distributed these guns. The company was paid a substantial royalty by Remington on each sale.

Model 3: Smith & Wesson's Russian Connection

Horace Smith and Daniel Wesson remained determined to build their own revolver, however. They decided that the tip-up design wasn't strong enough, and that solid-frame guns made loading too slow. An alternative was a break-open revolver with the hinge below the barrel and a mechanism that would kick all empty cartridges out simultaneously. Searching the patent records, Smith and Wesson found two that had been conferred to a W.C. Dodge on January 17 and 24, 1865, covering the simultaneous extraction of cases from a cylinder. In March of 1869, the partners paid Dodge $6,250 for those patents. They also bought from Louis Rodier (for $2,500) his 1865 patent for rotating a cylinder with a rachet mechanism integral with the extractor. And for another $5,000, Abram Gibson sold Smith & Wesson his 1860 patent for swinging both barrel and cylinder away from the recoil shield.

The first patent covering Smith & Wesson's new revolver, which integrated all these features, was issued to Robert Lake in London in May, 1869, and then assigned to Smith & Wesson. Plant superintendent Charles A. King was awarded a similar patent a few months later. Apparently unwilling to concede failure of the "Model 3" name that had graced its solid-frame .44 prototypes and the ill-fated .41 pocket pistol, Smith & Wesson used that label for its first top-break .44 revolver. From then on, "Model 3" denoted a frame size, not a specific design or model.

The first Model 3's, which Smith & Wesson released to the Army Ordnance Board in May, 1870, were chambered for the .44 Henry rimfire round and featured a standard 8-inch barrel (6- and 7-inch barrels were also available). The guns came in blued or nickel finish and, in a departure from previous Smith & Wesson models, featured a trigger inside a triggerguard. At the Army's request, the company changed the chambering to .44 centerfire, calling this cartridge the .44/100. Only about 200 copies of the .44 rimfires were built. Then, on December 28, 1870, Smith & Wesson received its first government contract, specifying 1,000 Model 3 revolvers. These were delivered to the Springfield Armory the following March.

During this same period, the Russian military attache in the U.S., General Alexander Gorloff, was living in Hartford, where he helped supervise the

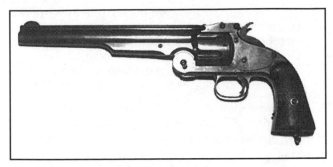

Dubbed the .44 S&W Russian, this revolver was produced by Smith & Wesson for the Russian government in 1871.

production of Berdan rifles being manufactured for his government by Colt. Smith & Wesson set about courting Gorloff for a revolver contract. Reluctant at first, the general was finally persuaded to order 20,000 Model 3's at just over $13 each. According to the contract, payment was to be paid in gold, with a $50,000 advance for tooling (also payable in gold). The Russians did not want their guns chambered in .44/100, however, and specified another cartridge, whose case was of greater diameter than its bullet. Chambers for these guns, therefore, were of two diameters—a new idea at that time. The cartridge was dubbed the .44 S&W Russian.

Many other changes were specified by the Russians, some of them minor at first glance but calling for substantial retooling. Russian inspectors were very thorough, too, which further slowed production. Smith & Wesson salvaged some of the rejected contract guns by grinding off the Russian inscriptions and marking them "Russian Model." Subsequently, guns without the Russian features were called "Americans." Many of the improvements specified by the Russians made good sense to Smith & Wesson, which incorporated them in its standard Model 3's for the domestic market.

The Russian contract established Smith & Wesson as an industry giant. Not only did it give the firm substantial capital for expansion, it prompted orders from other governments. In December, 1871, the Russian Grand Duke Alexis visited Smith & Wesson's plant and was given an engraved Model 3 with pearl grips. He carried this pistol on a subsequent tour of the American West with William F. "Buffalo Bill" Cody.

Smith & Wesson's Model 3 American proved popular with civilians as well; in fact, Smith & Wesson couldn't fill all the orders until its Russian contract had been completed. One order, from com-

pany distributor M.W. Robinson of New York City, totaled 25,000—more than had been ordered by the Russian government! Total production of the commercial Russian and American versions of First and Second Model 3's came to 32,800.

In 1873, Russia ordered 20,000 more revolvers, with a request for changes in the grip. Smith & Wesson quoted a price of $15.33 in gold for each gun. Because the company was not pleased with the new Russian grip, it continued to make guns in their original form for the domestic market. The contract guns, called "Model 3 Russian Second Models," were delivered by the end of 1873, when Russia ordered yet another 20,000 revolvers. Because Smith & Wesson was running its plant at full capacity and still couldn't keep pace with domestic demand, it discontinued the American version in 1874. Subsequently Russia placed yet another revolver order, its fourth.

In 1874, Turkey contracted with Smith & Wesson for 1,000 Second Model Russian revolvers chambered in .44 Henry Rim Fire. War with Russia in 1877 prompted Turkey to order 7,000 more. Smith & Wesson could not provide that many standard rimfire revolvers but agreed to supply center-fire guns altered to shoot rimfire ammunition. This alteration consisted of a blank to replace the firing pin bushing and a cut in the top of the recoil shield, to allow a hammer extension access to the cartridge in line to fire. The cylinder, bored for the .44 Russian round, was not replaced on these guns, probably due to the urgency of the order. This must have caused Smith & Wesson some problems, because the .44 Henry cartridge was smaller in diameter and some probably split in the oversize chambers.

The Japanese government also bought 5,000 Model 3 Russian Second Models, with commercial production adding another 6,200. More than 85,200 of these revolvers were made in all. In 1874, Smith & Wesson's Model 3 Russian Third Model, redesigned primarily to please Russian Ordnance, was announced. More than 41,000 of these guns were produced for Russia under four separate contracts. Turkey, Japan and the U.S. commercial market absorbed 19,500 more.

George Schofield's Quick-Firing Horse Pistol

The Schofield revolver, developed by Major George Schofield of the 10th U.S. Cavalry, was patterned after the Model 3. Major Schofield apparently heard about the Model 3 from his brother, General John Schofield, who headed the Small Arms Board in 1870. Smith & Wesson responded to the Major's interest in the gun by sending him a sample, plus 500 rounds of ammunition, at no charge. Schofield liked the design but saw room for improvements. Due to the press of Russian contracts, Smith & Wesson could not implement the changes but agreed to furnish parts if Schofield decided to have the changes made by another firm.

Following this tack, Major Schofield altered the cylinder latch so it could be operated easily by a soldier on horseback. After incorporating other refinements, he then promoted the gun to the military. In July, 1873, U.S. Ordnance adopted the Colt single-action revolver, but Smith & Wesson appealed for another testing of its Model 3. Finally, in December, Major Schofield convinced the Ordnance Department that it should take the Model 3 revolvers with his modifications. The following September, Smith & Wesson contracted to build 3,000 Schofield revolvers for the government, at a cost of $13.50 each. The government had requested them in .45 Colt, but accepted a shortened version of the round designed by Smith & Wesson because it worked better with Schofield's automatic extractor.

In the test that proved the Schofield revolver at the Springfield Armory in 1873, a timed reloading trial on horseback was included, as reported in the following excerpt from the government's report:

Major George Schofield adapted Smith & Wesson's Model 3 (above) so it could be operated easily by soldiers on horseback.

"The cartridges were taken from a cap-pouch on the belt. The horse was at a hand gallop, the Colt's pistol began loading [after ejection of six cases] in twenty-six seconds, [and was] loaded in sixty seconds. Major Schofield's pistol began loading in two seconds, [and was] loaded in twenty-six seconds."

The problem with the Schofield revolver was its cartridge. Shorter than the Colt's, it could be fired in a Colt chamber, but the reverse was not possible. Ammunition mixups inevitably occurred in battle, and the Schofield revolver was spurned by the same soldiers it should have benefited. By 1880, Schofields were being sold as surplus guns to firms like Schuyler, Hartley and Graham and Francis Bannerman, who commonly nickel-plated them and cut the barrels down to 5 inches. So altered, these revolvers became quite popular in the West. The Wells Fargo Express Company even bought some for its agents.

Fewer than 9,000 Schofield revolvers were produced by Smith & Wesson before the last one was assembled in 1878. This was due in part to the Army's dissatisfaction with the short cartridges. The gun still had potential on the civilian market, but Smith & Wesson may have balked at giving Major Schofield the 50-cent royalty per gun that had been set as payment for his design contributions.

The Schofield was followed by the New Model 3, destined to stay in production longer than any other single-action revolver made by Smith & Wesson. It appeared in 1878 in .44 S&W Russian, with a 6½-inch barrel and blued or nickel finish. Grips were red or black hard rubber or walnut. Soon the company offered the gun in other barrel lengths, from 3½ to 8 inches. Its most significant departure from earlier Model 3's was a hook-driven extractor that replaced a rack-and-pinion mechanism. This would have been done earlier, but Schofield had suggested the hook initially and would have demanded royalties for it. By contrast, J.H. Bullard of Smith & Wesson designed a hook of equal merit in 1877 and was given a $100 bonus! The New Model 3 stayed in production for 34 years with nearly 36,000 copies built in that time. Offered in 14 chamberings and a myriad of styles, it sold as well overseas as it did at home.

In 1879, Smith & Wesson introduced a rifle derived from the New Model 3. It featured a detachable stock, a red hard-rubber forend grip, and 16-, 18- or 20-inch barrels. Chambered for a .320 cartridge, this so-called "Revolving Rifle" never became popular. Only 977 were produced, all but 76 with blued finish (the rest were in nickel) and all but 17 in the first year of manufacture. The rifles were carried in Smith & Wesson catalogs through 1889, when the gun listed for $23, complete with hunting sight, case and cleaning kit.

While the Revolving Rifle failed to prosper, the top-break mechanism it featured had long ago proven itself in various large-frame revolvers. As early as 1870, Smith & Wesson began to adapt this design to its pocket pistols. Probably because of the hectic work pace dictated by military contracts for existing guns, plans for new small-frame guns were shelved until 1874. Originally designed for a .38 rimfire round, the new guns were redesigned before production for a .38 centerfire. This became the .38 Smith & Wesson cartridge that is still so popular.

The spur-trigger .38 Single Action and its Second and Third Model successors fared well in the marketplace. About half of the 108,225 .38's built left the factory in the first 2½ years. The Third Model, which Smith & Wesson listed in its catalog until 1911, featured a trigger guard instead of a spur. Concurrently, a .32 Single Action with a rebounding hammer (patented by Daniel Wesson and J.H. Bullard) was designed on a smaller frame. The .32 Smith & Wesson centerfire cartridge is still manufactured. Like the .38 Single Action, the .32 came in many styles. About 97,600 were produced before it was discontinued in 1892. By 1880, double-action revolvers had grown in popularity and became Smith & Wesson's ticket to the 20th century.

Double-Action Delayed; Hammerless Guns Follow

The first of the company's double-action guns was apparently built before November, 1872, because at that time Smith & Wesson sent a letter to Russian General Gorloff, offering him ". . . twenty thousand self-cocking revolvers . . . [for] $14.45. . . . If self-cocking revolvers are ordered, four months will be required to make the necessary preparation of tools. After which we can deliver an average of 100 per day."

The Russian reply is not found in factory records, but in any event the gun designed for this market was never manufactured. The prototype was a top-break revolver with a long latch. Because it differed substantially from the Model 3, it probably was engineered specifically for the Russians. Smith & Wesson all but ignored double-action mechanisms for six years. Then, in October, 1876, J.H. Bullard produced drawings of .38 and .44 self-cocking guns, featuring the long strap of the Russian prototype and the Schofield-inspired extractor.

Perhaps to avoid making royalty commitments to Schofield, Smith & Wesson rejected these designs, gave the matter more study, and finally approved a different type of revolver in August of 1878. For the first time, "double action" was used in place of "self-cocking" in the gun's catalog description. By October, 1879, Bullard had completed his blueprints for the new five-shot .38, and it was listed in the company's 1880 catalog. By the end of 1880, 17,691 revolvers had been shipped. Improvements resulted in six subsequent models, the last of which—the "Perfected Model"—came on the market in 1909. In addition to the knob at the rear of the top strap, it featured a thumb-latch for the cylinder. Both had to be worked simultaneously to open the gun. This innovation, implemented at the request of peace officers, prevented a suspect from grabbing an officer's gun by the latch and opening it.

Beginning about the same time, the company also offered a series of double-action guns in 32 caliber. A .44 double-action model, called the New Model Navy No. 3 (to distinguish it from the single-action Army Model), was introduced in 1881. While the .38 and .32 revolvers stayed in the Smith & Wesson line until 1919, the .44 double-action was dropped in 1913, after a run of 54,668.

Two variants on the large-frame gun included the 44-caliber Wesson Favorite and the Double Action Frontier. The Favorite was not cataloged, though 1,073 were manufactured between 1882 and 1885. It had a 5-inch barrel and contained parts that had been trimmed to reduce weight. Possibly built to service a military contract that did not

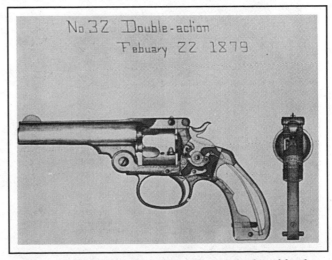

S&W's .32 Double Action revolver, as depicted in the original factory drawing above, was introduced in 1880.

prove out, the Favorite was priced at only $13.75 in 1889, the second and last year of its mention in Smith & Wesson literature. The remaining guns were sold as surplus.

The Double Action Frontier, introduced in 1886, was a copy of the .44 Double Action, except that it had a slightly longer cylinder and strap to accommodate the .44-40 WCF cartridge. A few were manufactured in .38-40 WCF.

By 1882, Joseph Wesson was working on a .38 hammerless revolver, and within two years he had a working model, which he called the "Safety Hammerless." Refining it took two more years, until in August of 1886 the first guns were produced, followed by four modified versions. A total of 261,493 of these medium-frame, top-break guns was built before the last one sold in 1940. A .32 Safety Hammerless, introduced in 1888, survived two model changes and stayed in production nearly 50 years, during which time almost 243,000 copies were made.

In the mid-1890's, Smith & Wesson began offering target barrels and sights designed to convert its small- and medium-bore single-action pistols into single-shot target guns. Soon requests came in for a pistol designed from the start for competition. Smith & Wesson responded with a line of single-shots in 22, 32 and 38 caliber. About 1,500 were

produced on revolver frames before the Second Model made its debut without a recoil shield or cuts for the hand and cylinder stop. The Second Model, in .22 rimfire only, was made from 1905 through 1909, with shipments totaling 4,617. The Third Model, with a production run of just over 7,000, stayed in Smith & Wesson catalogs from 1909 through 1923. It had walnut grips, in contrast to the hard rubber grips on earlier target guns. A few were made with short chambers, so that the bullet had to be pushed into the rifling. This feature was thought to enhance accuracy, and guns so equipped were called "Olympic Models." A 10-inch barrel and blued finish were standard on all Smith & Wesson target guns of this era. In 1920, the company circulated a questionnaire to find out what shooters looked for in a target pistol. Incorporating their most worthy responses, Smith & Wesson produced in 1925 its Straight Line .22 target model. This gun did not become popular, however, and after a production run of only 1,870 it was dropped in 1936.

The ''Hand Ejector'': S & W's Most Important Revolver

The most important development at Smith & Wesson during the 1890's came from company experiments with solid-frame revolvers. The first were carried out with the modified Colt 1892 Army

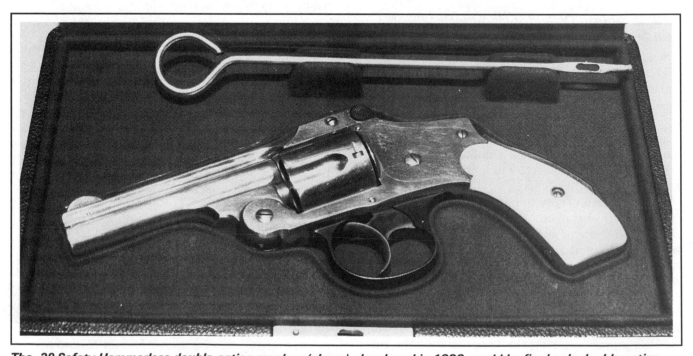

The .38 Safety Hammerless double-action revolver (above), developed in 1886, could be fired only double action.

gun, which Smith & Wesson crafted into a seven-shot .32 that it called a "Hand Ejector" model. The top-break revolvers that had carried the company for nearly three decades featured automatic ejection; that is, when the gun was fully opened, its own gearing pushed the extractor plate rearward to dump the empties. A Hand Ejector gun opened to the side, the cylinder swinging on an axis parallel to the barrel until its entire diameter was clear of the frame, and from which it pivoted in front of the trigger guard. There was no easy way to include automatic extraction with this design. The cartridges had to be removed manually by pulling back on the extractor rod, which in turn pushed back the extractor plate, kicking out the empties.

While hand ejection didn't seem desirable at first look, it offered a huge advantage by eliminating the hinge and movable strap of the top-break revolver. The Hand Ejector's solid frame also allowed the chambering of much more powerful cartridges, an important consideration at a time when smokeless powder was replacing black. In 1895, Smith & Wesson announced a six-shot 32-caliber "Model I" revolver, becoming the first guns available a year later. (Eventually, the letter designation for the model came to denote frame size, and the models were numbered.) The six-shot .32 got a luke-warm reception, but when several police departments chose it as a duty arm, sales picked up. The gun was modified in 1902 and became known as the "First Change" Hand Ejector (instead of being called the "First Model," as was the custom with earlier revolvers). The .32 went through five changes and nearly 537,000 copies before World War II interrupted production. It was revived in 1949 and revamped in 1960, when Smith & Wesson started using the "J" frame on all its small revolvers. The .32 Hand Ejector spawned several other important models, including the .22/32 Bekeart target gun, the .22/32 Kit Gun, and the .32 Regulation Police, all numbered consecutively with the parent .32. The .38 Regulation Police was built on the same frame but had its own serial number series.

In 1896, Smith & Wesson accelerated its efforts to improve the Hand Ejector revolvers—specifically, to eliminate the top-side cylinder stop and devise an easier-opening mechanism. At the same time, it experimented with a more powerful .38 cartridge. The .38 Long Colt then in common use lacked enough power to suit law officers and soldiers, so Smith & Wesson lengthened the case, boosting its capacity from 18 to 21½ grains of black powder. Bullets from the new round drove 25 percent deeper than those from the .38 Long Colt in pineboard penetration tests.

In 1899, the company combined its mechanical improvements in the Hand Ejector gun with this new cartridge. The result was Smith & Wesson's most famous gun—the .38 Military and Police. This six-shot double-action revolver featured a cylinder stop rising from the frame beneath the cylinder and a thumb-operated latch at the right rear of the frame to facilitate opening. Chambered in .38 Smith & Wesson Special, this model came in blued or nickel finishes and barrel lengths of 4, 5, 6, 6½ and 8 inches. It was built on what the company called its new "K" frame, a medium-size frame with a rounded butt. You could get the same gun chambered in .32/20; and while some of these were bought by sportsmen, they lagged far behind the .38 Military and Police in popularity.

The First Model Military and Police was produced from 1899 to 1902, when an improved Second Model was introduced. The Second Model, First Change appeared in 1903 and was revamped two years later with a new and more useful square butt. Four subsequent changes of the 1905 Model brought production of the .38 Military and Police up to serial number 1,000,000 in 1942. So good was the gun's basic design, and so popular the new cartridge, that nearly 21,000 .38's were sold before the first modifications were made less than three years into production.

The first military contract for this revolver came from the U.S. Navy, which purchased 1,000 pistols in June, 1900. Early the following year, Smith & Wesson received an order from the Army

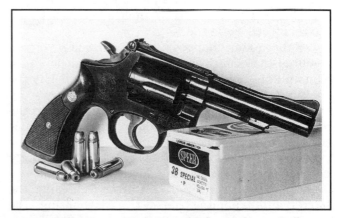

Smith & Wesson's Model 14 .38 Special was built on a mid-size K frame.

for 1,000 more. The only time production of this revolver stopped was from June 3, 1918, to February 6, 1919, when Smith & Wesson's plant was dedicated almost entirely to the production of .45 Hand Ejector guns, Model of 1917. In 1942, after serial number 1,000,000 was reached, a new serial sequence started. It had a "V" prefix, and guns so designated were called "Victory Models," a reference to the hope for a quick victory in World War II. Some Military and Police revolvers were chambered for the .38 Smith & Wesson cartridge, for shipment to Great Britain during the war. Because this round fired a 200-grain lead bullet, it was known as the .38/200 British Service cartridge.

Smith & Wesson's first large-frame Hand Ejector revolver was a 44-caliber, six-shot gun chambered for a new cartridge pushing a 246-grain bullet with 26 grains of black powder—three more than were used to fuel the old .44 Russian. In pineboard tests, the new bullet penetrated a little deeper than the lighter .38 Smith & Wesson Special bullet. Because of its increased power, the .44 Smith & Wesson Special required a big, strong gun. Accordingly, the company's "N" frame was engineered in 1905 and put into production in 1907. The first revolvers came off the line early in 1908 and were designated the ".44 Military Model of 1908."

Because this gun was designed to lock the cylinder in three places, it has become known as "Smith & Wesson's Triple Lock." The three points are: 1) at the center of the recoil shield, where the cylinder's spindle extends into the frame; 2) at the juncture of yoke and barrel; and 3) at the forward end of the extractor rod. These new large-frame Hand Ejectors, as listed in the 1908 catalog, were available in blue or nickel, in .44 Russian or .44 Special, at a cost of $21. A few Triple-Locks were chambered in .38-40, .44-40 and .45 Colt. The standard barrels were 5- and 6½ inches long, but 4-inch barrels were made too.

Subsequent changes to the N-frame revolvers resulted in Second, Third and Fourth Model .44's. The first big order for this gun was tendered by the British Government in 1914. Smith & Wesson responded by converting .44 Special cylinders to the .455 Mark II cartridge. Though British ordnance people objected to the gun's great weight and the precise fit of parts that invited malfunction in dirty conditions, they accepted all the guns Smith & Wesson could ship. In 1915, after lightening the barrel and trimming the extractor housing, the company continued to send these modified N-frame revolvers to England through the Union Metallic

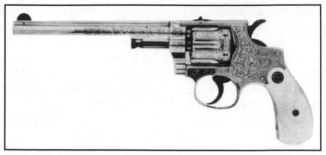

This S&W .32 Hand Ejector First Model is engraved by Oscar Young.

Cartridge Company (the British government's purchasing agent in the U.S.). A few guns went to Canada, possibly for issue to the Royal Canadian Mounted Police.

The .455 Mark II was the only .45 round Smith & Wesson had chambered since the Schofield. But as Europe's war threatened the United States, the company developed a revolver for the Colt .45 Automatic Pistol cartridge. The rimless case was kept from falling through the chamber by a thin halfmoon clip made of steel. Two of these clips, designed by Joseph Wesson, held three cartridges and fit against the rear of the cylinder. Besides enabling Smith & Wesson revolvers to use rimless ammunition, they speeded up the loading process.

The Great War and Harold Wesson's Big Task

Daniel B. Wesson, who had lived long enough to witness the initial success of his company's Hand Ejector guns, died on August 4, 1906, just before the N frame was introduced. For six years after his father's death, Walter Wesson served as president of the company. In January, 1912, a new trust arrangement for the management of the company named Walter Wesson as president and treasurer. Trustees included Walter and his brother Joseph, along with Harold Wesson, Frank Wesson, Douglas Wesson, Harcourt Bull, George Chapin and Adam Garrison. Between 1912 and 1915, power struggles within this group compromised its effectiveness. Walter and Joseph were in and out of the president's chair, until Walter's health failed in 1915 and Joseph became president.

Now 56 years old, Joseph Wesson had already contributed more than 20 patents to the improvement of firearms. His inventive genius rivaled that of his father, and he had become an accomplished gun mechanic. But Joseph's term as president was short. Ill health impeded his progress, and labor disputes arose just when the onset of World War I called for increased production.

In 1917, Smith & Wesson won several substantial contracts for military revolvers. By this time, the company had begun planning a new factory. Production of .455 revolvers for Great Britain had taxed the Stockbridge Street plant; clearly, it would be too small to meet wartime demands for U.S. guns. Construction of the new facility had just begun when the government ordered its first N-frame service revolvers in .45 ACP. The old factory turned out the first of these, designated "U.S. Army Model 1917." The guns were similar in design to the .44 Hand Ejector Second Model, but they had 5½-inch barrels, plain walnut grips and a lanyard ring on the butt.

Unfortunately, Joseph Wesson's poor health and other factors deprived Smith & Wesson of strong leadership during the first months of the war. Production did not accelerate fast enough to suit the U.S. government, and on September 13, 1918, it took control of the company. Smith & Wesson remained under the management of federal agents throughout the war.

The completion of its new Willow Street plant in 1918 enabled the firm to boost output of the Model 1917 Army revolver from 5,000 to 14,500 units a month. By Armistice Day, 1919, it had built 163,476. After the war, Smith & Wesson sold its unissued guns to civilians. By early 1921, this stock had been depleted, and the company began making a new model expressly for the civilian market. It differed from the military version only in its checkered grips. Sales were slow, but in 1937 the Brazilian Government gave business a boost with an order for 25,000 military .45's, to be delivered the following year. Smith & Wesson resumed production of the Model 1917 in May, 1946, but the revolver was discontinued three years later, after a total production of 210,782.

At the end of World War I, Joseph Wesson returned as company president. He faced many hurdles, including an abundance of surplus guns, which depressed the sales of new ones. Cheaply constructed foreign arms, having the same general features of superior American guns, stole another piece of the market. Finally, many people had become so disgusted with war that they actively campaigned against the tools of war. For the first time on record there were calls for firearm restrictions. Joseph Wesson tried unsuccessfully to pull his company through these rough times, but as Smith & Wesson continued to lose money his health deteriorated.

Joseph Wesson died on April 30, 1920, and the following month Harold Wesson, son of Frank L. Wesson, became the firm's fourth president.

Born October 17, 1878, Harold had been tutored in Springfield as a child, then earned an engineering degree from the Massachusetts Institute of Technology. From 1902 until 1909, he worked as an engineer for the New York Ship Building Company of Camden, New Jersey, before returning to Springfield and the family gun business. After working in various departments, he moved into management, then took leave during World War I to serve as a Lieutenant Commander in the U.S. Navy.

After Joseph's death, Harold's mandate as company president was to put Smith & Wesson in the black again. He started by directing the redesign of an automatic pistol. Though revolvers had brought great prosperity to the company, Harold's uncle, Joseph, knew back in 1890 that autoloading pistols would command an increasing share of the handgun market. He began experimenting, assembling a collection of existing mechanisms, then

Harold Wesson (1878-1946) became president of Smith & Wesson in May, 1920.

working to improve them. Nothing came of his efforts until 1909, when he met Charles Philibert Clement from Liege, Belgium. Clement had recently designed a 25-caliber autoloading pistol, one that gave Joseph Wesson a starting point. He bought the manufacturing rights to Clement's design and immediately set about improving it.

The first change he made was in the gun's safety—a thumb bar that had to be held down before firing and functioned only for right-handed shooters. Joseph patented a finger-activated safety that was accessible to all shooters. The second problem concerned the Clement model's heavy recoil spring, which was controlled by a lightweight slide. Pulling the slide to the rear proved a hard job even for strong men; and so, to make the gun easier for women to operate, Joseph developed a slide lock that disconnected the spring from the slide.

The Smith & Wesson autoloader that resulted from this work was planned as a .32 ACP, but the engineers grew concerned about the bore life of a gun fed a steady diet of jacketed bullets from the Colt cartridge. So Smith & Wesson developed its own, slightly larger round, the .35 Smith & Wesson Automatic. Its bullets featured a jacketed nose for smooth feeding, but an exposed lead base that gripped the rifling. The first .35 Automatic pistols were finished in May, 1913. Available in blue or nickel, they sold for $16.50. Though initial demand was strong, the company discontinued these little guns in April, 1915, in order to devote more of its factory to the production of military revolvers for England. In June, 1916, Smith & Wesson resumed manufacture of the Automatics, then stopped again in January, 1918, to throw its muscle into the American war effort. Postwar production of the gun amounted to only 50 a month in response to a weakened demand.

Thus, when Harold Wesson was installed as company president in 1920, he decided to drop this model because it lacked the sleek looks of its competition, and because its cartridge had no application elsewhere. The new president then asked for a new autoloader with a more attractive profile and chambering for the .32 ACP. The resulting pistol, which went to market in February, 1924, featured several improvements over the old Clement design. But it was still a bit more complex than the Colt—and, at $33.50, it was $11 more expensive. For that reason, and because of the Great Depression that followed, sales were slow. Fewer than 1,000 Smith & Wesson .32 Automatics were produced before the last one was sold in 1937.

During the 1920's, Harold Wesson tried several ways to cure his ailing firm. One of the earliest was a dissolution of the trust that controlled the company. He reincorporated Smith & Wesson in November, 1922, but remained its president. At this time target revolvers were selling better than autoloading pistols. Soon after the turn of the century, Smith & Wesson had earned a fine reputation among members of the U.S. Revolver Association, then the largest competitive handgun association in the world. In 1913, 27 of the 40 USRA records were shot with Smith & Wessons—probably almost all of them with the popular .38 Military and Police Target model. In the late 1920's, the company solicited suggestions from shooters for the development of another target gun. The consensus was to build a .22 just like the .38. And so, in 1930, Smith & Wesson introduced its "K-22 Outdoorsman," cannily named to draw sportsmen to the counter along with target shooters. The six-shot revolver featured checkered grips of Circassian walnut, a 6-inch barrel, target sights, and a trigger that broke at around 3 pounds. It weighed 35 ounces and was advertised to give inch-and-a-half groups at 50 yards.

The gun sold well, and in 1939, after a production run of just over 17,000, it was given some improvements, including a faster action and a micrometer rear sight. Called the K-22 Masterpiece, this exquisite revolver retailed for $40 in 1940, shortly before production was stopped to allow Smith & Wesson to gear up for more military guns.

Trinkets Fail; the .357 Triumphs

The success of its target revolvers failed to pull the company out of its financial pit, however. In an effort to give the firm better footing, Harold Wesson opted to diversify. His first project was a handcuff, designed and built in-house and sold at a good profit through the Peerless Handcuff Company. Peerless bought this product from Smith & Wesson until World War II, when it obtained all handcuff manufacturing equipment from the gun company.

Another venture was the production of "blade savers", a device patented by Harold Wesson for resharpening safety razor blades. Sold under the name, "Wesson Products," the blade savers didn't prove out and were discontinued in 1925 after a five-year run. A washing machine and a line of flush valves for toilets got no better reviews. As a result, by 1939 the company was close to bankruptcy.

During these troubling times, ironically, Smith & Wesson produced some of its finest revolvers. The .38/44 Heavy Duty was introduced in 1930 in re-

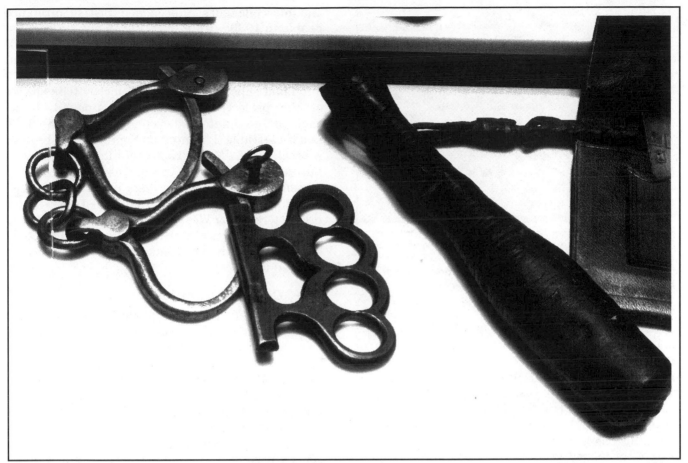

These handcuffs, brass knuckles and "Black Jack" were made by Smith & Wesson in the early 1880's.

sponse to law enforcement demands for a cartridge with even more punch than the .38 Special. Built on the "N" frame, this revolver had the strength to handle a powerful new cartridge, the .38/44, which was really a .38 Special loaded to higher velocity. A 5-inch barrel came standard, though other lengths were available. Finish was blue or nickel. The .38/44 Heavy Duty proved popular, with more than 11,000 guns produced before the model was discontinued in 1941.

A refined version of this heavy pistol—the .38/44 Outdoorsman—went into production in 1931. Available only with a blued finish, the Outdoorsman featured "Magna" walnut stocks that extended higher on the frame than standard grips. It came with a 6½-inch barrel and target sights but was dropped in 1941. Prewar production totalled 4,761.

During the 1930's, gun authority Philip B. Sharpe had worked to develop potent loads for the .38/44 Smith & Wesson Special round. He urged the company to design a new cartridge that would out-perform the .38 Special. Smith & Wesson took the idea to Winchester Repeating Arms and asked for help with the project. Subsequently, Winchester came up with a new case that was an eighth-inch longer than that of the .38 Special. It also held a heavier powder charge, one that could drive a 158-grain bullet over 1,500 fps.

Using the N frame, Smith & Wesson designed a revolver for Winchester's lively round. Because the company's marketers considered its sales potential limited, the first .357 Magnum revolvers were promoted as custom-order guns only, available in barrel lengths of 3½ to 8½ inches and a variety of sight combinations. Each gun was sighted in at the factory for 200 yards, and each owner received a registration certificate, numbered to match the gun. For this deluxe treatment, buyers shelled out $60, or about $15 more than they'd pay for any other Smith & Wesson revolver. The first .357 Magnum was presented to FBI director J. Edgar Hoover in 1935.

Demand for this powerful new gun far ex-

This large (N) frame .38-44 Outdoorsman was made just after World War II and dropped in 1966. Chambered for the .38 Special, it was built on the same frame as S&W's .44 Special revolvers.

ceeded expectations. At a first-year production rate of 120 guns a month, the company could barely keep up with orders. By 1941, when war intervened, 6,642 copies of the .357 Magnum had been built. In the hands of expert pistol shooters, the new revolver and its cartridge turned in astonishing performances. Ed McGivern, who in 1934 had used a .38 Smith & Wesson revolver to rattle five bullets into a card-sized group in two-fifths of a second, tried out the .357. After sighting in, he regularly hit man-size targets out to 600 yards.

The spectacular success of its K-22 and .357 Magnum revolvers did nothing to ease financial tensions at Smith & Wesson in the late 1930's. In an effort to salvage the company, Harold Wesson

This Model 27 .357 Magnum was first offered in 1935 by Smith & Wesson. Response was so overwhelming that demand exceeded supply for several months.

and his colleagues approached British ordnance people in 1939 with a proposal to build a new assault rifle. They convinced the British to forward $1 million in start-up money, and then scrambled to design a rifle.

Plant superintendent Ed Pomeroy took charge of the project, designing an 8¼-pound, blowback-operated autoloader chambered for the 9mm Luger cartridge. Patented on September 3, 1940, it was called the "Model 1940 Light Rifle." Tests with European ammunition (which was loaded to higher pressures than American 9mm cartridges) caused malfunctions. When the British asked for a better product, Smith & Wesson submitted two improved models—Mark I and Mark II. But before they could be produced in any quantity, Carl Hellstrom stepped in.

The "Carl Hellstrom" Era

Hellstrom, an accomplished mechanic, had worked with Smith & Wesson before as a consulting engineer assigned to improving the company's line of flush valves. Now he was called in to assist with the assault-rifle project. He began by informing management that Smith & Wesson had neither the background to design nor the capability to produce the kind of rifle required. The best course, he advised, was to petition the British to accept S&W service revolvers in payment for the million-dollar advance ($870,000 of which had already been spent). Reluctantly, Smith & Wesson followed Hellstrom's advice. The British were annoyed but accepted the proposal. Three years later, Hellstrom was elected vice president of Smith & Wesson; and when Harold Wesson died in 1946, he became the company's fifth president.

Born in Stockholm, Sweden, on January 29, 1895, Carl Reinhold Hellstrom attended Tensta School and Christiana University, where he studied civil engineering. Postgraduate work in Paris brought him an appointment as consulting engineer of the French Commission. He was sent to the United States and, in 1917, became assistant superintendent of shell production with the U.S. Army. Subsequently, he worked for Republic Steel and the Eastern Coal and Mining Corporation before being named president of the American Rack Company in 1922. His work as an independent consultant followed.

Besides salvaging the assault-rifle project, Hellstrom kept the company alive after the postwar slump. Priority was given to all orders received from police departments, and a new plant was built

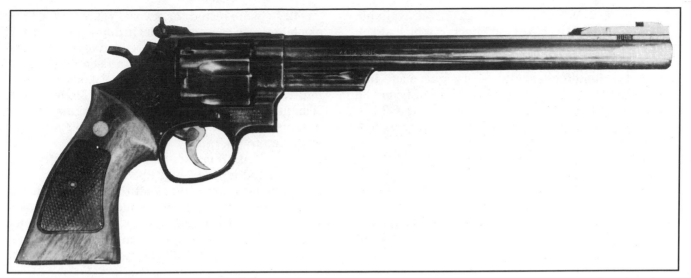

This long-barreled Smith & Wesson Model 29 .44 Magnum, which is ideal for hunting and silhouette shooting, has an adjustable front sight as well as an adjustable rear.

to revitalize the civilian line of Smith & Wesson guns. Completed in 1950, the 270,000-square-foot factory was paid for by profits from revolver sales. Hellstrom directed the renewed production of pre-war revolvers that had proven potential, but he carefully avoided the diversification that had se-

duced previous company presidents. The only exception to his "guns only" policy was the reintroduction of Smith & Wesson handcuffs in 1952.

The .44 Magnum got its start in the Hellstrom administration after Elmer Keith and other well known handgunners urged the development of a

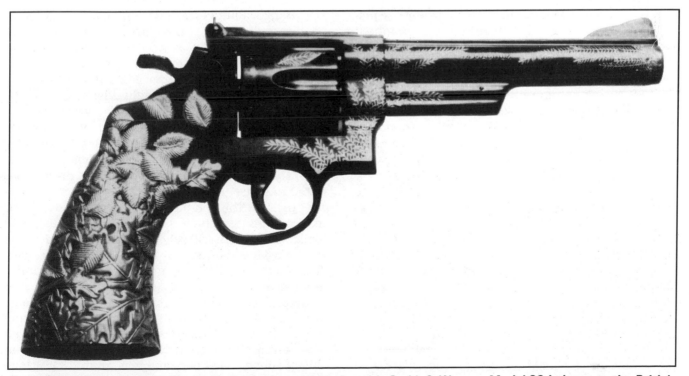

One of the most ornate revolvers existing in the world today, this Smith & Wesson Model 29 belongs to the British Royal Family. It was heavily adorned with three colors of gold at the request of the Queen's armorer.

big-bore round with more sauce than was available from the .44 Smith & Wesson Special, which at the time was chambered in the company's Model 1950 Target revolver. This gun had not sold well, but aggressive handloaders like Keith had made it a truly formidable revolver. The message from the field was: "Give the .44 what you gave the .38 in 1935. Make the gun more powerful and sales will climb."

Hellstrom listened, then consulted with Remington's R.H. Coleman. By the summer of 1954, Remington had delivered to Smith & Wesson a new .44 cartridge, one that was 1/8-inch longer than the .44 Special. Subsequent tests in a rechambered Model 1950 revolver indicated that the gun should be beefed up. A heavier barrel and stouter frame were added, boosting total weight from 40 to 47 ounces. The first commercial .44 Magnum revolver—called the Model 29—was sent to Coleman at Remington in January, 1956. Julian Hatcher of the NRA Technical Division got the second gun and Elmer Keith the third. That first year, 3,124 Model 29's were sold.

Another success during the Hellstrom era was Smith & Wesson's Model 39, a double-action 9mm autoloader (called the 52-A in civilian catalogs). Hellstrom had assigned company designer Joe Norman to develop a gun similar to the prewar Walther, and in October, 1948, he submitted a prototype pistol, stamped "X-46." Government tests prompted requests for a single-action version, to which Smith & Wesson complied in 1953. No contracts were issued, however.

Despite flagging military interest in both designs, Smith & Wesson decided in 1954 to build a double-action autoloader with an alloy frame for the civilian and police market. To hedge its bets on the acceptance of this gun, the company also continued work on a single-action. Both guns were produced—with both alloy and steel frames—late in 1955. The initial price was $65 for the single-action and $70 for the double-action. The single-action Model 44 was discontinued in 1959. Its sibling, Model 39, struggled along for a time before it eventually became a success. In 1960, the U.S. Army Marksmanship Training Unit at Fort Benning, Georgia, requested a prototype 39 chambered for a new rimless .38 cartridge, called the .38 AMU. A modest production run of 87 followed.

At the same time Joe Norman began work on Model 39, other Smith & Wesson designers had started experimenting with an autoloading .22 target pistol. The prototypes—stamped "X-41" and

"X-42"—were tested for several years before their official release as a new model in September of 1957. Model 41 met a surprisingly receptive market, and the factory was hard pressed to keep up with demand. By the end of 1958, nearly 10,000 had been built, and orders were still piling up. Model 41 has remained popular, a credit to the engineers who designed it as the best target autoloader available anywhere.

Carl Hellstrom directed other successful ventures, including the Chief Special and Bodyguard, the Highway Patrolman, and the Combat Masterpiece series. He continued to pilot Smith & Wesson through the prosperous 1950's, maintaining good relations with customers and employees alike. Then suddenly, on April 6, 1963, he died of a heart attack.

A Time of Conglomerates

The company's sixth president was William G. Gunn, a former plant superintendent and vice president. He'd started with Smith & Wesson in 1929 as a draftsman and worked his way up. A smart business manager, Gunn built on Hellstrom's postwar foundation, expanding the company's product line and increasing its profits. He was so successful that Bangor Punta, which was then actively pursuing mergers and acquisitions, tendered a stock offer that was accepted by Smith & Wesson.

Bangor Punta directed Gunn to diversify Smith & Wesson's product line through acquisitions of profitable smaller firms. Accordingly, Gunn bought Lake Erie Chemical Company (makers of tear gas munitions), General Ordnance Equipment Company (makers of "Mace" and night vision gear), Stephenson Corporation (the "Breathalyzer" people), Alcan (an ammunition and components manufacturer), and Wolfram (a maker of leather goods). Thus did the Smith & Wesson trademark subsequently appear on many products not directly related to guns.

In 1960 the company opened an academy for police training, which it expanded in 1970. There police officers are still schooled in the use and repair of firearms and other law enforcement equipment. This facility is part of a huge complex that includes a lawn with the size and look of a finely kept golf course. The factory has its own forges, unlike some other companies that buy forgings for use in making their frames and receivers. Partly because of its substantial police contracts, Smith & Wesson routinely runs three shifts and was, in mid-1991, one of the few U.S. armsmakers operating at capacity most of the time. The firm now produces 187 dis-

Though Smith & Wesson uses the most up-to-date equipment, skilled operators are still a necessity. This one readies a CNC machine for a milling operation.

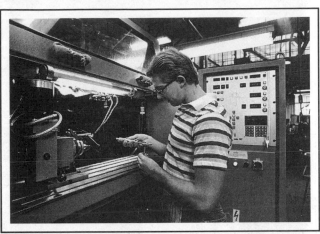

A clean workplace and sophisticated machines, as this photo demonstrates, help ensure precise shaping and proper fit of all parts.

Smith & Wesson's test tunnels swallow millions of rounds of handgun ammunition each year.

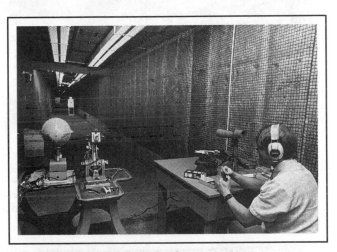

Charging the magazine of a Smith & Wesson autoloader, this shooter prepares to sight in his gun at one of the factory ranges.

These furnaces heat-treat small parts, with electronic controls and monitors ensuring proper temperatures.

Gauging and testing revolver parts, as shown above, are routine steps in the manufacturing process.

The sprawling Smith & Wesson plant in Springfield (MA) includes a police academy. The guard house facing the boulevard demonstrates the tight security common to all arms factories.

tinct shelf units (all variations of all models) and is by any measure the world's leading maker of handguns.

From a rifle that didn't work very well, and ammunition that left cork crumbs in the bore, has evolved a company that defined the American dou-ble-action revolver—and then refined the auto-loader. Smith & Wesson continues to fill the needs of hunters, competitive shooters, law officers—and people who will shoot only to protect their family, home or business. This public has indeed been well served.

CHAPTER 7

WINCHESTER: MOVING AMERICA WEST

Every arms company has its patriarch. Usually that man is the company's namesake and founder; almost always he achieved great personal success in the gun business before starting a corporation. In Remington's case, that man was a frontier mechanic determined to build a better rifle. Sam Colt secured his fame with marketing skills and initiative. And Browning Arms sprouted from the genius of a shy Mormon whose action designs changed an industry.

Winchester Repeating Arms, on the other hand, was named after a shirt salesman by the name of Oliver Fisher Winchester. He and the many people who worked with him consolidated major 19th century developments in the gun industry to give shooters the guns they wanted. Sound marketing and business practices in the early years provided this company a foothold. Now, 130 years later, the Winchester name has become a legend.

Like most other giants in the arms field, Oliver Winchester had help from history. About the time of the Civil War, opportunity called to anyone who could meld recent developments in cartridges, breech-loading and repeating mechanisms. Incorporating all of them in guns that could be produced on assembly lines would surely make a man rich. From this fertile environment Winchester and his contemporaries built the arms industry as we now know it.

When, in 1807, Alexander John Forsyth patented his method of igniting powder by hammering a loose priming mixture, external sparks were suddenly obsolete. Perfecting a percussion cap took some time, however, and half a century passed before anyone successfully marketed a useful, self-contained cartridge. The Hall rifle was America's first breechloader accepted for military service. Adopted in 1819, it used paper cartridges, but its flintlock mechanism was heavy and crude; and it was so weak that wrought-iron straps were bolted on to stiffen it.

When war with Mexico threatened to drain U.S. arsenals in 1845, American armsmakers scrambled to build more rifles. Standard issue of the day was the Harpers Ferry rifled musket, for which the John Griffiths Company of Cincinnati held a supply contract. Deliveries fell behind government needs, so to expedite manufacture of 5,000 muskets, Eliphalet Remington II was commissioned to augment Griffith's production. Remington immediately tooled up and sought talented people to help with production.

On a visit to Chicopee Falls, Massachusetts, Remington discovered the N.P. Ames Company, a sword manufacturer that had recently begun making rifles. But Ames was disenchanted with the gun business. His first government contract for a new repeating breechloader was languishing in red tape. Remington saw promise in the gun and in its buoyant Welsh designer, William Jenks. He bought the Ames gun business, including contracts, machinery, and stock, plus the services of William Jenks, for $2,581.

Walter Hunt's Cantankerous Breechloader

The first Jenks breechloaders had been flintlocks. Remington decided to fit the guns with Dr. Edward Maynard's percussion lock, which used caps on a strip of paper that advanced for each shot. In 1858, an improved breech mechanism designed by J.H. Merrill was adapted to the Jenks. Using tallow-coated cardboard cartridges, rifle and

Oliver Fisher Winchester (above) was a shirt manufacturer and one of the investors in the Volcanic Repeating Arms Company, which later became Winchester Repeating Arms.

U.S. Patent No. 6663. While his rocket balls were advancing from a tubular magazine, priming pellets were being fed by a pill-lock mechanism. The firing pin was driven by a coil spring, with the trigger doubling as a lever to move the breechbolt rearward during feeding.

Unfortunately, Hunt's rifle had several faults: the action consisted of several delicate parts within a diminutive receiver, it still relied on external priming, and the trigger's dual function limited its efficiency as a firing device. Two operating levers—one to cock the gun and another to convey a rocket ball from magazine to chamber—further complicated the operation. Nevertheless, Hunt went ahead and assigned manufacturing rights for his rifle to engine maker George A. Arrowsmith of New York. Arrowsmith saw the need for some improvements and hired gun designer Lewis Jennings to revamp the rifle. On Christmas Day, 1849, Jennings was issued U.S. Patent No. 6973 for an altered version of Hunt's repeater. It retained the tubular magazine and pill-lock primer advance but required only one operating lever to perform all the functions. It also substituted a rack-and-pinion gear for Hunt's pivoting lever, and its receiver was bigger. The Jennings could be easily converted to a single-shot breechloader or a muzzleloader as well. Despite these improvements, the gun still had serious flaws, causing Arrowsmith to look for a buyer. He found one in New York financier Courtland C. Palmer.

An aggressive businessman, Palmer quickly contracted with the Robbins and Lawrence Arms Company of Windsor, Vermont, for 5,000 Jennings rifles. The mechanism proved both troublesome to make and unreliable to use. Consequently, Palmer's early guns were marketed as single-shot breechloaders. He then turned to Horace Smith for a redesign of the Jennings action. In August, 1851, Smith was issued U.S. Patent No. 8317 for his improvements, which included a return to the pivoting ring used in the original Hunt rifle. Smith kept Jennings' single-lever mechanism, but he eliminated the trigger guard.

About this time, gun designer Benjamin Tyler Henry joined Horace Smith in his Norwich, Connecticut, shop. There the two men further refined the Jennings rifle and formed, along with Daniel B. Wesson, a new limited partnership under the name of Smith & Wesson. In February, 1854, U.S. Patent No. 10535 was granted to Horace Smith and Daniel Wesson for a much modified lever-action repeater and its metallic cartridge (patent No. 11496 was issued six months later to cover the cartridge).

ammunition alike performed flawlessly in government tests that included a one-minute submersion in water. This first truly successful breechloader made in the U.S. was followed only a year later by Walter Hunt's new rifle. Like Jenks, Hunt was an idea man whose inventions covered a broad field. Among other things, he designed a flax-spinner, an iceboat, a nail-making machine, a fountain pen, and even the safety pin. Hunt also perfected a lockstitch needle around 1833, but he never received a patent for it. Twelve years later, Elias Howe developed a similar device, which he patented. While Hunt lost the glory and wealth he could have had as inventor of the sewing machine, his contributions to the gun industry have been recognized as pivotal.

In August, 1848, Hunt received U.S. Patent No. 5701 for a conical lead bullet, which he called a "rocket ball" (see also Ch. 1 for details). The 54-caliber rifle Hunt built for this bullet—the Volition Repeater, as he called it—appeared in 1849, under

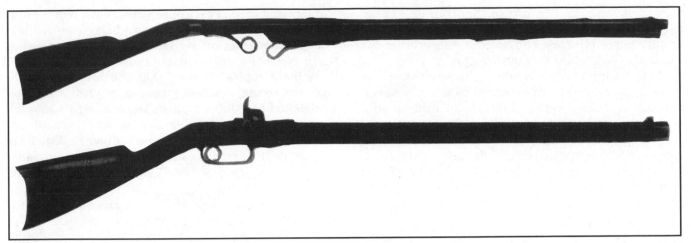

The 1848 Hunt rifle (top photo) fired a "rocket ball" with its propellant in a hollow base; this prompted later developments, such as the Jennings rifle (bottom photo) that helped spawn Winchester Repeating Arms.

While Benjamin Tyler Henry was not named in either patent, he strongly influenced the design of both rifle and ammunition.

The cartridge described in these patents had a metallic case tapering outward near its base (almost like a rim, but not folded). Priming mixture was first spread all over the inside of the cartridge head, then a metal disc was inserted to confine the primer and act as an anvil. Since a hit anywhere on the head would detonate the primer, this round served as both rimfire and centerfire.

Unfortunately for Smith and Wesson, the machinery of their day could not produce these cartridges economically. Undaunted, the partners unearthed Hunt's rocket ball design and reworked it. A fulminate-of-mercury primer was placed in a glass cup resting on an iron anvil within the bullet's cavity. A cork base wad sealed the propellant and helped seal the breech upon firing. In Hunt's repeaters, the wad, or its residue, was left in the barrel to be ejected by succeeding rounds. But Smith and his crew found the cork debris caused malfunctions; moreover, the internal primer kept misfiring because the cork cushioned the striker. The solution was a copper base cap, later changed to brass. The iron anvil was also changed to brass. These alterations prompted another improvement—a firing pin-extractor designed by Hicks—that came into use in 1856.

The first Smith & Wesson repeaters, built in 1854, were pistols built on the revamped Hunt-Jennings design. Designated "Number One" and "Number Two," they came in calibers 30 and 38, with 4- and 8-inch barrels, respectively. About a thousand copies were made before the company acquired Rollin White's revolver patents a year later.

In June of 1855, a group of 40 New York and New Haven businessmen formed the Volcanic Repeating Arms Company, and a month later they bought out Smith, Wesson and Palmer. Incorporated in Connecticut with a capitalization of $150,000 (6,000 shares of common stock at $25 a share), the company received "exclusive use and control of all patents and patent rights which the said Smith and the said Wesson or either of them can or may hereafter obtain or acquire for inventions or improvements in firearms or power of granting licenses, conveying shares and rights, receiving rents and royalties, and recovering and collecting damages

The Volcanic Repeating Arms Company, which operated from this building, was incorporated in 1855.

for infringements." In return, Smith and Wesson received $65,000 cash in three installments, plus 2,800 shares of stock and an undisclosed sum for their Norwich plant and machinery.

The financiers of this new venture included two bakers, two grocers, three carriage makers, seven clock makers and representatives of other manufacturing, marketing and shipping concerns. One of the biggest shareholders was shipping magnate Nelson B. Gaston, who became Volcanic's first president. Another investor was shirt maker Oliver Fisher Winchester, now 45 years old. Though he held only 80 shares of stock, he was elected the company's director.

Oliver Winchester and the Volcanics

Oliver Winchester's family had come early to America, starting in 1635, when John Winchester sailed from England at the age of 19 and landed near Boston. There he and his descendants remained for the most part. Oliver's father, a farmer named Samuel, had 10 children by two previous marriages before his third wife bore Oliver and his twin brother Samuel C., the youngest of her five children. Oliver's father died a year after the twins were born, and there was little money left to the family. So Oliver was forced to work on farms from the time he was seven, attending school only in winter. At 14, he was apprenticed to a carpenter and became a master builder.

In 1830, Winchester moved from Boston to Baltimore, where for three years he contracted for and supervised the construction of homes. After investigating the retail dry goods business, he opened a men's furnishings store in Baltimore in 1834. Despite a financial panic in 1837, Oliver expanded his business by opening a downtown store. It too was successful, and for 10 more years he prospered. During this time, he and his wife Jane Ellen had three children: Ann Rebecca, William Wirt, and Hannah Jane.

In 1847, Winchester decided the world could use a better shirt. In shirts of that era, the neckbands were notoriously uncomfortable, a problem he resolved with a curved seam on top of the shoulder. Subsequently, he sold his Baltimore business and moved to State Street in New Haven. A patent (U.S. 5421) for his new shirt design was granted in February, 1848.

The following year, Oliver Winchester teamed up with John M. Davies, a leading New York importer of men's furnishings. Their partnership, known as Winchester & Davies, built a new man-

ufacturing facility on Court Street, with Winchester supervising shirt production and Davies handling sales and marketing. By 1860, Winchester & Davies had become a substantial enterprise, with an investment capital of $400,000 and some 500 foot-pedal sewing machines plus a payroll that approached $17,000 a month. The company's annual production of 480,000 shirts was valued at $600,000. Thus, by 1855, when Oliver F. Winchester made his first investment in the arms company that would one day bear his name, he was living quite comfortably.

One of Winchester's first actions at Volcanic Repeating Arms was to move the company from Norwich to New Haven. Included with the gun-making machinery in that move were 600 finished and unfinished repeating pistols. Daniel Wesson stayed on as shop superintendent or plant manager until 1856, when he joined Horace Smith to build another now famous gun firm. He was succeeded at Volcanic by William C. Hicks, who later relinquished the shop superintendent job to B. Tyler Henry. The first Volcanic guns came off the line in February, 1856. At that time, the plant's labor force numbered about 50, including four young women who were responsible for the ammunition. The work week—six 10-hour days—was common for that period. Most parts were fabricated in-house, though outside firms supplied Volcanic with its cast bronze frames (receivers), mild steel barrels, and walnut stock blanks.

Volcanic offered a greater variety of pistols than Smith and Wesson had, but all came under the same heading: "Navy Pistols." Most were made in 38 caliber with barrels 6 and 8 inches long. Bronze receivers replaced the earlier steel ones because they proved easier to make. Customers could order detachable shoulder stocks and 16-inch barrels on request. Volcanic carbines were also sold with 16-, 20- and 24-inch barrels, but they did not sell well. The ammunition, while considered adequate for traditional handgun use, lacked the power and range shooters expected even of muzzleloading rifles. Volcanic's bullets and powder charges weighed only half as much as the popular big game loads of the day. Because smokeless powder and bottleneck cases were still 30 years in the future, it was common practice to assess the effectiveness of ammunition by weighing it.

Nonetheless, Volcanic's fabulous claims followed both pistols and carbines to market. On November 17, 1856, the New Haven Journal-Courier reported that "an accomplished marksman," a Col-

The tab in front of the receiver of this brass-framed Volcanic rifle is a magazine follower that moves the full length of the magazine tube.

onel Hay of the British Army, had used a Volcanic Repeating Pistol to fire nine balls in rapid succession "at an 8 inch diameter target at 100 yards." All hit the mark. "He [Hay] then moved back to a distance of 200 yards and fired 9 balls more, hitting the target seven times. He then moved back 100 yards further, a distance of 300 yards from the mark, and placed 5 of the 9 balls inside the ring, and hitting the bull's eye twice." Even Oliver Winchester couldn't swallow that. His ballisticians later indicated that Hay's chances against a perfect score at 100 yards were about 11 to 1. At 200 yards, a seven-for-nine score was likely only once in 70 tries; and at 300 yards, Hay had one chance in 7,140 of making five hits.

The poor performance of its carbines crippled Volcanic Repeating Arms. But even strong demand could not have sustained the firm's fragile financial base. Nearly half of Volcanic's 6,000 original shares had been allocated to Smith and Wesson, whose $65,000 cash claim depleted the $80,000 in stock value remaining. Machinery and operating costs, along with a controversial $11,000 demand by two clients for the shipment of faulty Volcanic guns, added to the burden. Soon Oliver Winchester and company president Gaston were securing their company's loans with personal mortgages. By August of 1856, Winchester had invested over $25,000.

When Gaston died in December, 1856, Winchester became president and purchased Gaston's mortgages. Although he planned to continue making Volcanic rifles and pistols, creditors forced the firm into receivership in February, 1857. On the 18th of that month, The Volcanic Repeating Arms Company was declared insolvent, with Samuel Talcott and

R.B. Bennett named as trustees. On March 15, Oliver Winchester purchased all company assets for just under $40,000, which was barely enough to cover claims against the corporation. Despite this setback, Winchester saw a bright future for the lever action repeater. In April, 1857, he reorganized Volcanic Repeating Arms into the New Haven Arms Company with an authorized capital of $50,000 (2,000 shares at $25 each). Eleven investors joined Winchester, seven of whom were carryovers from the Volcanic Arms venture.

Having purchased 800 shares of stock in the company, Winchester was a natural to become its president (he also served as treasurer). On May 1, 1857, The New Haven Arms Company purchased from Winchester for $25,000 all the tooling and machinery he'd acquired from Volcanic. Another $15,000 was assessed for the right to manufacture firearms and ammunition under Volcanic's patents, which had also been assigned to Winchester. The total roughly equaled the value of the claims Winchester had held against Volcanic. His 800 shares in the new company cost him $20,000, so he came away with $20,000 in cash, plus ownership of the patents and beneficial interest in the covenant signed by Smith and Wesson in 1855 (10 years later, he exchanged those rights for a substantial block of stock in Winchester Repeating Arms).

Henry's Rimfire Rescues Winchester

The New Haven Arms Company needed a shop foreman, and so Winchester turned to Benjamin Tyler Henry, who was then 36. Under Henry, the firm continued production of Volcanic guns with few significant changes. The 38-caliber Volcanic Navy Pistols were, by 1858, also available in 30 and 40 caliber (the .30's with barrels 4 and 6 inches long, the .40's with barrels of 6 and 8 inches). Pistols with 8- and 16-inch barrels could be ordered with shoulder stocks. Carbines retained their early barrel lengths (16, 21 and 25 inches) and finish (blued barrels with polished brass frames). Barrel lengths varied by as much as half an inch from specification, and no "rifle" versions were offered. Pistols sold better than carbines. Serial numbers ran from 1 to over 3,200. During this period, black powder was substituted for some of the fulminate in Volcanic ammunition.

A year after New Haven Repeating Arms began operations, Winchester wrote to Smith & Wesson: "We have in contemplation to open an office on Broadway, N.Y., for the sale of our arms and should perhaps like to make an arrangement with you to sell yours if we can do so in a manner mutually satisfactory. What do you think?'' When nothing came of this proposal, Winchester contracted with J.W. Storrs of New York to act as his company agent there. New Haven guns were discounted to dealers at rates determined by volume (a 20 percent discount applied on gun orders over $100, 25 percent on orders over $1,000, and 30 percent off on shipments totaling at least $5,000). Ammunition orders over $100 were given a 20 percent break. Winchester did not allow consignment sales, vigorously encouraging his dealers to sell New Haven products "at list price and in all cases for net cash." He tried to accommodate wholesalers and big, profitable dealerships that sought exclusive marketing rights.

In June, 1859, the factory was moved to No. 9 Artizan Street in New Haven, but no improvements were made in Volcanic ammunition—and improvements were needed. The bullet was too skinny and light. Compared to the performance of contemporary bullets in single-shot rifles like the Sharps, it had no pep. Its shallow base cavity limited the powder charge and velocity. Besides, the gun's mechanism didn't seal gas, and firing pins (nipples) wore out quickly.

These serious flaws worried Oliver Winchester, who knew his firm's reputation lay with its ammunition. And so, in 1858, he directed B. Tyler Henry to adapt the Volcanic rifle to metallic rimfire cartridges. Having labored over the Hunt and Jennings designs for 10 years without patent recognition, Henry was finally rewarded in 1860 with U.S. patent 30,446. It covered a lever action rimfire repeating rifle with a 15-round tubular magazine and a two-pronged firing pin that came down on both sides of the rim of a chambered case. A movable breech pin that fit loosely in the breechblock transmitted nearly the entire thrust of the hammer to the firing pin (in previous rifles the block had absorbed much of the blow). Henry's spring-steel extractor was mounted on the bolt face, as with many of today's rifles, and its barrel-length magazine was the slotted, front-loading tube of its forebears.

Several of these first few hundred "Henrys" had iron frames, but brass quickly became standard. Engraving, plating, special sights and other options were available on all Henry rifles but were not encouraged. Brisk demand kept the guns plain. Early Henrys had jointed hickory wiping rods stored under a trap in the crescent buttplate. Later rifles came with jointed steel rods. Each Henry rifle

bore a serial number, starting with 1, continuing an uninterrupted sequence for about six years. After that, serial numbers for Model 1866 Winchester were mixed with numbers for the Henry, with most high numbers in the series going to the former.

The Henry's cartridge featured a .44 caliber, 216-grain pointed bullet astride 26 grains of black powder, for a muzzle velocity of about 1,025 fps. Later, the bullet was lightened to 200 grains to boost speed. The .44 Flat, also with a 200-grain bullet, was developed about this time as an alternative. Chamber dimensions were identical. Both cartridges were subsequently chambered in Winchester's Model 1866 rifle, and the .44 Pointed round was listed for some Colt revolvers. Anemic by modern standards, the .44 Henry rimfires developed 10 times the muzzle energy of the old Volcanic bullets. In fact, this cartridge drew as much attention in its time as the complex and revolutionary rifle chambered for it.

Volcanic bullets featured grease grooves that, filled with tallow, helped prevent bore leading and improved accuracy. A new tallow-based lubricant was used in the .44 rimfire ammunition. It had a higher melting point to prevent it from running into the powder when it got warm. Bullets were crimped in the .44 Henry to prevent loosening under recoil or the press of the magazine spring. Originally, pointed ammunition sold for $25 per 1,000, with cartridges packed in cases of 2,000 each.

Because the Henry rifle required new tooling, commercial production was delayed until 1862. The rifle was assembled at the New Haven plant, but its parts came from other firms—barrel steel from English and Atwater locally, and swivels from Colt in Hartford. In addition, spring steel came from Ichabod, Washburn and Moen, and lever blanks from the Arcade Malleable Iron Company, both of Worcester, Massachusetts. Gunsmiths working for New Haven Repeating Arms earned $2 per day in 1860, but only two years later they were making as much as $4.50 per day. A plain Henry rifle then cost around $40.

In return for Benjamin Tyler Henry's design work, for which Winchester admitted "difficulties of estimating the real value," the company had agreed to pay its chief engineer $12,500 for his patent, in addition to an annual salary of $1,500. On behalf of New Haven Arms, Winchester then offered Henry the option of a 5,000-rifle contract in lieu of salary. In-house contract work had become commonplace at other plants of that era, and Winchester had already experimented with it. Contracted workmen were responsible for producing a part or assembly for a certain price. They bore all production costs, including the wages of people they deemed necessary to complete the project (although company employees were paid directly by the firm). Under this arrangement, B. Tyler Henry earned $15,000 in five years, double what he would have made from regular wages.

No patents were taken out on Henry's rimfire cartridges, which were head-stamped "H" in his honor, probably because Henry did not believe the design patentable. He may even have been unaware of the work done by Smith and Wesson that resulted in the manufacture of .22 rimfire cartridges beginning in January of 1858. Henry began engineering his .44 rounds in the fall of that same year. When his rifle and its ammunition made their debut in 1860, it was just in time to prop up a nearly bankrupt New Haven Repeating Arms. The slide had begun not long after the company was formed; indeed, if Tyler Henry and the Civil War had not intervened, Winchester and his company might have perished.

Repeating Rifles Change the Pace of War

"Probably it will modify the art of war; possibly it may revolutionize the whole science of war," Winchester wrote sometime in the early 1860's. "Where is the military genius . . . (to) so modify the science of war as to best develop the capacities of this terrible engine—the exclusive use of which would enable any government . . . to rule the world?"

In ancient times this might have been written about the horse; a modern essayist might so describe the atomic bomb. But the hyperbole came from Oliver Winchester's appeal to the U.S. Government for military adoption of the Henry repeater. In addition to the advantages of its increased firepower, the breech-loading repeater was proving safer to operate in battle. After the war, a Navy Ordnance report showed how battle tensions rendered muzzleloading rifles dangerous:

"Of the whole number (27,574 guns collected after the battle) . . . we found at least 24,000 of these loaded; about one half of these contained two loads each, one fourth from three to ten loads each and the balance one load each. . . . In many of these guns, from two to six balls have been found with only one charge of powder. In some, the balls have been found at the bottom of the bore with the charge of powder on top of the ball. In some as many as six paper regulation-caliber 58 cartridges have been found, the cartridges having been put in the guns without being torn or broken. Twenty-three loads were found in one Springfield rifle-musket, each loaded in regular order."

A bright future certainly existed for cartridge repeaters, but Winchester immediately ran into fierce competition from the seven-shot Spencer lever action repeating rifle. Designed by Christopher Spencer in 1860, it quickly became the most popular breechloader in the Civil War. While 1,731 Henrys were bought for use by Union soldiers, 12,471 Spencer rifles and 94,196 Spencer carbines saw service during the war. The only other repeater of significance was Colt's Revolving Rifle, of which 4,612 were issued. At a unit price of $37.50, a Spencer rifle cost only 50 cents more than the Henry and $6.50 less than the Colt. Spencer carbines, at $25.40 each, were a real bargain. Ammunition for the Spencer, which fired a 56 caliber, 350-grain bullet driven by 45 grains of powder, cost a tenth of a cent more per round (2.44¢) than a .44 Henry cartridge. By war's end, 58,238,924 Spencer rounds had been bought, compared with only 4,610,000 cartridges for the Henry.

Christopher Spencer had learned the gun trade early on. Now in his 30's, he'd worked at the Colt armory during the 1850's, when Colt was expanding its facility and experimenting with mass-production techniques. Spencer soon began work on his own gun designs. Anticipating conflict-of-interest problems with Colt management, he left the company to work for Cheney Silk Mills in Manchester, Connecticut. The owner, Charles Cheney, wisely let his talented young employee work on gun projects at the company's machine shop during off hours. By 1859, while Christian Sharps was still adapting his breech-loading carbine for combustible ammu-

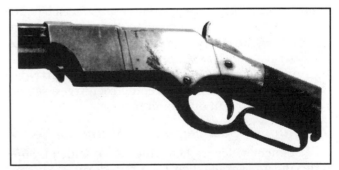

This Henry rifle fired a .44 rimfire cartridge that generated much more power than the Volcanic's bullet. Though the Spencer repeater saw more action in the Civil War, many Henry's were bought privately by Union soldiers who preferred them to the Spencer.

nition, Christopher Spencer had built several wooden models for a new repeating rifle. The mechanism was patented (No. 27,393) on March 6, 1860.

Soon after, Spencer joined the flood of inventors and armsmakers hounding the government for contracts in the first months of the Civil War. He had no luck until Charles Cheney intervened in the form of a personal recommendation to Gideon Wells, Secretary of the Navy. In June, 1861, Spencer's rifle was tested at the Washington Navy Yard and passed muster. With the Navy's admonition that the extractor seemed to be his rifle's weakest feature, Spencer received the first of many contracts. A year later, he replaced the original sawtooth extractor with a leaf arrangement that worked much better.

The then-Chief of Ordnance, General Ripley, strongly opposed the military use of any breechloaders, claiming the rifles were too heavy when loaded. Moreover, these rifles and their ammunition together were much more expensive than the muzzleloading armament in service. A high rate of fire encouraged waste in battle, the general said, creating supply problems. So when President Lincoln finally told Ripley to contract with Spencer for 10,000 rifles, it was like a crack in the dam for the ambitious inventor, as well as other gun designers of the day.

Spencer spent most of 1862 tooling up. The rifles were to be chambered for his .56/56 rimfire cartridge. This round was named, strangely enough, for the case diameters in front of the rim and at the mouth. Rifles from Spencer's first production run had 30-inch barrels and weighed 10 pounds empty. Later, he offered an 8³⁄₄-pound carbine version with a 22-inch barrel. It proved hugely popular, especially with the Union cavalry, who used it to supplement their .44 percussion revolvers and a saber. A cartridge box, patented on December 20, 1864, allowed the Spencer to be reloaded very quickly. While the buttstock magazines common to both Army and Navy Spencers could be fed with individual cartridges, the new wooden cartridge box with its tin-lined tubes could recharge a seven-round magazine in one hand motion.

The Rugged Spencer vs. the Mercurial Henry

Spencer rifles and carbines gave Union troops a terrific advantage over the Confederates who, by war's end, were still armed largely with muzzleloading guns. Colonel John T. Wilder of the 17th Indiana regiment, Army of the Cumberland, wrote to the Spencer Company describing how, on June 24, 1863, at Hoover's Gap in Tennessee, ". . . one of my regiments fairly defeated a rebel brigade of five regiments, they admitting a loss of over 500, while our loss was forty-seven."

In his experience, Wilder continued, the Spencer ammunition is ". . . the cheapest kind for the service as it does not wear out in the cartridge boxes and has the quality of being waterproof—the men of my command carry 100 rounds of ammunition in their saddle bags, and in two instances went into a fight immediately after swimming their horses across streams twelve feet deep and it is very rare that a single cartridge fails to fire."

Captain Barber, commanding the First Battalion of Ohio Volunteer Sharpshooters, had similar praise. Of a Kentucky battle in 1863, he wrote: "We found by actual trial that our guns had longer range and greater accuracy. We seldom missed at 700 yards. I had 125 men with me, and for two weeks kept 600 Rebels at bay, and as I afterwards learned, killed and wounded over thirty, with a loss of one man wounded. . . . General Reynolds, Chief of staff, said to me, [The Spencer] is the best rifle on the face of the earth, and I am fully convinced that his remark is literally true."

The Army preferred the Spencer to the Henry mainly because it was a sturdier gun. However, many Henrys were bought by soldiers with money from their own pockets, with the understanding that the government would furnish ammunition for them. In fact, of 10,000-odd Henry rifles produced during the Civil War, some 8,500 probably were carried into battle. According to Winchester records, orders for 100,000 Henrys received during the last half of the war could not be filled because of low production capacity.

The Henry's major fault was its long underbarrel magazine tube, further weakened by a full-length slot. Dents rendered the follower unreliable, and debris worked its way into the slot. But the rifle had two advantages over the Spencer: one, it held 15 rounds to the Spencer's seven; and two, a single motion of the lever both reloaded and cocked the gun, while the Spencer required a separate cocking motion after the lever closed. With its "delicate" 15-shot magazine and blistering speed of fire, many soldiers opted to baby their Henrys. Major Joel W. Cloudman of the First D.C. Cavalry observed that the Spencer was "a good arm," but not the equal of the Henry. "The Henry excels all others in accuracy and force. It is also the most durable arm. . . . [and] almost any soldier can repair one if needed. . . . It is a very safe arm, as there is no half cock to it. The hammer is either down or clear back. Great danger attends the use of common arms from the fact of their going off so often at half cock. Another advantage is that it is so easily and quickly loaded. . . .

"But the best evidence in favor of the Henry rifle," Major Cloudman continued, "does not come from its friends or from our own people who use it. It comes from the enemy. I was captured last season and was for a time in the Libby Prison. Several of these rifles were taken when I was, and I often heard the enemy discuss its merits. They all feared it more than any arm in our service and I have heard them say, 'Give us anything but your d----d Yankee rifle that can be loaded on Sunday and fired all week.' "

Winchester became the best-known name in guns all over the world due in part to its link with the romance of the American West.

Ever the entrepreneur, Winchester traveled to Switzerland after the war to enter the Henry in Swiss ordnance trials. Its high marks earned a first place showing and recommendation for adoption, but no sale was ever completed. One problem common to both Spencer and Henry rifles was the sickly performance of their ammunition compared to that delivered by the Sharps and other stout single-shots. Nineteenth-century metallurgy simply couldn't produce a rimfire case strong enough to take higher pressures without making the rim too stiff for indentation by the striker. Once case alloys and forming procedures were improved, this situation was corrected, but for many years it kept repeating rifles from clearing the market of single-shots. Another factor that kept pressures—and velocities—so low was action strength. To make a repeating rifle portable, action parts had to be made as compact as possible; and once again, metals of the day weren't up to the task.

To boost the performance of military cartridges, U.S. Ordnance Board members recommended (September 24, 1863) that ". . . a minimum [powder] charge be established at 1/10 the weight of the ball." The 1862 Henry bullet, at 216 grains, was comfortably below maximum weight for its 34-grain powder charge; i.e., the charge was sufficient to thrust the little bullet at acceptable velocity. The Spencer bullet of that period, however, weighed more than 10 times its 34-grain powder charge. It's unclear how this determination would have affected future contracts, given such glowing reports of Spencer ammunition in battle. But commercial .56/56 Spencer ammunition subsequently featured a 45-grain powder charge behind the 350-grain bullet. Muzzle velocity then equaled that of the much lighter Henry. Neither could compete with bullets pushed by 60 grains of powder in the Sharps.

Despite its brilliant design, the Spencer rifle did not fare well after the war—nor did the company, which remained in business only 10 years (1860 through 1869). Part of the problem was that rimfire ammunition had limited potential, even with stronger cases and loading techniques that ensured more uniform priming. But even before centerfire ammunition made its debut, Winchester had forced the Spencer Company out of business with a new rifle.

Winchester's "Yellow Boy" Anchors a Dynasty

In 1865, Oliver Winchester asked the state legislature for a charter to change his firm's name to the Henry Repeating Arms Company. One year later the legislature also approved Winchester's application for a second name change to Winchester Repeating Arms, and on December 30, 1866, the first stock was issued. The incorporators—Oliver Winchester, E.A. Mitchell, Morris Tyler and Henry Hooker—set the first stockholders meeting for February 20, 1867. At that time, they adopted bylaws and elected directors Winchester, Mitchell, Nathaniel Wheeler and John Davies. Davies had been Winchester's shirt partner, and all the men had strong business credentials; but none except Winchester had been in any way connected with the New Haven Arms Company. In a directors' meeting that followed, James Wilson was added to the group and Winchester became president and treasurer. Mitchell was elected vice-president and Oliver Davis secretary.

Shareholders in the New Haven (or Henry Repeating) Arms Company were given the option of a cash buyout of stocks at $182 per share, or an exchange for shares of Winchester Repeating Arms at a par value of $100. About a third of the stocks were cashed out. Oliver Winchester owned 2,040 shares in the company, and his family held an additional 450. The new firm began operations with a net worth of about $450,000—but only $71,000 in working capital. The credit available to Winchester and others on the board no doubt proved crucial during the first months of production.

In 1867, the New Haven company transferred its plant equipment to a building in Bridgeport owned by Wheeler and Wilson's Sewing Machine Company. This move allowed Winchester Repeating Arms to expand from a work force of 100 men to one of over 250 at little cost. By this time, B. Tyler Henry had left the company, and Nelson King was shop foreman. In 1866, King redesigned the Henry rifle's troublesome magazine by engineering a spring-loaded port into the receiver. Cartridges could then be thumbed in, just as they are on today's Winchester 94 and Marlin 336 rifles. King was issued a patent for this change which, with the addition of a wooden forend, gave the Winchester Repeating Arms Company a brand new rifle.

Like the Henry, the Winchester Model 1866 was chambered for .44 Pointed and .44 Flat rimfire cartridges. It retained the Henry's brass frame and buttplate and was offered in carbine, rifle and musket styles (muskets did not appear until the fourth year of production). Model 66 featured 20-, 24- and 27-inch barrels (all round), with magazine capacities of 17 for the rifle and musket, 13 for the carbine. The guns weighed from 7¾ to 9½ pounds. While

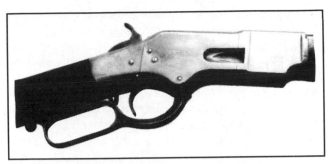

The Winchester Model 66 (above), called "Yellow Boy" for its brass frame, featured a loading gate and solid magazine tube.

the components and ammunition of this famous rifle were grossly inferior to those found in modern guns, its overall design and handling characteristics proved good enough to survive a dozen decades of gun-building. Indeed, some rifles still in production look very much like the old Model 66 that gave Winchester its first secure grip in the market.

After Model 1866 was introduced, Winchester stopped making Henry rifles. The company's 1867 catalog assured the public that the new gun "remains in the mechanism for loading and firing precisely the same as the Henry," but it also had some improvements. These improvements did not, the catalog emphasized, affect its rate of fire. "The whole fifteen cartridges can be fired in fifteen and a half seconds," it claimed, "or at a rate of sixty shots a minute, or in double-quick time, in seven and a half seconds, or at a rate of one hundred and twenty shots per minute, or two shots per second."

The Model 1866 effectively killed off the Spencer. Henrys had always been a little trimmer and easier to handle on horseback, so when America's pioneers headed west after the war, they chose the Henry. Its quicker operation and larger magazine capacity no doubt added to the settlers' peace of mind as they remained on the lookout for hostile Indians. And when Nelson King corrected the Henry's magazine problem, Winchester was guaranteed an impregnable spot in the market. Thousands of rifle buyers turned down war-surplus Spencers for as little as $7 to pick up a Winchester 66 that cost $50 (cartridges cost $20 a thousand). Later, when Winchester's Model 1873 supplanted the 66, the latter's price was cut to $28; and in 1878 it was again reduced, to $22. By 1884 you could buy one for $14.50, and enough people took advantage of this bargain to keep the 66 in production until 1898. In all, about 170,000 were built. Now even a well-worn 66 (also called "Yellow Boy" for its brass receiver) can fetch several thousand dollars.

In 1868, Winchester acquired the Spencer Repeating Rifle Company, and a year later it bought the American Repeating Rifle Company (formerly the Fogarty Arms Company). Since Winchester did not manufacture guns from either company, these purchases were apparently made to eliminate the competition.

Encouraged by public demand for its Model 66 in the U.S., Winchester took it to England to compete in ordnance trials there. The Henry had been tested previously by the British and earned favorable comments; now Winchester hoped the King improvement would bring sales. But even though the 66 beat all other repeating rifles submitted, British ordnance officers were obviously not ready for a repeater. "There may, however, be occasions when a repeating arm might be useful," they assured Winchester, "and, if such should be the opinion of the military authorities, the Committee recommends that the Winchester arm should be taken as being the best." But not yet.

Foreign Deals, Super Salesmen, A New Plant

Foreign sales were bound to pick up, though. Winchester got its big break in 1866, when Benito Juarez, the Mexican leader who opposed Emperor Maximillian, ordered 1,000 rifles and 500,000 rounds of ammunition. When Winchester salesman Thomas Emmett Addis received the goods, he waited in Brownsville, Texas, to hear from Juarez, who'd promised to pay on delivery. Defying company orders not to leave the country, Addis smuggled the arms across the Rio Grande to Monterrey. There he rented an empty store, where he could guard the guns and ammo until Juarez's people arrived.

The buyers finally arrived—but they refused to pay, whereupon Addis threatened to sell the guns to Maximillian if the money wasn't forthcoming. The next day, Addis left town in a hired coach with $57,000 in his pockets. During the grueling three-day trip home, he kept sticking a scarf pin in his thigh lest he fall asleep and become easy prey for the driver and his guards.

Born Thomas O'Connor, Addis was truly one of Winchester's most colorful salesmen. After running away from home at the age of 12, he found work as a filer at Remington's Ilion (NY) plant. Later he moved over to Winchester, eventually becoming the company's first salesman with unlimited territory and the authority to conduct any company

Thomas Emmett Addis (above) engineered the first big foreign sale for the New Haven Arms Company, receiving $57,000 in silver for 1000 rifles sold to Mexico in 1866.

the Americans, an Armenian Turk and naturalized U.S. citizen named Oscanyan accompanied Bey. In a suit he brought later against Winchester, Oscanyan claimed he steered Bey toward Winchester rifles instead, and that without his help Bey would have bought Spencers instead of Model 66's. In November, 1870, the order came in from the Turkish government: 15,000 muskets at $28 each and 5,000 carbines at $20 each (a second contract in August, 1871, specified an additional 30,000 muskets) for a total sale of $1.36 million.

Spurred by these foreign government orders, Winchester stockholders voted to buy land in New Haven for a new plant. The Bridgeport facility was dismantled and, in 1871, a new one completed at the corner of Munson and Canal Street (later changed to Winchester Avenue) in New Haven. The land cost about $12,000, and the three-story, 103,000-square-foot brick plant came in at just under $80,000.

During the late 1820's and early '30s, New Haven had become one of New England's leading ports. A canal had recently been dug from the harbor all the way to Massachusetts, allowing goods from the clipper ships to be ferried up the canal to various ports. The canal's charter permitted the construction of a railway along its tow path, however, and by the time Winchester moved to New Haven, the railroad had already taken over as the city's primary means of transportation. Parts of the old canal are still visible a few miles north of the old Winchester plant.

In 1870, Thomas Gray Bennett, a recent Yale graduate, began work for Winchester. The following year, when Oliver Winchester's son William became vice president, Bennett was elected company secretary, later becoming a vice president, and finally president. When Winchester bought a half-interest in E. Remington & Sons in 1888, Bennett served as vice president of the reorganized Remington Arms Company under Marcellus Hartley. He retained that post until Winchester withdrew its interest in 1896.

Bennett's work was crucial to the design of the Winchester Model 1873, which was an improvement on the Model 1866 and, more importantly, the company's first centerfire rifle. This new gun, which was chambered for the .44 WCF or .44-40, launched a 200-grain bullet with 28 grains of black powder. With a muzzle velocity of 1300 fps, this bullet generated nearly 30 percent more energy than the .44 Henry—and over 12 times the energy of the old Volcanic bullet. The brass frame of the 1866 was

business without approval. He would accept coffee, lumber and other commodities in exchange for rifles, and he often negotiated with other arms companies and with foreign governments. He tried to change his name to Thomas Addis Emmett, after the celebrated Irish patriot, but a clerk recorded it as Thomas Emmett Addis. He worked for Winchester for 35 years, until 1901.

In 1870, Winchester struck more lucrative foreign deals. The Peruvian government ordered $36,000 in goods, and then a French order came in for 3,000 muskets, 3,000 carbines and 4.5 million cartridges. Remington was so busy filling other contracts, however, it had to pass this French work along to others. The real plum that year was an order from Turkey. Anticipating war with Russia in the late 1860's, Turkey was in the market for rifles. Accordingly, a Turkish Army officer named Ruston Bey was sent to the U.S. in 1869 to inquire about Spencer rifles. To help him negotiate with

Thomas Gray Bennett was Oliver Winchester's son-in-law and company president from 1890 to 1910, when he retired at age 65 following 40 years of service.

dropped in favor of forged iron, which was replaced in turn with steel in 1884. A sliding action lid kept out dust and snow. Standard barrels were round and 20, 24 and 30 inches long (special barrels of 14, 16 and 18 inches also became popular with rubber workers in South America). Though Model 1873 was ready for market in its name year, manufacturing problems with both rifle and ammunition limited its production. Only 18 rifles were shipped in 1873, but by 1875 the problems had been solved and the new gun was offered in quantity to an eager public.

During the early 1870's, Winchester gained the services of a German immigrant and gun designer named Hugo Borchardt whose main interest was in revolvers. He engineered five 44-caliber revolvers, all with features that put them ahead of their time. Winchester submitted samples of each to the U.S. Navy and Russian Ordnances, but no orders came and the guns were not produced. Borchardt left

Winchester to join the Sharps Rifle Company, which introduced the famous Sharps-Borchardt rifle in 1877. Ten years later, the inventor returned to Germany, where he designed the Borchardt automatic pistol, forerunner of the even more famous Luger.

A Cartridge Enterprise; Lever Guns Get Bigger

At the end of 1872, Winchester's net worth had soared to nearly $1.18 million, almost all from company profits. That same year, the company's board of directors doubled Oliver Winchester's salary, from $5,000 to $10,000, as a reward for steering the company successfully through the perilous half-decade following the Civil War (when 25 less successful New England firearms firms had disappeared). Winchester Repeating Arms Company was financially healthy and poised for expansion, part of which involved ammunition. In its 1873 catalog, the company claimed it was "prepared to manufacture 250,000 cartridges per day, embracing every size and description. . . ." Only two years later, a million cartridges were being packaged daily, including 25 different kinds of rimfire and centerfire rounds, and 8 shotshell varieties. Part of this expansion was to fill military contracts, like those signed with Turkey (calling for 87.5 million primed cases and bullets for Martini-Henry rifles in 1874, with 112.5 million more in 1875). The Ottoman Empire meanwhile ordered 80.1 million loaded Snider cartridges, and substantial (but unrecorded) numbers of Model 1873 rifles and matching ammunition went to China as well.

After this flood of military business in the 1870's, Winchester saw its rising profit line level off in 1878, when annual sales dipped slightly to $1.3 million. For the next 36 years, excepting the brief Spanish-American War, Winchester targeted its expansion to the sales of sporting guns and ammunition. Many gunmakers started offering options at small additional cost—mostly in stocks, buttplates, barrels, triggers, sights and almost anything else that could be changed with minimal effort. Winchester's Model 1873 lent itself well to this diversity, an asset that helped Winchester sell rifles as production passed demand during the final years of 19th-century America. Some of these Model 73's—the ones that demonstrated exceptional accuracy on proof targets—were marked "One of a thousand" on the barrel. They wore set triggers and a fine finish and sold for $100 more than a standard Model 1873. The next grade of barrels was marked,

"One of a hundred." Less flossy than the others, they commanded a $20 premium.

In 1880, Winchester augmented the .44 WCF chambering in its Model 1873 with the .38 WCF; and two years later the .32 WCF was added. Between 1884 and 1904, some 19,552 Model 1873's in .22 rimfire were produced. It was, in fact, the first American .22 rimfire repeating rifle ever made. Model 1873 parts were manufactured until 1919, though a few rifles were put together as late as 1925. In all, 720,610 copies were produced. Incidentally, Model 1873 was the first lever action Winchester to be called by its model number; so popular and distinctive was the 1866 that everyone knew it simply as "the Winchester."

The company's next new product—Model 1876—was nothing more than a big Model 1873 chambered for a new cartridge—the 45-75—designed to rival those used in single-shot rifles. Later, Winchester added the .50-95 Express, .45-60 WCF, and .40-60 WCF. Model 1876, which Winchester dropped in 1897, was for many years the official rifle of the Royal Canadian Mounted Police.

Despite substantial profits from foreign arms sales, most American gun firms experienced tough sledding during the period 1873 through 1879. Business was poor, forcing Winchester to lower its prices significantly during this time. In 1874, a new Model 1873 rifle cost $50, but by 1879 the price had fallen to $25. Despite its steady, conservative course for most of the 1870's, Winchester did buy the Adirondack Arms Company of Plattsburg, New York, in 1874. The following year, William Converse (who had married the sister of William Winchester's wife), came onto the board of directors, later becoming treasurer. By 1880, Converse was making $7,500, William Winchester was drawing $4,500 in salary, and Thomas Bennett made $3,500. The company's flagship rifle that year was Model 1876, which bore a massive look but lacked

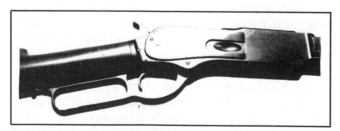

This Winchester Model 76 featured an iron frame and accommodated much longer cartridges than the Models 66 and 73 which preceded it.

the strength to handle cartridges like the potent .45-70 Government.

The rifle that proved it could handle relatively high pressures was Winchester's Model 1883 Hotchkiss, the first U.S. bolt rifle. Invented by B.B. Hotchkiss, an American living in Paris, Model 1883 featured a tubular magazine in its buttstock and, with its relatively strong action, raised Oliver Winchester's hopes that at last he would be chosen to supply U.S. military rifles. Tests by ordnance officers in 1878 gave the Hotchkiss a superior rating, and the cherished contract was tendered. Due to flaws in workmanship, however, the first shipment of Winchester-Hotchkiss rifles proved unacceptable. Moreover, the U.S. soldiers disliked the unfamiliar bolt action. Later, the Government tested the Hotchkiss again, but sadly Oliver Winchester was not there to witness it. In robust health during the early 1870's, he began to feel the effects of his age as 1880 approached. At a board meeting that year, he asked that his salary be reduced to $5,000 a year, because he could no longer handle the workload. On December 10, 1880, a month after turning 70, Oliver Winchester died at his home in New Haven. His son, William Wirt Winchester, who'd been groomed to succeed him, outlived Oliver only a few months, succumbing to tuberculosis late in March, 1881.

The choice of another president for Winchester Repeating Arms was strictly a family matter. Of the 10,000 shares of stock outstanding, Mrs. Oliver Winchester held 4,440, Mrs. William Winchester 777, and Mrs. Thomas Bennett 400. William Converse, then 46, was elected president after several ballots, also serving as treasurer. Thomas Bennett, then 37, was given the secretary post and, after the death of William Winchester, became the vice-president.

The 1880's were boom years for Winchester. Its ammunition business, especially, showed great growth. Between 1881 and 1889, the types of available centerfire cartridges increased four-fold. Winchester's market position for both rifles and ammunition was strengthened by the company's ability to design one for the other, and to follow its advertising with ample supplies. In 1888, Winchester teamed up with Marcellus Hartley and the Union Metallic Cartridge Company to buy Remington Arms. Mainly because of the Sherman Anti-Trust Act, however, that marriage was brief.

In 1880, Winchester announced its first breech-loading shotguns—imported double barrels, priced from $20 to $85. The Tariff Act of 1883, which assessed an added-value tax of 35 percent on such products, may have prompted Winchester's decision to drop the guns in 1884 (another factor was the competition Winchester gave its own jobbers, who also handled imports). Subsequently, Winchester built a lever action shotgun on a design supplied by John Browning in 1886. First cataloged in 1888, this was the fourth repeating shotgun made in the U.S., following designs by Colt, Roper and Spencer. It was the first successful repeater, however, and launched the New Haven firm into another promising market. The lever action shotgun, which sold initially for $25, was discontinued in 1919 after a production run of 79,000.

The 1880's also spawned the first factory-loaded shotshells, which proved an immediate and stunning success. Soon Winchester and other companies were offering hundreds of loads. A less dramatic but equally important development had occurred in 1878, when Winchester cartridge superintendent John Gardner invented a folded anvil for use in centerfire primers of all types. Replacing the solid anvil in use at that time, Gardner's design imparted enough spring to grip the primer cup walls securely. It made primer manufacture easier and cheaper and was later found to work equally as well with smokeless powders.

During that same decade, the number of Winchester employees doubled, with women now comprising roughly 25 percent of the work force. Mostly, they handled ammunition production and were paid about 60 percent of the wages earned in the gun shop. Ammunition work was more seasonal than gun manufacture, and Winchester found women more amenable than men to part-time work. Inside contracting, begun in the 1870's, became a popular and productive manufacturing scheme. By the mid-1880's, about half the people working on rifles consisted of inside contractors. But Winchester, pressured by stiff competition, reduced its contracting rates steadily to cut operating expenses, until by 1889 rates had been chopped 25 percent. Workers and contractors alike complained of large discrepancies in the profitability of contracts within the shop. Often Winchester's management had too little information with which to establish fair, equitable pricing.

In 1887, Winchester purchased the Whitney Arms Company of nearby Whitneyville, Connecticut. Founded by Eli Whitney in 1798 and run by him until his death in 1826, this company had subsequently been transferred to the uncles of heir apparent, six-year-old Eli Whitney, Jr. In 1842, at 22,

Eli Jr. assumed control, incorporating the business as the Whitney Arms Company in 1864. After the Civil War, Whitney offered two single shot and two repeating rifles to sportsmen. Winchester paid $65,000 for the company, mostly to take its rifles out of circulation, then leased the property and buildings until 1903, when the New Haven Water Company bought the land.

A year after the Whitney acquisition, Winchester joined Hartley and Graham in a bid for the estate of E. Remington & Sons, its giant competitor from Ilion, New York, with Winchester anteing up half the $200,000 purchase price. The Remington plant was then run by both buyers, with Marcellus Hartley acting as president and Thomas Bennett as vice president. Winchester sold Hartley its interest in Remington in September, 1896. A few years later, in 1899, Winchester bought the Burgess Gun Company, which had actively pursued repeating shotguns. True to form, Winchester did not reproduce the Burgess, but only shelved its designs.

Smokeless Cartridges and a Genius from Utah

By 1890, gun design in the United States had eclipsed cartridge development. Barrel steels and rifling technology, action strength, and the precision of available sights and triggers had little chance to prove their capabilities with the short range cartridges of the day. The problem lay in the propellant. Black powder was essentially the same mixture that the Chinese had used back in the 14th century. Advances in granulation had boosted efficiency, as had the metallic cartridge; but to achieve significantly more range, the only option was to lengthen cases and use more powder. The biggest black-powder rifle cartridge then measured nearly four inches! Fouling still ate away at accuracy, and clouds of smoke prevented quick followup shots from the new repeaters.

Following the work of Swiss chemist Christian Frederick Schoenbein and the Italian Sobero, who discovered nitrocellulose and nitroglycerin, black powder became obsolete. Then in 1885 Paul Vielle, a Frenchman, found that dissolving nitrocellulose in ether or alcohol produced a stable colloid which could be dried and used as a propellant. This compound became single-base or bulk smokeless powder. Alfred Nobel and Frederick Able later added nitroglycerin to form double-base smokeless.

Beginning in 1888, Winchester experimented with smokeless powder; but its catalog did not list smokeless ammunition until 1893, when it adver-

Winchester's lever-action shotgun was designed by John Browning in the late 1890's (Browning thought a slide-action would sell better).

tised shotshells charged with the new "nitro" propellant. Until 1905, Winchester "Leader" shotshells used smokeless powder, while the company's "Rival" brand was loaded with black. Loading metallic rifle cases with smokeless proved troublesome, but the 1894 Winchester catalog listed the new .30-40 Krag rifle with smokeless ammunition. Within a year, the company was offering 17 smokeless centerfire cartridges. In all but four of these, the new propellant was substituted for the old without any attempt at improving ballistic performance. The exceptions were the .236 Navy, .25-35 Winchester, .30 Winchester (.30-30) and .30 U.S. Army (.30-40 Krag).

Winchester had published its first ballistics table in 1889, by which time Thomas Bennett and Winchester's top sales agent, Thomas Emmett Addis, were building an on-site laboratory for powder development. The laboratory enabled Winchester to update its primer manufacturing as well. The new propellants required different primers than did black powder, and primer uniformity became much more important. Seeking stronger actions to handle more powerful cartridges, Bennett had traveled to Ogden, Utah, in 1883 to negotiate with the Browning brothers on a single-shot rifle. While there, he examined a sketch of a new lever action mechanism. In 1884, John and Matthew Browning had been granted U.S. patent 306,577 for that mechanism and assigned it to Winchester. Bennett secured the rights to the two Browning rifle designs for a total of $8,000: one became Model 1885 single shot (High Wall), and the other Model 1886 lever action. That rich haul paled in comparison to the profits derived from other Browning guns over the next decades. In that time, Browning sold Winchester plans for more than 40 mechanisms, from which Winchester eventually spawned seven important rifles and three shotguns.

Initially, Model 1886 was offered only in .45-70 Government, .45-90 WCF and .40-82 WCF, with seven other chamberings added later. Sliding vertical locks made the action much stronger than in previous lever guns. Nearly 160,000 Model 86's were produced before the last one left the plant in 1935. The last Winchester rifle to be designed for black powder cartridges, it remains an elegant rifle indeed.

By the sunset days of western expansion in the U.S., Winchester had become America's premier maker of long guns. The balky Hunt repeater had changed rifle design as only the Mauser and a few others would. Steering the thriving company into the 20th century required less invention than it did care. No one wanted to change the formula, least of all conservative Thomas G. Bennett. His election to the presidency of Winchester Repeating Arms came in February, 1890. Not yet 45, he was a mature, intelligent man with 20 years of experience in the company. He'd started staking out building sites for Winchester's move to New Haven in 1871.

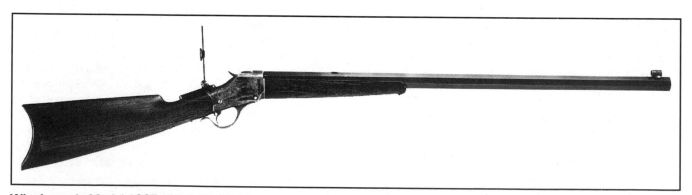

Winchester's Model 1885 "High Wall" (above) was the first Browning-designed rifle in the company's line. Winchester President Thomas Bennett traveled to Browning's shop in Utah to buy manufacturing and marketing rights for this gun.

A stint in the production shops, followed by valuable time spent with gun designers, gave him practical experience. From there he climbed through the various levels of management. A competent, but not an open man, he consulted the board of directors very little. Still, the company prospered under his leadership.

In 1899, John Browning presented Bennett with a radical new design: an autoloading shotgun. At a time when lever actions and pumps were fattening the company, Bennett was reluctant to risk money in this venture. To complicate things, Browning did not want to sell his design outright—he wanted a royalty contract. When the two men could not come to terms, Browning commented about the split:

"It was not a very dignified parting, I admit, but I was younger then. Bennett was the most conservative of men, and admittedly the automatic was something of an innovation. To put it simply, he was afraid of it, and so were the few men in his confidence. They were afraid that it would take ten years to develop such a gun to the point where it would be a profitable manufacturing article."

And so Browning, having waited a long time to be told "no," stalked out of Bennett's office in a huff. The Browning-Winchester bond never healed completely thereafter. Browning conceded later that the new automatic would have competed directly with Winchester's popular Model 97 pump, and he understood Bennett's hesitation. "Don't think of him as a coward," he admonished later. "He enlisted at 16 and fought in the Civil War, coming out a captain." He acknowledged, too, that

"Winchester had a fine record. It was their boast at one time that the company had not borrowed a cent in 40 years." Caught between opportunity and security, Bennett, in Browning's words, would have "shelled out a hundred thousand dollars just to have had it [the autoloader] banished forever from the earth."

The 20th century brought great changes in firearms metallurgy. Because the balance of hardness and elasticity in gun steel and cartridge brass was critical with smokeless powders, Winchester created its own chemical division, headed by Joseph Wild, a graduate of the Yale Sheffield Scientific School. By 1905, Winchester was loading 100 different smokeless cartridges; and by 1914, the number swelled to 175. Many were still held to black powder pressures for use in weak actions like the Model 73; while others, with a bit more sauce, were approved for the stronger Model 86 and bolt action guns by other makers. Cartridges designed as smokeless rounds—namely, the .30-40, .303 British, .33 and .35 and .405 Winchesters—could be used only in barrels of modern steel and the stoutest of lever and bolt action mechanisms.

243 Million Shotshells; 72,500 Wooden Blocks

During the transition from black to smokeless powder, Winchester supplied both kinds of ammunition. It also catered to handloaders; in fact, the 1914 catalog had about the same number of black powder accessories that were listed in the company's 1890 book. Some shooters wanted to roll their own rifle cartridges using smokeless powder,

This photo from an old Winchester catalog shows a line of desert-hardened Texas Rangers with their Model 1895 Winchesters (the lone exception, fifth from the right, appears to be holding a Krag).

but Winchester discouraged this. The company called the handloading of smokeless cartridges, "impractical." A desire to sell factory-made ammunition, combined with an alarming accident rate among careless handloaders, prompted other ammunition firms to echo Winchester's warning. In 1918, Townsend Whelen observed that, of the "thousands of riflemen" he knew, "very few of them load their own ammunition."

Overcharging, while only a minor fault with black powder, could prove disastrous with smokeless. Another problem was the mercury residue left in the case from primers of that day. Mercury weakened the brass so that even modest loads could split a case, spilling gas. Shotshells also were strained by smokeless, often separating just in front of the metal. To remedy this, Winchester's John Gardner patented a grooved metal shotshell head in 1896. The circumferential grooves not only gripped the paper more tightly, they absorbed some of the shock of firing by flattening against the chamber wall.

Winchester issued no warnings concerning the reloading of smokeless shotshells. Indeed, the company did not market loaded shells aggressively until 1895, because profits were higher in the sale of components. Many of the shotguns in use then were built for black powder, and some guns blew up when fed the new factory loads or smokeless handloads. But the subsequent dive in the popularity of handloading resulted mostly from Winchester's expansion of factory loads, not from fear of accidents. The first loading machines for smokeless shells were pretty crude, and production lagged, driving up the price of shells. As late as 1914, the cost of Leader shotshells was almost double that of black powder Nublack shells.

In 1900, Winchester's ammunition works benefited a great deal from a two-hour visit made one day by employee Henry Brewer to the Union Metallic Cartridge Company plant. U.M.C. was being sued by an injured workman and invited Brewer to inspect its operation. The company wanted an outsider familiar with loading procedures to testify on its behalf that the loading rooms were safe. Brewer, the only Winchester employee allowed anywhere near U.M.C. in several years, found the loading machines far more automated than Winchester's. On his return, he urged Bennett to update, claiming cost savings of $50,000 a year. Bennett laughed at Brewer's estimate but agreed to install the automatic feeds. The company was soon saving $200,000 each year in shotshell production!

Before 1911, Winchester had bought its shot from the National Lead Company; but that year National Lead acquired the U.S. Cartridge Company and thus became Winchester's direct competitor. Immediately, the New Haven firm began building its own 154-foot shot tower, which was completed in 1912 at a cost of $190,000.

Between 1900 and 1905, Winchester shotshell sales tripled—from 23 million to 67 million. This growth prompted the company to offer still more choices in shotshells, and by 1907 sales had jumped to 243 million rounds. The reliability and uniformity of factory shells, combined with competitive pricing and a broad selection of shot charges, thinned the ranks of handloaders. On the other hand, the development of new powders and wads meant that shotshell inventories would increase beyond reason unless some loads were eliminated. Winchester alone already listed 14,383 different loads!

About that time, the company began charging premium prices for all but a few standard loads. Significant savings came in 1921, when the major U.S. ammunition companies collectively dropped 5,200 loads, accounting for about 10 percent of total sales. By 1925, available factory loads numbered 1,747; by 1947, only 137 remained. Handloading had suddenly become attractive again.

Between the advent of smokeless powder and the start of World War I, Winchester developed and marketed some of its most famous guns, including Model 1890 (a .22 rimfire pump rifle) and its Model 1897 pump shotgun, plus models 1892 and 1894 (both lever action rifles). Model 1903, an autoloading .22 rimfire, was the first successful self-loader produced in quantity in the U.S.; and Winchester's Model 12, a pump shotgun (first listed at $20), became one of the most popular smoothbores ever.

During the 1920's, Winchester pioneered the use of nickel steel barrels in its centerfire rifles. The mild steels used for black powder arms comprised about 99 percent iron and one percent carbon—

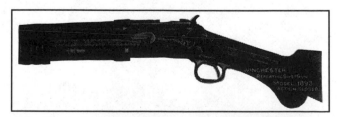

John Browning's Winchester Model 1893 slide-action shotgun (above) became Model 1897, which later evolved into the hugely successful Model 12.

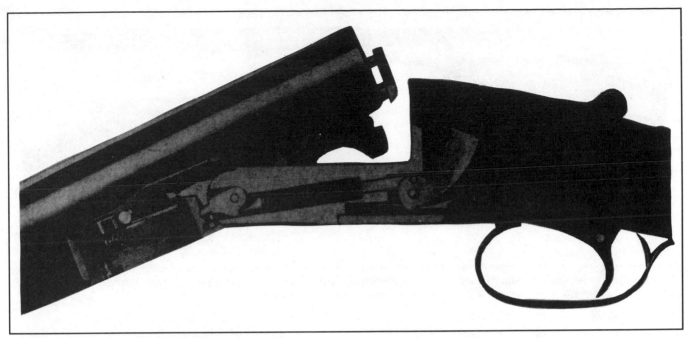

This Model 21 double shotgun, widely regarded as one of the sturdiest of American doubles, is now available only through Winchester's Custom Shop.

strong enough to contain pressures of 25,000 psi. But even the first smokeless loads jacked pressures to 38,000 psi, and by World War I some rounds routinely developed 48,000 psi. Nickel steel offered higher tensile strength and more resistance to erosion. By August, 1895, after Winchester engineer William Mason had designed new tooling to machine, drill and rifle nickel steel, the company's new catalog listed for the first time its Model 94 with a nickel steel barrel. It was priced at $18 and soon became a hunter's favorite. It carried well in hand or in a scabbard, and its smokeless .30-30 round was ideal for deer. Its predecessor, Model 92, was chambered for shorter, less potent rounds (like the .44-40) and proved equally popular with explorers, especially in its 14-inch barrel form. Winchester advertised it as, "The rifle that helped Peary reach the North Pole."

Around 1900, Winchester began employing "missionary" salesmen. They'd call on dealers for orders, then turn them over to appropriate jobbers. These salesmen, who also represented Winchester to the dealers and the public, were often trick shots and expert entertainers. Among them was Adolph Topperwein, who began his shooting career with the circus at age six. A Texas native, Topperwein began work at Winchester in 1901, when he was 32. There he met Elizabeth Servaty, who worked in the loading rooms, and two years later they were

married. Soon Winchester sent "Ad" on the road as an exhibition shooter, leaving Elizabeth at home. Finding life dull with her husband away so much, she asked Ad to give her shooting lessons. She learned fast and was soon accompanying him on the circuit, under the nickname "Plinky." At the 1904 World's Fair in St. Louis, "Plinky" broke 967 of 1,000 targets at trap; and three years later, she hit 1,952 out of 2,000.

Meanwhile, her husband became famous for his endurance shooting at hand-thrown wooden blocks measuring only 2½ inches square. In 1907, while shooting steadily with a .22 rifle for 10 eight-hour days, Ad missed only nine out of 72,500 blocks. In the first 50,000 shots, he missed just four, and his longest run without a miss was 14,540!

Competition Among the Cartridge Companies

Winchester Repeating Arms Company had been a member of the Ammunition Manufacturers' Association since the group's incorporation in New Jersey on September 27, 1883. Other charter members included U.M.C., the U.S. Cartridge Company, and the Phoenix Metallic Cartridge Company. All were New England firms, and each bought stock in the Association. Winchester and U.M.C. each held 374 shares, U.S. Cartridge 179, and Phoenix 79. The

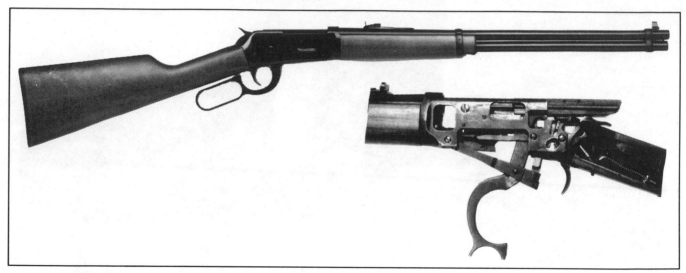

The Winchester Model 94 (above), which is the gun most people think of when they hear the name, "Winchester," has been in production for nearly a century. Few have seen its innards (below).

percentage of stock held by a company determined its share of profits.

The Association served ". . . to buy and sell ammunition of all kinds and act as agent for others in the purchase and sale thereof; to make contracts with Manufacturers and Dealers in Ammunition for the purpose of producing and securing uniformity and certainty in their customs and usages and preventing serious competition between them; to settle differences between those engaged in the manufacture of or in dealing in ammunition, and to devise and take measures to foster and protect their trade and business."

While the Association fixed retail prices and dealer and jobber discounts, it did not eliminate competition among its members. The apportionment of profits depended on periodic reviews of actual sales, so brand competition was brisk. Furthermore, the members could not afford to have one of their group develop such a strong market that it broke with the Association.

During the 1880's, ammunition production in the U.S. more than doubled, and income from the sales of cartridges more than tripled. Winchester's ammunition sales during the last half of this decade totaled $4.9 million, returning an "Association profit" of about $1.2 million. At this time, Winchester ammunition was generating slightly more than half the company's total net profits.

When the Sherman Anti-Trust Act was signed by President Benjamin Harrison in 1889, the Association's activities came under review. But with the exception of minor changes in its complex pric-

ing, discount and "salary" programs, the Association continued to operate as it always had. By 1900, ammunition sales were climbing sharply, and in 1901 shotshell receipts jumped to $2.2 million—seven times what they'd been in 1887. During these boom years, Association members produced a large volume of components for shooters who wanted to load their own ammunition, and for "loading companies" that assembled and packaged cartridges.

Shortly after the turn of the century, the Association stopped supporting the loading companies. For one reason, its members were now marketing their own loaded ammunition more aggressively; and for another, prosperous loading companies could themselves develop into ammunition firms and thus become direct competitors of Association members.

The Peters Cartridge Company provided an early cause for concern. Established in 1887 for the purpose of loading empty shotshells for the trade, Peters got its powder from the King Powder Company, and its hulls came from members of the Association. Then, in 1889, Peters purchased patent rights and machinery for paper shell manufacture from the American Buckle and Cartridge Company, which had just sold out to Winchester Repeating Arms. Thus, when Peters started making shotshells, Winchester sued. The fight was a bitter one, ending in victory for Winchester in 1900, and a payment of $1,000. But Peters had continued making shotshells in the interim on equipment not open to patent litigation.

Another loading company that began manufacturing ammunition at this time was the Western Cartridge Company. Formed in February, 1898, by Franklin W. Olin in East Alton, Illinois, Western evolved from The Equitable Powder Manufacturing Company, which Olin started in 1892. It used the powder produced by Equitable and other components supplied by Association members to make shotshells until 1900, when the Association cut off Olin's supply of primers.

Undaunted, Olin turned to Eley in England for primers and kept on making shotshells, developing his own wad and hull machinery at great expense. By 1904, Western had a shot tower and was distributing its shells through the Simmons Hardware Company of St. Louis. And a few years later, Olin's firm began making metallic cartridges.

The Savage Arms Company, formed in Utica, New York, in 1894 to make rifles, also bought ammunition components from Association members. These it assembled and sold as loaded ammunition under the Savage name. When Western's primer supply was cut off in 1900, Savage lost its primers too. The Utica firm struggled to develop its own cartridge firm and eventually succeeded. While Savage's ammunition department was small, and the Peters and Western firms eventually joined with Remington and Winchester, the growth of independent ammunition concerns outside the Association showed that it could not long continue. Pressure from antitrust forces added to the strain, and in 1906 and 1907 a merger proposition within the Association was finally scuttled by Winchester. The Ammunition Manufacturers' Association was finally dissolved on November 7, 1907. Between then and the outbreak of World War I, ammunition manufacture and distribution among the big companies did not change significantly. But after the war, competition between these firms, in the absence of a moderating group, grew fierce.

Winchester's First Autoloading Shotgun

The 20th century brought new men and products to Winchester's gun department. Thomas Bennett's split with John Browning hurt the company, but Winchester found another gifted engineer in Thomas Crossly Johnson. Born in 1862, Johnson graduated from the Yale Sheffield Scientific School in 1884, worked a year for his father's firm (Yale Safe and Iron Company), then joined Winchester in 1885. He remained there until his death in 1934. In the early years, Johnson spent most of his time designing guns with Thomas Bennett and William

The Winchester factory, shown here at the turn of the century, formed a bustling industrial complex taking up several city blocks in New Haven, Connecticut.

Mason. Later he specialized in autoloading mechanisms, developing Winchester's recoil-operated, self-loading rifles, (Models 03, 05, 07 and 10). Johnson was also given the tough job of engineering Winchester's first autoloading shotgun, called Model 11, a "recoil operated, hammerless, takedown, five shot repeater." It was a tough assignment because Johnson had to work around several Browning patents, which he himself had helped articulate. In the end, he succeeded in producing a sound shotgun, but it proved only moderately popular. Priced at $38 in 1911, it was then the most expensive Winchester gun on the market.

Remington's announcement of its Browning-designed Model 11 preceded Johnson's gun by six years, so Winchester could not complain of unfair competition from Ilion. When Remington started work on autoloading rifles in 1906, however, Winchester was quick to point out that, at the time it relinquished interest in Remington, it had been assured no direct competition would be allowed from either side. If true, the agreement must have been a verbal one between Bennett and Marcellus Hartley. Hartley was now dead, and Remington's new management was making its own path. In a much earlier example of business conduct in the Victorian era, Winchester had casually shown Colt samples of revolvers produced in its shop but not yet ready for market. Colt immediately stopped development of a competing lever action rifle, and in return Winchester did not pursue the revolver.

Pricing proved as hard to regulate as competition. In 1904, Sears, Roebuck defied Bennett's minimum pricing policy by offering a Winchester take-down shotgun as a premium for customers who spent $300 at Sears. Bennett promptly denied the mail order firm access to the Winchester warehouses. When Sears tried to buy Winchester products elsewhere, Bennett countered by warning that jobbers who sold to Sears would themselves be cut off. Sears continued to list a few Winchester items, but in 1906 it established its own firearms plant in Meriden, Connecticut, where it made and promoted the long defunct "Aubrey" guns.

By 1912, the right of a manufacturer to enforce retail pricing had been challenged in court, and a year later Winchester was compelled to rewrite its price restrictions. But the controversy was renewed following World War I and wasn't settled until the passage of the Miller-Tydings Act of 1937, which legalized national retail pricing.

Meanwhile, the Winchester and Bennett families continued to give generously to educational causes, mainly through Yale University. Oliver Winchester donated an observatory site there in 1871 and added a building in 1879. Twelve years later, Oliver's widow donated Winchester Hall to the University in memory of her husband. The family subsequently established memorial funds in the art and medical schools as well.

Sarah Winchester, William's widow, became known as an eccentric after building onto a house she bought near San Jose, California, in 1892. The eight-room home eventually grew to 160 rooms covering six of the estate's 160 acres. But the character of the building, not its size, engendered most of the gossip. There were screens on blank walls, barred windows between rooms, staircases that dead-ended, and outside water faucets beneath second-story windows. Some rooms had 13 windows and 13 walls, and an inlaid mahogany newel post was installed upside down. Nonetheless, having invested income from her Winchester stock, Sarah profited greatly from her California real estate. In 1911, she contributed $300,000 to a New Haven group for a tuberculosis sanatorium in her husband's memory. Her total donations to this cause, in fact, came to $1.2 million.

In 1911, Thomas Bennett relinquished the presidency of Winchester to George E. Hodson, who, along with Arthur Hooper, had helped Bennett steer the company for 21 years. Hodson's starting salary of $20,000 reflected the doubling of salaries at that time to most company officers. Four years later, Hodson resigned for health reasons and Thomas Bennett's son, Winchester, took over. Only a few months before that change, John Otterson was appointed general plant superintendent, becoming the first man outside the Winchester family to hold that post.

Unfortunately, Winchester Bennett contracted typhoid fever, which was followed by pneumonia and an appendectomy. His condition forced Thomas Bennett to step back in as president *pro tem*, a job he had no inclination to handle on a day to day basis. As a result, John Otterson assumed increasing responsibilities, leading to his election to the board in 1916 and, a few months later, the vice presidency. Winchester Bennett remained as company president through the war years, but took little active part in its management.

War Debt and Drugstores

Winchester's huge wartime commitments included more than 50,000 Browning automatic rifles. The New Haven firm also supplied short-barreled Model 97 shotguns for trench fighting. Each shell, with its six 34-caliber pellets, proved so devastating that the German government protested, warning that any American carrying a shotgun when captured would be shot. The war ended before such threats and counterthreats could be carried out. Other military contracts called for 44 million .303

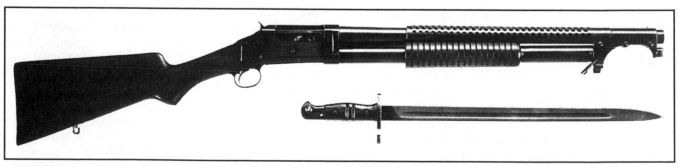

This Winchester Model 1897 shotgun with bayonet was designed especially for trench fighting during World War I. The Germans feared the buckshot loads from these guns so much, they threatened to kill any Allied soldier caught armed with a shotgun.

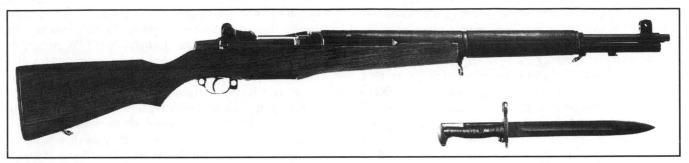

During both World Wars, Winchester produced huge quantities of ammunition and military arms, including this M1 Garand infantry rifle.

British cartridges and 400,000 Enfield rifles for the British government, which also procured 9 million .44 WCF cartridges (for the British Home Guard's Winchester 92 rifles) and 50 million .22 Long Rifle cartridges. In addition, Winchester sold 300 million 7.62mm cartridges and 200,000 Model 95 rifles to Russia, and another 1.5 million 7mm rounds to the French. By December of 1915, these contracts—all negotiated by J.P. Morgan & Company—totaled $47.5 million, from which Winchester expected to take $5 million in profits.

Filling these huge orders required expansion, of course. In tooling up for war, Winchester spent $13.3 million that first year and soon felt an acute need for more operating capital. Turning to J.P. Morgan, it soon received a loan of $8.25 million; then, in February of 1916, it negotiated a loan of $16 million with Kidder, Peabody of Boston (half of which went to pay off the Morgan debt). By July, the Winchester plant had doubled in size.

Serious problems with the Enfield contract ensued. British inspectors held unswervingly to specifications that could not be met at a wartime production pace. When deliveries fell behind, Winchester blamed it on the inspectors. The company maintained that its contracts called for rifles that would shoot and function well. Minor differences between production rifles and the contract models should, it insisted, be expected and ignored. The British felt otherwise. J.P. Morgan advised them that Winchester—and Remington, too, which was also affected—would take legal action to recover expenses. And so it happened that a $10.8 million cash settlement was reached for the 235,000 rifles already shipped and for those not yet delivered.

By early 1917, Winchester was free of foreign contracts and had reduced its work force by 5,000. On April 23, the company started manufacturing Enfield rifles for the U.S. government—a month before the gun, which had been modified for the .30-06 cartridge, was approved. By December, it had delivered 80,000 Enfields at a cost of about $26 each (not including the bayonet). Winchester manufactured these and other guns on "cost-plus" contracts, wherein the company was guaranteed (by the U.S. government) production costs plus 10 percent. A Navy contract for 40 million rounds of ammunition was among the first of several orders that kept Winchester's loading machines operating. By war's end, the firm had shipped 525 million .30-06 cartridges.

During the war, Winchester employed a record 17,549 people, with average weekly plant wages rising from $16.22 to $19.50. But quick expansion created problems. The plant grew with little planning, draining efficiency, and long-term price contracts failed to reflect steeply rising labor costs. By war's end, with demand on a sharp downward slide, these oversights crippled Winchester. With some 17 million dollars in debt, the company borrowed another $3 million from Kidder, Peabody just to pay taxes on its wartime profits.

Into the Postwar Era

In 1920, Thomas Bennett and other company patriarchs reorganized their empire to form The Winchester Repeating Arms Company (under John Otterson) and its sister firm, the Winchester Company. The arms branch made guns and ammunition, while the other manufactured a variety of consumer products, including gas refrigerators, skates, cutlery, flashlights, fishing gear, hand tools, washing machines, skis, baseball bats, paints, batteries and household brushes. This diversification failed to reduce the corporate debt; in fact, Winchester's debt load increased as hardware sales sagged. Ironically, the firearms division prospered.

Fortunately, Louis Liggett, who in 1903 engineered the United Drug Company and created the "Rexall" brand, was on Winchester's board of directors. His marketing ideas helped the company develop its dealer-agency plan, which enabled Winchester to bypass jobbers in small communities. Thus, the best equipped hardware store became the exclusive Winchester outlet for that area. In return, each dealer had to buy a small amount of Winchester preferred stock and pay a nominal annual fee. Despite some opposition, Winchester managed to gain support for this program, partly by hosting 1,000 hardware dealers at a lavish five-day convention in New Haven.

In towns with populations over 50,000, the company sought to establish its own retail stores, after the manner of Liggett's United Drug Company. While carrying other merchandise as well, these stores would serve Winchester as primary outlets without the cost of jobbing. The first such store opened in Providence, Rhode Island, in April, 1920, with Winchester's name appearing in big red letters against a gray background. The company couldn't meet its proposed schedule of opening a store a week, however, and deteriorating economic conditions forced it to postpone expansion after only 11 stores were operating. By 1921, it had dropped the hardware merchandise from these retail outlets. The company found that Liggett's successful United Drug program could not be applied without modification to the arms industry. In the last months of 1921, Winchester executives had to admit, in the face of rising production costs, that neither the dealer-agent nor retail store program had proven itself.

Early in 1922, the Simmons Hardware Company of St. Louis asked that Winchester acquire it in a $9.3 million merger. A well established firm that was incorporated in 1873, Simmons had vociferously opposed Winchester's dealer-agent plan; but new management at the hardware giant saw some benefits in cooperation. On June 26, 1922, Ot-

terson announced that the two companies had combined "under a common management" and would thereafter be operated jointly, with Winchester handling the manufacturing and Simmons the distributing.

Still, this new alliance was not enough to brake Winchester's slow but noticeable slide after the war. Finally, Liggett ordered an accounting of both company branches and the result was dire indeed: a recommendation for receivership. In June of 1924, John Otterson tendered his resignation, and Frank Drew was promoted from his position as vice president to Winchester's top spot. Kidder, Peabody & Company, which held most of the company stock, immediately chose Louis Liggett as president of Simmons Hardware. When Thomas Bennett resigned as chairman of the board of the Winchester Repeating Arms Company that August, Liggett was given that job too.

Two Fine Rifles—and a Bankruptcy

In the early 1920's, Winchester's gun designers had almost no budget. Nonetheless, they came up with two fine rifles: Model 52, a bolt-action rimfire (1920), and Model 54, a centerfire (1924). Model 54 gave Winchester its first grip on the promising market for bolt action centerfire rifles. The company had never succeeded with a bolt gun, despite the military's preference for this design over the past 30 years. Clearly, Paul Mauser's stout action showed great potential, and the powerful cartridges developed by Charles Newton had no future in lever guns.

Winchester's early efforts in bolt actions included the .45-70 Hotchkiss, which was discontinued in 1900, and the Lee Straight Pull, which lasted from 1897 to 1903. When company designers started on the 54, they ignored those designs for the most part and concentrated on the successful 1903 Springfield. In 1925, three years after the project began, Model 54 was introduced. It had a nickel-

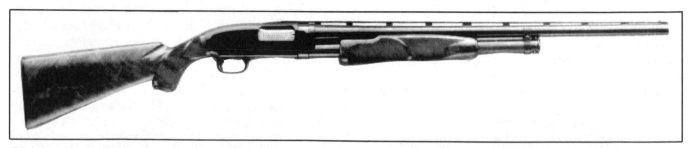

Perhaps not as elegant as a Parker double, but certainly less costly, Winchester's Model 12 pump shotgun (above) has often been called the greatest American-built shotgun. The model shown here is a Pigeon Grade skeet model.

Tools and refrigerators, as indicated in these Winchester ads, were among the many consumer products marketed as part of Winchester's unsuccessful post-Depression attempts to diversify.

steel barrel and cyanide-hardened receiver to bottle pressures from the .30-06 and brand-new .270 WCF cartridges. It also featured the coned breech of the Springfield and an ejector by Newton, with Mauser-style bolt, extractor and safety. Its stock was patterned after the popular Sedgely sporters of the period, with a slender, schnabel forend and shotgun butt.

Winchester's Model 54, which was eventually offered in 10 styles and 10 chamberings, drew quick applause from shooters. It was lightweight, good-looking, and fast-handling—with just enough Springfield in its bloodline to interest ex-G.I.'s. The .270 cartridge, with its 130-grain bullet moving at 3,000 fps, awed hunters who were used to .30-30-class deer rounds. In 1932, a "speed lock" was added; and a year later chrome-molybdenum barrels replaced those made of nickel-steel.

In 1926, Winchester bought the manufacturing assets of the U.S. Cartridge Company of Lowell, Massachusetts. Some 83 freight-carloads of the company's machinery were shipped to New Haven, where it was installed and operated to produce ammunition under the U.S. Cartridge brand name and distributed as it always had been. Winchester then sold the ammunition back to U.S. Cartridge on a cost-plus basis. Included in the deal were patents covering the manufacture of radiators, which Winchester eventually used (in 1929, all Rolls Royce autos were equipped with Winchester-built radiators).

When the Great Depression hit, Winchester was too weak to stand. During the mid-1920's, it had merely sustained the level of net sales that had proved unsatisfactory at the start of the decade. By 1927, a series of cost-cutting moves had increased profitability only slightly—but interest charges on funds borrowed before 1924 had kept the company operating at a loss of nearly $1 million a year. In February, 1929, the old organization was dissolved, and The Winchester Repeating Arms Company of Delaware took its place. Its prospects for success seemed reasonably good—until the stock market collapsed. A year later, Kidder, Peabody told the directors that it could lend Winchester no more money. With debt accrual continuing at $1 million a year, the company had no choice but to fold, and on January 22, 1931, it went bankrupt. The following December, Winchester was acquired by the Western Cartridge Company. Ironically, Winchester's Model 21, the last product created by the now defunct company, has been called the best double gun ever built in the United States. Also ironic was the fact that Winchester, once the undisputed leader in the firearms industry, had been bought by a company that had struggled so hard to compete with its ammunition branch.

Western Cartridge assumed the Winchester company with all "its properties, assets, business and good will" for $3 million cash and $4.8 million (par value) of 6 percent cumulative preferred Western stock. Of course, Western also inherited Winchester's liabilities, and it agreed to accept the costs of receivership up to $300,000. The purchase reduced the book value of fixed Winchester assets from $24 million to $3.5 million.

As Western entered the Depression, it was piloted by Franklin Olin's son, John, who shared his father's active interest in the development of firearms and ammunition. With the purchase of Winchester, he now led the biggest firm of its kind in the world. In the next decade, 23 new Winchester guns would be announced, among them the Model 54's successor, Model 70. The decision to replace Model 54 with another rifle was prompted largely by a desire for a better centerfire target gun. Since its introduction in 1919, the Model 52 rimfire rifle had steadily built an unassailable record on small-bore ranges, and Winchester designers wanted centerfire laurels to match. Besides, a good target action with a hunting-style stock and barrel would likely be popular with sportsmen.

But the Depression had battered rifle sales, and Winchester took a long time developing its new gun. The company's supply of Model 54 parts still far exceeded demand, and releasing a new rifle into an economic abyss didn't seem like the smart thing to do. Sales of Model 54 rifles picked up in 1935, however, and in January, 1936, the first receivers for Winchester Model 70 rifles were given their serial numbers. By New Year's Day, 1937, 2,238 rifles were ready to be shipped.

Model 70 offered many refinements lacking in the 54, including an override trigger mechanism borrowed from Model 52. The trigger was adjust-

Don Pind, manager of Winchester's custom shop, examines an exquisite Model 70 (above) built to customer specifications. Model 70's account for 90 percent of custom work, which produces engraving like that found on the gold inlaid floorplate shown below.

able for weight of pull and overtravel; and its bolt stop was a separate device that engaged either the left locking lug or a bar attached to the bolt body by an extractor clip. Cartridge length determined the need for, and length of, the bar, which in turn allowed shooters to choose cartridges ranging from the .22 Hornet to the .375 H&H Magnum in size. Receivers for all 70's had the same outside dimensions; but the shape and size of various parts within the mechanism could be changed to accommodate cases of varying lengths and diameters.

The bolt handle on Model 70 was lowered to a 45-degree angle and rested in a groove milled in the receiver. Later, its shoulder was ground off to clear low-riding scopes with big ocular bells. A low, rear-mounted safety allowed for the use of most scopes (this was changed later to the clever and even more practical three-position, side-swing safety). A machined, hinged floorplate replaced the sheet steel magazine cover used in Model 54. The hook rifling process used in other Winchester barrels was retained. Most Model 70 barrels were made of chrome-molybdenum steel, but some chamberings were still routinely furnished in stainless. The first rifles, cataloged at $61.25, came in nine chamberings, but seven more were added in the 1950's and early 1960's before a drastic reconfiguration of the gun took place in 1964. Of the 581,471 rifles made before 1964, more than 330,000 were .30-06's and .270's, the former accounting for two thirds of these.

Aptly called, "The rifleman's rifle," Winchester's Model 70 gave the company a much needed post-Depression boost. Indeed, it became to modern hunters what the Winchester 66 had been to our pioneers.

World War II and Corporate Restructuring

Back in 1936, U.S. Ordnance decided the M1 Garand rifle should supplant the 1903A3 Springfield as America's primary infantry weapon. When Government arsenals delayed production of the first Garands, Ordnance asked for bids from private firms. As a result, Winchester won a 500-rifle contract, an experience that helped the company underbid competitors for a 65,000-gun contract a few years later. The first New Haven-built Garands were delivered a year before the attack on Pearl Harbor in December of 1941.

In 1940, Winchester also developed a lightweight carbine at the government's request. In his preliminary work, Winchester designer David "Carbine" Williams used a new short-stroke piston to operate the action of a 7½-pound rifle firing the standard .30-06 cartridge. This gun was later scaled down in size and chambered for the less powerful .30 Carbine round. The five-pound rifle passed muster at Aberdeen Proving Grounds just 34 days after its first official firing. During the ensuing war, Winchester built 818,059 of these M1 Carbines.

Meanwhile, the company's ammunition plant was developing a 60-caliber machine gun round for the U.S. government, delivered Finnish military cartridges at less cost than domestic makers charged during peacetime, and turned out huge quantities of .303 British ammunition. Total wartime production from Winchester-Western amounted to 1.45 million guns and more than 15 billion rounds of ammunition.

After the war, John Olin's ammunition firm concentrated on the development of sporting ammunition, including ball powders (1946), Baby Magnum shotshells (1954), the .22 Winchester Magnum Rimfire round (1959), and a compression-formed shotshell (1964).

In August, 1954, Olin was swallowed by the huge Mattheson Chemical Corporation. Ten years later, Winchester guns were redesigned to take advantage of cheaper materials and manufacturing processes. Though the principle was sound on paper, its implementation triggered a colossal revolt in the marketplace. Pre-1964 Winchesters suddenly commanded premiums on the used gun market. The new guns were sound—in some ways, even superior to early models—but they lacked the detailing, fit and finish shooters had come to expect from Winchester Repeating Arms.

Scrambling to correct its blunder, the company quickly offered guns with the traditional features shooters wanted, but without the hand finishing that had become prohibitively expensive. When Olin-Mattheson sold the Winchester Sporting Arms business in July, 1981, the new company—U.S. Repeating Arms—continued to improve its products. Although most Winchester guns are still made in this country, Olin-Kodensha (OK Firearms Company) of Japan has recently manufactured Winchester's double shotguns. Winchester ammunition is still made in East Alton by Winchester-Western.

In 1984, beset by rising costs and lowering demand, USRAC filed for Chapter 11. Five investors bought the company in 1987, among them Fabrique Nationale (FN), the Belgian firm that also owns Browning. FN originally acquired 38 percent of US-RAC, but eventually wound up with 44 percent. A huge enterprise, FN is itself owned by Societe Gen-

These Winchester Model 94's, their receivers protected by adhesive paper, have almost cleared the assembly line at the USRAC plant.

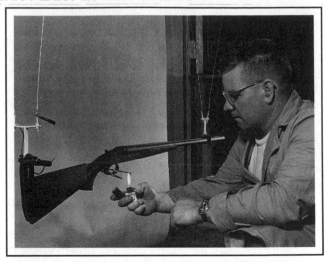

A Winchester engineer burns through the filament that binds a trigger-tripping device on a Winchester Model 21 shotgun set up for recoil measurement.

This Winchester pantograph, or duplicating machine, is finishing a batch of Model 70 stocks.

This bar stock is formed in the shape of Winchester Model 70 sears, which are cut from it like slices of bread.

erale, which controls 75 percent of Belgium's GNP. Early in 1991, Giat, a French conglomerate, bought FN and, with it, USRAC.

The corporate forces that shape gun companies today had their beginnings long after Walter Hunt started making his Rocket Balls. These same forces might have indeed been imagined by such astute businessmen of their time as Oliver Winchester and Thomas Bennett. But in those early days, engineering and production took priority over marketing. "Produce a better gun and people will buy all you can make" was the prevailing belief then. By the 1970's, Winchester and other huge corporations were taking marketing lessons from companies whose products didn't even exist in those earlier glory days of gunmaking.

The president of USRAC in 1991 was Jack Mattan, an aggressive entrepreneur who came from Belgium to manage the Giat acquisition and was later named its chief executive. By his own admission, Mattan is no connoisseur of firearms, but he obviously wants very much to see the company succeed. That means listening to people who know the gun business.

"Winchester is the greatest name in the world of guns," he declares. "But the company has concentrated too long on production at the expense of marketing. This isn't the 1940's, when we had 20,000 people working here and every gun was sold before it was built. Now the market is very competitive, and demand has slipped. Guns are durable. You don't need a new one every year, so steady sales depend on good customer recruitment—marketing!"

Mattan has little patience for employees who don't share his vision or enthusiasm. The 700-odd people who work at USRAC have been shifted since Giat gained control, and some have fallen out and been replaced. As Mattan points out, when the company benefits, everybody benefits. The reverse is also true, so if an employee is not pulling hard in the harness, he's considered a liability. In Jack Mattan's Winchester, everybody is a salesman.

Not that selling is the only thing going on at USRAC. Recent additions to the design staff and an expanded custom shop creating several new products indicate that this company is geared up for the long haul. Production times have also been shortened, with manufacturing tailored to smaller lots for quicker market response. Jack Mattan knows that quality, timeliness and price determine the success of any product. He and his staff are committed to keeping the Winchester name in its honored place among the world's great armsmakers.

CHAPTER 8

MARLIN: SOLID GUNS FOR THE MASSES

In 1853, the year that John Mahlon Marlin turned 18 years old, he signed on as an apprentice machinist with the American Machine Works. His contract provided the Connecticut youth with a job until he reached the "full and entire age of twenty-one years." In return, Marlin agreed to work for no wages during his first six months, then join the payroll at $1.50 per week. After a year, he'd be raised to $2.50, then receive 50-cent increases for each six-month period, provided he was not discharged, "without recourse or complaint, for any disobedience or insubordination."

Born May 6, 1836, near Windsor Locks in Hartford County, Connecticut, Marlin may have worked in Colt's Hartford plant as toolmaker and machinist. In 1863, the New Haven (Ct.) directory listed John M. Marlin's home address as 130 James Street. He changed quarters at least six times in the next 10 years but was probably living in Hartford from 1867 to 1869. His first two gun patents—dated February 8 and April 5, 1870—show a Hartford address.

We do know that by 1864 John Marlin was married to Martha Susan Moore, who bore him four children: Mahlon Henry, Burton Louis, Jennette Bradford, and John Howard. Burton died before age two and Jennette at 12, but Mahlon and John Howard lived long lives.

Before he became a husband and father, John Mahlon Marlin was a gunmaker. His first products were single-shot, deringer-style pistols named "Never Miss" and "Victor." The Never Miss came in rimfire calibers 22, 32 Short and 41; the Victor was chambered in .38 Short rimfire. Their barrels rotated sideways for loading. Between 1863 and 1880, Marlin marketed 16,000 of these pistols. In 1870, he expanded his line to include single-action revolvers. The "OK" and "Little Joker" were solid frame pocket models with spur triggers and 7-shot capacity chambered for the .22 Short. Models XX, XXX, No. 32 (and 38, which followed two years later) were heavier, tip-up revolvers with slightly longer, ribbed barrels. Chamberings were .22 long, .30 long, .32 short or long and .38. Five of the six models had brass frames, with the 38 (the only gun chambered for a centerfire round) wearing a steel frame.

The Marlin tip-ups most likely descended from a mechanism designed by Rollin White and patented in 1855. In 1861, a near copy of the White revolver (manufactured by Smith & Wesson) was marketed by the Manhattan Firearms Company, which had already built .31 and .36 percussion revolvers similar to those made by Colt. In 1863, Manhattan Firearms moved from New York to New Jersey, and five years later it folded. The American Standard Tool Company took its place and manufactured Manhattan-style .22 revolvers until its dissolution in 1873. The year before, John Marlin probably acquired the rights to build the Smith & Wesson revolver then manufactured by American Standard Tool. Rollin White's original patent had by that time expired.

Double-Action Revolvers to Scheutzen Rifles

In 1887, Marlin introduced a double-action, tip-up revolver in .38 centerfire. It remained in production only two years, despite some heavy advertisements, one of which read:

"The style is identical with the Smith & Wesson revolver, and in no respect whatever is it inferior.

These tip-up revolvers and "Victor" derringer were made by Marlin in the mid-1870's.

Our rifles have enjoyed the reputation of being superior in workmanship, finish and accuracy of shooting to any others in the world; this position we mean to hold, and the Marlin revolvers will be found to be in these points, so essential to a high-class arm, equal to anything we have heretofore made. Realizing the immense hold that S&W revolvers have on the markets of the world, by having for a long series of years stood alone as perfectly made weapons, we have made our price sufficiently low to attract the notice of the trade and of the public. . . ."

When it was introduced, Marlin's DA revolver sold for $11. Engraving was extra ($1.50 or more), and full silver plating or gold trim cost $2.75. Prices dropped later, and by 1899 (a year after the .32 rimfire was added as a chambering) a DA revolver went for $7.50. In 1882, Marlin's single action revolvers listed for as little as $4.66.

By 1889, John Marlin, now 53, had registered 10 handgun patents. He embellished many of his pistols with engraving and gold, silver and nickel plating, with grips of ivory, pearl and rosewood. Ornate Marlin handguns in excellent condition have become exceptionally rare and command a high price. Marlin began his next venture in 1875 with the manufacture of Ballard rifles. C.H. Ballard had designed the rifle in 1861 and peddled 1,000 to the government for use by Union troops. After the Civil War, Joseph Merwin and Edward Bray engineered a mechanism for loading the Ballard with either cartridges or loose powder and ball. Subsequently,

Ballards were produced by several firms. The last, Brown Manufacturing, sold its rights to Schoverling and Daly, who asked John Marlin to make the rifles. Rejecting the Merwin-Bray design, Marlin used mostly leftover Brown parts; but he kept his own reversible firing pin that allowed the use of both centerfire and rimfire cartridges. Twenty versions of the Ballard were cataloged by Marlin, in chamberings from .22 rimfires to .45-100. A "gallery rifle" cost $18; Spartan hunting guns listed for about $22; and target rifles with checkered Schuetzen stocks and spirit-level sights went for $75 to $90. It wasn't uncommon for customers to place special orders for rifles with features not listed in the catalogs. Consequently, many Ballards don't fit catalog descriptions. Marlin ceased Ballard production in 1889 or 1890, after producing about 40,000 rifles.

At the 1893 Chicago World's Fair, an observer remarked that the Marlin display featured a single-shot rifle touted as being "better than the old Ballard." However, the prototype model believed to

John Mahlon Marlin (1836-1901) first designed pistols, then founded a company that has emphasized the production of rifles.

have been on display at the exhibit does not bear the Marlin stamp, nor does it have any numbers. It looks a lot like a Winchester Model 1885 (Highwall), but the internal parts are quite different. Marlin apparently did not make any of these rifles for the market; no doubt he recognized even then that single-shot rifles would not drive the gun business much longer.

John Marlin's first repeating rifle, with its underhammer lever action and tubular magazine, didn't sell. Its faulty feeding and locking mechanisms prompted Marlin to design a better rifle, which he first marketed in 1882 (six years later it was designated as Model 1881). Incorporating features patented by Andrew Burgess, H.F. Wheller and E.A.F. Topperwein, the new Marlin lever-action was a side-loading, top-ejecting repeater in .45-70 and .40-60. A 28-inch octagonal barrel with a 10-round magazine was standard; 24- and 30-inch barrels of various weights and contours came later, with 8- and 10-round magazines. Marlin trimmed the rifle's receiver in 1885 and paired it with shorter barrel lengths to yield, at 8½ pounds, a gun two pounds lighter than the original. At the same time, a small frame model, another pound lighter still, was made in .32-40 and .38-55. First priced at $32, Model 1881 was later made available with a set trigger, special sights, checkering, engraving, case-hardening and gold and silver plating.

When John Marlin submitted his 1881 rifle to the chief of ordnance for military trials, it fired 10 shots in seven seconds. Despite its solid performance, the rifle was eliminated when a cartridge exploded in the magazine. There were no injuries and the cause was not determined.

Marlin's Model 1881 had two major faults: top ejection, which was eliminated in subsequent Marlins beginning with the Model 1889, and unreliable feeding from magazine to carrier. This second problem was particularly bothersome. A split carrier with a wedge that expanded the carrier in operation eventually solved it. This rifle was offered in many versions, including one with a smooth bore. It was discontinued in 1891, after some 20,000 copies were produced.

Lewis Hepburn, Annie Oakley and Accurate Barrels

In 1884, Marlin was issued patents for a top-ejecting lever-action .22 rifle, similar to Winchester's Model 73. Although it was never manufactured, patents granted that year to a Remington

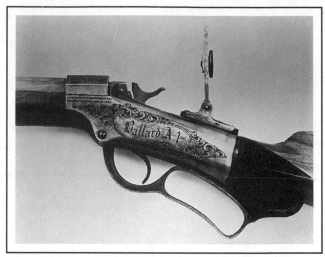

This Marlin-Ballard target rifle with its folding tang sight was made between 1875 and 1890.

designer in Ilion, Lewis L. Hepburn, helped establish for Marlin a leading spot in the arms industry.

Born in 1832, Hepburn had built muzzleloading rifles in his own shop from 1855 until 1871, the year he went to work for Remington. A champion marksman as well as a prolific designer, Lewis fired with the first Creedmore team to beat the defending Irish sharpshooters in 1874. He also developed the Remington-Hepburn No. 3 single-shot breechloading rifle. When Remington faced financial ruin in 1886, Lewis joined Marlin to design and produce lever-action guns, including Models 1888, 1889, 1891, 1892, 1893, 1894, 1895 and 1897. He also worked on slide-action shotguns, .22's and autoloading rifles, not to mention various magazines, safeties, sights and takedown mechanisms. Hepburn worked

Annie Oakley was one of many trick shooters who used and promoted Marlin rifles. This Model 1889 (above) was engraved especially for her.

Marlin's first successful lever-action rifle was Model 1881 (top). Models 1888 (center) and 1889 (bottom) featured several mechanical improvements.

at Marlin until January 6, 1910, when he slipped on ice and broke his hip. It refused to heal. Bedridden but uncomplaining, he lingered four more years before dying on August 13, 1914.

While Marlin initially marketed Hepburn's Model 1881 as superior because of the powerful cartridges it chambered, the popularity of smaller rounds in the lightweight version promised even greater success for the Hepburn-designed Model 1888. Chambered in .32-20, .38-40 and .44-40, with barrels ranging between 16 and 44 inches, it was available in many configurations. The 24-inch model held 16 rounds, weighed 6½ pounds and cost $18. Fewer than 5,000 copies were made before Model 1888 was discontinued in 1892.

Its successor—and Marlin's first side-ejecting lever rifle—was Model 1889, chambered for the same Winchester centerfire (WCF) cartridges that fed Marlin's Model 1888. By this time, the second pair of numbers, which heretofore had referenced the standard charge of black powder used in a case, was often deleted from cartridge designations. For

example, "W" now sufficed for "WCF." The most popular model was a .44-40 (.44W) with a 24-inch octagonal barrel. One customer even ordered a 54-inch barrel, and Marlin made quantities of other 1889 rifles with short magazines, half magazines, pistol grips and other options. Musket and takedown versions were also available. A saddle-ring carbine was also listed, with a 15- or 20-inch barrel. All standard 1889's featured a tab at the rear of the lever to lock it closed. This great Marlin rifle was discontinued in 1895; and eight years later, the last of 55,119 Model 1889's produced by Marlin were assembled and shipped.

Lewis L. Hepburn contributed a great deal as well to Model 1891, Marlin's first successful .22 rimfire lever rifle. His design was evident in features adopted from Models 1888 and 1889, but what sold the gun was side ejection, easy access to the mechanism, and exhibition shooting by Annie Oakley. The first version, priced at $18, featured a straight grip and 24-inch barrel. A 32-caliber rimfire Model 1891 appeared in 1892, complete with tube feed

Predecessors of Marlin's Model 39 .22 include (top to bottom) Models 1892, 1891 and 1897. Model 97 came standard with a shotgun butt; the one shown here has a special-order rifle-style butt.

and the same interchangeability of Long and Short ammunition that had boosted .22 rimfire sales. Best of all, .32 centerfire rounds could be used after changing the firing pin. Marlin ads emphasized the .32 rifle's utility as follows:

> "This ammunition is cheap, and as compared with repeaters using the .32-20 or .32 WCF cartridges, will save the entire cost of the rifle on the first two or three thousand cartridges. The ammunition is what costs in the long run. Get the best rifle made to shoot cheap cartridges."

Even then, Marlin was quick to point out the reputation it had established for accurate barrels:

> "They are rifled deep, and will not foul as quickly as barrels not rifled as deep. This also adds to the life of the barrel, as they will not become shot out as quickly. The accuracy of our barrels has been a standard of excellency for years."

Ten-Dollar Deer Rifles and Bicycle Guns

In 1896, after a production run of 18,000, Model 1891 was replaced by Model 1892. Although the new rifle lacked a lever-operated trigger safety, its improved trigger mechanism and a blocking device for the firing pin prevented accidental firings. Cosmetically, the 1892 was much like its predecessor, and its starting price was the same. More than 40,000 copies were made, all in .22 and .32 rimfire, before Marlin dropped this model in 1915.

The next Marlin rifles—Models 1893, 1894 and 1895—were essentially the same except for action dimensions. Introduced in its same year, Model 1893 handled the long .32-40-165 and .38-55-255 cartridges. Its stronger lock-up and two-piece firing pin distinguished it from Model 1889. A musket version (with bayonet) was also offered. The standard

Model 1893 had a 26-inch round barrel marked for smokeless powder loads. In 1905, a "Grade B" rifle in .32-40 and .38-55 was offered. Its barrel, marked "For Black Powder," was not made of the "Special Smokeless Steel" advertised by Marlin for its other rifles of this period. Starting with Model 1893 (which sold for $13.35 and up), Marlin listed case-hardened receivers as standard on its lever rifles. Previously, blued finishes had been standard, with case-hardening available at extra cost. In 1922, when Marlin resumed production of this model, some of the optional features were no longer available, but the .30-30 and .32 Special were added as chamberings.

Model 1893 had a counterpart—Model 1894—to handle smaller centerfire rounds (the .25-20, .32-20, .38-40 and .44-40). It came with a 24-inch round barrel, had case-colored fittings, and sold for $18. The lightweight carbine configuration, with half-magazine and 20-inch barrel in .44-40, scaled only 5½ pounds. This delightful rifle, with its slide-elevated rear sight, apparently did not create the stampedes of customers then that it would now. The price of this Model 1894, like that of its contemporaries, dropped later on, so that in 1901 one

could buy a standard model for $10.40. Model 1893 remained in production until 1917, when war changed the company's priorities. It came right back in 1922 and continued to sell until 1936, reappearing only briefly between 1929 and 1933.

Model 1895 was a beefed-up version of Model 1893 designed for fatter cases: the .38-56, .40-65, .45-70 and .45-90. The .40-70 and .33 WCF were added in 1897 and 1912, respectively. A takedown barrel could be ordered for a Model 1895 for $3.50 additional, bringing the base price of the gun to $22. Barrel lengths ran from 20 to 32 inches in 2-inch increments. For longer tubes, a customer was charged $1 per inch. As always, full-length magazines were standard, but half and short magazines (which held only three cartridges) sold well. Both 15- and 22-inch barreled carbines were cataloged from the start. A lightweight version, chambered for the .33 Winchester, appeared in 1912, matching the regular carbine's weight at 7½ pounds despite a 24-inch barrel. After 1913, this lightweight was the only Model 1895 still being advertised by Marlin.

Marlin's takedown rifles sold well and, in 1897, prompted the introduction of a .22 takedown. It

Marlin's Model 93 (top photo) was a side-ejecting rifle, whereas Winchester's Model 94 ejected from the top, a difference that favored Marlin when scopes came into use. The company's Model 27S slide-action .22 (bottom photo) roughly resembles Winchester's Model 62.

Marlin made its popular Model 1893 centerfire rifle in several versions, including a take-down (top) and musket (center). The Model 1894 shown at bottom is a carbine with short magazine.

looked like a Model 1892, but loosening a thumb-screw on the receiver and removing a sideplate exposed the action parts and unlocked the barrel. A special bicycle version with a 16-inch barrel could

Marlin employees pose in front of the Willow Street factory in New Haven in 1905.

be stowed in a leather-bound canvas case and strapped inside a bicycle frame. Like most Marlins of the period, Model 1897 .22 came standard with case-hardened receiver, hammer, lever and magazine cap. A half magazine was offered in 1899, the same year a magazine cutoff was featured to improve feeding of mixed-length cartridges. Model 1897's were made until 1916.

John Mahlon Marlin died in 1901, leaving his sons, Mahlon and John Howard, in charge of the company. On May 16, 1910, Marlin acquired Ideal Manufacturing, a New Haven toolmaker. Ideal had been established in 1884 by John Barlow, an immigrant who had fought in the Civil War, then worked for Parker and Winchester. When Marlin took charge, few things changed. Ideal's loading tools, many of them designed by Barlow, had already earned a good reputation among handloaders.

During its ownership of Ideal, Marlin stamped the tools with its own name and added it to the Ideal Handbook, a popular source book for hand-loaders. When Marlin sold Ideal to Phineas Talcott

Mahlon Henry Marlin (1864–1949) assumed leadership of the company following his father's death in 1901.

later on, he followed the same course. Ideal was bought by the Lyman Gun Sight Company in 1925.

While lever rifles and reloading tools kept Marlin prosperous at the dawn of America's automobile era, political events in Europe soon demanded other hardware from this New Haven armsmaker. As early as the spring of 1915, Marlin had been asked by arms broker J.P. Morgan to bid on the manufacture of 100,000 7mm Mauser rifles. Mahlon Marlin demurred, saying Marlin's facilities were not suited to such a large scale of production, and that refurbishing the plant would cost too much. But J.P. Morgan & Company had committed heavily to supplying the Allies with arms and ammunition; in fact, this aggressive firm was then the sole purchaser of war materials for England. Tenaciously, Morgan pursued Marlin and other companies with whatever

machinery was needed to make guns. When rebuffed, it encouraged the formation of syndicates by investment houses for the purpose of buying out the manufacturers. Two years earlier, a one-percent Federal Graduated Income Tax had taken effect as a "temporary" measure to replenish government coffers. This may have given Mahlon Marlin, who knew there was no such thing as a "temporary" tax, the nudge he needed to sell his firm.

The Rockwell Era and World War I

A syndicate comprising William P. Bonbright & Company and Kissell-Kinnicutt & Company bought the Marlin Firearms Company and—on December 9, 1915—formed the Marlin Arms Corporation. The new firm showed 35,000 shares of preferred stock at $100 par value and 60,000 shares of common stock with no par value. There were no outstanding debts, and the company treasury was to retain $1.3 million in cash. Preferred stock was to be retired at par in three equal portions on December 1, 1916, March 1, 1917, and June 1, 1917. Common and preferred stock were to be placed in a voting trust, with a majority interest determined by the syndicate. Albert F. Rockwell, then president of the Bristol Brass Company, was chosen as president of the new Marlin Arms Corporation.

One of the conditions specified by Bonbright was the receipt from J.P. Morgan of a British contract for 12,000 machine guns. These Model 1914 Colts were to be made under exclusive license from Colt and delivered at a minimum price of $650 per gun. Royalty payments to Colt added $100 to the price of each gun. This fee also procured the services of John Browning, who invented the 1914 Colt. Marlin president Rockwell would receive as part of his compensation a portion of "the saving in cost of manufacture of the Colt gun below the figure of $300 per gun."

As fighting in Europe drew the U.S. closer to a declaration of war, Rockwell reorganized the company, changing its name in 1916 to the Marlin-Rockwell Corporation. No sporting guns were now inscribed with the Marlin Arms Corporation name, although a handtrap built just before World War I still carried it, as did a 1915 retail price list for existing Marlin guns. The names of both firms were stamped on all military arms.

Rockwell's formal education ended at age 13, but he had already proven himself an able entrepreneur by the time he joined Marlin Arms Corporation as its president in 1915. He had managed a hardware store and fruit business, and with his brother had formed the New Departure Bell Company of Bristol, Connecticut. From there, the Rockwells ventured into various markets: bicycle lamps and coaster brakes, springs, and eventually ball bearings. In 1907, A.F. Rockwell established the Bristol Engineering Company to make the first domestic cast engine blocks for automobiles, and the following year, at New York's Auto Show, Rockwell launched his new Public Service Cab. Produced by New Departure, which had taken over car production from Bristol Engineering, the cab was painted yellow in deference to Mrs. Rockwell's choice of color. What better name for the new taxi than "Yellow Cab"?

Unfortunately, A.F. Rockwell's optimism for his cars exceeded their performance in the market. He spent too freely promoting and producing them, until in 1911 he was forced to halt production (the company's automobile assets were acquired in 1915 by General Motors). Automobile buffs still remember well the old Houpt-Rockwell cars: the Landaulet, Limosine, Raceabout, Touring Car and Close-Coupled Runabout.

Between 1913 and 1915, A.F. Rockwell served as president of Bristol Brass. A generous man, he donated a park to the city of Bristol and gave to other civic causes. He relinquished Marlin's top job in 1920, and on February 17, 1925, he died. His son, Hugh, who had joined Rockwell at Marlin during the war, contributed to the company with some patented inventions and continued working at the Bristol plant.

During the armament years prior to World War I, Marlin-Rockwell and the Savage Arms Company were the only two U.S. gun firms producing machine guns in quantity. Marlin-Rockwell was awarded a government order in 1917 for 2,500 Colt training guns, followed by additional contracts for 5,000 aircraft machine guns, 20,000 Browning Automatic Rifles (BARs) and 10,000 new Browning aircraft guns. To meet production schedules, Marlin used the Hopkins & Allen Arms Company works in Norwich, Connecticut, which was then finishing up a military rifle contract for Belgium. Marlin also bought and retooled the Mayo Radiator Company of New Haven.

While manufacturing Colt machine guns, Marlin also developed a lightweight gas piston mechanism to replace Browning's "potato digger" design. A synchronizer built by Marlin enabled the gun to be fired through whirling propeller blades without striking them. Contracts were subsequently awarded Marlin for its Model 1917 gas-operated machine gun. On the battlefront in 1918, Marlin aircraft guns were fired successfully on four separate air raids at 13,000- and 15,000-foot altitudes, and at temperatures of minus 20 degrees F. On one trip, the guns were completely covered with ice, yet all metallic links and fabric belts performed satisfactorily. By October 1, 1918, Marlin had fulfilled its contract for 38,000 synchronized aircraft guns—21,000 of those being made in the last five months of production.

Marlin also made belt-loading equipment for its machine guns. A verbal agreement in 1916 between Marlin, Colt and John and Matt Browning committed a $3.75 royalty each to Colt and the Brownings for every loading machine manufactured by Marlin. Many of these, marked "Shaw Loading Machine," were later sold to Russia. Then, in the spring of 1918, the Ordnance Department asked Marlin to modify its Model 1917 machine gun for tank use. It was to have a heavier barrel, aluminum fins to radiate heat, a slower rate of fire, and new sights, handgrips, triggers, and charging handles. Hindered by bureaucratic and technical problems, work progressed slowly. By autumn of 1918, only 171 tank guns had been made; but by war's end in November, the total had soared to 1,470. In all, Marlin Arms Corporation and Marlin-Rockwell Corporation con-

Marlin's Model 15YN single-shot .22 (above) is proportioned specially for youngsters.

This Model 1995SS in .45-70 Government remains Marlin's most powerful lever-action gun.

tributed heavily to the war effort, producing 2,500 Colt Model 1914 machine guns, 1,605 Marlin Navy Mark V machine guns, 38,000 Marlin Model 1917 aircraft machine guns, 2,646 Marlin Model 1918 tank machine guns and 16,000 BARs.

Postwar Reorganization: Birth of the Model 39

Now, as it faced the post-war era, Marlin-Rockwell had become an industrial conglomerate comprising 10 divisions, as follows:

Braeburn Steel Company, Pittsburgh, Pa.
Heany Laboratory, New Haven, Ct.
Insulated Wire Division, New Haven, Ct.
Marlin Arms Division, New Haven, Ct.
Marlin-Rockwell Loading Company, New Haven, Ct.
Marlin-Rockwell Machine Shop, Tacony, Pa.
Norwich Division (Hopkins & Allen), Norwich, Ct.
Plainville Division, Plainville, Ct.
Radiator Division (Mayo), New Haven, Ct.
Standard Roller Bearings, Philadelphia, Pa.

The only armsmaker in this list was Hopkins & Allen, which evolved from Merwyn, Hulbert and Company after that company stopped building guns in 1898. By then, Hopkins & Allen, which was founded in 1867, had already established a business with its acquisition of the Davenport Fire Arms Company of Norwich, Ct., and the Forehand Arms Company of Worcester, Mass. At the beginning of World War I, H&A was a growing firm; but when it failed to make good on a contract to build Model 1889 Mauser rifles for the Belgian government the company went into bankruptcy. Marlin-Rockwell Corporation acquired it in a court foreclosure on October 17, 1917, and continued to manufacture automatic military arms at the Norwich plant. After

the war, this plant was closed down and its machinery moved to Marlin's New Haven facility.

About this time, J. Allen Heany, an engineer with Marlin's Heany Laboratory and Insulated Wire Division, found a way to make strong asbestos wire by using cotton in its core. Early wiring for heaters, flat irons, stoves and other appliances was manufactured in the old Ely Whitney gun works in Whitneyville (Ct.). In 1920, when Marlin divested itself of all peripheral enterprises (with the exception of its Plainville ball bearing branch, which later became Standard Roller Bearing Company), Heany Laboratory and the Insulated Wire Division were sold. Eventually, they became the Rockbestos Products Corporation (New Haven, Ct.), which still manufactures products, from .053-inch aircraft ca-

This big broaching machine makes the major cuts in Marlin's receivers.

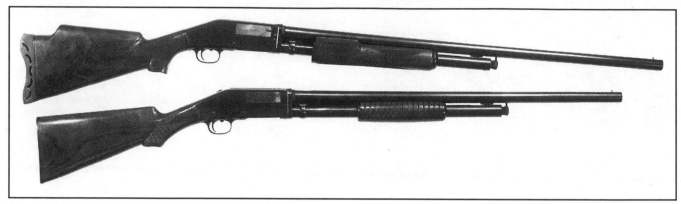

While noted more for its rifles, Marlin also made several shotguns, among them the Model 43 (bottom) and Model 43 Trap hammerless slide-actions shown here.

ble to 3½-inch electric transmission lines. The Standard Roller Bearing Company, meanwhile, continued to operate under the Marlin-Rockwell name. Much later, in 1982, TRW bought the firm and retired the name. It now functions as the Bearing Division of TRW.

During World War I, the Marlin-Rockwell Loading Company, also located in New Haven, designed and manufactured bombs for the U.S. military. An early contract called for 28,000 Barlow bombs, but a complex firing mechanism slowed production, forcing cancellation of the contract after only 9,000 bombs had been produced. In December, 1917, Marlin was awarded another contract for 70,000 Mark II bombs, but soon thereafter the order was reduced to 40,000 when front-line fighters demanded a bigger explosive charge. The surplus bombs were then used for training. During World War I, Marlin maintained its own hangars and airplanes in New Haven, where it tested bombs, bomb racks and triggering devices.

In 1914, Carl Gustaf Swebilius, one of Marlin's greatest engineers, began designing guns for the company. Born in Sweden in 1879, Swebilius came to America 17 years later and began his career as a barrel driller for the Marlin Firearms company. Later, he became a toolmaker and eventually chief engineer. Throughout the war and during the 1920's, Swebilius strongly influenced the design of Marlin shotguns, slide-action .22 and centerfire rifles, and autoloading mechanisms for both sporting and machine guns. This industrious and affable Swede also worked for the Winchester Repeating Arms Company, and in 1926 he formed the High Standard Manufacturing Company, which made deep-hole drills. Swebilius bought the defunct

Hartford Arms Company in 1931 to manufacture High Standard pistols. He died in October, 1948.

The Postwar Slump

Beginning in 1919, Marlin-Rockwell began to divest itself of its holdings. During the next two years, it used up most of its stock of pre-war gun parts. On July 23, 1921, the Marlin Firearms Corporation was formed in Delaware, supplanting the Marlin-Rockwell Corporation. Insurable assets at the time totaled over $2 million. The balance sheets showed just over $182,000 in available cash and almost $734,000 in inventory. Plant machinery, tools and fixtures came to $1.9 million. Capitalization included 14,000 shares of preferred stock with a par value of $50 a share, and 27,500 shares of common stock.

The new company's president was John F. Moran, who had joined Marlin as ordnance manager during the war. A salesman by nature and training, Moran said he intended to make Marlin a leader in the firearms industry. To fulfill his pledge, he used Marlin-Rockwell's earlier acquisition of Hopkins & Allen to promote new Marlin guns built on H&A designs. Among them was the Safety Police .38 revolver, a top-break gun identical to H&A's Safety Police. Another successful product from Marlin Firearms was its Model 60 single-shot shotgun, which was essentially H&A's Model 712 with a revamped stock. A year after its formation, Marlin resurrected a single-shot target pistol first marketed by H&A in 1913. Like its contemporaries, this gun (about 50 were made in all) was built largely from parts on hand. It included a detachable skeleton stock offered by H&A in 1914 (when the pistol listed for $10).

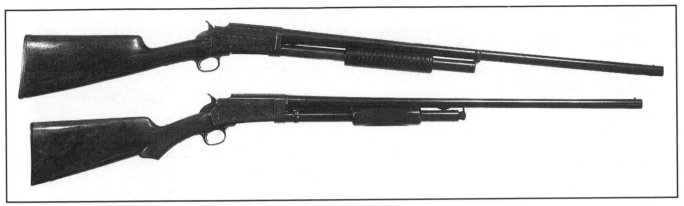

These early exposed-hammer, slide-action shotguns—Marlin Models 17 (top) and 30 (bottom)—look very much like Winchester's Browning-designed Model 97.

The Marlin Firearms Corporation issued its first catalog in 1922. That year, Marlin offered two slide-action 22 caliber models—20 and 38—and also introduced its Model 39, a lever-action .22 based on the prewar models 1892 and 1897. A few Model 39's were made by Marlin-Rockwell before the sporting arms business was sold, but officially this rifle was born in 1922. With its standard 24-inch octagon barrel and distinctive curve in the bottom of its pistol grip, Model 39 retailed for $26.50. It also featured quick takedown and the ability to feed mixed loads of different length cartridges. Bolts on these early 39's were weakened by a cut just aft of the locking lug, causing some bolts to crack when used with high-speed ammunition. As a result, bolt manufacture was changed in 1932 to eliminate the cut. Bolts made after 1932 were marked "HS" and were considered safe when used with any ammunition. Model 39A was introduced in 1939, featuring a coil mainspring (replacing Model 39's leaf), a round barrel, and beefier forend (list price was $26.95). After World War II, the case coloring on Model 1939's receiver was dropped for a blued finish; and except for wartime breaks in production, this famous .22 lever rifle has remained essentially the same since its inception in 1891. In its many forms, it has become the world's oldest rifle still in production.

Neither the engineering genius of Gus Swebilius nor John Moran's marketing skills could keep the Marlin Firearms Corporation from feeling the postwar slump. Eventually, a large mortgage, back taxes, and heavy re-organization costs pulled the company into court. Payments due totaled more than $162,000, and a tepid sporting gun market promised no relief. Charles Haskell, the ex-governor from Oklahoma who had led the group buyout of Marlin-Rockwell's Insulated Wire and Heany Laboratory sections (which became Rockbestos) in 1920, still held a $200,000 mortgage on the real estate of the Marlin Firearms Corporation. Accordingly, on February 4, 1924, Superior Court of New Haven awarded a foreclosure judgment to Charles and Lillian Haskell. On May 10 of that year, the Haskells conveyed to Frank Kenna, for the price of $1, all of Marlin's land and buildings. Kenna then conveyed to a newly organized Marlin Firearms Company the same property for the same price. Tax obligations and the mortgage were transferred in the deal.

Frank Kenna, the Great Depression, and Charles Newton

Born in New Haven on June 22, 1874, Frank Kenna, Sr., graduated from the Yale School of Law in 1905. He was admitted to the bar that same year and quickly established a law practice, which he continued until 1939. While in school, Kenna published the *Yale Law Journal*, ran the Kenna Advertising Agency, and worked part-time at a newspaper. His news experience prompted the founding later on of the Marlin Industrial Division's "Illustrated Current News." Kenna dealt in real estate, too, buying up land on which to develop housing projects (one 19-acre tract was parlayed into 70 homesites). Risking capital when the odds looked good, he had the drive and savvy to succeed at whatever he tried. For example, Kenna helped organize the American Bank and Trust Company, founded the Race Brook Country Club, was a member of the board of aldermen and the state legislature, and served as president of several companies,

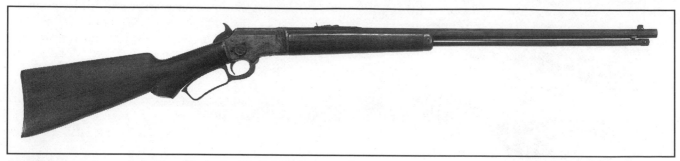

Marlin's most famous rimfire rifle is the Model 39 lever-action shown here.

including the Associated Realty Company, M.J. Jordan Company, Connecticut Finance Company, Mortgage Loan Company, and Groton Park Development.

Frank Kenna, Jr., recalled once that his father believed in the Edward Harriman rule: "Borrow when money is tight, hoard when money is easy." But there was more borrowing than hoarding ahead for Frank Kenna in 1923. When the ailing Marlin Firearms Corporation was offered at a local sheriff's sale in 1924, he bid $100 for the real estate, which included 13 buildings with 140,000 feet of floor space, as well as the land beneath it all. The only hitch: it carried a $100,000 mortgage. When nobody topped his bid, Kenna bought the business and in the process negotiated the mortgage down to $95,000. On January 15, 1926, Frank Kenna incorporated his enterprise in Connecticut as the Marlin Firearms Company, with partners Thomas W. Cahill and Harold G. Wayne.

Kenna promptly leased some of the office space to other businesses and issued $100,000 of preferred stock at 8 percent, wooing investors by reminding them of Marlin's great tradition in the gun industry. He boasted of "putting the New England conscience into every gun," and declared, "Every gun that leaves the factory is the kind of firearm you can use with the assurance that you have the best in material, workmanship, accuracy and safety." In 1928, Kenna was able to report "an increase of more than $45,000 in sales for the first ten months of this year, contrasted to the same period of 1926, with a consequent increase in net profits of 80 percent."

Indeed, Kenna's unfailing entrepreneurship carried Marlin through some grueling times. In a 1944 shareholder report, he unabashedly told of his efforts on behalf of the company during the Depression: "As a matter of fact, the investment of every stockholder in The Marlin Firearms Com-

pany, both the preferred and the common, was entirely lost in 1933. . . . For more than 80 days we were operating with a sheriff in legal possession of the plant. The real estate was in fact advertised for sale by the first mortgagee.

"In the meantime, by means of a loan made to me for which I paid a large bonus, and for which I

Frank Kenna, Sr. (1874–1947) saved the Marlin Firearms Company from bankruptcy in 1924 and rebuilt the firm.

was personally responsible, by draining other companies which I owned personally, of every dollar they could spare, by pledging my insurance policies, by putting in all of the personal cash I could raise . . . I managed to prevent the sale of the properties. . . ."

During the darkest days of the Depression, when the prime rate bottomed at 1.5 percent, foreclosure notices on Marlin by first and second mortgage trustees totaled about $193,000. The City of New Haven claimed an additional $22,000 in back taxes. Kenna spent most of his time in court and raising money, but he never appealed to the stockholders for a bailout. A Reconstruction Finance Corporation mortgage of $70,000 arrived just in time to help Marlin limp into the 1940's, and it was then that Frank Kenna reminded his shareholders that, in tough times, "Each preferred stockholder who purchased four shares of stock paid $100. He received a $52 shotgun and $14 in dividends. His net investment on each $100 was $34. Today his stock is worth the full par value. . . ."

In March, 1929, a frustrated rifle designer named Charles Newton approached Frank Kenna and pleaded to have Marlin build his new Leverbolt Rifle. He even offered to split the profits. The idea sounded good, but Kenna was a shrewd bargainer and agreed at first only to test the market. Newton claimed his Leverbolt "has all the strength and simplicity of the bolt action type combined with the speed and ease of operation of the lever action. . . ."

Kenna agreed to accept orders and deposits for the Leverbolt Rifles, and if enough came in to cover start-up costs, Marlin would go ahead and produce them. In 1932, Newton's Leverbolt Company published a notice to sportsmen asking for orders: "The Marlin Co. is very conservative and cannot see why anyone should want a rifle more powerful than their .30-30, Model 1893. Once they are shown, they are ready, willing and able to build them for us to sell. You alone can show them."

Nevertheless, Newton's advertising failed to generate the 500 orders Frank Kenna needed to convince him the Leverbolt would succeed. The Depression had begun just as the new rifle was announced, and in the end Kenna's caution proved well-founded.

During the Depression, Marlin's main objective—and that of other American armsmakers—was simply to stay in business. In addition to slumping demand, which idled machines and shrunk profits, the 11 percent Pittman-Robertson firearms tax first levied in 1937 was an extra burden. Frank Kenna's zealous recruiting of small businesses to fill his idling Marlin plant rated an article in the March, 1945, edition of *Collier's* magazine. It described how, with less than $2,000 start-up money, he filled 39 buildings and 700,000 square feet with 110 small industries, some of which paid as little as $15 a month in rent (and which he often waived). Over a 15-year period, Kenna lost only $1,759 in uncollected funds; conversely, his rent receipts during that time totaled nearly $2.5 million.

Collier's reported that Kenna even traveled to communities around New Haven, seeking out businesses that had failed and finding out why. If he thought a move to New Haven would give the owner a better start, he said so. After attending a foremen's association meeting once, he marched a selected few down to the bank and helped them borrow enough money to set up competing businesses of their own. As president of the bank,

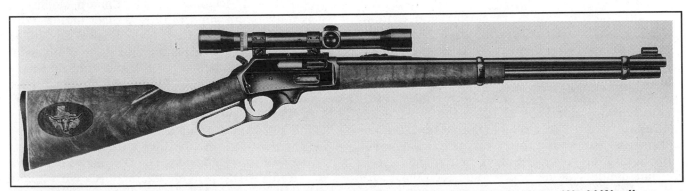

Marlin's Model 336 has appeared in many configurations since it supplanted Model 36 prior to World War II. Among them was this DT (Deluxe Texan) carbine (made in 1962 and 1963 only).

Kenna could extend credit freely, and he did so for people who showed some ambition. He thought little of guaranteed jobs and admonished young men to shape their own futures. "I almost hate the word *security*," he once declared, observing that government programs might be a good thing for people who lacked initiative, but they also squelched initiative.

Model 336, "Micro-Groove" Rifling, and the UDM

In 1936, Marlin improved its workhorse Model 1893, adding a fuller forend, fluted stock comb, and new sights. The rifle, carbine and sporting carbine versions of this new Model 1936 were offered in 1937 at $32 each. Later that year, the Model 1936 designation was shortened to Model 36. Although steel buttplates were listed for it, apparently only hard rubber ones were provided, completing a change that began with shotgun-style rubber buttplates as options on the old Model 1889 rifles.

Model 36 retailed for $61.45 in 1948, when it was replaced by Model 336. It remains in production and has, in its varied forms, become what many hunters picture when they think of Marlin. In 1955, "Micro-Groove" rifling replaced the cut Ballard-type rifling used in earlier Marlin Model 336 rifles. Developed in 1950, Micro-Groove barrels were subsequently installed on every Marlin rifle. The shallow, multiple-grooved rifling was ironed in with a hardened tungsten carbide button; thus a bore could be finished in about five seconds, compared to 15 minutes for the old cut method. Micro-Groove rifling has since become a catchword with shooters, as purely "Marlin" as "Silvertip" bullets are to Winchester and "Golden Ring" scopes are to Leupold.

When Micro-Groove rifling came on the market, a Marlin 336 could be bought for $74. In addition to .30-30 WCF, .32 Winchester Special and .35 Remington, the rifle was offered in .219 Zipper. Only 3,230 Zippers were made before a soft market stopped their manufacture in 1959. Besides, claimed shooters, lever actions were not varmint guns. In fact, Marlin had announced a more traditional varmint rifle back in 1954. Built on a Sako action, its Model 322 was chambered in .222 Remington and came equipped with a Sako receiver sight and Micro-Groove barrel. When the barrels did not deliver the accuracy expected, Marlin replaced them with slimmer, stainless steel barrels

Marlin rifles are found wherever hunters go. This Inuit seal hunter keeps his Model 336 at the ready.

and called the new rifle, "Model 422 Varmint King." Production of Model 322 and Model 422 together totaled only 6,213 before the 422 was dropped in 1958.

Marlin's only big-bore bolt rifle to date arrived on the scene in 1955. Stocked by Bishop, Model 455 was built on an imported FN Mauser action, with its stainless Marlin barrel chambered in .30-06. Later, the .308 Winchester and .270 Winchester were cataloged, but no .270's and only 59 .308's were built. Accordingly, Model 455 died in 1959.

Deer hunters continued to buy Model 336, however. During the last three decades, Marlin has given this gun a great deal of attention, offering more styles and chamberings without changing its basic well-proven design. The Glenfield line, introduced in 1964 to provide chain stores with "plain vanilla" versions of these popular rifles, lasted until

This "Micro-Groove" rifling machine draws barrels over a button that irons the lands and grooves into the bore.

1983. In 1963, Marlin began offering its Model 336 for the .44 Magnum revolver cartridge. Other new lever rifle chamberings since have included .444 Marlin, .375 Winchester, .45-70 and .356 Winchester. Model .356, a rimmed version of the compact (but potent) .358 Winchester, was developed for the Model 94 Angle-Eject rifles introduced earlier by Winchester's successor in the gun field, U.S. Repeating Arms (USRA). A companion cartridge—the .307 Winchester—performs much like the .308. It is chambered in Model 94 (Big Bore Walnut) and was planned for Model 336, but Marlin has made no rifles for it. USRA's Angle-Eject feature, incidentally, came nearly a century after John Mahlon Marlin decided to do away with top ejection in his Model 1889 rifle. Scopes probably didn't figure into his decision as they have Winchester's; but keeping empties out of the line of sight and dirt out of the

action remain important concerns. The closed-top receiver also provided greater strength.

World War II offered a business boost to beleaguered American armsmakers. Marlin was soon under contract to produce submachine guns and 20mm cannon links. In addition, the company manufactured 50,000 M1 Garand and 314,000 M1 carbine barrels, delivering up to 500 a day. It made other parts for the carbine, and such diverse items as wooden blocks, foot pedals and idler shafts for various military applications. Carl Swebilius, Marlin's aging engineer, designed a submachine gun, a functional but expensive model known as "UDM '42." A few prototypes were built by High Standard, but Marlin later produced over 15,000 UDMs for the United Defense Supply Corporation. Chambered in 9mm Parabellum (not .45 ACP), most were shipped into France or distributed in China. Swebilius' gun was not accepted for U.S. military use. Marlin also built the Hyde-Inland .45 submachine gun, approved by Ordnance as substitute standard in April 1942. While Marlin tooled up for this model, further development on the gun resulted in the famous M3 "Grease Gun." As a result, only 500 M2's were manufactured. The Korean War provided Marlin with contracts for 25,000 M3 barrels. The company also made 3,000 charging mechanisms for the 20mm wing-mounted Orlikon gun and contracted to supply 50,000 M1 Garand barrels. Nearly 10,000 of these barrels were rejected because of cracks, which Marlin people thought were due to faults in the supplied steel. Republic Steel made allowances for 2,500 barrels and Marlin used new blanks to complete delivery on a protracted schedule.

Almost any gun firm can prosper during war, but Frank Kenna knew by experience that diversification was required to help armsmakers get by when the peacetime market for sporting goods

The .444 Marlin cartridge was developed and is factory-loaded (by Remington) for only one rifle: Marlin's Model 444 SS.

sagged. During the tough post-Depression times, Marlin had started a razor blade business that lasted until 1968, when, as Frank's son remarked, "All these young fellows were letting their beards grow long." Next to guns, razor blades were among the most heavily promoted Marlin goods. The company also marketed cartridge belts, clay target throwers, gun racks and "Red Head" gun cases. Other domestic products included shaving cream, watch fobs, bicycles, bicycle locks, paperweights, buckles, hair brushes, calendars, baby carriages, handcuffs and whistles. A plastic grip cap with the owner's initials came with all Marlin lever rifles sold in 1951 and 1952, a program that proved much too costly. Marlin fared better with such gun accoutrements as slings, swivels, recoil pads, hammer spurs, scopes, mounts and iron sights.

Shotguns to Scholarships; A Family Enterprise

On December 26, 1947, Frank Kenna died, leaving the company to two of his sons, Roger and Frank, Jr. Roger assumed the presidency first. He had been initiated in 1945 when Marlin bought the Hunter Arms Company, and was appointed president of the L.C. Smith Gun Company. He'd tried to save L.C. Smith, keeping the fine shotgun on line until January 16, 1949, when flood damage caused the Fulton (NY) factory's first floor to collapse, spilling 14 milling machines into a lower-level raceway. With damage estimates at $75,000 and structural repairs needed for work to resume on the

Marlin's marketing manager, Tony Aeschliman (left), and company president Frank Kenna, Jr., examine a Model 39 rifle, a flagship product since World War II.

Frank Kenna, Jr., took over the company in 1947 and continues as its president.

second, third and fourth floors, the Fulton plant had closed.

Like his father, Roger was an aggressive salesman and civic leader. He founded the exclusive Young Presidents Organization for men who reached the top spot in a million-dollar company before the age of 39. In 1952, he moved the Marlin sales office to 715 Fifth Avenue in New York, where he expanded the Sears, Roebuck account by 50 percent at a time when other companies were struggling to break even in the postwar slump. Roger used mostly radio and cartoon advertising to boost razor blade sales and promote Marlin guns.

When Roger Kenna died on March 29, 1959, at the age of 49, he left his brother, Frank Jr., in charge. Frank had been on Marlin's board of directors since 1951, and upon Roger's death he became company president. Born in 1923, Frank, Jr., was the youngest of the five Kenna children. He attended Yale but left school to serve with the Marines in the Pacific Theatre in World War II. Upon his return, he entered Clarkson College of Technology in Potsdam, New York, to study mechanical engineering, then began a career with Marlin as a toolmaker. His rise through management positions was predictable but earned.

Young Frank's civic contributions and business accomplishments also read like those of his father. He has served as chairman of various campaigns to help the disadvantaged, and was a director of the New Haven Rehabilitation Center. He has lectured on business subjects at Boston College and the University of Massachusetts, and he continues

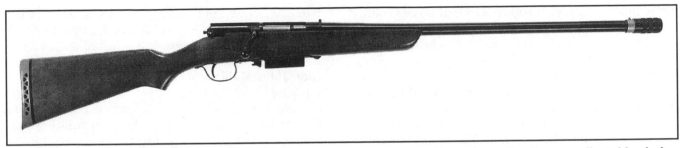

For hunters on a budget, Marlin offers its bolt-action Model 55 shotgun. This early version has an adjustable choke.

the Kenna tradition of helping young entrepreneurs get a start.

During the 1960's, computers and gun control legislation forced all armsmakers to redesign and modernize their operations. Business was no longer a matter of simply matching production to demand. Personnel management suddenly became as important as parts flow; and corporate image mattered almost as much as gun performance. When gun legislation made the headlines in 1968, Frank Kenna joined forces with O.F. Mossberg & Sons (New Haven) in opposing local, state and federal gun registration. Their views, as reported in the *New Haven Journal-Courier*, expressed why laws requiring registration wouldn't work. They stopped short of condemning all gun control, conceding that waiting periods and owner identification cards might have merit, and they supported a closer scrutiny of dealer licensing and mail-order gun sales.

Marlin's stately Willow Street complex in New Haven is still in use, mostly by small firms that rent office space.

Earlier, during the 1950's, Marlin had announced its hammerless Model 56 and 57 lever action rifles and Model 99 autoloaders. All three were rimfires; but Model 62, a variation of Models 56 and 57, arrived later in .256 Winchester and .30 Carbine (it was designed to chamber the .22 Jet as well, but no rifles were made for it).

With the 1960's came the bolt-action Model 980 rifle in .22 WMR, and a single-shot Model 122 Auto-Safe .22. Both were based on the Model 81C action that had been used for various rimfire rifles since 1939. Though inexpensive, the Auto-Safe couldn't match the sales appeal of Marlin's Tom Mix Special (Model 100S), which was marketed to youngsters for only $5.95 in 1937 and 1938. Marlin had advertised the little bolt gun as "a sensational value" at only "10 cents a day." That kind of innovative marketing is hardly practical now, but Marlin still builds and sells more .22 rimfire rifles than anyone else.

The postwar years also found Marlin engineers busy designing new shotguns. In 1955, the bolt-action Model 55 made its debut, followed by a single-shot, bolt-operated .410, named Model 59. Both were dropped in 1965. Marlin re-introduced the lamented L.C. Smith double in 1968, but a few years (and 2,000 guns) later, Kenna decided the market would not justify its expense and it was dropped. In 1971, Marlin announced its Model 120 pump shotgun, to be supplanted in eight years by Model 778, the last of a series of Marlin pumps that began in 1898, including 10 exposed-hammer and nine hammerless models. Marlin's Model 90 over/under, designed in 1936 for sale through Sears, had been discontinued by 1959. A lever action .410, introduced in 1929, did not survive the Depression.

The most popular gun in Marlin's line currently is Model 60, a .22 autoloader. Its alloy receiver gives it quickness in the hand, and also makes it relatively inexpensive to produce. Its racy lines have little in common with the traditional boxy profiles of the lever-action big game rifles John Mahlon Marlin engineered, but the low price—under $100—reflects the value he sought to give his very first customers.

Marlin still thrives on those exposed-hammer lever guns. If anything, they have become less contemporary. White stock spacers are being abandoned, and the short-action Model 94, recently reintroduced, has proven quite popular. Unfortunately for the purist, all traditional Marlin centerfire rifles are now made with a cross-bolt safety. This is an unabashed concession to a litigation-prone public; moreover, it perpetuates a feature that is contrary in design to the purpose for which a rifle is built.

Marlin's growth rate between 1959 and 1974 compounded at 14.3 percent. In 1969, the manufacturing plant was moved to a 240,000-square-foot building in North Haven, greatly favoring production. Four years later, Marlin pioneered a four-day work week, giving employees a choice of work schedules. In 1974, Frank Kenna, Jr., predicted the company would generate $28 million, with $2 million dollars in after-tax profits—the kind of money that John Mahlon Marlin could never have even imagined back in 1863.

Marlin remains a family-owned business, and though it's big enough now to keep on building more shoulder-fired guns than any other domestic maker, it still shows concern for the people who keep it competitive. In 1980, Frank, Jr., started a competitive scholarship fund for children of Marlin employees with at least two years of service, with more than 80 students benefitting so far.

The late Roger Kenna's son, Steve, is now Marlin's vice president of operations and manufacturing. DuPont-owned Remington and other industry giants continue to offer Marlin plenty of challenges, but the shrewd management and perceptive vision that have kept Marlin guns on dealer racks for 126 years remain evident in North Haven.

CHAPTER 9

JOHN BROWNING: UTAH'S MOUNTAIN MECHANIC

The last years of the 18th century were perilous ones for the pioneer farmers in north-central Tennessee. Local Indians had come to realize that the white men who were clearing fields and building cabins meant to stay there. The tolerance of the red man for white traffic soon gave way to hostility; between 1787 and 1793 at least 83 settlers were killed by Indians.

Among the farmers of Sumner County during that period was Edmund Browning, a descendant of Captain John Browning, who'd come to America in 1622 aboard the Abigail and had helped found an early Virginia settlement. After the Revolutionary War, Edmund Browning married and moved to Tennessee, establishing a farm near Brushy Fork.

Despite the hardships of that time and place, Edmund was by all accounts a gentle man. He played the violin expertly and treated his wife Sarah and seven children well. The Browning farm, like others in the area, produced barely enough to live on; but game was plentiful. Deprived of formal schooling, young boys quickly learned the skills necessary for survival on the frontier. Marksmanship was among the most important of these.

Edmund's son Jonathan, it seems, had more than a passing interest in guns. At the age of 13, he accepted a neighbor's broken flintlock rifle as payment for a week's farm work. Jonathan knew a blacksmith nearby who agreed to tutor the lad in return for help around the smithy. After a while, Jonathan brought his newly acquired firearm there and, to the surprise of his mentor, fixed the gun. Then he sold it for four dollars—to its original owner!

Jonathan continued to work at the smithy, learning how to weld, braze, solder, forge and tem-

per. He received little money but had the run of the shop for his own projects, which were mostly guns. By age 19, Jonathan had repaired many guns, using tools he'd made in the smithy, and dreamed now of building his own guns from scratch. The actions of the simple flintlocks, he knew, would be easy to make; he'd already been called upon at the smithy to fashion most of the common parts. Any difficulty he might encounter would come in drilling and rifling the barrel. Recognizing this was no job for a rural blacksmith, Jonathan decided to go to Nashville and watch a real gunmaker at work. He'd been impressed by a gun barrel bearing the mark of Samuel Porter, so one day Jonathan hiked the 30 miles to Nashville and found Porter's shop.

"No sir, I don't want a job. I just want to help you make barrels," Jonathan told the barrel maker. When Porter asked what he expected in return, the strapping six-foot lad insisted, "Nothing, sir, except I'd eventually like to make a few barrels myself." If the gunsmith had any reservations, he quickly dismissed them. The young man obviously knew metalworking; he asked only to gain more experience. Porter told Jonathan his meals would be provided and that he could sleep in the hay loft. Soon he started paying his apprentice two dollars a week, which Jonathan saved. He'd made it clear that he did not want a permanent job, and that he hoped to set up a gun business himself back home.

In three months, Jonathan had learned what he'd come to learn and was eager to be on his own. Besides, a girl back home was waiting to marry him. Reluctantly, Samuel Porter wished him well. "Here's a bit o' my shop to take home with thee," he said, offering Jonathan several mandrels, drills and cutters. With the tools Jonathan had already

Jonathan Browning, John's father, is credited with recognizing and encouraging his young son's genius for invention.

purchased, these made a heavy pack for his horse. He topped the load with a barrel bearing the proud inscription, "JONATHAN BROWNING 1824."

Back on Brushy Fork, the young mechanic built a shop next to his small house. In November, 1826, Jonathan Browning turned 21 and married Elizabeth Stalcup; and in August of the following year she bore the first of many Browning youngsters. While the family had no luxuries, Jonathan's gun business kept it from want. The West was calling to adventurers and farmers alike who were looking for better land. Streams of travelers came by the Browning gunshop, and because guns were so important on the frontier, Jonathan stayed busy.

Eventually, his parents and brothers joined the exodus. In 1834, a year after Edmund Browning's death, Jonathan and his family moved 400 miles away, to Quincy, Illinois. A growing town of 753 people, Quincy shadowed the Mississippi River, the hem of the West. In just a few years, its population would triple.

One of Jonathan's first projects at his new home was the development of a repeating rifle. The percussion cap had just recently been invented, prompting many gunsmiths to design guns that would hold several charges. The revolving cylinder came of age in the 1850's, but boring and aligning the chambers, then fitting the cylinder tightly to the barrel, all required a great deal of equipment. Jonathan Browning tried with his limited tools to build a revolving rifle, but the results were unsatisfactory. Not one to despair, he redirected his efforts to a simpler type of gun. It proved successful and would probably have been widely adopted had not metallic cartridges followed shortly.

Browning's new "slide gun" featured a rectangular bar that moved sideways through a slot in the frame, which in turn held the breech end of the barrel. The bar was bored lengthwise, with each cavity—usually there were five—making a chamber. For people who wanted more capacity and didn't mind the protrusion on either side of the gun, Jonathan would make longer bars. A small thumb lever advanced the bar, aligning it with the barrel and pushing it against the breech to make a gastight seal. The hammer, which lay underneath and swung up, was powered by a mainspring that also served as a triggerguard. The gun worked well and reflected Jonathan's penchant for straightforward designs.

At 35, Jonathan Browning had built a flourishing gun business and had been elected the local justice of the peace. One of his cousins, Orville, had made good as a Kentucky lawyer, and through him, Jonathan met another lawyer, named Abraham Lincoln. Lincoln took dinner with Jonathan one evening and marveled that young Browning could set the broken arm of a neighborhood waif as easily as he could weld pieces of metal together to make a gun part. With differences between North and South becoming ever more acute, Lincoln likened broken bones to the fracturing of the country. "It will take a lot of mending, Mr. Browning," surmised the future president.

Browning Joins the Mormons and Heads West

About 43 miles north of Quincy lay the new settlement of Nauvoo, which then consisted of 250 houses. It was a Mormon settlement started by Joseph Smith in 1839, after he'd escaped across the Mississippi from jail in Liberty, Missouri. Religious persecutions were not new to the Mormons, but as the sect gathered converts and sought to found its own religious community, resistance to the new settlement grew. Jonathan Browning had learned of The Prophet and his group from a Mormon customer who stopped at his gun shop in 1840. The Mormon literature left by his customer convinced

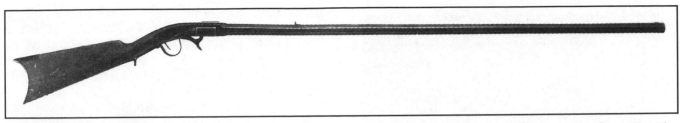

This under-hammer percussion rifle (c. 1855), a crude but functional repeater, was made by Jonathan Browning; it featured a sliding bar with several chambers.

Jonathan that here indeed was a true plan for salvation—a direct route to heaven. And so, in 1842, Jonathan joined the Mormon community and moved his family to Nauvoo, setting up shop on the first floor of a two-story brick home.

On June 25, 1844, Joseph Smith and his brother Hyrum were arrested and jailed in Carthage, Illinois. Despite a promise of protection from Governor Thomas Ford, a mob of over 20 armed men stormed the jail and killed both men. The panic that ensued among the Mormons was squelched by the efforts of Brigham Young, who saw little hope of restoring peace with the outside world east of the Mississippi. Accordingly, church leaders began to plan a mass exodus from Nauvoo.

Young figured the community could move by the spring of 1846, as soon as weather permitted. In the meantime, everyone contributed to the preparations. Timbers, having been cut and slabbed for wagons, were kiln-dried or boiled in salt water. Wheelwrights and blacksmiths, seamstresses, hunters and carpenters worked furiously. And well they did, for hostile neighbors forced the Mormons to move earlier than planned, in February, across a frozen Mississippi. Many of their household goods had to be left behind, and only a small part of their land had been sold, mostly because their persecutors had threatened anyone who dealt in Mormon-held property.

The group camped for a time on Sugar Creek, on the Iowa side of the big river, but within a month were forced to move again. According to one historian, the March weather "was extremely cold and stormy, and a great number of the people were without proper clothing and necessary shelter. Many of the wagons were without covers, while others had covers that failed to shed the rain. Several members of the camps died from exposure and lack of proper care. The roads were almost impassable. . . ."

In June, the travelers penetrated the land of the Omaha and Pottawattamie Indians, whom they found friendly. Near Kanesville (Council Bluffs), the Mormons halted for several months. There, in July, a U.S. Army officer approached the settlement and asked for 500 volunteers to help fight in the war against Mexico. This must have stunned the Mormons, who had repeatedly pleaded with the government without success to stem the injustices done them by religious persecutors and others. Dutifully, Brigham Young called for and got the volunteers. As for Jonathan Browning, who hoped he'd be chosen, Young told him, "You're too valuable a gunsmith to lose."

He said the same thing the next spring, when the Mormons again took to the trail. Browning was to stay behind with others to provision new followers and send much-needed firearms west. In Kanesville (Iowa), he set up a prosperous business, making slide guns that held up to 25 shots. These were particularly effective on the plains Indians, who liked to draw fire with a small detachment of warriors, then attack with the main contingent while their enemy tried furiously to reload. Browning's repeating guns allowed no break in the fire.

On July 24, 1847, when The great Mormon Exodus completed the final leg of its journey at Salt Lake, Utah, only 143 people were left. Jonathan Browning followed five years later, over ruts worn deep by the Mormon pioneers and other men bound for the gold of California.

An Ogden Gun Shop and Tannery

Jonathan and his family settled in Ogden, then known as Peter Skene Ogden, after a Canadian who explored vast areas of the West for the Hudson's Bay Company. By 1852, the town's settlers had already channeled the Ogden and Weber rivers into outlying farm fields and had platted the land into one-acre homesites. Jonathan Browning chose one of these parcels and parked his six wagons there. The $600 he'd hidden under the floor of the lead wagon helped buy building materials and food for his wife and 11 surviving children. Jonathan soon

This house in Nauvoo, Illinois, was home to the Brownings between 1842 and 1846.

followed the Mormon practice of polygamy, taking two more wives and siring 11 more children, including John Moses. By then, most of the children from Jonathan's first marriage were grown, with families of their own. Jonathan was 71 when his last child entered the world.

As soon as John Moses Browning could walk, he began toddling about his father's rough-hewn shop, later making fish hooks of shop scrap with which to catch suckers in the nearby irrigation canals. In 1862, about the time young John Moses turned seven, his father built a tannery. John helped him operate it, riding a harnessed horse in a circular track to keep the crude machinery operating. He'd sometimes fall asleep on the horse's bare back, then tumble to the ground. After only a month of this, John's mother insisted he start school. Jonathan didn't keep the tannery long, though. He was in his late 50's when he built it, and while it proved a viable enterprise, he had no interest in running a business. He preferred instead to work on guns and various building projects.

John's schooling lasted until he was 15. During that time, he spent as much time in his father's gunshop as in the classroom, waiting on customers and later fixing their firearms. He was only 10 when he built his first gun, a flintlock made from a smashed musket barrel, a piece of board, and some scrap metal and wire. Fashioning a crude, funnel-shaped pan out of the scrap, he screwed it to the wood, which he'd shaped with a hatchet. The barrel was held in place with wrappings of wire, soldered here and there. John stuffed it with a heavy charge of powder and some rough shot he'd made in the

shop. Next, he heated a small batch of coke on the forge, scooping it into a perforated tin can. The gun had no trigger or lock. Fire in the touchhole would come from the coke. So to keep air flowing to the coke he had to keep swinging the tin can on a wire leash.

John recruited his brother Matt to swing the can and together they moved into the fields bordering Odgen on the south. Soon the youngsters spied three prairie chickens and prepared the assault. John instructed Matt to thrust a long pine splinter into the hot coals. When the splinter caught fire, Matt lifted it to the touchhole. John, meanwhile, aimed his rifle somewhere in the middle of the dusting prairie chickens. The recoil was fierce—as John later put it, "I went down on my hunkers"—but all three birds were hit!

At the breakfast table the next morning, John and Matt broke the news to their father. "Let's see this magnificent gun," Jonathan said. After John had fetched the rifle, his father examined it carefully, then rose from the table. "John Mose," he sighed as he walked to the door, "you're almost eleven. Can't you make a better gun than that?"

Young John took that reprimand as hard as any he'd later remember. It was true, the gun wasn't much, but he didn't want to hear that from his father. Quickly, he unwound the wire holding metal to wood, broke the stock in two with his foot, and threw the pieces in the forge. After that, John often went hunting so he could test guns for his father, stalking bunches of quail and prairie chickens in the tall grass and weeds along the ditch banks. He always tried to get as many birds as possible with one shot. "Shooting then wasn't sport; it was a way to get meat," he'd explain later. "You didn't waste shot on singles or flying birds."

John's talents weren't directed only to guns. He learned to repair household utensils, sharpen knives, solder small tools, even sew. When eventually he designed a belt-fed machine gun, he stitched the cartridge loops for the prototype himself. He also made moccasins, a craft he'd learned from an itinerant Indian who spoke no English but periodically showed up at the Browning's barn. Getting buckskin for those moccasins took much more time than making them did. John and Matt decided they'd barter their way into more buckskin, which local Indians seemed able to find at will. John had fashioned bows and arrows in his father's shop, and he used them frequently to trade for home-grown produce or other items within the community. Now he courted the attention of a passing In-

John Moses Browning, the most prolific firearms designer in U.S. history, founded his own company and supplied many important gun designs to Winchester, Remington and other gun companies as well as the U.S. military.

dian by shooting arrows into a soft piece of pine. The Indian drew near, obviously interested. Through crude sign language, John told him the bow was his if he'd fetch a deer hide. A handful of arrows clinched the deal, and the Indian returned the next day with buckskin.

Just after John turned 13, a wagon freighter stopped at the shop with a badly damaged gun. The stock was broken and the mechanism no longer functioned. A few seconds' examination told Jonathan all he needed to know. "It'll cost more to fix than it's worth," he told the owner.

The damage was obviously severe and the freighter was in a hurry, so he bought a second-hand gun for $10 and headed for the door. But when he spotted John, he stopped. Laughing, he tossed the mangled firearm at the youngster and said, "Here, you might have some fun with this."

Salvaging that percussion smoothbore was the first real gunsmithing job John ever had. He spent a great deal of time just looking at the piece. Its svelte barrel—perhaps a 20-bore—had a fine finish,

as did the buttstock. Though the mechanism was smashed, John had handled enough guns to recognize superior craftsmanship. He vowed to rebuild it if he had to make every part new! He began by stripping the lock down to the smallest part and examining the pieces. The only components he couldn't fabricate were the barrel and breechplug, but both had been spared serious damage. To encourage him further, Jonathan presented his son with a cherished walnut blank for the new stock.

From Gunsmith to Designer and Manufacturer

This project brought John Browning out of boyhood. While his father, who was now in his 60's, dabbled in local politics, John kept the shop humming. He shouldered an increasing amount of the repair work and in his spare time made play guns that could be traded for produce or sold outright for a nickel apiece. Matt helped as much as he could. Five years younger than John and a faithful companion, he finally asked his brother to build him a gun. John agreed to do this only if Matt would provide the barrel.

That would be hard for a 10-year-old, and Matt had almost despaired of ever having his own gun when, upon cleaning under the bench one day, he discovered a new 32-caliber barrel that had been left behind by a customer months before. Using slide-rifle parts that had been brought from Missouri, John built Matt a .32 rifle. For years after, it complemented John's shotgun on hunts with Matt around Ogden and helped feed the Browning family.

When the transcontinental railway was finished in 1869, the last spike was driven in Promontory, Utah, only 50 miles from Ogden. The celebration repeated itself the following January, when Brigham Young's Utah Central Line connected Salt Lake City to Ogden. School ended that year, as always, when the frost left the ground. The demands of farming kept semesters short. But this would also be John's last semester in the one-room school. His teacher, a man of sketchy education himself, told him, "There's little use coming back next fall. You know about as much as I do now."

Determined not to make his father's mistake of squandering his mechanical talents on odd jobs, John concentrated on firearms. He knew he wanted to work on guns, and he was too independent to ask someone else for a job. His recurring problem was boredom—once he'd fixed one gun, there was another one to fix just like it. Repetition had sapped the challenge; he needed to find something new.

The fresh motivation John sought came in the form of breechloading mechanisms, pioneered as early as the Revolutionary War. British army major Patrick Ferguson had invented a serviceable breechloader in 1776 that was used against American troops in the Carolina campaign. In 1811, Captain John Hall of Maine developed another gun that could be charged from the rear. Sharps, Remington and other breechloading rifles arrived in mid-century, following the refinement of metallic cartridges. And soon after that, Walter Hunt's "Rocket Ball" repeater made its debut. While flawed in many ways, it became the template for guns that helped subdue America's rowdy frontier and changed the name of a New England shirt salesman—Oliver Winchester—into an American legend. Actually, Winchester had nothing to do with Hunt's rifle directly, but through the efforts of B. Tyler Henry, Dan Wesson, Horace Smith and other brilliant mechanics, the repeater evolved into Winchester's flagship product. It eventually took many forms, and John Browning's skills helped in furthering its development.

The shop John was gradually inheriting from his father had little to recommend it in the physical sense; but between referrals and name recognition, the Brownings always had plenty of business. One day in 1873, John realized the shop needed an overhaul. His father had bought some cheap charcoal, and to test it John threw it in the hot forge. The charcoal was wet, and as it hit the heat, it began to explode, scattering fragments over the shavings on the floor. Soon the place was on fire. John yelled for help, and his mother came running with water, arriving just in time to help save the building. Then she added a little heat of her own. "If you don't clean up this mess, you'll have another fire soon—and maybe you should. Look at this shack! I wouldn't keep *pigs* in this place!"

John felt duly ashamed. His mother was right—if he was going to work here he'd have to spruce up the building. His father agreed. "Son," Jonathan said, "why don't we do a little cleaning?" And so they did, rebuilding much of the structure in the process. It was there, five years later that John invented the first of his many gun mechanisms.

Early in 1878, just after John turned 23, his father encouraged him to spend some time designing a gun. "You've a good head, John Mose. Use it." So John did. With no drafting tools or blueprints,

he designed a single-shot rifle action. And with no milling machine, he hand-forged and trimmed most of the parts with file and chisel. The foot-lathe his father had carted by ox-team from Missouri helped fashion the remainder.

Late in the year, the young designer had a prototype, but no idea what to do with it. Patenting was a mysterious process even then. He finally wrote to Schoverling, Daly and Gales, a New York jobber from whom he'd bought shop supplies. "Please tell me how to patent a gun, and oblige." His letter got a fast response, including the name of a patent attorney to whom John wrote the same note. After complying with instructions, he filed for his first patent on May 12, 1879. The patent for his breechloading single-shot rifle was issued on October 7. Its big, simple parts, designed for ease of manufacture on a frontier forge, also made the gun sturdy and reliable. The design would later be sold to Winchester and marketed as "Model 1885."

While John Browning was waiting for action on his patent, his father, then 74, died. Because John was the oldest among Jonathan's two surviving families, he became head of those households. His family duties, however, were minimal, and he spent most of his time in the shop. Ogden was growing, giving the Browning brothers more gun business. In addition, John recruited freighters to bring in disabled guns from remote homesteads. The freighter paid the bill when the gun was fixed, then delivered it to the owner, who reimbursed the freighter for repair and delivery.

By the fall of 1879, there was so much work that John and Matt had no spare time. Brother Ed quit his job with the railroad to help out, and within a year he too became a competent gunsmith. John was already thinking of a bigger shop—maybe a small factory—in the middle of town. He had designed a gun, and now he wanted to build it. Matt and Ed were soon busy helping John build his factory on a 30-foot lot on the edge of Ogden's business district. None of the boys had any experience as masons or carpenters; and none had ever operated power-driven machinery. But they knew how to work hard and to improvise. The finished structure measured 25 by 50 feet, with a low ceiling to conserve heat and materials. Shafts and pulleys rose just high enough to clear the head of a workman. Because the town had no drainage system, the factory had no basement. John's New York supplier— Schoverling, Daly and Gales—offered to furnish rough forgings for the receivers that went into his rifle, and they also put him in touch with two barrel makers.

The first sign at the factory hailed it as the "New Browning Gun Shop." Most of Ogden knew about the Brownings and their fine gun work, but the announcement of a new shop hardly made headlines. What awed people in this or any other western town was the mere mention of *patents*. A patent came from the East, after all—you couldn't get it anywhere else. How you got it, nobody could say. That's why John Browning's patented rifle stirred immediate interest, enabling him to take several orders even before he started up the machinery in his new facility. Even he could not help feeling a thrill when the first 10-dollar gold piece was plunked down by a backwoodsman. "I want the first one you make," the man declared, eyeing the prototype one day. "This'll make it a deal." Though he desperately needed it, John did not take the money—but he did promise him the first rifle.

Frank Rushton and the New Browning Shop

When the last wagonload of tools from the old shop had been heaped on the floor of the new Browning factory, it offered little evidence of accomplishment. Strewn about the building were parts and pulleys, power machinery with no one to run it, and only the idea of a patented rifle to patch it all together. Somehow, this mess had to generate a finished product. As if on cue, a slightly-built Englishman wandered onto the scene one day. He was Frank Rushton, on his first exploratory trip to the American West, and he came with impressive credentials as a British gunsmith. A few minutes in the new Browning factory told him all he needed to know. "It'll take some work, but you ought to be perking shortly. Would you like some help?" He did not have to ask twice. John later attributed most of his early production expertise to what he learned at the hand of Frank Rushton. Quick to learn and unhampered by Old World habits, John soon became even more adept at machine-work than his mentor. He took what shortcuts he could and found new, more efficient ways to accomplish old tasks.

For the first run of 25 rifles, Rushton helped set up the machines and taught Ed to run the mill. Brothers Sam and George drilled and rough-filed the receivers, while John completed the filing and fitted the parts and Matt made the stocks. Frank also mounted the barrels and sights of that first lot, a demanding task. In three months, the guns were finished and a 20-foot space that had been walled

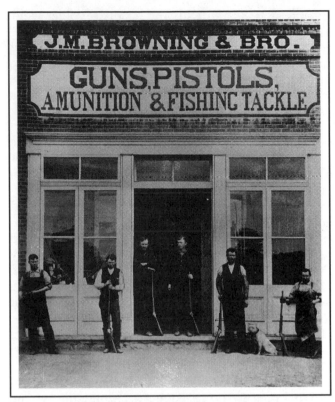

The staff of "The Largest Arms Factory Between Omaha and The Pacific" poses in front of the Browning Brothers Factory in Ogden, Utah.

off at the front of the store for retail sales had its first product display.

The rifles sold for $25 each, but with ammunition and accessories added the brothers usually took in $30 from a transaction. In one week, all the guns were gone. If John Browning had any doubts about his ability as a designer or manufacturer, they were buried by the money accumulating in the cash drawer. With no debts outstanding and material on hand for 75 more rifles, John was able to relax a bit. Even if the flood of early buyers reflected pent-up local demand, he had sold enough to establish the credibility of Browning's factory. He ordered components for 100 more rifles and relented when Matt pressed him for money to stock the retail corner of the shop with more merchandise. A retail store had long been Matt's goal, impeded so far by insufficient funds. John would not allow any borrowing, having seen his father suffer for the bad debts of others. For the same reason, all sales and repair work at the Browning shops were strictly cash transactions.

About $250 was allocated to stocking the shelves for retail customers. In 1880, even the best rifles cost less than $30, and a Colt revolver went for $15 or so. Schoverling supplied most of the merchandise, but unfortunately, on the night after all the merchandise had been arranged, thieves broke in and stole everything—including the prototype of John's rifle. There would be no more retail sales now, at least not until rifle production met demand.

Demand, like Ogden, was growing, and the orders came as fast as a full crew could handle. The railroad brought a mix of people to the shop—not just Mormon farmers, but professional people from the East. Among them were Dr. A.L. Ulrich, a German physician, and Professor H.W. Ring, who'd come west to organize a school for the Congregational Church. These men were both shooters and together they proposed the establishment of a city rifle club. The range they laid out west of town along the Weber River is where John Browning eventually thought up a way to use the energy of a fired round to cycle a gun's mechanism.

In the factory's second year, John made Matt a partner. The two worked well as a team, and Matt slowly assumed more daily production responsibilities. Frank Rushton stayed with them until his untimely death. Ed Ensign, a promising young gunsmith, worked at the shop more than 40 years. The younger Browning brothers had all gained enough experience by now so that the shop ran smoothly. Even on those days when little or no money came in, guns were being built at the rate of up to three a day. As a result, John decided to spend more time designing.

Actually, while refining his first single-shot rifle for a patent, he'd developed another single-shot action, this one with a fixed trigger guard and a separate, forward-mounted lever that dropped the block and cocked the hammer. It was never produced, and the only example left is the prototype, which is still in the family. By 1882, John had drawn up plans for a repeating rifle with a tubular magazine. He built a model and applied for a patent, which was quickly granted. But John was already at work on another repeater, and in September (1882) he filed for a patent on this design as well. His true genius was blossoming now. Even for capable engineers, designing a complex rifle from scratch demands a great deal of thought, incurring huge blocks of time and many tests. John Browning completed patent requirements for two repeating rifles in the space of a year, while working full time at the factory as its manager.

Still, John considered the patents—and all the efforts that went into them—meaningless should the guns prove less than satisfactory. And so, as his own most uncompromising critic, he shelved both designs. The second held promise, as it was engineered much like his single-shot, with extraordinarily few parts for a repeater. The parts were big and easy to make, too. But both mechanisms displeased their inventor, who already had in mind a much better idea for a repeating rifle. It would become Winchester's Model 1886.

Thomas Bennett Buys a Rifle

In 1883, a Winchester salesman named Andrew McAusland bought a used Browning single-shot rifle and sent it to Winchester president Thomas G. Bennett, who didn't know what to make of it. To his experienced eye, Browning's model seemed unusually sophisticated—and the serial number (463) was high enough to suggest that quite a few others were about. He'd never heard of Browning, and he wasn't even sure where Ogden was. He did know that the rifle was good enough to threaten Winchester sales; and that, while Winchester had a stranglehold on the market for lever-action repeaters, it had no big, strong actions adapted to rounds

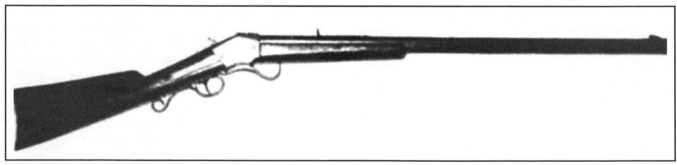

At 23, Browning designed this single-shot rifle, an experimental model with fixed trigger guard and separate finger lever.

This cluttered workbench was the scene of John Browning's many brainstorms.

like the .45/70/405 Government. Granted, buffalo hunting was all but over; still, the .45/70 was a common and popular round in the West, chambered in most Sharps rifles and other stout single-shots. If Browning could be induced to sell this model, Winchester would lose a competitor and gain an important addition to its line of firearms. Consequently, Bennett took the next train to Utah.

He probably didn't expect what he found. Billed as the biggest gun establishment between Omaha and the Pacific, the Browning Brothers factory hardly looked imposing. When Matt met Bennett at the door, he looked more like an apprentice than a partner; and John, now in his mid-20's, hardly fit the image of a gun designer. But Bennett saw past the farm-boy facade and recognized in John an extraordinary talent—talent that Winchester could use.

"I want to buy rights to your single-shot rifle," he said. There was no argument, for John was ready to sell. The price? "Ten thousand," declared John. It must have seemed an enormous sum to him. Bennett, who was no doubt prepared to pay more, countered with an offer of $8,000, plus jobbing grants, which, he said, would more than make up the difference. He also required first look at the repeating rifle John had told him about, to which John agreed. Bennett wrote a check for $1,000, with the rest to come later. Then he and John each wrote a short note describing their obligation to the other. That was the only contract necessary and the only one drawn up for manufacturing rights to Browning's rifle. Bennett was on the train for the six-day trip back East by nightfall, having spent less than six hours in Ogden.

Did telling Bennett about the shelved patents, along with his plans for a repeater that would handle the big cartridges then reserved for single-shots, become the perfect bait with which to hook the powerful man from Winchester? Perhaps John Browning knew that, perhaps he didn't. Bennett asked him enough pointed questions to confirm that John had indeed sound ideas for this important step in rifle development. Such a gun would give Winchester an enormous edge in the frontier market, where a man had to choose between a rifle that fired short-range cartridges in rapid succession or more powerful rounds one at a time. Combining a repeating mechanism with the most potent ammunition of the day had proven difficult. Somehow, Bennett thought, this young man had the answer.

For the Browning brothers, Bennett's visit brought the best kind of news. Now the overloaded repair and fabrication shop could catch up with business. The retail store, restocked a year after the loss there, could be expanded. Between the two, profit and cash flow would equal, perhaps even exceed, what the manufacturing plant had generated. Ed Browning was delighted that he could make models for John, and John at last had the freedom to pursue his true love: designing firearms.

The contract with Bennett spurred the Brownings to accelerate production. They had parts on hand to build a lot of single-shot rifles, and enough orders that none would go begging. While Bennett's attorneys used their 30 days to examine the Browning patents, John and his brothers worked feverishly. The balance of $7,000 came when it was due, and before the Ogden shop had used all its components. Manufacturing never stopped, forcing Bennett to write to John Browning, reminding him of the terms of their contract. His letter proved an embarrassment to John, who ruefully shut down the machines. By that time, all the orders had been filled and only a handful of parts remained.

Winchester named Browning's single-shot rifle after the year of its debut in the Winchester catalog: Model 1885. Billed as a powerful, durable rifle for hunters, it offered a choice of two receivers. The "high-wall" receiver from Browning, which used big cartridges, offered lots of metal and great strength to the area supporting the breechblock. The "low-wall" rifles made loading easier with smaller rounds. Discontinued in 1920 in the face of stiff competition from repeaters, Model 1885 outlasted many other single-shots. It was eventually resurrected by Browning as the Japanese-made Model 78 and later renamed Model 1885.

When the Browning brothers stopped making single-shot rifles in 1883, John immediately began work on his lever-action repeater. He applied for the patent in May, 1884, and five months later he got it. He and Matt then made their first trip to Connecticut to sell Thomas Bennett their new rifle, which became Model 86. By then, John had already designed another lever rifle, one with a mechanism all its own. For the rest of his life, John Browning's urge to design firearms continued to drive him at a furious pace. His ambition was matched by a brilliant mechanical mind and an inborn sense of practicality. No other inventor contributed as much to the development of firearms. None other would be so fast, so prolific, and so versatile in his work. Recognizing this genius, Thomas Bennett wasn't about to send the Brownings to a competitor during their visit to New Haven.

According to most sources, Winchester paid $50,000 for Browning's Model 86 lever-action rifle. "More money than there was in Ogden," John commented later. Before seeing Bennett, he and Matt had stopped in New York to visit Schoverling, Daly and Gales. Their salesman, long familiar with the Utah family and a gun expert himself, got the first look at the new lever-action. After examining the gun, he handed it back to John and said matter-of-factly that it was the best rifle in the world. "Right now," he'd said, "you're holding the future of the Winchester Company in your hands."

Before their trip, John and his brother hadn't traveled much farther than the 35 miles between Ogden and Salt Lake City. Now they saw the New York shipyards, tasted mixed drinks, and attended the theater. And not only did they receive a huge sum for the 86, but Thomas Bennett gave them the directive to start work on a lever-action shotgun.

"Can you do it?" Bennett asked.

"Yes," John said. "But I think a pump-action gun, operated by a sliding forend, would look and sell better."

Bennett, aware that Winchester's reputation was built on the lever action, did not want to stray far from that course. He asked how long it would take to develop the lever shotgun. John Browning thought it could be done in two years. Eight months later—in June, 1885—he filed for a patent. His lever-action shotgun would be called the Model 1887 Winchester. While it wasn't the first repeating shotgun, it is commonly considered the first practical model. It was one of 11 guns John designed and sold to Winchester between October, 1884, and September, 1886.

John Browning: Winchester's Wonder Boy

By this time, John and his wife Rachel had started a family. Sadly, their second and third sons both died as infants. When John was called by the Mormon church to accept his two-year tour of duty as a missionary, the couple was raising a son and a daughter. That was in 1887, just after John turned 32. While Mormon missionary work today is required only of single young men, in John's day married men were also called. He was obliged to leave Rachel and the children to carry the Mormon message to Georgia.

People there proved, on the whole, unreceptive to John and his companion, who were not provisioned by the church. They sang for their suppers and lived on whatever people offered them. It was a lean time. During their travels, however, John saw his first Model 1887 shotgun in the window of a Georgia town. The gun had been released to market after he'd left Ogden. Only reluctantly did the shopkeeper let this dusty traveler handle his new merchandise, commenting that John seemed familiar with the shotgun.

Returning to Utah in March, 1889, John Browning spent long hours at his workbench. In the next three and a half years, he was awarded 20 patents. As in the past, he worked without blueprints, his mind bringing a concept to fruition with the help only of rough sketches and templates from brother Ed. John dealt in approximations, whereas traditional engineering required exact measurement. One of his shop foremen once remarked how pleasant it was at the Browning shop, where the chief talked in inches instead of thousandths. Indeed, John's designs were so good that his guns worked despite a lumberman's precision at the template stage. When a model was completed, it usually functioned extremely well. Given the fantastic rate at which Browning produced new mechanisms during this time, there must have been relatively few failures.

Winchester bought all John's guns during this time. The money helped the Brownings erect a new two-story retail outlet on Ogden's Main Street. In the back of the new store John built a small shop—much like the old one, except that it was plastered and whitewashed. Here he'd sing or whistle snatches of tunes while he worked. He liked the place warm, and there were no blinds to stop the summer sun. If a problem impeded his progress, John fell silent, then scowled and muttered as his impatience grew. Until they heard him whistle again, his brothers kept their distance. Once he'd tested a model to his satisfaction, he took it home and asked his wife to operate it. He wanted each gun to work flawlessly, even in weak or inexperienced hands.

For nearly 20 years, Winchester relied on John Browning to design its guns, largely because Thomas Bennett thought so much of the Utah inventor and his products. Besides serving as company president, Bennett was Oliver Winchester's son-in-law. He voted the stock of his wife and her sister, Winchester's only two daughters, and was able to do pretty much what pleased him—and it pleased him that John Browning was working for Winchester, not someone else. During the most fertile 17 years of their relationship, Bennett bought 44 guns from Browning, 10 of which were manufactured. The others, while not producing income for Winchester, were not gaining market share for someone else, either. "Fences," John called the guns that didn't sell. "They're fences to protect Winchester from competition. They're worth a little money for that."

John Browning apparently got his asking price for every new design. There were no royalties and no dickering. Once or twice a year, he'd travel to New Haven to deliver his working models, which he'd wrapped in brown paper packages and tied with string. He made a great show of cutting the string for Bennett and explaining the guns to Winchester engineers.

One of the guns John delivered in this manner was the pump-action shotgun he'd tried to talk Bennett into substituting for the lever-action model, the one that became Model 1887. The pump, introduced as Model 1893, was later modified and renamed Model 1897. It stayed in production for 60 years. No other repeating shotgun had a fighting chance in the market for several years after its debut.

The pump action, so well suited to shotguns, was first used successfully on Winchester's Model 1890 .22 rimfire rifle. It became an instant success at shooting galleries in the U.S. and Great Britain, and proved equally useful in the hunting field. When John Browning proposed this gun to Winchester, he did it through the mail, with only a few rough sketches. Company engineers didn't like the idea and wrote back, suggesting he discontinue his efforts on the design. In characteristic fashion, John built a prototype and shipped it to New Haven with the following note: "You said it wouldn't work, but it seems to shoot pretty fair for me."

John enjoyed doing what others thought impossible. Around 1890, on a pilgrimage to New Haven, he talked with Bennett about designing a short-action rifle along the lines of Model 1886. Winchester still had Model 1873 in its line—a direct descendant of the first successful lever rifle developed by Walter Hunt. Model 73 was outdated, and Bennett wanted a gun to replace it. "I want it soon, too," he told John. "If you can get it to me in three months, I'll pay ten thousand dollars. Make it two months and you'll have fifteen thousand."

John Browning scratched his head as he figured train times between Connecticut and Utah. He said he'd sell the design for $20,000, with delivery in 30 days or Winchester could have the rifle at no charge. In disbelief, Bennett agreed. John and his brothers started work on the new gun as soon as he got home. Within two weeks, they'd built a working action. The first rifle arrived in New Haven well before the two-month deadline. It must have pleased Thomas Bennett, because he immediately sent John a check for $20,000. Called Winchester Model 1892, it featured Model 86's double vertical locking bolts and sold over a million copies.

All of the designs John Browning sold Winchester during this period were for black powder cartridges, including the famous Model 1894. Originally, this gun came as either .32/40 or .38/55; but soon after its introduction, it was also listed in .30/

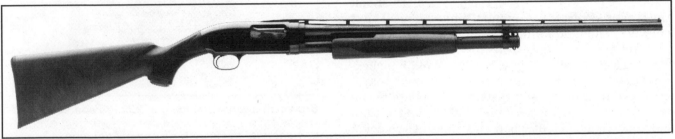

Browning now offers several reproductions of discontinued Winchester guns designed by John Browning, among them the famous Model 12 pump shotgun shown here.

30, becoming the first smokeless centerfire sporting cartridge in America. While black powder pressures seldom exceeded 25,000 psi and smokeless pressures ran to about 40,000, Browning guns seemed to handle the new propellant as easily as they did the old. Barrels built for black powder generally did not have the structural strength required for smokeless, but the actions held. All one had to do was screw on a new barrel of high-tensile steel.

The last Browning gun bought by Winchester was, like the first, a single-shot rifle. Thomas Bennett approached John about developing a lightweight rimfire rifle that would complement the hugely-popular Model 1890 pump but sell at half the price. An inexpensive Belgian single-shot, the Flobert, was getting lots of attention from buyers who didn't want to pay for a repeater. Bennett wanted Winchester rifles to replace the Flobert.

John had already built a gun like that; in fact, he'd invented five of them. He now sent them all to Winchester, and Bennett bought them (although only the latest model was ever brought to market). Bennett squirreled them away, knowing they had no future as Winchesters, but fearful lest another company would get them and build a gun too cheap to compete with. Model 1900, Browning's last design, was a 4-pound bolt-action that sold for five dollars and almost immediately buried the Flobert. Subsequently, Winchester developed nine improved versions of the 1900 and sold nearly 1,500,000 of them.

Automatics That Work

During the 19 years he worked for Winchester—from 1883 to 1902—John Browning also delved into other projects, chief among them the self-loading gun. This mechanism would soon change the way wars were fought; but its immediate effect was the breakup of the alliance between John Browning and Thomas Bennett. John allegedly got his idea for self-loading (or automatic) guns from watching riflemen at a local shooting match. Each time one of them fired, the muzzle blast shook the weeds several feet away. "Why waste all that energy?" thought John.

Always quick to test his ideas, Browning hurried back to his shop. First, he laid an old Winchester Model 73 rifle on its side on a heavy board, strapped it in place, and fastened the board to the floor. Next, he drilled a hole slightly larger than bore size in a block of wood and placed the block a quarter inch in front of the muzzle, lined up so that a bullet passed clean through the hole. When John

Browning is shown holding a .22 autoloading rifle, whose buttstock magazine and bottom ejection demonstrate the inventor's original thinking.

Browning's machine guns were used with deadly effect in both World Wars, in airplanes as well as on the ground. He designed 30- and 50-caliber models in addition to a 37mm automatic cannon.

fired the gun, the blast of escaping gas sent the block of wood caroming around the room. He predicted then that within a few years he'd have a gun "that keeps firing by itself as long as you feed it ammunition."

Automatic guns weren't new. Before the widespread use of firearms, the Greeks had built a contraption that launched arrows in rapid succession without reloading. Multiple-barrel guns date to the Middle Ages. In the early 1860's, Dr. R.J. Gatling of Indianapolis devised a tripod-mounted, six-barrel repeater that fed cartridges from a hopper into each barrel in turn as it rotated on a spindle. Once it was indexed to a single firing position, the gun discharged. The mechanism itself was driven by a crank turned by the shooter. None of these weapons used the force of firing to cycle the action and, in accordance with Browning's theory, enabling the gun to keep firing as long as ammunition held out.

On November 22, 1890, John Browning sent a letter to Colt's Patent Firearms Manufacturing Company. It described an "Automatic Machine Gun" that could be made "as cheaply as a common sporting rifle." The Brownings had developed a lightweight model that fired 16 .44 WCF rounds per second, and a heavier prototype that discharged .45 Government (Colt) cartridges at six per second. Would Colt be interested in a demonstration?

Though John's tie to Winchester at this time was well established, Colt may have seemed the more appropriate market channel for a machine gun. The Hartford firm had manufactured all the U.S.-built Gatling guns beginning in 1866. Colt's reply was cordial but not altogether promising. The Gatling guns had been expensive to market, and more of them had gone abroad than had been sold to the U.S. government. But the Browning-designed Model 1886 Winchester had proven John's ability as a designer, so Colt sent back a somewhat loose invitation. Whether it was born of a sincere interest in machine guns or of an obligation to be nice to a major retailer of Colt revolvers isn't known.

Colt president John Hall gave the Brownings a gracious welcome. When John and Matt unwrapped the crude model they had hammered out in Utah, they regretted not having spent more time in its finishing. But the gun was meant to shoot, not look at, and John promptly suggested they do just that.

The Brownings had brought with them four belts, each containing 50 .45-70 cartridges. In a firing tunnel, they chambered the first round and pressed the trigger. Two hundred rounds rattled through the gun without a hitch. While the quickest Gatling had a slightly higher rate of fire, the operator had to keep cranking in order to keep shooting. Browning's gas-driven, belt-fed gun required only one pull of the trigger! Besides, the Browning weighed only 40 pounds compared to the 90 pounds carried by Gatling's 10-barrel repeater. To Colt people in attendance, this new mechanism looked suddenly very attractive, despite its rough finish. Hall remarked that not only did Browning's mechanism look easy to operate, it probably had no more parts than a Colt revolver. Certainly it was one of the simplest automatic mechanisms ever devised.

Several months later, back in Utah, Browning received a letter from Hall asking him to demonstrate the machine gun for U.S. Naval Ordnance. The test required three minutes of uninterrupted fire—something the Navy thought reasonable in the event two ships came close enough for sustained deck-raking. John thought this was an unnecessarily tough standard. "Who's going to stitch 1,800 canvas cartridge loops in a belt?" he complained. "And who's going to thumb in 1,800 .45-70 rounds?"

Persuaded by his brothers, John accepted the challenge and contracted with a local tent-maker to create 10 belts with a capacity of 200 rounds each. The Browning brothers then loaded each belt by hand, positioning each cartridge carefully. At the appointed time, John traveled to Hartford, where he engaged a carpenter to build nine feed-boxes, each holding a belt folded to expose a dozen cartridges per layer. The box was clipped under the feedway of the gun and a brass tab was riveted to the end of each belt, so the shooter could hand-feed the first round.

In the shooting tunnel, John passed out cotton earplugs to the observers, warning them that there'd be lots of smoke and noise. Then he released the bolt on the first round and held back the trigger. The gun roared to life and kept roaring. Soon the barrel glowed as its muzzle spewed a blue mist of lead from bullets melting in their passage through the bore. John was sure the extractor, hammering the red-hot breech 10 times a second, would break. When the gun suddenly stopped firing, however, it was only because the last belt box was empty. The observers descended on John Browning with hearty congratulations, and that evening they toasted him at Hartford's famed Heublein Hotel.

Still, this was 1891. The U.S. was at peace and saw no need for a new machine gun. Fifteen years earlier, when George Custer and his detachment met their end on the Little Bighorn, four Gatlings had languished in their boxes at Custer's head-quarters. Machine guns were too cumbersome and ill-favored by cavalry units who fought brief skir-mishes with Indians between long treks over rough western terrain. Besides, changes in weaponry usually come slowly in conservative military cir-cles. To an 1890's horse soldier, a machine gun wasted a lot of ammunition that could be more ac-curately fired from a trapdoor Springfield. The bat-tlegrounds of World War I some 25 years hence could not yet be imagined. In the end, John Brown-ing declined Hall's offer of a contract to produce a machine gun for review by the Army. He did prom-ise, though, that Colt would get first crack at the next machine gun he developed.

The next model appeared in 1893. Like the first, it was gas-operated, channeling a portion of the ex-panding powder gas from each round through a port in the barrel, then into a mechanism that moved the bolt back against spring tension. Extraction, ejection and cocking were all accomplished by this one motion. Slamming forward, the bolt picked up another cartridge, which fired as soon as it was chambered—provided, of course, the shooter kept the trigger depressed. Colt started making this gun in 1895 and called it the Model 1895. Chambered for the .30/40 Krag and 6mm Lee Navy cartridges, these new smokeless rounds created a great deal of extra design work for Browning and his crew.

The new gun went up against two others in Navy tests—the Gatling itself, and a two-barrel, crank-operated model made by Pratt and Whitney. In January, 1896, the Browning (Colt) design won Navy approval, and 50 guns were ordered. Shipped in 1897, they comprised the first automatic guns ever purchased by the U.S. government. In 1898, the Navy requested 150 more, but the Army stuck doggedly with its Gatling for another decade.

Browning started work on another, recoil-op-erated machine gun in 1900, maintaining that Eu-rope's military had pursued machine gun design far more aggressively than had the U.S. armed services. "The Colt 1895 will be obsolete before long," he declared, "and I want to have one ready to replace it." In less than three months, he had a firing model ready, the first of many. In both world wars and Korea, every machine gun used by U.S. forces—on land or sea or in the air—was of Browning design.

Thomas Bennett's Biggest Mistake

While he was developing the first automatic mechanisms for military sale, John kept busy filling Winchester's catalogs with new sporting guns. By 1900, three of every four repeating rifles and shot-guns sold to American sportsmen had originated in Browning's shop. But the Utah inventor wasn't satisfied with building new pump- and lever-action guns. He wanted to apply his knowledge of auto-loading mechanisms to build a self-loading shotgun.

The turn of the century was a poor time for this, given the transition of shotshells from black to smokeless powder. The ammunition companies were still experimenting, and several loads that performed admirably in double guns caused trouble in repeaters. Case separations occurred, the brass head pulling off the paper shell body. Water swelled the paper, making feeding and ejection difficult. These were problems even in guns operated by hand, where a shooter could feel and force his way through a cycle if need be. An autoloader depended on perfectly-sized ammunition to function. If there was a hitch or stall in the movement of parts, the gun would jam. In addition, autoloaders used the force of the fired round to make things work; if that force varied, the action might operate too violently or fail to open far enough to eject the spent case.

Hand-operated repeaters were not affected by moderate variations in breech pressures because the action moved after pressures had dissipated.

While ammunition firms worked to make shotshells tougher and more uniform, Browning developed a simple inexpensive device to counter changes in breech pressures. Called a friction ring, or shock absorber, it proved useful for decades to come, metering the force delivered to operate recoil-activated shotguns. At the same time, he eliminated the exposed hammer. John's first autoloading shotgun was also the first commercially successful repeating shotgun made with a closed breech.

During the development of this gun, Browning made a second autoloader that featured a different kind of mechanism. In March, 1899, he wrote Thomas Bennett at Winchester, stating he had an autoloading shotgun ready to demonstrate. The new model was delivered to New Haven, and over the next several months Winchester engineers and patent attorneys conducted their usual inspections. On October 11, Bennett wrote John that a prior patent applied to one of the small parts. John changed it immediately. Several more months went by. Finally, in July of 1900, Bennett returned the gun to John for more minor changes, but with no mention of price. John shipped the altered gun within a month, including a letter reflecting his growing impatience. Winchester's people had already started filing for patents, but still Bennett refused to move ahead with this project. With that, Browning decided to visit New Haven and settle the matter once and for all.

Their meeting was tense. Though they'd worked together for 19 years and had a great deal of respect for each other, the two men still lacked a first-name relationship. Now, the conversation was even more formal. John was incensed at Bennett's seemingly unwarranted delays; and Bennett was in turn furious at the terms John demanded, which included royalties on top of a huge cash advance. Winchester had never paid royalties to Browning, and it wasn't about to start.

As John recalled later, "It was not a very dignified parting." He observed that "Bennett was the most conservative of men, and admittedly the automatic was something of an innovation. To put it simply, he was afraid of it, and so were the few men in his confidence. They were afraid that it would take ten years to develop such a gun to the point where it would be profitable."

Winchester had a sterling reputation at that time, not only among shooters, but within the business community. It hadn't borrowed a nickel in 40 years. There was something unassailable about the firm, and Bennett, this time, felt John Browning was being presumptuous. John admitted in retrospect that "the automatic shotgun put Bennett in a tough position. I'll bet he'd have shelled out a hundred thousand dollars just to have had it banished forever from the earth, leaving him with his levers and pumps. If he made the gun and it proved a failure, as he and his advisors seemed to have half suspected, it would leave a blot on the Winchester name. Even if he made it and it proved a big success, it would seriously hurt one of the best-

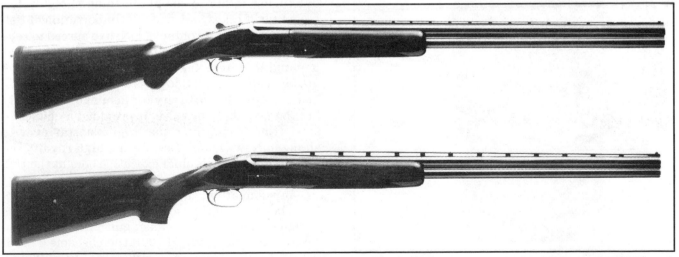

Browning's famous Superposed over/under shotgun, which is still made in Belgium, was the predecessor to several other over/under designs, among them the Lightning Sporting Clays (top photo) and the Special Sporting Clays (bottom photo).

paying arms in his line—the 97 shotgun [another Browning design]. If a competitor got it, and it caught the popular fancy, he'd be left a long jump behind in an important branch of the business.''

John left New Haven in a huff, and without a commitment from Winchester on the new shotgun. On January 8, 1902, he and Matt traveled to Ilion, New York, to show the autoloader to Marcellus Hartley, president of Remington. While they waited in his office, Hartley died suddenly of a heart attack. Reluctantly, the Browning brothers took their design overseas, to Fabrique Nationale de Guerre in Belgium. F.N., as it was known, had established ties with the Ogden shop back in 1897, when its commercial director, Hart O. Berg, had visited the U.S. His purpose then was to learn new ways to build bicycles, but he was intrigued with a self-loading pistol recently patented by John Browning. The fine factory he commanded in Belgium had everything needed to produce guns, but it had so far made only bicycles, motorcycles and miscellaneous munitions. Berg negotiated with John for the manufacturing

John Browning cradles a Belgium-made Auto-5, which he designed in 1900 (and which Winchester refused to build).

rights to his pistol and tried unsuccessfully to talk Browning into coming over to Belgium and supervising the startup. The Belgian returned to Europe alone, but with a contract, and in 1899 F.N. built the first Browning-designed autoloading pistols. They sold for 30 francs apiece and proved so serviceable that in 1900 the .32 Automatic Pistol became Belgium's official military sidearm.

When John Browning came calling early in 1902, Berg was no longer with F.N., but no matter. Browning's pistol had assured him of a warm welcome. Once arrangements were completed for producing Browning's autoloading shotgun, John stayed another three months in Belgium, supervising the tooling and production of pilot models for F.N. The initial production run of autoloading shotguns came off the line in autumn, 1903, and soon 10,000 units were on their way to Schoverling, Daly and Gales in New York. Any doubts about the gun's value in the marketplace soon vanished as the entire inventory sold out in one year.

Meanwhile, John decided to visit Remington again. The company had changed hands, and Browning hoped the new president—Marcus Hartley Dodge—might offer new opportunities. Dodge was only 20 years old when his grandfather, Marcellus Hartley, died. The estate was settled while young Marcy finished his schooling at Columbia University, and on his 21st birthday he was elected president of M. Hartley and Company. From that post he administered, with their respective presidents, both Remington Arms and the Union Metallic Cartridge Company.

John Browning had sold F.N. world-wide manufacturing rights to the autoloading shotgun, but recent tariff hikes had made the importation of Belgian-built guns unprofitable. F.N. had agreed to cede U.S. rights to the shotgun to an American firm. Was Remington interested? A smart and aggressive young man, Marcy Dodge saw in this new autoloader a great opportunity for Remington. Not only did the gun show promise, it provided a chance to steal from Winchester the brightest star ever to shine on New Haven. Despite the high royalty demands, Remington's chief executive bought the U.S. manufacturing rights to John's shotgun.

In summation, the F.N.-made Browning Auto-5 has been one of the most successful of all firearms designed by Utah's premier gunsmith. Manufactured in Belgium until 1972, it then became a product of Japan, where it is still made. Remington's first version—Model 11—eventually took on a more streamlined form as Model 11-48, which evolved

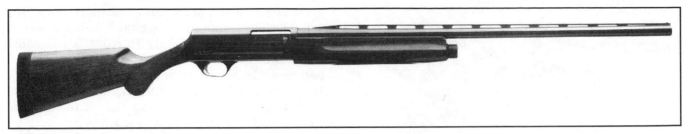

John Browning's first autoloading shotguns were operated by recoil. Some later models, like this A-500G, are gas-driven.

into the gas-operated Model 1100. The Browning Auto-5 shotguns, however, retained the distinctive square receiver profile of the original design.

Self-Loading Pistols and the BAR

As important as his work was in the development of long guns, John Browning proved equally brilliant in designing pistols. He began building his first autoloading handgun in 1894, and he had an exposed-hammer, .38 self-loader ready to market in mid-1895. Colt expressed interest in it and signed a royalty agreement for manufacturing rights to the pistol a year later. Actually, Colt got four pistols from the prolific inventor, one of them (another .38) appearing in Colt's line in 1900 as the first auto-loading pistol manufactured in the U.S. Every Colt self-loading pistol manufactured after that date was of Browning design.

Among the greatest achievements in Browning's development of the autoloading pistol was his idea for an operating slide—in short, a housing mated to the frame by rails. The slide added mass to the recoil mechanism, thus absorbing shock and also served as an action housing, sighting rib and bolt. It has since been employed on most centerfire autoloading pistols of all makes and ranks with the revolver cylinder as crucial to the development of modern handguns.

Browning also helped design pistol cartridges, specifically the .25, .32, .380 and .45 Automatic Colt

Pistol (ACP). Given the adaptability of self-loading mechanisms to powerful rounds like the .45, he was convinced the next military sidearm should be an autoloader. As early as 1902, John developed a .38 that he called the Military Model. Aware by that time of the prolonged discussions, delays and testing that any gun proposed for military service must endure, Browning simply offered up his ideas and turned to other projects.

Eventually, he was called before the review board, which agreed that his Military Model seemed a good idea—but could Browning chamber it for a more powerful cartridge? The Moro insurrection in the Phillipines had soured officers on the .38 Colt, which lacked the power to stop a frenzied attacker. High velocity was not required, because all pistols at that time were short-range guns; but bullet weight and diameter had to be increased.

John produced two designs for the board's inspection in short order. Both were 45-caliber self-loaders, one with an exposed hammer, and the other without. While ordnance offices made their way slowly through the bureaucratic rituals, John refined and marketed (through Colt) his Model 1905 .45 Automatic Pistol. It became quite popular. Eventually the government opted for Browning's exposed-hammer model and scheduled its tests for March 3, 1911.

Anxious to perfect his .45 before that date, John worked hard and long at Colt's Hartford plant,

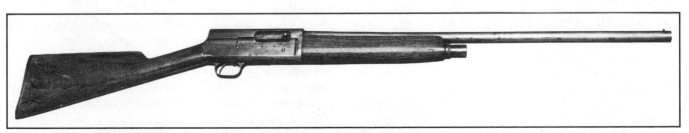

This example of the first Browning autoloading shotgun, built in 1900, has a straight grip but otherwise looks much like the Auto-5's still being made for Browning in Japan.

Browning's .45-caliber self-loading pistol (above) featuring an exposed hammer and a 5″ barrel, was invented in 1905.

usually with Fred Moore, his protegé and friend. Moore was chief of Colt's machine gun division and had become a competent engineer by this time. The two men altered some parts of the pistol and prepared it for a grueling trial—6,000 rounds in 100-round strings followed by an acid bath, a sprinkling of dust, and still more shooting. After that, damaged ammunition, such as might be found on a battlefield, would be fired. It was a lot to ask of any gun, even revolvers, which had the advantage of past service to shield them from criticism. Autoloaders were untried machines that might or might not work.

John Browning's did work, for all 6,000 rounds, plus the abuse of acid, dust and deformed cartridges that occurred later. The examining board subsequently recommended this 45 Automatic Pistol for military service, a position it held for over half a century. Indeed, Colt's Model 1911 has become one of the most celebrated of all hand-held firearms.

After his break with Winchester, John Browning spent a lot of time on military projects, though he continued to work on several sporting guns as well. Automatic mechanisms continued to intrigue him. In 1910, he completed a new machine gun, and as the thunder of approaching war echoed in Europe, he perfected an automatic rifle for use by infantrymen. The machine gun became known as the Browning Heavy Water Cooled Machine Gun, while the rifle was given a simpler title: Browning Automatic Rifle, or B.A.R. Both were chambered for the standard .30 Government 1906 round issued for 1903 Springfield rifles.

The B.A.R. elicited immediate interest from the Army, mostly because it provided for "walking fire"—the ability to move forward without interrupting a heavy barrage of bullets. The B.A.R. could cycle at a rate of 480 rounds per minute, emptying a 20-shot magazine in 2½ seconds. Besides that, it was a simple gun, with only 70 parts. A gun could be disassembled and reassembled by trained armory personnel in less than a minute. In February of 1917, the B.A.R. became the second Browning-designed gun adopted by all branches of the service. (Colt's Model 1911 pistol was the first.)

A 48-Minute Machine Gun

Ordnance people delayed a decision on the machine gun, but when the U.S. declared war in Europe on April 6, 1917, additional tests were quickly scheduled. America's stock of war weapons was abysmally low, and most of the existing machine guns were outdated. The government hurriedly ordered more Colt Model 1895's and directed Browning to bring his new water-cooled gun to the proving grounds at Springfield Armory. Probably not even John could have anticipated the results.

The Browning machine gun gave a most remarkable performance that day, firing 20,000 rounds without a sniffle. No parts failed or even showed signs of fatigue. Satisfied that the stunned onlookers had seen enough to convince them of the gun's reliability, John decided to try another burst. Another 20,000 cartridges chattered through the gun in a steady stream. The audience by now was so incredulous that John had to unpack another gun, just to prove that no special alterations had been made to the first. The tests had gone too smoothly—surely there must be a trick.

But nothing had been rigged. If the initial show was impressive, the encore was unbelievable. John's second gun fired continuously for 48 minutes and 12 seconds, an unprecedented feat. The seven-member examination board promptly declared the Browning Heavy Water Cooled Machine Guns "the most effective guns of their type known to [us]." Like the B.A.R., this machine gun had relatively few parts, enabling armorers to disassemble and reassemble it blindfolded. In fact, the blindfold test thereafter became a routine part of ordnance training.

Browning was still in New England in the fall of 1917 when ordnance officials made an offer for the manufacturing rights to his new machine gun, the B.A.R., and the Colt .45 Automatic Pistol. The sum was $750,000, nearly $12 million less than John could have demanded in royalties from private firms. But he didn't hesitate to accept, observing that if he were 20 years younger he'd be among the other Yanks ducking German fire in French mud.

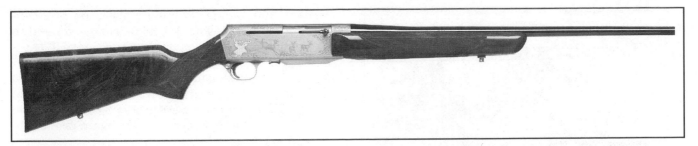

Browning's BAR (Browning Automatic Rifle) was first used in France during World War I and continued in use through World War II. Different in form but similar in function is this gas-driven BAR autoloader for sportsmen.

His generous action prompted Secretary of War Newton Baker to write to John: "You have performed, as you must realize, a very distinct service to this country in inventions and contributed to the strength and effectiveness of our armies. You have added to that service by the attitude you have taken in the financial arrangements necessary to have your inventions available to the Government."

John rented an apartment in Hartford and stayed in the East for two years, making only one brief trip to Ogden. He kept busy supervising the production of his military weapons in six factories, five of which were nearby. Colt had plants in Meriden and Hartford; New England Westinghouse was in Springfield; Winchester and Marlin-Rockwell operated in New Haven. Only Remington's plant in Ilion, New York, took John away from home.

Tooling up for the machine guns took less time than clearing the contracts through Washington. Westinghouse didn't get a contract until January 1, 1918, and changes John required in the manufacture of parts had to be approved by people in Washington. Always a pragmatist, John objected. "If there's anybody down there who understands these guns better than I do, send him up and I'll go home." Soon after that, he was given authority to direct all aspects of production of the guns he'd designed, and Westinghouse had its production line operating nine weeks later.

Browning's machine gun hadn't even been shipped overseas when American Commander General John J. Pershing demanded a more powerful weapon to penetrate the armor on German tanks. Attempts to adapt the 30-caliber gun to a bigger 11mm French round had failed, and the cartridge was abandoned altogether when it was found lacking the bullet weight and velocity necessary for use against armor. The government asked John for help: could he make a 50-caliber machine gun that would stop tanks? John replied that as soon

as he had the ammunition, there'd be a gun to fire it.

Ordnance engineers went to work, producing what looked like an overgrown .30-06 cartridge, with a 50-caliber 800-grain bullet at 2700 fps—the same velocity given a 173-grain 30-caliber bullet. It could penetrate $1\frac{1}{8}$-inch armor plate at 25 yards.

In September, 1918, Colt delivered the last Browning-designed parts for the new gun, and John assembled it. Tests scheduled for November 11 were postponed when Armistice was announced on that day. Four days later, at Aberdeen Proving Ground, John fired 877 rounds in several extended bursts from the .50 with no malfunctions. Made essentially along the same design as John's 30-caliber Water Cooled Machine Gun, this weapon incorporated an oil buffer that tamed its vicious recoil and made its parts last longer. Both guns spawned air-cooled versions that weighed less and were quickly adapted for use in aircraft. The first to see combat was the .30, rigged to fire in line with the path of

The "Four B's," Ogden's premium live-bird shooting team (above), included John Browning, second from left.

John Browning shared the joys of elk hunting in Montana with his brother Matt. Both men are shown here holding Remington Model 8 autoloading rifles.

the airplane and timed to put bullets through the arc of a nose propellor without hitting the blades.

The Commander of the U.S. Air Force called the Browning light machine gun "the backbone of offensive and defensive guns for American aircraft." During the Tunisian campaign in World War II, it was used by 35 allied planes to down 72 enemy fighters, with an average of less than 200 rounds of ammunition fired per gun. And when Field Marshal Erwin Rommel captured Tobruk in 1942, seizing thousands of Browning 50-caliber guns, the German high command got a good look at its nemesis. "If we'd had these," commented Field Marshal Herman Goering, "the Battle of Britain would have taken a different turn."

The Japanese were so impressed they did what American engineers had insisted was unfeasible: they built a 20mm machine gun on the Browning design. Though of inferior workmanship and materials, the gun worked, firing 960 rounds per minute. Subsequent variations of those original Browning guns totaled more than 66. The latest 30-caliber models for use in airplanes boast a cyclic rate of 1300 rounds per minute, with the .50's generating 1200 rpm. The B.A.R. also showed itself to be battle-worthy. Its maneuverability gave it a special advantage in the jungles of the Pacific Theater. Many were shipped to England following the Allied evacuation of Dunkirk in 1940. In all, close to 180,000 of these rifles were produced during World War II. Later, in Korea, they once again proved invaluable to U.S. infantry divisions.

The grim side of gun-making didn't noticeably affect John Browning. The grisly harvest reaped by machine guns on columns of soldiers was a fact of war—and the quickest way to stop a war, he knew, was to dominate the battlefield. If the enemy had machine guns, the only sensible thing to do was equip our troops with better machine guns. Escalation seemed part of the price of winning.

While John never used his guns in combat, he enjoyed shooting and hunting the waterfowl-rich lakes and streams near his home. He and his brother Matt teamed up with two other Ogden shooters to become Utah's premier live-bird shooting team, known as the "Four B's." John would also on occasion pick out a gun from a production run and take it afield for some shooting, just to make sure every gun of his design worked the way it was supposed to. As he acquired more and more responsibilities, hunting became a sometime thing for the inventor. There wasn't enough time for inventing, he'd complain.

A 37mm Encore

Browning's last project for the military came at a time when he bore a particularly heavy load of other commitments. He begged off, but the government persisted. The armed services needed a 37mm cannon, and two prototypes developed by their own engineers had failed. Chief of Ordnance General C.C. Williams made another plea for Browning's help in 1920. Again John demurred, pointing out that he was happy working on sporting arms, which made him a lot of money. If he opted for the cannon project, his gun would be a long time getting approved and he'd realize little profit. Besides, there was no war going on now, and no immediate threat of one. Even if he did make a gun that pleased some ordnance people, it wouldn't please them all. Besides, the 66-year-old inventor concluded, this was a job for a young man.

Predictably, John couldn't let the subject drop like that. He found himself thinking about the 37mm while he worked on other projects, until finally he caved in and accepted this new challenge.

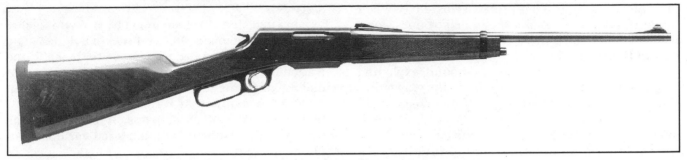

Model 81 BLR (above) is a modern front-locking lever gun offered by the Browning Arms Company.

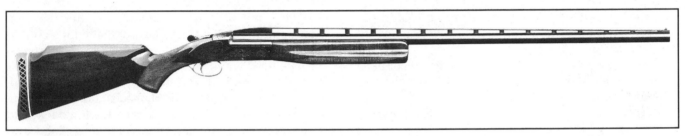

Browning's premium competition gun is this fine single-barrel trap model.

Browning's 9mm Hi-Power pistol is a long-standing favorite with sportsmen and law officers in Europe and the U.S., partly because of its 13-shot capacity.

Browning now carries guns designed especially for women and youngsters, such as this 20-gauge Model BPS shotgun.

But designing a gun meant first having cartridges for which to build it. That problem was solved when General Williams sent him six dummy rounds. John responded with an order for 500 live cartridges within three months.

The big shell, with its one-pound exploding projectile, really belonged with artillery ammunition, not small arms cartridges. It dwarfed the .50 Belted Machine Gun round, the largest John had ever worked with. Moreover, traditional autoloading mechanisms didn't seem appropriate. John began serious work on the cannon in January of 1921, and a prototype was ready for firing by March. As he'd predicted, the live ammunition was not forthcoming. "Just like the .50-caliber project," Matt observed. "We had the gun before Uncle Sam could produce ammunition."

But John knew of a military storage depot near Ogden. On a whim, he called to see if it housed any 37mm rounds. "Two railcars worth," said the officer in charge. "You won't want it though. It has explosive heads."

Immediately John requisitioned some of the ammunition, vowing to take the necessary precautions. Loading the gun in a pickup truck, he drove to the range with his brothers. There he placed a heavy plank shield around the gun and fastened a wire lanyard to the trigger. Then he stepped back and fired a five-round magazine into the distant mountains. The TNT-filled projectiles threw geysers of snow where they hit. A few months later John demonstrated his prototype at Aberdeen. True to his predictions, the successful test was followed by a barrage of questions from ordnance officers. Do you think this gun could be made to fire a more powerful round? What about moving this shell at 2,000 instead of 1,400 feet per second?

John had anticipated their queries and already had plans for an even more potent 37mm cannon. Soon he had a working model, which met military standards. After that, he devised yet another automatic cannon, built around a 14-inch cartridge that drove its projectile over 3,000 fps.

Once again, John's prophesy came true. In the tranquil times between world wars, military projects got little attention. A few of the cannons were produced for England in 1929, but not until 1935 did the American forces equip themselves with the big Browning guns. Colt, which had again provided the workplace for development of these weapons, turned in peacetime to the manufacture of domestic appliances. As a result, Browning received next to nothing for his last government project.

A Legend's Last Days, A Company's New Era

In 1926, John, accompanied by his wife Rachel and his son Val, made his 61st trip to Belgium. The day after Thanksgiving, they drove to the Fabrique Nationale plant, where John checked on the production of the new Browning Superposed Shotgun. After a few minutes, he returned to the office, complaining to Val of chest pains. A physician was summoned and quickly administered various stimulants to John.

"I wouldn't be surprised if I am dying," he told Val. And a few minutes later, at the age of 71, John Browning's heart stopped beating.

The military ceremonies for his passing couldn't fully reflect the man's tremendous contributions to the development of modern weapons. He'd devised ways to make guns operate with levers and slide handles and had proven his ideas by berthing them in steel. He'd used the force of firing to design long-recoil, short-recoil, blowback and gas-driven mechanisms that made guns load and fire themselves. He'd been issued 128 patents for some 80 distinct firearms. None of the guns he'd submitted for military tests had ever failed them. In his nearly 50 working years, John Browning had so dominated the frontiers of gunmaking that his influence could be felt and seen on most sporting and military small arms long after his death. Since the turn of the century, no armsmaker can claim to have been unaffected by the ideas of John Moses Browning.

The arms company that now carries the Browning name is still headquartered in Utah, though manufacturing has been done almost entirely overseas. Belgium's F.N. plant continued producing the Auto-5 and Superposed shotguns after John's death, adding self-loading pistols and sporting rifles later on. A big-game rifle built on the Mauser bolt action and a clever .22 with a straight-pull bolt followed. Production stopped only for a time during World War II.

In the early 1970's, Miroku Firearms Manufacturing Company of Tokyo started making some Browning guns on contract. European inflation had boosted the Superposed shotgun beyond the reach of most shooters, so the Browning Company introduced its Japanese-built Citori as an affordable alternative. The F.N. plant also reached a point where it had to retool for other guns, so eventually Miroku absorbed most of the Browning line. The fine Belgian-made High Power rifle, with its Mauser and Sako actions, did not survive the move. It was re-

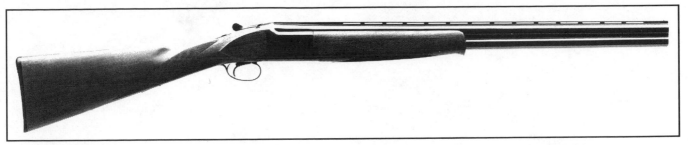

Browning's racy, Superlight version of its Japanese-built Citori shotgun is popular with upland bird hunters.

placed by the more easily manufactured BBR, later to become the A-Bolt.

Only the custom-built Superposed shotgun, the 9mm pistol, and a few parts for the BAR sporting rifle are still made in Belgium. Since the switch, several new Brownings have been introduced, most of them for Japanese manufacture. Recently, Browning's Buck Mark and 9mm BDM pistols have been built in a Utah factory. And when Fabrique Nationale bought Browning in 1977, Morgan, Utah, became U.S. headquarters for a much-diversified international enterprise, one that began in a frontier fix-it shop with a broken single-shot rifle more than a century before.

PART III

THE INNOVATORS: PAST AND PRESENT

AN INTRODUCTORY NOTE

Only 18 gunmakers appear in this book. The choice was to cover the most important companies well, or try to write something about every incorporated American gunmaker. The first option appeared by far the best. Giving all entries equal coverage seemed at the outset both unfair and untenable. Unfair because contributions from some men and their companies have proven far more influential and enduring than those of others. Untenable because some companies have short, unremarkable histories, while others have deep, convoluted roots. Weighting a chapter to reflect the firm's stature seemed reasonable—hence the separation of this book into Parts II and III.

The companies in this section sprouted after the frenetic race to develop the first cartridge guns and early repeaters. Their histories have a lesser impact on the arms industry than, say, Colt, if only because they came later. Famous men like Lincoln and Churchill owe at least part of their fame to the times that bore them. So it is in the gun industry.

Innovation is the essential factor in this section. The 11 companies whose histories appear here boast leaders of uncommon enterprise. These are men who pursued not only profit but new ideas, developing guns that were demonstrably superior for their time. Parker shotguns are still a standard of excellence; Savage's Model 99 remains essentially the same after nearly 100 years; and Bill Ruger's pioneering work in stamped and investment-cast parts helped him muscle the giants aside to become a giant himself.

Limiting this book's chapter count to a manageable number obviously means leaving out some armsmakers we'd like to have included. Perhaps their stories will merit another book like this one.

CHAPTER 10

UNCLE DAN LEFEVER'S ENDURING DESIGNS

Daniel Myron Lefever was a contemporary of John Moses Browning, and some say he was just as gifted. That Browning became a legend while Lefever's name has been lost—except among gun collectors—stems mostly from the direction taken by gun development in the U.S. during the late 19th century. John Browning refined the lever-action repeating rifle, designed the first successful pump shotgun, and pioneered autoloading mechanisms. He channeled his efforts where the shooting public and the military could best use them. Dan Lefever, on the other hand, focused his attention on the breech-loading double-barrel shotgun, a costly firearm whose popularity plummeted when reliable repeaters became available at the turn of the century.

Born on August 27, 1835—probably in upper New York state (though some historians contend his birthplace was Ohio)—Lefever's first significant work on guns was completed for the well-known riflemaker, William Billinghurst of Canandaigua, New York, for whom Lefever served a five-year apprenticeship beginning in 1848. Two years after his marriage to Sara Stead in 1857, he'd become a gunmaker of note in Canandaigua County, where Boyd's State Business Directory listed him as a gunsmith. By 1860, Lefever had a partner, J.A. Ellis, who was four years his junior and had been apprenticed to a riflemaker named Calvin Miller of Honeyoye, New York.

Lefever and Ellis apparently stayed together for several years, as their partnership appears in the business directories of 1864, 1865 and 1867. By 1870, they had split up, and Lefever returned to Auburn to become a partner in F.S. Dangerfield and Company. While with Ellis, Lefever had built mostly percussion guns, but his work with Danger-field centered on the new and promising cartridge breechloaders. Besides trying to improve the primitive breeching mechanisms of the day, Lefever converted muzzleloaders to the new system.

One such job came from an Illinois waterfowler, who sent the New York partners a worn-out gun that had cost him $250. Lefever refurbished and converted the battered smoothbore, cutting the 40-inch barrels to 30. After he'd returned the gun, Lefever received a note of thanks: ". . . I will say it is the finest shotgun I have ever owned. I have killed fox squirrels dead from the tallest bean trees that grow in the river bottoms and kill duck and geese higher. . . ."

Considering the wages of the day, Dangerfield and Lefever commanded high prices for their guns. An 1872 catalog lists their shotguns up to $250 (oddly enough, breech-loading double rifles retailed for only $100). The partners separated in 1873, with Lefever later moving to Syracuse, New York, to join with a man named L. Barber. Barber had been an agent for the Mutual Benefit Life Insurance Company and, while living in Troy (New York), he'd asked Lefever to do a conversion and build him a new 10-gauge shotgun. Subsequently, he wrote a complimentary letter to Lefever regarding his work, but no other connection is recorded between the two men. In 1875, Barber and Lefever operated under the name, "L. Barber and Company," located at "House 57 Johnson." Their first catalog, issued in 1876, bore the longwinded title, "Barber and Lefever Patented Breech Loading Double Barrel and Single Barrel Sporting Shotguns and Rifles." It listed a sidelock double shotgun ($250) with "the finest Laminated Damascus steel barrel, nice quality, forward action, rebounding locks, best English walnut,

This photo of Dan Lefever appeared in the 1905 Lefever catalog.

ently were still popular and profitable. A new service provided was the fabrication of rifle barrels for shotguns. "We insert a rifle barrel into our breech loading shotguns when desired," so stated their catalog. The price was $25. During this time, the famous barrelmaker, A.O. Zischang, worked for Nichols and Lefever, but he left in 1879 to open his own shop in Syracuse.

Nichols and Lefever soon began stamping the grade letter of their guns on the breech face. This was to prevent agents from selling low-priced guns as "best quality" and in so doing give the firm a bad reputation. There were five grades of Nichols and Lefever shotguns in 1877, ranging from "first

pistol grip stock, very finely engraved." Prices for other guns were about the same as those listed earlier by Dangerfield and Lefever. Converting a percussion double gun to a breechloader cost $45; changing a pinfire mechanism was half that.

The Nichols-Lefever Alliance, a Hammerless Gun

Dan Lefever didn't stay long in this partnership, either. In 1876, he teamed up with gunsmith John A. Nichols to form "Nichols and Lefever, successors to L. Barber and Co." Nichols must have provided the capital for this venture, since the partnership agreement obligated him to "furnish Six Thousand Dollars from time to time as the same shall be needed." Lefever, in turn, pledged "one undivided half of any [gun] patent that he now has or shall have" during the life of the union. Lefever also could "draw out from the concern one hundred dollars a month for the first year of the partnership, and one hundred twenty-five dollars a month the second year provided two-fifths of the profits will allow it." All notes, checks and drafts were to be signed only by John Nichols.

The partners produced a 35-page catalog in 1877, listing double rifles and shotguns and Creedmore rifles, as well as the conversions that appar-

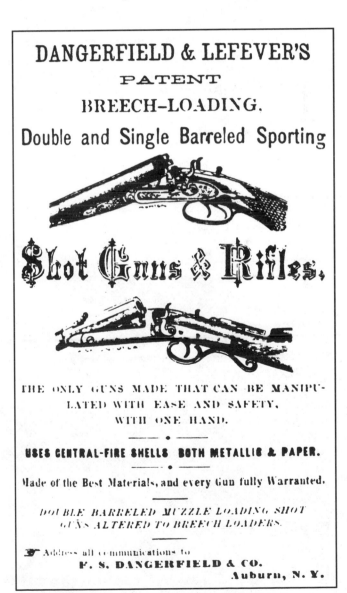

Front cover of the Dangerfield & Lefever catalog around 1872.

quality" A grade that retailed for $250 to an E model that sold for $100.

Predictably, the Nichols-Lefever bond quickly dissolved, and in 1879 the Syracuse directory listed Dan Lefever as "Sole manufacturer of the celebrated Lefever shotgun." John Nichols subsequently produced a few shotguns under his own name, but he went bankrupt in 1880 and thereafter worked with W.H. Baker of Ithaca, New York (Baker later marketed his own guns, starting a firm that lasted until 1933).

In his shop at 78 East Water Street, Dan Lefever worked diligently on a design he'd started in 1878. He'd won a prize at the St. Louis Bench show that year for a breechloading shotgun with no visible hammers. W.W. Greener had displayed a hammerless double at the Philadelphia Centennial two years earlier, and in so doing had borrowed heavily from a patent issued in 1871 to one Theophills Murcott. So the concept of hammerless guns wasn't new. Still, Lefever's rendition of this design impressed the judges.

On June 20, 1880, Lefever was granted a patent for the first hammerless double shotgun built in the U.S. It had the standard top opening lever of hammer guns, but also featured a thumb-operated tab on the left side of the frame for cocking. A lightweight, finely balanced gun, it was initially offered in 12-gauge only, but later came in 8 and 10 gauge as well. Between 1880 and 1883, Lefever manufactured 3,049 of these "side-cockers" in six grades (including a fancy AA grade). He replaced the manual cocking lever in 1883 with internal cocking rods that automatically compressed the mainsprings when the barrels were swung down. The 1892 catalog also mentions the new engine-turned rib, describing it as an "absolute dead surface of velvety softness . . . generally considered to be the most beautiful engine-turned rib ever to be brought to the public." Ribs on all other double barrels prior to that time were hand-cut; Lefever claimed that his ribs were more accurate than those made by any other manufacturer.

Automatic Ejectors and Single Triggers

This new shotgun must have sold well. Surely it promised future sales, for in 1884 Dan Lefever incorporated the Lefever Arms Company of Syra-

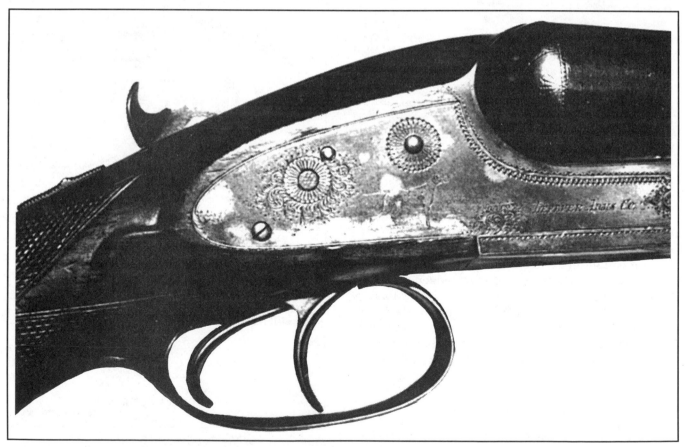

Lefever's first hammerless shotgun, similar to this 10 gauge model, was patented in 1880.

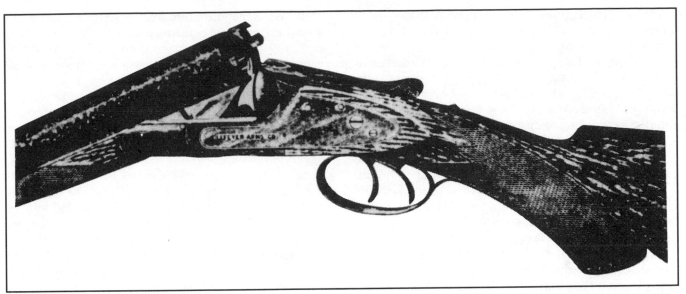

In 1892, Lefever's Ideal or G Grade was described as a "medium-priced hammerless gun" with damascus barrels in 12 or 10 gauge. No price was listed, but it appeared in a 1904 catalog for $57.00 without ejectors ($72.00 with).

cuse, New York. An 1889 catalog listed eight grades of Lefever hammerless guns, from an "F" on the bottom to the "Optimus," one notch above the AA. During the next 30 years, few basic changes were made in the mechanism of this shotgun, despite a confusing list of grades that was periodically trimmed and augmented. A collector must know manufacturing dates as well as grade designations to place with accuracy a gun's value. During the last years of the 19th century, all shotgun manufacturers were switching from Damascus to fluid-steel barrels. Fluid steel was stronger and necessary for smokeless powder loads. On the other hand, Damascus barrels—formed by winding strips of iron and steel around a mandrel and welding the joints— offered striking colors and patterns. For this reason, Damascus barrels were generally chosen for high-grade double guns, at least until black powder became obsolete. Now most collectors agree that fluid-steel barrels don't command a premium price for the best shotguns from that era because they won't be fired anyway.

"Uncle Dan" Lefever, as people came to call him, had great engineering talent. In his early guns he designed (but did not patent) a quick-release forend fastener that ranks with the best ever used on double guns. Lefever forends feature keys, levers and buttons, depending on their date of manufacture. Another clever device was an adjustment screw to compensate for action wear and to keep the gun tight. One of the most significant Lefever achievements was the introduction in 1892 of the automatic ejector. If Lefever did not invent automatic ejectors, he was certainly the first American to offer them (for $15) on a commercial scale in shotguns. Lefever's chief competitor, Parker Brothers, did not list automatic ejectors until 1902.

Several types of slide safeties were used on Lefever guns, along with a roll-type tang safety on some boxlocks. Dan Lefever did not like automatic safeties and would not install them except at a customer's request. "Live bird" shooters and some

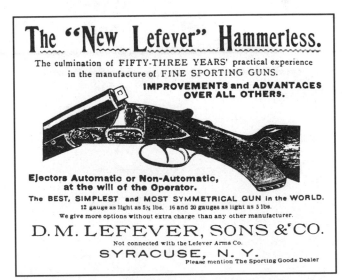

This 1899 ad heralded ejector guns at low prices. Dan Lefever apparently designed the first American ejector gun in 1889, marketing it three years later (Parker's ejector gun followed in 1902).

hunters—Nash Buckingham among them—preferred guns without safeties, and Uncle Dan accommodated them, too.

During the late 1890's, probably 10,000 Lefever shotguns were produced. All wore sideplates, but none were true sidelocks. The early Lefevers (below serial number 12,000) had the firing mechanism on sideplates, but later guns were really boxlocks that looked like sidelocks. Between numbers 12,000 and 25,000, part of the lock hung on the sideplate and part was pinned to the frame. Above number 25,000, no functioning parts were found on the plates. While these guns were in effect boxlocks, they're not to be confused with later guns of different design that lacked sideplates.

In 1898, Dan Lefever unveiled a single trigger he'd designed and offered it as a $15 option on his guns. During this time, the original officers—President A. Ames Howlett and Treasurer J.F. Durston—apparently continued to run the firm, with Lefever serving as superintendent. Although the company prospered, Dan Lefever must have become unhappy, because in 1900 he sold his stock to the Durston family, withdrew his assets, and left.

Lefever's independence may have prompted his exit, or perhaps he simply wanted to try another arrangement. Some say he was forced out. Whatever his reasons, he and his three sons—Charles, Frank and George—established D.M. Lefever and Sons in 1901. This new Syracuse company immediately introduced a boxlock shotgun, called the "Cross Bolt" (to distinguish it from earlier guns with false sideplates). Lefever took on S.H. Hale as his partner the following year and changed the name of the firm to D.M. Lefever, Sons and Co. It was a short-lived union.

This Lefever ad (above, left) appeared in the "Sporting Goods Dealer" in 1898. The offer to rebuild old Lefevers is noteworthy—the kind of option that is no longer available. The poster (above, right) dates from 1898 also.

LEFEVER

HAMMERLESS DOUBLE BARREL SHOT GUNS

	List Price	Net Factory Price
Durston Special	$ 37.00	$ 25.00
Durston Special, with Ejector	52.00	35.00
H Grade	44.00	33.00
H, with Ejector	59.00	44.25
G Grade	57.00	42.75
G, with Ejector	72.00	54.00
F Grade	80.00	56.00
F, with Ejector	95.00	66.50
E Grade	100.00	70.00
E, with Ejector	115.00	80.50
D Grade	125.00	87.50
D, with Ejector	140.00	98.00
C Grade	150.00	105.00
C, with Ejector	165.00	115.50
B Grade	200.00	140.00
B, with Ejector	215.00	150.50
A Grade	250.00	175.00
AA Grade	300.00	210.00
Optimus Grade	400.00	280.00
$1,000 Grade	1,000.00	700.00

The Durston name in this 1913 price list is that of the controlling family in the Lefever Company following Dan Lefever's death in 1906.

A Final Move, the Durstons, Ithaca's Nitro Special

In 1903, Lefever and his boys moved to Defiance, Ohio, where they formed the D.M. Lefever Company. Dan's partners included M.B. Chidester (vice president), J.G. Hickox (treasurer) and F.W. Thurstin (secretary). The company's 1905 catalog showed more changes than usual, omitting two of the six grades of cross bolt boxlock guns that had been listed, the 7D and 3 Optimus, and including three new grades—O Excelsior, 9F, and Uncle Dan, the last being an exquisite shotgun that sold for $400. About this time, Lefever also introduced a single-barrel boxlock trap gun for $38. The catalog also listed bicycle chains, which Lefever had begun marketing in the 1890's. In August, 1905, this ever restless entrepreneur, now 70, started yet another

firm: the D.M. Lefever Arms Company of Bowling Green, Ohio. A year later, in poor health, he moved back to Syracuse. And there, after battling a stomach ulcer, Daniel Lefever died on October 29, 1906.

Meanwhile, the Durston family continued to build its Lefever guns in Syracuse, offering in 1910 the "One Thousand Dollar" grade, the last word in double shotguns and purported to be, at least according to the company catalog, "The finest gun that can be made at any price." A turn-of-the-century shotgun listing for $1000 obviously had a limited market. The average factory wage then was 20 cents an hour, and most bird guns sold for well under $100. Even in the Lefever line, the One Thousand Dollar grade had no close rivals. The exquisite Optimus cost $400 in 1910, and the Parker A1 Special then listed for $750, as did the L.C. Smith A3. Until the Parker Invincible came on the scene in 1929 at a price of $1500, this Lefever remained the most expensive shotgun made in America. Adjusting for inflation, it may still be the most expensive gun ever cataloged by a U.S. firm. At least two specimens—both 10 gauges—are known to have survived.

In 1915, for reasons that remain obscure, the Ithaca Gun Company bought all Lefever company assets from the Durstons. Two years later, Ithaca distributed the last Lefever catalog, offering discounts of 40 percent on all Lefever guns. Between 1915 and 1919, Ithaca sold some Lefevers under its own name, and in 1921 the company marked its boxlock Nitro Special shotgun with the Lefever name.

The Nitro Special sold initially for only $28.25, roughly $9 less than the lowest-grade Durston Lefever had commanded in 1917. By 1933, the price had inched up to $30.50, with a single trigger option costing $4.60 additional. Available in 12, 16, 20 and .410 chamberings, the Lefever Nitro Special stayed in Ithaca's line until 1947. For hunters on a budget, the "Long Range Single Barrel" bird gun, priced at $16, was announced in 1927. A trap gun on the same action, but with competition rib and other frills, came out the same year at a price of $35. The field gun was available in 12, 16 and 20 gauges, and .410 bore, while the trap model was offered in 12 gauge only. Like the Nitro Special, these guns were cataloged as Lefevers.

The design and workmanship of Lefevers put them in the top ranks of American double shotguns. The independent nature of Dan Lefever and the course of American gun design during his career have conspired to deny them the attention afforded

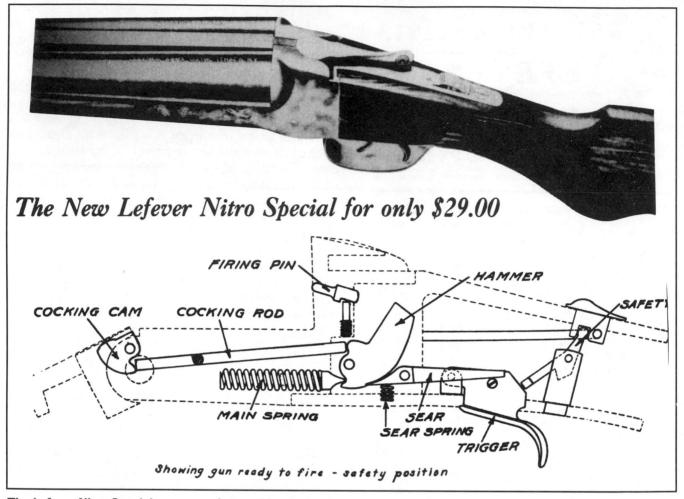

The New Lefever Nitro Special for only $29.00

The Lefever Nitro Special was manufactured beginning in 1921 (after serial number 100,000), following acquisition of the Lefever Company by Ithaca.

comparable firearms. Later, Dan's grandson, Fred, also worked as a gunsmith, but his name was forever shadowed by that of the company he worked for. Moreover, the 60 patents he earned never bore his name, either. While Dan Lefever's shotguns are still prized for their rarity, Fred Lefever's designs can be found almost anywhere, for it was he who developed the pump-action BB gun produced by Daisy.

Dan Lefever proved a restless genius whose inability to sustain relationships compromised the progress of his companies. But his mechanical wizardry produced some of America's truly great double shotguns. They comprised an important link between 19th and 20th century gunmaking—the last of the hand-built doubles that a working man could afford.

CHAPTER 11

CHARLES PARKER AND HIS SHOWCASE SHOTGUN

Some things are made merely to function. A ball bearing is beautiful only if it works. Nobody looks at one except to replace it, so the fewer bearings we see, the better. Other objects—from fine art to cheap wax fruit—have no worth apart from their appearance. A few toys and tools, however, when properly made, manage to combine both utility and beauty. Guns belong to this last group, as do automobiles. When asked to name the finest automobile ever engineered, one would be hard pressed. Choosing the best American shotgun would be comparatively easy. All you'd have to say is "Parker"—or defend your alternative against an army of Parker shotgun enthusiasts who insist there *is* no alternative.

Parker shotguns aren't the sturdiest ever built, nor the lightest. Their stocks have too much drop for shooters used to straight modern combs. And yet, they've become celebrated guns—a legendary line that comprises not just steel and walnut, but the elusive ingredients of great art. To many connoisseurs, Parkers are simply what shotguns ought to be.

Their story begins with the birth of Charles Parker on January 2, 1809, in Cheshire, Connecticut. As a youngster, Charles was apprenticed in a nearby Southington shop, where he cast buttons. He moved to Meriden in 1828 to make coffee mills. Four years later, with a starting capital of $70, Parker launched his own coffee mill business. His first "power plant" was a blind horse attached to a pole sweep. The horse was replaced in 1844 by a steam engine, one of the first in Meriden.

Charles Parker was quick to diversify his product line. The growing population of southern New England demanded a variety of tools and utensils. By 1862, the Parker Company Catalog listed several hundred items—among them hinges, vises, door knockers, locks, waffle irons, tobacco tins, piano stools and German silver tableware. The merchandise sold well, and some reached foreign countries. As early as 1859, a sailor reported seeing a Parker coffee mill in Melbourne, Australia.

Ever in search of new opportunities, Charles Parker did not closet himself in his office. He dabbled in other businesses, too, sometimes as partner, sometimes as investor. His most noteworthy outside venture began in 1844, when he became a partner in Snow, Hotchkiss and Company. Just five years old, this machine jobbing business had been started by brothers Oliver and Heman Snow. Heman soon sold his share of the firm to a Lucas Hotchkiss, who withdrew a year after Parker came in. For the next nine years, the company manufactured and sold machinery of all kinds.

A joint stock enterprise called the Meriden Machine Company was formed in 1853, employing 120 men in a foundry, smithy and machine shop. Additional capital in 1854 brought expansion and a new name: Snow, Brooks and Company. Gamaliel F. Snow, a shareholder and superintendent, designed many of the buildings that were later used by the firm to fill government contracts for rifles for the Union Army, and eventually to build Parker shotguns. Apparently, Parker had a substantial interest in Snow's machine works, because by the start of the Civil War its name had been changed to "Parker, Snow, Brooks and Company." At war's end, the firm became Meriden Manufacturing Company, with Charles Parker as its president.

A Family Business in Battle Rifles

In 1868, Parker and his sons—Wilbur, Charles, Jr., and Dexter—formed the Parker Brothers corporation to manufacture sporting guns. The first Parker Brothers shotgun had been built in 1865 and was featured that year on the frontispiece of the Meriden Manufacturing Company Catalog. During the next three years, Parker worked hard to perfect the gun. In 1868, the first factory-built Parker shotgun was sold, and the Snow family relinquished its share of the business. John Parker, Charles's brother, arranged for the sale of the company to Charles, who soon discontinued many of its products and expanded the sporting gun section.

Before the Civil War, Parker had apparently never made a gun. He was an industrialist and an entrepreneur whose main interest seemed to lie in the manufacture of profitable items and the expansion of corporate holdings. The source of his government rifle contract isn't documented, but his facilities invited such business. Just as Singer Sewing Machine was tapped for the manufacture of Model 1911 Colt pistols in World War II, any company that could easily accommodate gun manufacture in 1860 had a ready buyer in Uncle Sam. If Charles Parker had wanted to get into the gun business, this was an excellent chance to acquire tooling and experience with little risk. If he considered arms contracts simply lucrative projects, that was reason enough to participate.

The first contract, for 5,000 rifles, came from the Kentucky Home Guard, or North Kentucky Militia, in 1860. It was filled by Parker, Snow, Brooks and Company with a 50-caliber cartridge rifle, called the "Triplett and Scott." Produced by the several Meriden factories then under Charles Parker's influence, the gun featured a tube magazine in its stock and a lever that released the barrel, which could now be turned to free a fired case. After a fresh round was inserted and the action locked, the rifle was again ready to fire.

Because it could be reloaded so rapidly, the

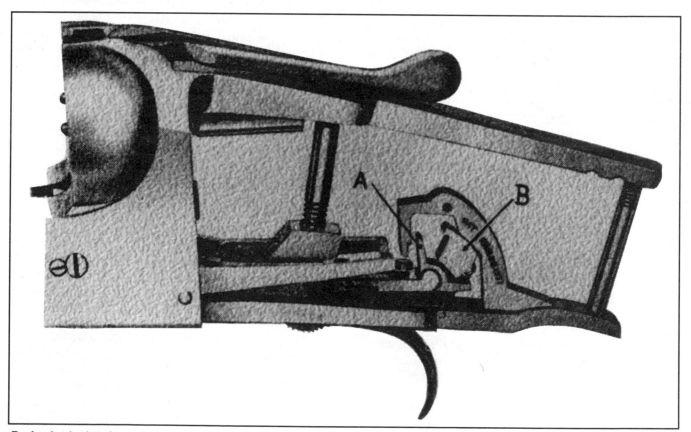

Parker's single trigger had a detent lever (A) that moved up into the hook of its housing when the first barrel fired. The housing stopped its movement until the trigger was released. A rebound block (B) prevented doubling under heavy recoil by backing into the housing.

Confederacy appealed to President Lincoln to withdraw this gun from service on humanitarian grounds. Apparently Lincoln thought the complaint had merit, because he referred it to the Hague International Tribunal for a decision. The war ended before the Tribunal delivered its verdict.

The second Parker rifle was produced for the U.S. Government in 1864. Similar in appearance to the Colt and Whitney rifles of that day, Parker's was, by contrast, a breechloader. Very few of these 55-caliber guns saw service before Appomattox, though records show the contract was initiated on September 28, 1963, and the order for 15,000 rifles (at $19 each) was filled. Conflicting reports indicate that Parker and his companies built about 1,000 rifles for Union troops during the war, shipping as many as 100 per day. The new design and controversial nature of the first gun may have limited its use in battle, however, and the second model was barely off the boards before the fighting stopped.

Perfecting the Double Shotgun

Why, after decades of successfully making and marketing small household items and industrial machinery, and grinding out hundreds (if not thousands) of infantry rifles during the war, did Charles Parker decide to build double-barrel shotguns? After all, manufacturing guns for the military demanded only a few of the talents needed in the production of fine sporting arms. Moreover, the double shotgun had at best limited application on the frontier. Pioneers were heading west armed with *rifles*—plain, sturdy guns with enough range and power to kill big game or fend off Indians. Conversely, Parker's expensive smoothbores smacked of southern plantations, still smoldering after America's devastating Civil War.

Parker's choice may have been dictated first by his own avid interest in the double shotgun. Second, his pragmatic, conservative approach to manufacturing may have steered him to a gun design that had been proven for over a century. While his Civil War rifles embodied new—even radical—ideas, most of Parker's prewar products were of conventional design. And finally, while double shotguns had a solid history, they also offered a huge potential for improvements.

Whatever his reasons, Charles Parker set about his new project right after the war. A three-year hiatus between his announcement and the actual production of guns was no doubt spent tooling up and perfecting the mechanism. Despite this prep-

aration, the final product—a 14-gauge with 29-inch barrels—came out with the same crude-looking lock common among breech-loading shotguns in those days. Apparently, shooters liked it anyway, because it stayed in use another 30 years. All Parkers were breechloaders, by the way. The double shotgun was the first sporting arm to be built in quantity for cartridges, and by the time Charles Parker got into the business, all "doubles" were assumed to be breechloaders.

The Parker gun came on the scene when loose black powder components were giving way to the self-contained shotshell. Its ammunition, like that of its contemporaries, comprised a brass hull containing powder, shot and wads. Priming was still external, consisting of percussion caps on hollow nipples that absorbed the blows of a hammer and channeled sparks to an opening at the base of the shell.

Parker's new double stayed on the market for six years before it was overhauled. As a shrewd businessman, Charles Parker must have been aware of the huge changes convulsing gun design during the 1870's, surely the most productive decade ever for America's armsmakers. In that period, Colt introduced its Single Action Army revolverys; Smith & Wesson produced its Schofield; John Marlin patented his first repeating mechanism; John Browning started to build his single-shot cartridge rifles; Winchester began pedaling its model 1873; and Remington had its Rolling Block. And yet, more and better gun designs were needed, if only as a mandate to keep up with the leaders.

King Develops the Auto Ejector; Imitations Intrude

To give his gun new life, Charles Parker sought a top-drawer engineer. He found one in Charles A. King, who left Smith & Wesson in 1874 to join Parker. There King developed a hammerless shotgun and designed the first Parker gun with automatic ejectors. But his best known and most important contributions were to the gun's locking mechanism. Working closely with Charles Parker, he reviewed the double-gun locking arrangements then in common use, including the Anson & Dealy, Dealy & Edge, and various rotary bolt designs. Some were successful and would remain so, but King and Parker wanted something different. Eventually they came up with their own bolting, incorporating a combination bolt plate that prevented a gun from blowing open. It was so effective, in fact, that a

Parker fired without the bolt engaged would not open. A Dealy & Edge-style forend lock replaced the earlier key design in 1880, and two years later the sliding lifter bar in front of the trigger guard was abandoned. In its place was a top-lever mechanism that locked the action by means of a pivoting lever and auxiliary roundbolt.

Within six years of its introduction—shortly after King's new bolting and lifter had been adopted—Parker claimed to have the "best and hardest shooting gun in the world." Sales supported the claim. By then, Parker was listing 11 models, priced from $45 to $250.

Early in the company's history, Charles's brother, Wilbur F. Parker, published a weekly sporting journal, entitled "The American Sportsman." Printed in newspaper format, it covered a variety of topics of interest to hunters and anglers. Contributors included high-ranking officials from the Smithsonian Institution, the U.S. Departments of Agriculture and Interior, as well as prominent naturalists and ballisticians. Advertising came from all quarters. Of course, other double shotguns appeared as well. U.S. buyers were warned of "utterly undependable" imitation doubles from Germany "descending on the States in a flood." A Pittsburgh dealer named J.H. Johnston warned his customers (through a catalog printed in the 1890's) that Parker imitations were being sold for as little as $20. All genuine Parkers, he reminded them, were stamped: "Parker Bros., Meriden, Conn."

"Grading" of Parker guns started as early as 1872, but while later grades were based primarily on embellishments, the first Parkers were priced according to the steel in their barrels. All barrel steel, initially imported from Belgium, consisted of "Damascus" blanks, made by twisting alternate strands of steel and wrought iron wire together to form a cable. This cable was then wound about a mandrel and furnace-welded. When etched or blued, the steel and iron reacted differently to the acids. The resulting patterns were marvelously intricate, adding beauty to the gun. Now Damascus barrels are considered unsafe for shooting, but at the time they were considered amply strong.

New Steel, No Hammers: "Old Reliable"

The first grades listed by Parker were, in ascending order, "PH," "GH," "DH" and "CH." The PH grade included "plain twist" barrels, while the better grades featured more complex patterns. The CH grade had a fancy "Bernard twist" and was

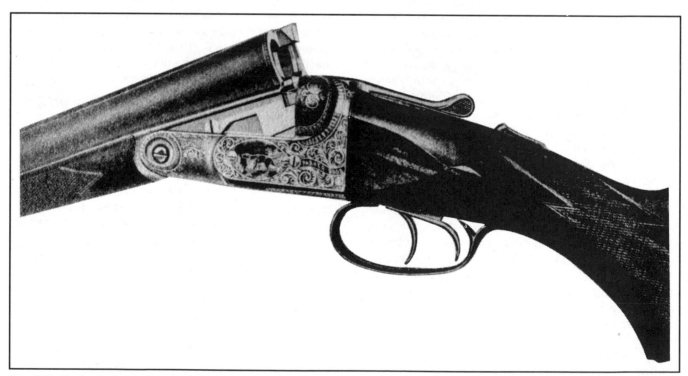

The DH, Parker's most popular mid-priced gun, accounted for about 41,000 sales. Its steel barrel was marked "Titanic," the company's own trade name.

considered Parker's best gun until Damascus barrels were replaced by those made of fluid steel right after World War I. Fluid steel barrels were stout enough to handle the pressures generated by smokeless powders, then new on the market, but they were less comely than Damascus tubes. They lacked not only the latter's surface patterns but its traditional "swamped" shape—thick at the breech, with a graceful, swooping taper forward. Fluid steel barrels had only a straight taper.

Parker's first hammerless guns appeared in 1889. The hammers were not actually abandoned; they were simply reshaped and moved inside. Unlike some hammerless guns, Parker's did not feature separate firing pins; rather, the hammer had an integral pin. A rebounding device on the base of each hammer brought the pin back away from the breech face as soon as it dented the primer. While Parker was not the first American firm to manufacture hammerless double shotguns, it marketed a successful design that lasted, essentially unchanged, for 25 years. Colt brought out a hammerless double in 1883, but it was quickly dropped because of poor sales.

Except for the change in barrel steels, the hammerless Parkers of 1889 differed little in appearance from those built after World War I. All were built of steel forgings and coil springs. Then, in 1910, Parker technician James P. Hayes, who'd engineered and patented the top-lever bolting system, came up with a simpler design. The old mechanism had 18 parts, the new one only four! Hayes maintained that "a gun so remodeled cocks much smoother and easier than the regular Parker guns do. . . . The 18 pieces may be discarded and the 4 new pieces put into a completed gun without having to alter the frame except to provide holes and slots for the new pieces."

The nickname, "Old Reliable," has stuck to the Parker shotgun for many years—principally, say Parker owners, because the bolting mechanism is so strong and foolproof. Parkers close crisply, and even prolonged hard use won't cause discernible looseness.

Parker steel was case-hardened for a time by Frederick Storm, a gunsmith whose father, George Storm, had been hired by Charles Parker after the Civil War. George had been a lieutenant in the Virginia State Militia and was stationed at Harper's Ferry when John Brown made his famous raid on the arsenal. He stayed with Parker the rest of his life, with his son Frederick following the same path. By packing the parts in bone dust and firing them in a coal furnace, Frederick achieved better case colors than his contemporaries. But he apparently did not pass along all his procedures, for his secrets died with him in 1952.

Building Parkers at Fifty Cents a Day

Most early Parker checkering was done by women (who were not allowed in other parts of the factory, except the business office). Records show that a 16-year-old girl named Elizabeth Hanson was hired in 1908 as a "checker" for Parker. She learned at the plant on her own time, then submitted her work to a foreman, who'd authorize wages if he found it satisfactory. Starting pay was 50 cents a day for 10 hours at the cradle.

Like other gun companies during the first years of the 20th century, Parker used inside contracting to give employees extra incentive. A company employee—often, but not always a foreman—would contract for a certain job and be paid when the job was completed. Expenses, including the wages of shop people involved, came out of his check. This arrangement not only gave ambitious workers a chance to make extra money, it provided management with precise cost figures. The system worked well until labor unions evolved. By and large, Parker employees down through the years remained loyal. In 1934, the average length of service among the firm's gun mechanics—many of whom began work for 25 cents an hour—was 36 years!

At the height of Parker production, fewer than 300 people worked at the Meriden plant. Compared with the 17,000 employed by Winchester during a wartime peak, this was a small operation indeed. But Parkers were not guns meant for the masses. Charles Parker might have said they were—he claimed his least expensive model had been designed for blue-collar bird shooters—but only 20 to 25 guns per day (not all of them economy models) were ever inspected, and many of these were sent back for touching up.

Parker guns were made largely by hand. The barrels were filed to reduce weight or change their shape; stocks were selected by weight to ensure proper balance on individual guns; and all locks and ribs were hand-fitted. Barrels had to be "soft-fitted" to the standing breech so closely that two pieces of tissue paper placed between them would be held tight, but without any metal contact. This and other ways in which these guns were made prevented them from becoming as affordable or available as repeating shotguns that were built in quantity and quickly on war surplus machinery.

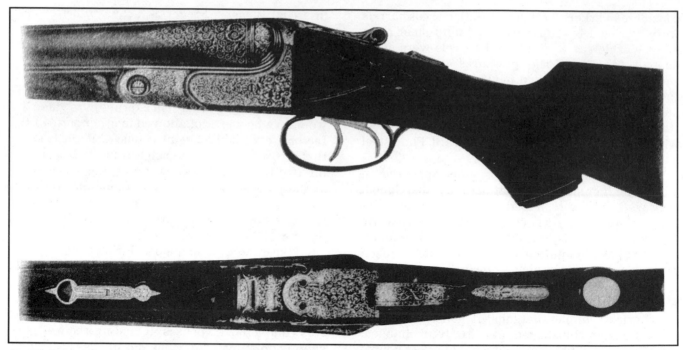

Parker's A1 Special (above) was the most valuable shotgun ever cataloged in the U.S. Only about 300 were made in 10, 12, 16, 20 and 28 gauge.

The American walnut used for most Parker stocks was selected by Walter King on his annual visits to the Des Moines (Iowa) Saw Mills. Linseed oil, hand-rubbed, was the most common stock finish. As with other parts, stocks bore the serial number of the action to which they were matched.

All Parker shotguns were targeted at the plant. Each was clamped in a rest and fired at a white, 30-inch steel plate mounted on a trolley parked 40 yards away. A black bolt head in the middle of the plate served as an aiming point. After each shot, the pellet marks were counted and a fresh coat of paint applied. A gun that failed to shoot well had its barrels straightened or rebored.

While the company worked hard to build fine shotguns, it did relatively little to promote them. Parker literature is comparatively scarce, and few Parker magazine ads have surfaced. The gun's reputation and a relatively small output kept orders coming in fast enough to fill without extensive advertising. Parkers were handled by such well known jobbers as Belknap, Shapleigh, Weed & Co., and were sold primarily through small but reputable gun dealerships. In addition, Parkers were marketed as specialty items by Abercrombie & Fitch, Stoeger, Simmons Hardware, Phil Baekert and other companies known for carrying high-grade sporting goods. Overseas orders were discouraged

by many big armsmakers, but as a semi-custom shop, Parker welcomed them. The French were particularly fond of Parkers. The company had only two sales rooms—one in Meriden, the other in New York City. Its salesmen, like those of other gun firms in pre-Depression days, often doubled as trick shooters. They not only talked a good line, they could shoot well enough to impress anyone in search of a better shotgun.

Frames, Grades and Prices

For nearly 50 years, Parker maintained the most comprehensive line of double-barrel shotguns ever produced in America. Lefever, Ansley Fox, L.C. Smith and others offered credible competition in this era, but none earned the reputation afforded Parker. The firm stuck to a narrow path, experimenting with repeating mechanisms and over/under shotguns but never producing them. A single-barrel trap gun, introduced late in the company's life, was its only deviation from the manufacture of side-by-side doubles. Shotgun accessories were featured at Parker stores, but they were made elsewhere. The company never assembled ammunition—though some brass shotshells were manufactured for it by contractors prior to 1900.

From the turn of the century to the Depression,

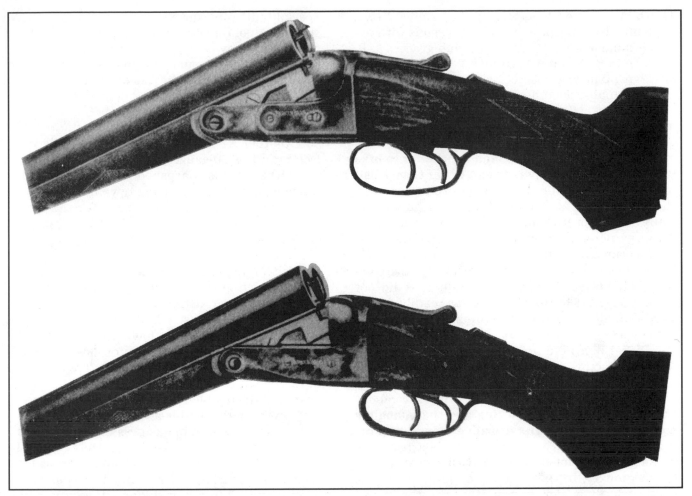

Parker Models VHE (with ejectors) and VH (without ejectors) accounted for more sales—58,000—than any other Parker. The bottom-grade Trojan (shown here below the VH) ran a close second at 50,000.

remarkably few changes were made in the Parker shotgun line. Guns were built on six frame sizes:

#3 (8- and heavy 10-gauge)
#2 (10- and heavy 12-gauge)
#1½ (12- and heavy 16-gauge)
#1 (16-gauge)
#0 (20-gauge)
#00 (28-gauge)

This extensive selection of frames compelled Parker to keep a large inventory of parts on hand, but it also ensured buyers that any reasonable order could be filled with a perfectly balanced shotgun. The firm also listed its grades by number as well as by name, as follows (with average annual production percentages):

Trojan (Trojan)—40%
#0 (Vulcan)—25%
#1 (PHE)—3%

#2 (GHE)—10%
#3 (DHE)—15%
#4 (CHE)—1%
#5 (BHE)—5%
#7 (AHE)—½%
#8 (A1 Special)—½%

The 1899 catalog also listed "E" and "N" Parkers, but these grades were quickly dropped. A normal year's production totaled about 4,000 shotguns of all grades.

Parker's VHE (Vulcan) and A1 Special grades did not appear in company literature until after the turn of the century—sometime between 1899 and 1912. During this period, the old lifter mechanism was finally discontinued, having been kept alive as an option for roughly 20 years after the introduction of King's superior bolting system. The conservative, tradition-bound buying habits of double-gun connoisseurs also kept outside hammers available.

These lasted even longer than the original lifter, expiring after World War I. In 1912, guns with exposed hammers were offered in nine grades: T, R, H, G, D, C, B, A and AA. Grades T through G came only with Damascus barrels, with fluid steel barrels made available on guns graded D or higher.

The Parker Trojan first appeared in 1915, when a flyer inside the Parker catalog noted a price increase brought on by the war. The new prices took effect on January 24, 1916, and another price hike was declared the following year. Other than boosting production costs and paring output, however, the "Great War" passed by Parker without materially changing it. Remington and other industry giants garnered huge profits (and ran up huge debts) on government contracts, but no record of Parker taking such contracts exists. Certainly, the company's facilities for building double guns did not lend themselves to the war effort as readily as factories already geared for the production of repeating rifles.

World War I did prompt changes in the design and manufacture of sporting guns, though. Parker's products changed less than some, because they were still built mostly for people who cared about tradition, balance, hand-fitting and the intangible qualities that make a gun feel alive. However, three years after armistice, Damascus steel barrels were no longer an option at Meriden. Other changes followed quickly. In 1922, Parker announced its first single trigger model, and in 1923 the beaver-tail forend made its appearance. A ventilated rib arrived in 1926, followed by the first .410 Parker in 1927. By 1929, Parker was building about 5,000 guns a year.

The 200,000th Parker shotgun was numbered in the first months of the Great Depression. That shotgun, a 12-gauge with a straight grip, was given even more lavish treatment than the A1 Special. Parker called it "The Invincible," a top-of-the-line gun that was to be produced regularly but in small quantities and sold for $1,500. While such a price for the most ornate of double shotguns seems reasonable indeed by modern standards, it was comparatively high in 1930. An L.C. Smith Monogram Grade sold for $400 that year, a Purdey cost $650, and Parker's own A1 listed for $750.

The Depression smashed hopes for The Invincible, unfortunately. The company's planned steady production of three or four guns a year did not happen. Only two of these Parkers were built, and the gun was not listed after 1930. The only Parker rivaling The Invincible in appearance was an A1

Special built for Tsar Nicholas of Russia, an avid shooter. A gold-inlaid stock of imported walnut and a gold Romanov eagle set in the trigger guard distinguished this unusual gun. Just before it was finished, though, the Bolsheviks overran the Russian palace and the gun was never delivered.

A No-Frills Economy and Narrow Company

Another A1 with similar appeal to modern collectors is the 20-gauge presented by Buffalo Bill Cody, the famous sharpshooter, to Annie Oakley. A much plainer, though equally valuable Parker is a 24-gauge Trojan that was made for the United States Cartridge Company. Of the dozen Trojans so chambered, only one is known to have survived. The others were ordered destroyed when Parker decided not to produce any more 24-gauge guns. At its introduction in 1915, the Trojan was the least expensive Parker, listing at only $27.50. It quickly became the firm's best seller, differing from other Parkers in that it did not have automatic ejectors and wore double triggers only for most of its life. Single triggers became an option for Trojan buyers in 1934—but the Parker Skeet gun introduced that year, and the double-barrel Trap model released in 1937, were not available as Trojans.

Parker had been in business 47 years before it introduced the Trojan. This long delay seems unwarranted now, but there were good reasons for it then. First, Charles Parker wanted to build a high-quality gun. Before World War I, the only way to do that was to use lots of hand labor, which made any gun expensive. The extra work necessary to make a gun look good became a relatively minor additional cost. Secondly, several armsmakers offered cheaply-built doubles toward the end of the 19th century, some selling for as little as $10. Charles Parker would not risk the Parker name in an effort to compete in this arena, where volume mattered more than a reputation for high quality. When war prompted engineers to come up with more efficient manufacturing methods, Parker applied the new technology to double guns, offering the famous Parker balance and bolting system in a workingman's shotgun.

A Parker Trojan came standard with a hard rubber butt, pistol-grip stock, and spartan finish. It was sold only in 12, 16 and 20 gauges, but any choke was available. The Trojan's forend was attached in such a way that only an extremely heavy force could snap it loose. Its case-hardened frame lacked the gracefully curved forward shoulders of other Parkers. In 1939, its last year of production,

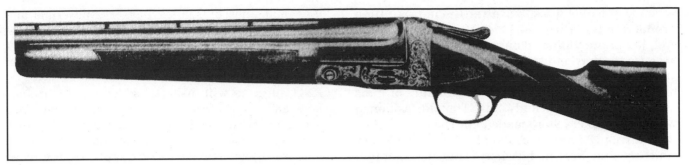

This Single Barrel Trap Gun was offered by Parker in five grades—but only one gauge (12).

the Trojan listed for $80—three times its introductory price and much higher than the prices of its competitors.

Except for the Trojan, Parker shotguns offered many options. Stocks came with the buyer's choice of straight grip, pistol grip, or semi-pistol grip. Checkered butts, steel skeleton plates, hard rubber and soft rubber buttpads were also optional. Almost any stock dimensions were possible, but a $10 charge applied to unusual orders. Barrel lengths ranged from 24 to 40 inches, the most popular being 26, 28, 30, 32 and 34 (chambered in 8, 10, 12, 14, 16, 20, 28 and .410 gauges). Few 8-gauge guns were built after 1900; and 10-gauge Magnum guns chambered for 3½-inch shells were built to special order only. In 1903, Parker became the first American firm to offer a 28-gauge shotgun. All grades (except the Trojan) were available in this gauge, but few were produced, and most of those were in the higher grades. Gun weights varied from 5¾ to 11 pounds, depending mainly on gauge and barrel length.

In 1917, Parker introduced its first competition model—the Single-Barrel Trap Gun. Available only with a 12-gauge, 2¾-inch chamber in barrel lengths of 30, 32 and 34 inches, this Parker came in several grades, with a beavertail forend and single trigger. It quickly proved itself on clay targets and remained unchanged and unchallenged until Parker announced its Double-Barrel Trap Gun in 1937. This double, which was manufactured for no more than seven years, became the last shotgun developed by Parker. It followed the Parker Skeet Gun, introduced in 1934. Cataloged with 26-inch barrels in 12, 16, 20, 28 and .410 chamberings, the Skeet Gun could be ordered with a ventilated rib at no extra charge. Both the Trap and Skeet models came with automatic ejectors.

The Great Depression may have summarily smashed many corporations, but gun firms weathered the blow surprisingly well. In fact, all the major armsmakers in business in 1929 were still in business at the start of World War II. Some had been absorbed by other firms, but their names and products were not swept away in the economic rubble of the early '30s. Of the gun companies, Parker was perhaps rocked the hardest. Its line comprised essentially one product—albeit in a heady number of configurations—that nobody needed. Many sportsmen wanted a Parker, true, but when money became tight such fine double shotguns simply did not sell.

Remington Takes Over

In 1934, the Charles Parker Company still had a variety of manufacturing interests in addition to its shotgun enterprise. Carrying this branch during an extended economic slump strained the other interests, however. Thus, when the Remington Arms Company offered to buy manufacturing and marketing rights to Parker shotguns that year, the board of directors agreed and on June 1, 1934, the deal was done. Other armsmakers had previously approached Parker—most notably Winchester, in 1920—but there was no reason to sell at that time. Winchester, determined not to be without a double shotgun, then developed its famous Model 21, which is still in production (on special order only).

When Remington assumed control of Parker, only 104 guns existed at the plant. During the next 3½ years, Remington continued to build shotguns at the Meriden facility, turning out 5,562 Parkers before transferring the operation to its Ilion factory in 1937. During this transition, Parker shotguns were manufactured exactly as before, by the same people with the same tools and machines. Nearly 80 percent of the original Parker work force made the move to Ilion, and for the next six years no substantial changes were made in the guns. Parkers were built regularly until 1944, with the last being shipped in 1947. Post-Remington Meriden Parkers and Ilion Parkers were built to the same standards as early Meriden guns, but after the move to Ilion production was throttled back. From 1938 to war's end, Remington finished only 1,723 Parkers, partly because the market had shifted heavily to repeating shotguns and partly because Remington's plant was better suited to high-volume manufacture of guns designed for the assembly line. The old-fashioned way that Parkers were made kept them in production during the first years of the war, when other sporting guns were all but discontinued so that military arms could take over the assembly lines.

The last Parker shotgun assembled bore the serial number 242,385—a low number, considering the firm was in business for nearly 80 years. Recently, Remington and Winchester have built limited quantities of replica Parkers. Materials and workmanship are surprisingly good, and prices—roughly, from $2,300 to $3,000—are about what you'd expect to pay for a well-built American double.

Collectors will insist these are not really Parkers, and that there's nothing like the original. They are right, of course. It is this same deep allegiance that made Charles Parker so successful with a gun built to higher standards of quality than anyone else dared risk in pioneer times. Parkers still bring to mind buckboards, magnolia blossoms and bobwhites; and sinkboxes bobbing under sky-dimming squadrons of waterfowl. In a Parker glow the glory days of shotgunning.

CHAPTER 12

SAVAGE: AN ADVENTURER'S PRACTICAL GUNS

The 19th-century gun designs that launched America's most famous armsmakers were obsolete only a few years after their inception. Eliphalet Remington's hand-forged long rifle, Samuel Colt's Patterson revolver, the Henry repeater and Marlin's "Never Miss" derringer, all are prime examples. A remarkable exception was Arthur Savage's Model 99 lever-action rifle, a gun so far ahead of its time that now, nearly 100 years later, it is still in production!

Its inventor—Arthur William Savage, born June 13, 1857, in Kingston, Jamaica—was no less remarkable. His father was England's Special Commissioner there, assigned to establish schooling for newly freed slaves. Intelligent and studious, young Arthur received a fine education in England and the United States. Immediately after finishing college, he sailed for Australia, where he found work managing a cattle ranch. Arthur stayed there for 11 years, long enough to marry and start a family that eventually comprised four sons and four daughters. One of his sons was born in a wagon during a pioneering venture, and once Arthur was captured and held prisoner for several months by aborigines. By the time he decided to return to Jamaica, this enterprising young man was said to own the biggest cattle ranch in Australia.

The sale of his ranch enabled Savage to buy a Jamaican coffee plantation, which he ran while experimenting to improve firearms, explosives and various types of machinery. Among his best-known products was the Savage-Halpine torpedo, designed cooperatively with another inventor. The U.S. Navy tested this weapon and found it quite satisfactory, but political factors prevented its adoption. Savage subsequently sold the torpedo to the Brazilian government and later contributed to the design of recoilless rifles.

Savage's greatest interest lay in small arms. Despite terrific advancements in firearms manufacture during the first years of his life, he concluded there were still fortunes to be made for people with ideas for better sporting guns. The competition was severe. One could not simply offer an improved product; it had to be substantially different and clearly superior.

A Brilliant Designer is Beaten—and Rebounds

Savage was only 35 years old when, in 1892, he developed a rifle that met these criteria. Called "Savage No. 1" in blueprint, the gun was a hammerless, lever-action with the lever accommodating only one—the near—finger. The middle finger(s) wrapped around an extension of the trigger guard that lay flat along the bottom of the grip and formed the forward part of the lever. The magazine held eight rounds of unspecified dimensions. Two bands held the musket-style stock to the 29-inch barrel.

In 1892, Savage, then living in the U.S., submitted his rifle for testing at the U.S. ordnance trials at Governor's Island, New York. It was judged inferior to the Krag-Jorgensen, which subsequently became the official U.S. infantry rifle. The next year, Savage refined his rifle for commercial markets, reducing magazine capacity to five for the sake of trimmer lines and redesigning the lever to accept all three grip fingers. He followed immediately with a new, smokeless powder cartridge for the gun.

Arthur Savage, shown here as a young man, raised cattle, grew coffee and citrus, and prospected for oil, in addition to founding one of America's great arms companies.

Arthur Savage formed the Savage Arms Company in Utica, New York, in 1894, and began producing his rifle the following year. Called the Model 1895, Savage's first sporting arm featured a truly hammerless mechanism with a rear-locking bolt adjoining a wall of steel. This stout steel barricade was machined into the tail of a streamlined receiver that began as one solid block.

Savage's action had great strength and served better than any competing lever mechanism to protect the shooter in the event of case failure. The new rifle also had a coil mainspring, the first ever offered on a commercial lever gun. It also featured a through-bolt to mate the buttstock to the re-

ceiver—a much stronger, more rigid arrangement than the traditional use of wood screws inserted through a tang extension. Savage surely had no inkling that in a few generations almost everyone would equip their rifles with scopes, but the Model 1895 featured side ejection that was destined to make scope mounting easy. For the time being, it kept empties out of the sight line.

This revolutionary gun featured the same rotary magazine engineered for Savage's 1892 rifle. A spring-loaded spool housed neatly in the receiver, it incorporated a cartridge counter visible through a small window on the left side of the frame. The gun could be loaded with single cartridges merely by dropping one in the breech opening, then levering the action shut. The magazine had no external components, so when the action was closed dirt and water had no access. There was almost no way to mishandle Savage's 1895 rifle so as to damage its feeding mechanism.

By eliminating the under-barrel tubular magazine pioneered by Walter Hunt (and sustained by Winchester in its lever guns), Savage offered a sturdier, better protected magazine design, one that did not affect barrel vibrations (hence, accuracy). Unlike tube magazines when they were full, the spool did not alter rifle balance, either. Its biggest advantage, however, would not become a key selling point for several years, when the superior ballistic qualities of pointed bullets in military rifles brought striking changes in sporting bullet design. Arthur Savage's magazine accommodated pointed bullets, while tubular magazines did not. A pointed bullet resting on the primer of the cartridge ahead of it could detonate that primer under the jar of recoil; thus, flatnose bullets were the only safe bullets in traditional lever rifles.

The slow, heavy bullets of the late 19th century, fired from big-bore, low-pressure, black powder cartridges, could as well be flat on the nose as round or pointed. Their large diameter and low initial velocity, along with the mediocre accuracy of early repeaters, limited the range at which they could be used. A pointed bullet extended that range somewhat but not significantly. Besides, hunters were used to shooting up close—but Arthur Savage was about to change all that. He began by developing a cartridge he called the .303 Savage. It wasn't really a .303, though. The .303 British, which had just been adopted for use in Great Britain's Enfield rifle, had a .311 bullet. Savage's cartridge featured a .308 bullet, which was standard for 30-caliber rifles (the .30-30 is properly a .307

bullet, but .308's are widely substituted). The case was about the same size as that of a .30-30, but Savage designed a long, roundnose 190-grain bullet to give his .303 an edge in penetrating power over the 170-grain, .30-30 flatnose. Given the short shooting ranges of the day, this extra weight helped more than a jump in velocity would.

Accolades from the Field; Charles Newton Contributes

Savage's new cartridge quickly gained converts. After firing his Model 1895, E.E. Jones of Townsend, Montana, said he'd bet $50 he could "shoot through a grizzly endwise" with the .303 Savage. Apparently no one came up with a carcass to call Jones on his bet, and even live grizzlies must have had second thoughts. Another big game hunter and backwoodsman from British Columbia claimed 18 kills (including grizzlies) with a box of 20 .303 cartridges. In its 1900 catalog, Savage ran an excerpt from a letter written by E.T. Ezekiel of Wood Island, Alaska, telling how the mighty .303 had even killed a whale!

Dr. W.T. Hornady, author of "Campfires in the Canadian Rockies," wrote: "I have just returned from my hunting trip with one bull moose and two bull caribou, all killed stone dead in their tracks with one of your incomparable .303 rifles. I shot the moose at a distance of 350 yards.

"Last fall [I killed] two bull moose with one of your .303-caliber Savage rifles. I hurriedly estimated the distance to be between 300 and 400 yards, and we afterwards found it to be 280. . . . In both instances the animals were killed with a single bullet.

"[My guide] thinks more of his Savage now than ever and would not lay it down for any rifle. . . . In November [he] killed a very fine large mountain sheep [with] the first shot 237 yards off and in a very strong wind. He says he likes the Savage to shoot in the wind as the barrel is small and [has] no long magazine to catch the wind and blow your rifle to one side."

Savage's Model 1895 was offered with a 22- and 30-inch barrel chambered only for the .303 cartridge. About 6,000 rifles were made between 1895 and 1899, when Savage modified the action slightly and changed its name to Model 1899. A year later, the gun became available in .30 WCF (.30-30); and in 1903, the .25-35, .32-40 and .38-55 made the list of chamberings (but they were dropped in 1919).

The first Model 99, which Savage produced in 1920, looked very much like a Model 95, with straight-grip stock and schnable forend. Barrels came in lengths of 20 to 28 inches, with letter des-

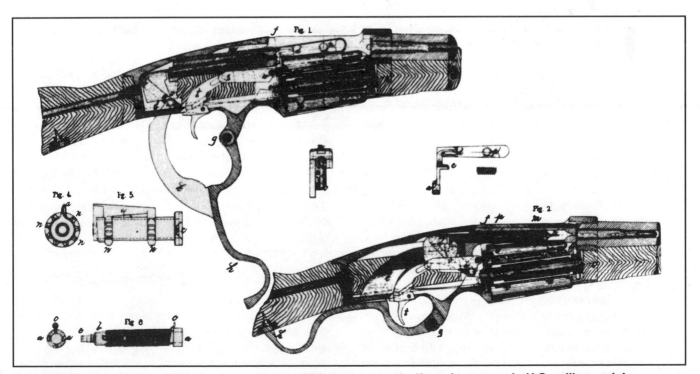

Savage's Model 1892, predecessor to its Model 1899, lost out to the Krag-Jorgensen in U.S. military trials.

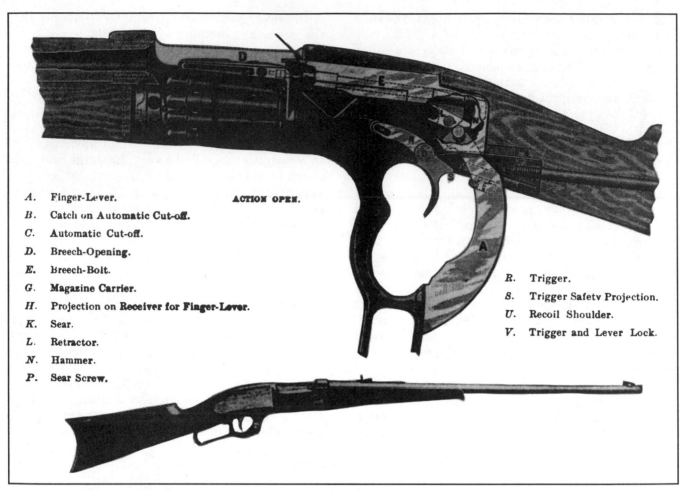

A. Finger-Lever.
B. Catch on Automatic Cut-off.
C. Automatic Cut-off.
D. Breech-Opening.
E. Breech-Bolt.
G. Magazine Carrier.
H. Projection on Receiver for Finger-Lever.
K. Sear.
L. Retractor.
N. Hammer.
P. Sear Screw.

ACTION OPEN.

R. Trigger.
S. Trigger Safety Projection.
U. Recoil Shoulder.
V. Trigger and Lever Lock.

The Savage Model 1895 shown here, chambered in .303 Savage, made its debut a year after the birth of the Savage Repeating Arms Company.

ignations denoting barrel shapes: "A" for round, "B" for octagonal, "C" for half-octagonal. A Model 99-D, featuring a full-length military stock, was available only in .303 Savage and died in 1905. The more popular 99-F was a saddle-ring carbine with a 20-inch barrel. In 1903, Savage's Model 99-A, featuring a short 22-inch barrel, came to be known as the "saddle gun." Its .25-35 chambering was dropped in 1913, when the .250-3000 supplanted it.

Beginning in 1912, Charles Newton, the brilliant ballistician and rifle designer (see following chapter), developed the .250-3000 for Savage. The case had the same head dimensions as the .30-06, but it was much shorter. Newton recommended a 100-grain bullet loaded to about 2800 fps, but Savage chose instead an 87-grain bullet at higher velocity. That velocity—3000 fps—became part of the cartridge designation to help spur sales. Later, the round was called simply the ".250 Savage."

Factory loads with 100-grain bullets, having proved more practical for all-around deer hunting, have now replaced those original 87-grain loadings.

Newton also gave Savage the "Imp," or .22 High Power cartridge. First offered in the Model 99-CD deluxe rifle in 1912, its 70-grain, .228-inch bullet achieved 2700 fps and became an instant hit with big game hunters, who used it on such unlikely quarry as lions and tigers. The High Power lacked bullet weight and energy for reliable kills on even deer-size game, however, and was muscled out of this arena by the .250-3000.

New Cartridges, An Enduring Design

By 1920, the Savage Model 99 was available in five styles: solid frame standard rifle, solid frame saddle gun, takedown standard rifle, takedown saddle gun and takedown featherweight. That same year, the .300 Savage cartridge was added to Model 99's list of chamberings. If the company's original intent was to offer .30-06 performance in a short case for rifles with compact actions, the .300 Savage cannot claim to have lived up to its billing. After all, there's a difference of 250 fps between the muzzle velocity of this round and that of the .30-06. Still, it had plenty of muscle for deer and, at moderate ranges with heavy bullets, elk and moose as well. It became a very popular chambering in the Savage lever-action, yielding in sales somewhat to the more powerful .308 Winchester after its appearance in 1952.

As the story goes, the .308 owes its existence to Savage's .300. In the early 1950's, when ordnance experts were looking for a cartridge to replace the .30-06 in battle rifles, they turned first to the .300 Savage. They knew it would function well in short actions and that it had enough punch for most applications. But when they found its neck was too short for reliable functioning in some mechanisms, they redesigned the cartridge by lengthening the neck and reducing the shoulder angle by 10 degrees. This experimental round was called the T-65 at first, then the .308 Winchester. The U.S. Army adopted it as the 7.62 NATO in 1955.

During its first 90 years of production, Savage's flagship Model 99 has been offered in 31 versions and 14 chamberings—not including a takedown model that came with a .410 shotgun barrel. The action has remained the same, with two exceptions: its safety was moved from the lever to the tang hump in 1961, and a detachable box magazine was introduced as an alternative to the lovely spool in 1965. Now Model 99 comes only with the box mag-

azine, and only in .308 and .243 Winchester chamberings. Other modern rounds that have been offered in Model 99 (but are no longer available) include the .284, .358 and .375 Winchester and the .22-250 Remington.

Savage's first catalog, issued around 1900, listed Model 99's for $20, with engraving available from $5 and checkering from $2. By contrast, a standard Model 99 now retails for nearly $550. A Lyman tang peep sight (or its wind-gauge globe front sight) cost an extra $3.50 originally, with sling and swivels adding $1.50 to the bill. Stocks of almost any dimensions could be special-ordered, but the 1905 catalog reminded buyers that: "Any deviation from [standard dimensions] requires the stock to be cut from the solid block by hand. This is expensive work and there is an extra charge of $10 for altering the length or drop of a stock."

Savage's rifle and ammunition quickly gained reputations for fine accuracy. The 1903 catalog showed a 10-shot, 100-yard group measuring only $1^5/_{16}$ inches. As Savage pointed out in its early literature, smokeless powder not only produced higher velocities with smaller charges, it reduced bore fouling. Additional claims of a 45 percent reduction in recoil for smokeless must have raised some questions—but they also helped wean shooters away from black powder and steered them to the sleek new Savage rifle.

Endorsements from famous outdoorsmen have always been welcomed by gun firms. In 1901, Savage got a personal letter from Theodore Roosevelt, recommending Model 99 as "the handsomest and

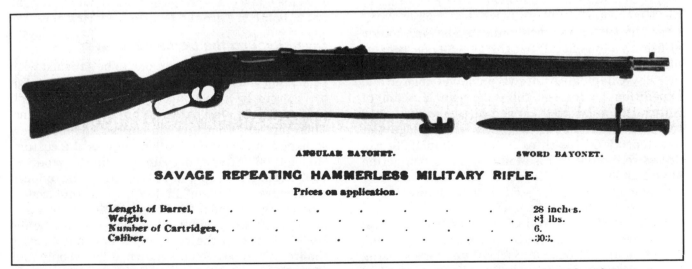

This military-style Model 99 was cataloged in .303 Savage, but large quantities could be ordered in other chamberings. The gun was dropped in 1905, but a late production run followed in 1915.

The author shoots a Savage Model 99—the company's most famous gun. The only 99 still being produced is made overseas for Savage.

best turned out rifle I have ever had." T.R.'s affinity for Winchester's 1886 and 1895 lever actions and, later, the 1903 Springfield indicate his appreciation of firearms in general, but the .303 Savage became his favorite.

Roy Chapman Andrews, famous explorer and expedition leader for the American Museum of Natural History, also carried a Savage. He called the .250-3000, "The most wonderful cartridge ever developed." On his third Asiatic trek in 1920, Andrews relinquished his Model 99 for a bolt-action Model 1920 Savage. However, another member of that same expedition, noted big game hunter Harry Caldwell, brought along his 99.

One of the best-known woodsmen ever to espouse Savage rifles was Frank Buck, who filmed the popular "Bring 'Em Back Alive" series, using his favorite gun to capture wild animals. Buck liked to fire his Model 99 into the branch of a tree that held his quarry, severing the limb and dumping the animal onto the ground or into a waiting net.

Diversity; and the Demands of War

Arthur Savage was not one to be satisfied with producing one rifle, no matter how sound its design or vigorous its sales. Success in the firearms business came only with a diverse line of sporting guns. Therefore, the company announced in 1903 a new slide-action .22 rimfire called, as was the custom, Model 1903. After short runs of slightly modified 1903's (Models 1909 and 1914), Savage introduced a takedown .22 pump in 1925, to be replaced in four years by Model 29. Savage's Model 1904 and 1905 .22's were single-shot bolt-actions, while Model 1912 was the company's first autoloading rimfire rifle. A box-fed takedown, it lasted only four years. Model 19 NRA, a box-fed bolt-action repeater, did much better, with catalog listings from 1919

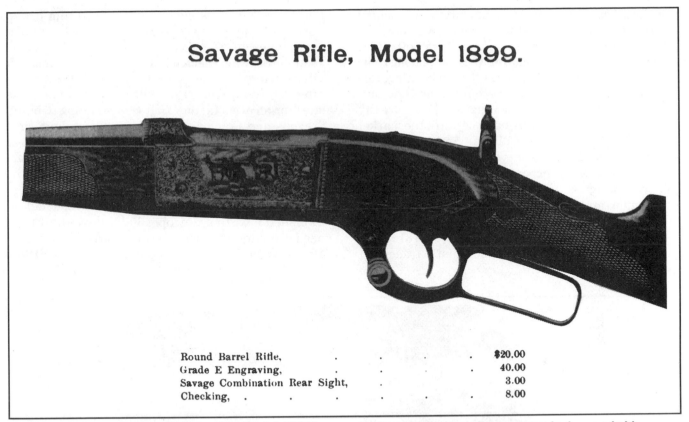

Savage Rifle, Model 1899.

Round Barrel Rifle,	.	.	.	$20.00
Grade E Engraving,	.	.	.	40.00
Savage Combination Rear Sight,	.	.		3.00
Checking, .	.	.	.	8.00

Despite their original low price, Savage Model 1899's were finely crafted guns whose strong lockup and side ejection put them ahead of their time.

through 1937. About 6,000 of these military-stocked rifles (total production came to about 50,000) were used to train American troops.

In 1907, Savage plunged into the pistol business with its Model 1907 single-action autoloader in .32 ACP and .380 ACP. With its 10- and 9-round magazine and barrel length of around four inches, this businesslike gun was potent yet concealable. Refinements produced Models 1915 and 1917 later on, but the company stopped making autoloading pistols entirely in 1928.

When the United States entered World War I in 1917, Savage Arms put all of its production capacity into government service, merging with the Driggs-Seabury Ordnance Company of Pennsylvania to manufacture a huge number of Lewis machine guns. Designed for use in aircraft, this weapon's firing mechanism was synchronized with a biplane's engine so that its bullets could fire between spinning propeller blades.

After the war, Savage faced the same problems that haunted larger arms firms. Production capacity had been expanded for the war effort, but no new sporting guns had been introduced. Tooling up for

machine guns was not, after all, easily adapted to the manufacture of hunting rifles. Debts incurred by factory growth were hard to erase when the company had no guns to sell civilians nor any new designs to convince buyers they needed its products. Moreover, scaling back a work force that was no longer needed in full strength placed an added burden on management.

To bolster its market position, Savage introduced a new centerfire rifle: Model 1920. Offered in .250 or .300 Savage, this gun featured a Mauser-type action and a checkered stock with schnabel forend. It did not prove as popular as Model 99 and was discontinued in 1926. In 1928, a successor—Model 40—was listed in .30-30 and .30-06, plus the two Savage rounds. Along with a fancier Model 45 Super, it survived until 1940.

Savage Buys Stevens, Fox, Davis-Warner and Crescent

In 1920, consistent with its bid for diversity in a product line, Savage bought the J. Stevens Arms Company of Chicopee Falls, Massachusetts. About the time Arthur Savage was entering grade school in the early 1860's, Joshua Stevens was opening his first gunshop. Soon, survivors from both sides of the Civil War began heading West, replacing their battle rifles with guns better suited to hunting, target shooting, and protection from Indians and outlaws. Winchester and Remington had already roared ahead of smaller firms to capture the market for hunting rifles, while Colt and Smith & Wesson cornered the market for revolvers. Joshua Stevens wisely chose another path: manufacturing inexpensive shotguns, pistols and small-bore rifles for sportsmen and fine target rifles for competitive shooters.

Born in Chelsea, Massachusetts, in 1814, Stevens grew up learning the machinist's trade; but his interest in guns eventually steered him to the Springfield shop of Cyrus B. Allen, a well-known armsmaker of the day. Under Allen's tutelage, Joshua Stevens became a competent gunsmith whose work so impressed Samuel Colt that he invited the young man to join him on a tour of possible sites for an arms factory Colt was planning to build. Stevens and Colt parted friends, but a short time later Joshua invented—apparently on his own—a revolver that was found in court to infringe on Sam Colt's patents. With that, Stevens was out of the revolver business.

Years later, the one-room shop Stevens had established next to a Chicopee Falls sawmill in 1864 needed enlarging. Business was so brisk that within 10 years the shop had doubled in size. By 1886,

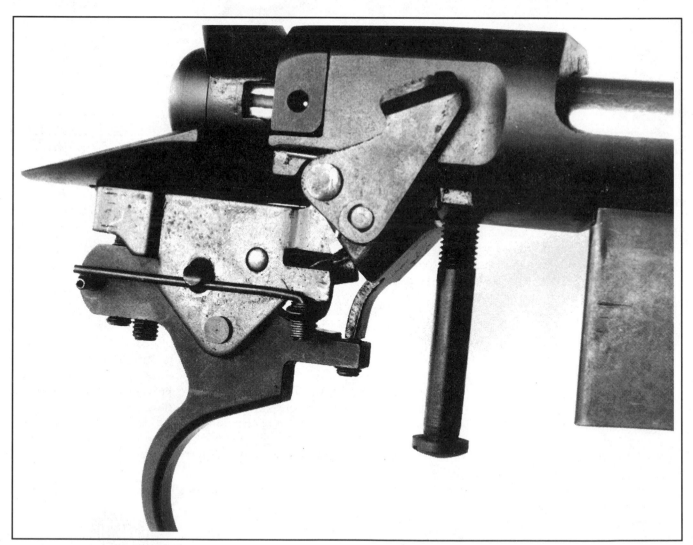

The Savage Model 110 trigger mechanism and bolt release (above) are made largely of stamped parts, but the trigger is adjustable and dependable.

Stevens' business was incorporated as the J. Stevens Arms and Tool Company, and a decade later his gun factory covered eight acres. Stevens' single shot "tip-up" pistols and single-barrel shotguns proved hugely popular. He was the first American to forge a break-action shotgun barrel and lug in one piece, still considered the strongest method of construction. Stevens also established a fine reputation for single-shot target rifles and, prior to World War I, claimed to be the world's largest producer of sporting arms.

A good businessman as well as a brilliant inventor, Stevens maintained a diversity of gun and ammunition products as a hedge against market fluctuations. A rimfire cartridge developed by the J. Stevens Arms and Tool Company in 1887—the .22 Long Rifle—is still available. The firm also built single- and double-barrel shotguns and engineered the .25 Stevens rimfire cartridge, introducing this round in a single-shot, falling-block sporting rifle called the "Ideal." Stevens' "Favorite" model, which came along later, was available in .22, .25

and .32 rimfire. These relatively inexpensive hunting and plinking guns completed a line of rifles that included the 22-caliber "Walnut Hill," acknowledged for many years prior to World War II as the finest target rifle made in America.

By the time Joshua Stevens died in 1907 at the age of 92, his gun company had become well known among sportsmen. Two years later, it produced a 12-gauge repeating shotgun under a Browning patent, and in 1913 it announced the first .410 shotgun made in America.

Savage's purchase of the Stevens firm in 1920 promised to beef up the Savage line with top-quality products already accepted by U.S. sportsmen. In 1929, Savage bought another enterprise—the A.H. Fox Gun Company of Philadelphia—whose double shotguns were among the best available in the United States. In fact, some shooters rated them higher than Lefevers and even Parkers. The name, "Savage-Stevens-Fox," appeared on later catalogs to indicate these mergers and to inform gun buyers that here was a company with deep roots in building

When Savage bought the J. Stevens Arms and Tool Company and the Ideal Tool Company, the new acquisitions broadened the firm's product line and helped it weather the post-World War II slump in sales.

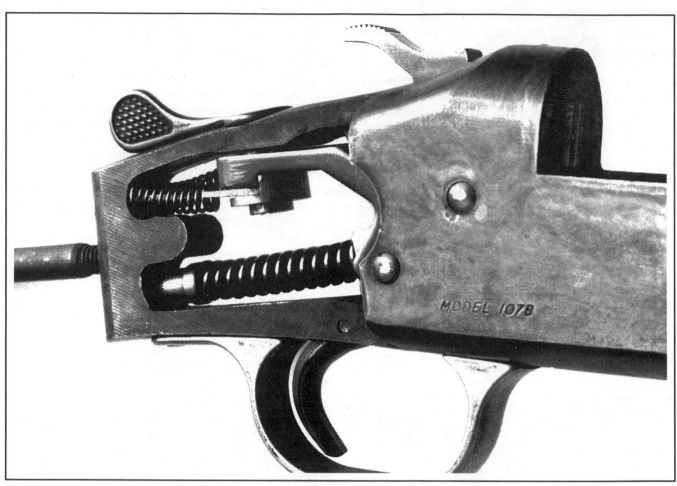

The Stevens Model 107B single-barrel shotgun shown here was one of several useful and popular guns produced at the Chicopee Falls (MA) plant following Savage's acquisition of the J. Stevens Arms & Tool Company.

three kinds of firearms: hunting and target rifles and double shotguns.

Savage further expanded its holdings by purchasing the Davis-Warner Arms Company in 1930 and the Crescent Firearms Company in 1931. Despite the Depression, it designed and introduced many new sporting arms in the 1930's, including Models 19L and 19M, which offered different sight and barrel options for the old Model 19 NRA. Model 19H was chambered during this same period for the .22 Hornet cartridge. Savage's Model 3 single-shot bolt-action .22 and its box-fed and tube-fed variations were also introduced in the mid-1930's. The Model 10 .22 target rifle made its debut in 1936, followed by Models 6 and 7 autoloading .22's in 1938 and 1939. Savage's Model 220 single-shot break-action shotgun was announced in 1938, as was its Model 420 boxlock over/under. These shotguns came on the heels of an autoloader built on Browning's "hump-back" action—Model 720—

which came out in 1930 and survived in the face of stiff competition for 19 years. It was succeeded by a similar gun, Model 755, which Savage manufactured from 1949 through 1958. Each had a lightweight sister with an alloy frame, Models 745 and 775, respectively. The final version of this series and the last autoloading shotgun produced by Savage—Model 750—died in 1967.

Machine Guns to Lawn Mowers

Shortly after the start of World War II, the Auto-Ordnance Corporation, which had arranged to supply the government with Thompson submachine guns, requested help from Savage, which contracted to manufacture 10,000 of the 45-caliber Thompsons. The first guns were ready in early 1940, and Savage promptly got additional orders. At peak production, the company completed 55,000 submachine guns a month, along with many spare parts. Its last order was filled in 1944, after a total production run of 1,250,000 Thompsons.

In September of 1940, Savage contracted directly with the U.S. government to manufacture 10,000 30-caliber and 25,000 50-caliber Browning aircraft machine guns. Savage shipped its first 50-caliber gun in July, 1941, four months ahead of schedule, and a year later the company was awarded its first of several Army-Navy "E" awards for high efficiency in the production of military equipment. At its peak, Savage was turning out 8,500 guns a month, plus spare parts; and by June of 1945 it had manufactured more than 300,000 50-calibers and huge quantities of stellite-lined barrels. During 1944 and the first part of 1945, Savage also manufactured Springfield rifle barrels, nose and tail bomb fuses, rocket nozzle assemblies and other military hardware. With war's end in Europe, the government halted all machine gun production but directed Savage to continue making stellite-lined barrels for the Pacific theatre and to tool up for the new M3 50-caliber Browning machine gun. When Japan capitulated in August, preparations for high quantity production of the M3 stopped.

Early in 1941, Savage responded to Great Britain's request for 330,000 additional Lee-Enfield rifles to re-equip its troops after their huge losses at Dunkirk (France). By converting the Stevens plant for this project and buying two new factories in Chicopee Falls, Savage found the needed room. The new buildings were outfitted especially for Lee-Enfield manufacture and by July—three months ahead of schedule—the first rifles came off the line. After the Lend-Lease Act was implemented, a new contract with the U.S. government superseded the original agreement with Great Britain. It called for a doubling of production, to 60,000 guns per month, and specified a higher total. Savage complied, and on May 8, 1944, presented its one-millionth Lee-Enfield to Army Brigadier General Guy H. Drewry.

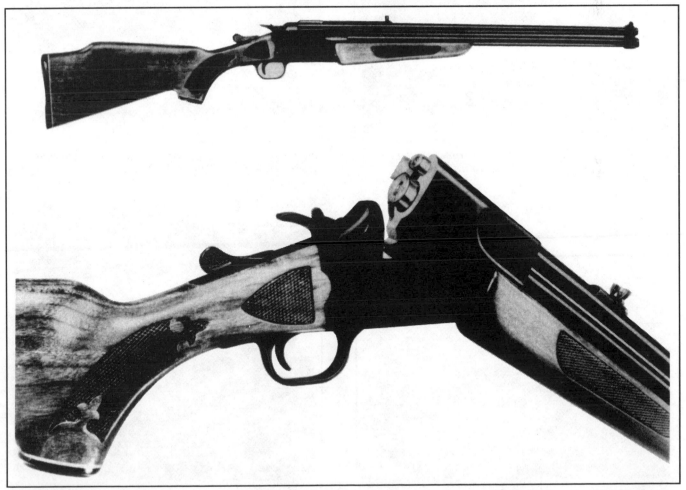

Savage's popular Model 24 over/under combination gun is one of only two models still being built in the Westfield, Massachusetts, plant. The other is the centerfire bolt-action Model 110.

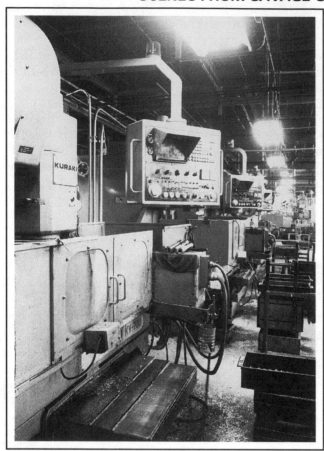

Along Savage's "Robot Row," CNC machines make a series of precise cuts in bolt parts and receivers.

Special jigs (above) hold each part so that pin and screw holes are drilled at the proper angle.

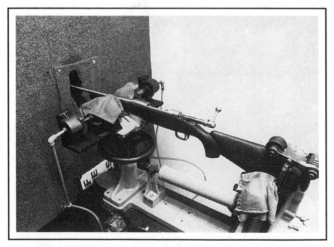

This Savage rifle is being fired to test function. Proof firing takes place in a steel "casket" by remote control.

These Savage Model 110 bolts are held in wooden racks to protect their finish.

A few weeks later, Savage stopped production of the rifles.

By the end of the war, Savage had produced 2.5 million aircraft machine guns, submachine guns and infantry rifles. Company employment during the heaviest work periods reached 13,000— roughly 10 times the peacetime payroll. Between 1941 and 1943, the production lines operated around the clock, seven days a week. Before the war, factory floor space in Utica and Chicopee Falls had totaled 930,000 square feet; purchase of the two facilities for the Enfield contract and other expansion nearly doubled that figure.

Predictably, peace brought its problems. Wartime expansion had activated so many people and so much equipment that they could no longer be supported once the military contracts stopped coming. Braking gently even before the end, Savage bought (in March, 1944) the capital stock of Worcester Lawnmower Company. The assets of this 50-year-old firm were then moved to Chicopee Falls, and the Worcester corporate structure was dismantled. The fine reputation of the Worcester lawnmowers dictated that the name be retained; but Savage added to the line with lawnmowers bearing its own name as well. The venture succeeded for a time, with strong sales for both brands.

Consolidation, Conglomerates—and Citrus

In 1946, Savage Arms consolidated its gun production at Chicopee Falls and closed the Utica operation. This enabled the firm to utilize its equipment (including the tooling acquired from the government during the war) more efficiently. By 1950, the company was vigorously marketing several new guns. Its Model 340 series, for one, offered a serviceable bolt rifle at little expense. Chambered in the .22 Hornet, .222 Remington and .30-30, this dependable workhorse stayed in the Savage line for 35 years.

Another popular Savage product was Model 24, an over/under combination gun in .22/.410 chamberings (several variations and other chamberings followed). First sold in 1950, Model 24 was dropped in 1965 but later made a comeback. The current Savage catalog lists an updated Model 24, along with modern versions of Model 110, a bolt-action centerfire rifle introduced in 1958 to compete with Remington Models 721 and 722. Since then, the 110 has been offered in most popular centerfire chamberings and several configurations, including heavy barrel and synthetic-stocked rifles. It is less expensive to build than Model 99 and has thrived because most American hunters now prefer bolt actions.

Between 1960 and 1968, the company marketed its only handgun since the Model 1917 autoloader. The Model 101 pistol, which looked like a single-action revolver, held only one .22 cartridge at a time. Savage took another run at autoloading rimfire rifles in 1969, with its Models 60, 88 and 90, but they lasted only into the early 1970's.

In 1968, Savage introduced an Italian-made over/under shotgun, Model 440, and imported a Valmet over/under from Finland in 1969. The 440 lasted only a couple of years, but the Finnish Model 330 and its offspring stayed in the Savage line until 1980.

In 1960, Savage moved to a more modern facility in Westfield, Massachusetts, comprising 480,000 square feet. Formerly the place where Fruehauf truck equipment and (later) prefab homes were manufactured, this plant is much more than Savage needs for the production of its two main models, the 110 and 24. Here, all Savage receivers are machined from bar stock. Those destined for Model 110 are drilled and broached, then heat-treated at both ends so the temper can be "drawn" to the middle (to relieve stress). As in many other major arms plants, computer-driven milling machines (CNCs) work in tandem with older mills to generate an orderly parts flow to the assembly area. All of Savage's Model 99 production, by the way, now takes place outside the country.

In 1963, Savage sold out to the American Hardware Corporation, becoming Savage Industries, a subsidiary of the Emhart Corporation. This conglomerate relinquished ownership in 1980, and Savage remained under private ownership until 1989, when Challenger International, a corporation headquartered in Bermuda, agreed to assume its assets and liabilities. The company name—Savage Industries—was not changed and it continues to operate at Westfield, producing Models 24, 99 and 110.

Until his death in 1941 at the age of 84, Arthur Savage continued to indulge his native curiosity and ambition, investing in such things as a tire company, a citrus plantation, and oil exploration. His most famous invention, the Model 99 lever-action rifle, has outlived him by more than 50 years, a remarkable accomplishment for a turn-of-the-century entrepreneur who spent his best years herding cattle. It was the well-deserved bounty of a brilliant inventor and a man whose eyes were always turned toward the horizon.

CHAPTER 13

CHARLES NEWTON: A MAN OF GENIUS—AND FAILURE

In the late 19th century, America's industrial center lay in New England. Among the many prominent gun designers of that time and place was Charles Newton. Born in Delevan, New York, on January 8, 1870, Newton apparently worked on his father's farm until he finished his formal schooling at age 16. He then taught school for two years, studied law, and was admitted to the state bar at age 26.

Charles Newton had more on his mind than law, however. Sometime before his 30th birthday, he'd grown fascinated by guns. It may have been during a six-year stint in the New York National Guard, where he earned the rank of sergeant. In any event, his first noteworthy accomplishment came in 1905, when he designed a .22 centerfire by necking down the .25-25 Stevens case. Not satisfied with the results, he changed the parent case to the .28-30 Stevens, then to Winchester's .25-35. In 1911, he convinced Savage Arms Corporation to load the round and chamber it in its Model 99 lever action rifle.

Capped with a .227-inch, 70-grain bullet, this Newton cartridge became the .22 Savage High Power (in Europe, the 5.6x52R). Riflemen affectionately called it the "Imp" and praised its performance on big game. Hunters shot everything from deer to tigers with the tiny bullet. At this time a velocity of 2800 fps gave a bullet a thunderbolt image, no matter what its weight or internal construction.

Ballisticians like Newton knew the Imp was no big game cartridge. His next project—probably started before the High Power had even been introduced—successfully married high velocity to a bullet better suited to deer-size animals. Savage brought this Newton cartridge to market in 1912 as the .250-3000. Later called simply the .250 Savage, it launched an 87-grain bullet at 3000 fps. Though Newton had designed it for a 100-grain bullet at 2800, the Savage people thought higher speed would attract more attention. Thus, Model 99 was chambered in .250-3000 in March of 1914.

The .250 was not Newton's first big game round. Between 1909 and 1912, he'd changed the neck on the .30-06 Springfield to make a .25 Special. This was later redesigned by other engineers (principally Neidner) and marketed as the .25-06 Remington. Newton also designed a 7mm Special, which, on the .30-06 case, would have been the great-grandfather of Remington's .280.

In any event, Charles Newton experimented with many parent rounds. A single-shot enthusiast, he used the .405 Winchester case to make rimmed versions of his .25 and 7mm Specials for dropping-block single-shot rifles. He also designed .30, 8mm, .35, .40 and .45 Express cartridges for dropping-block and hinged-breech guns. The first three of these were fashioned from a 3¼-inch Sharps hull; the .40 derived from a .40-110-3¼ Winchester case; and the .45 came from a .45-125-3¼ Winchester.

When foreign cartridges offered more of what Newton wanted—which was usually powder capacity—he used them. Together with Fred Adolph, a gunsmith from Genoa, New York, he developed the .30 Adolph Express on a case about the size of the British .404 Jeffery. Eventually, the Adolph series of Express cartridges included a .280, .35 and .40, all with rebated rims to fit Mauser bolt heads. The parent case for these cartridges was Germany's 11.2x72 Schuler. Because the Schuler cartridge did not appear until 1920 or so, Adolph's cartridge line

Charles Newton designed rifles and cartridges that failed during the World War I era but boasted many attributes lauded by shooters today. In this photo, Newton shoulders a three-barrel gun built for him by Fred Adolph.

came after Newton had worked extensively with rimless rounds like the Jeffery, which was designed around 1910. At first, the semi-rimmed .30 Adolph was also called the .30 Newton. More recent examples of rimless Adolph and Newton cartridges mike just under .530-inch at the base, while the .404 Jeffery is a bit over .540. If Newton fashioned these cartridges from the Jeffery, he may have swaged down, or even turned down experimental rounds.

Besides the .22 Savage High Power, Charles Newton developed a .22 Newton, which was a 7×57 case necked to .228. According to Newton, it launched a 90-grain bullet at 3100 fps from a barrel rifled one turn in 8 inches. He also experimented with a .22 Special, a necked-down Krag case that gave a 68-grain bullet nearly 3300 fps. Newton's

.256 was actually a .264, or a shortened 6.5-06. He chose to promote this cartridge instead of the .25-06 for two reasons: (1) the Mauser factory that initially manufactured rifles for his company was already set up to bore and rifle 6.5mm barrels; and (2) the .25-06 chambers cut by Neidner and others were occasionally tight, thereby boosting pressures. Since some period rifles built for the .30-06 would not handle hotter loads, Newton wanted nothing to do with rifles that came apart (or cartridges that reportedly made them come apart).

While the .256 Newton can be handloaded to provide a 129-grain bullet with 2900 fps—thereby beating the factory load by 140 fps—it doesn't quite match the .270 Winchester ballistically and so has limited utility. The .30 Newton, however, blows right by the .30-06. Its 180-grain factory load matches that of the .300 H&H and it's shaped more efficiently, with a sharper shoulder and a straighter case. Handloaded, it is the unbelted equivalent of a .308 Norma Magnum. The .33 Newton, with its 200-grain bullet 3000 fps, preceded by 40 years the popular .338 Winchester Magnum, which barely equals that performance. The .33 was dropped (because nobody wanted it) and the .35 Newton replaced it. Not many shooters bought the .35 either, but it stayed in Newton's line until the end. The .40 Newton was simply a necked-up .35 and has no modern counterpart. Remington and Weatherby's .416 Magnums, with their greater powder capacities, outperform it; and the .400 Whelen, an old and almost forgotten wildcat, can't match it.

Two 7mm Newton's—the .276 and .280—had little if any exposure outside company literature. The .276 was a lot like the .276 Pedersen in its various forms, and just a trifle longer than the .276 British. It was designed to fit the Newton Mauser rifles, whose magazines were a bit shorter than those found in rifles built by Newton. The .276 was not listed as a standard chambering. The .280 was cataloged but probably not manufactured, even though it would have been one of the most useful cartridges in the Newton line. Reportedly, it could drive a 160-grain bullet at 3000 fps, which would have equaled the punch of Remington's 7mm Magnum.

Starting A Company with Mausers

Newton has been rightly called the "Father of high velocity" for his development of cartridges that proved decades ahead of their time. In necking

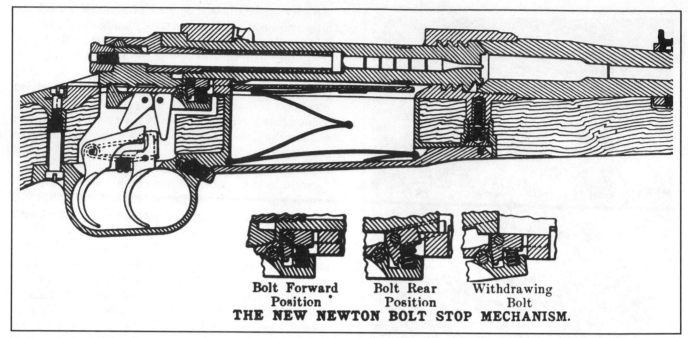

THE NEW NEWTON BOLT STOP MECHANISM.

Bolt Forward Position   Bolt Rear Position   Withdrawing Bolt

Before designing his first rifle, Newton considered using modified Springfield actions (Mausers had become hard to find during the war). He eventually decided to start from scratch; only the mainspring was borrowed.

big cases to accept small bullets and boosting pressures from the accepted 40,000 psi to 50,000 and more, he was handicapped by a lack of suitable powders. After World War II, surplus IMR 4831 and 4350 gave shooters of that era the slow-burning propellants Newton could have used earlier in his

These Newton Express rounds were designed for single, double and combination guns. From left: .30, 8mm, .40, and .45. The cartridge shown at right is a .30-06.

racy rounds. Bullets were also a problem. Designed for lower velocities, the big-game bullets of his day broke up when driven into bone or heavy muscle at high speed.

Despite these hurdles, Charles Newton had enough confidence in his products to start a company. His firm was incorporated as the Newton Arms Company on August 4, 1914. Capital stock totaled $10,000 and an office was established at 506 Mutual Life Building, Buffalo, New York. Directors included Charles Newton, Christopher Bierbaum, and Dayton Evans. Ads for Newton rifles and Adolph Express cartridges had appeared the previous month and ran until March, 1915, when Newton began cataloging cartridges under his own name. His rifles came from Germany, where he'd negotiated a contract early in 1914 with the Mauser factory. Two dozen rifles were to arrive on August 15, and another two dozen by September 15. The first Newton catalog, produced soon after the deal was made, listed three grades of rifles:

Grade A: a DWM Mauser in .30, 8mm or .35 Adolph Express for $42.50; and in .33 or .40 Express for $62.50.

Grade B: a DWM Mauser in .256, .30, 8mm or .35 for $55; and in .33 or .40 for $75 (double set triggers, $2.50 extra).

Grade C: a Sauer Mauser with double set trig-

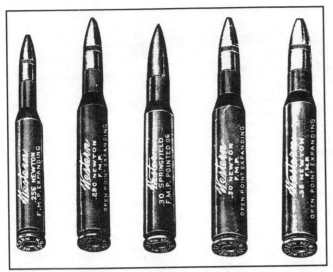

These rimless Newton cartridges have modern profiles and high ballistic performance. The .256 and .280 almost equal the .25-06 and Remington's 7mm Magnum, respectively. The .30 and .35 Newtons correspond ballistically to the .308 and .358 Norma Magnums.

gers, half-octagon barrel, matted rib, sporting sights; in .30, 8mm or .35 for $60; and in .33 and .40 for $80.

Curiously, the only 8mm Newton described in the available literature is the rimmed round on the 3¼-inch Sharps case, recommended for use in single shot rifles but much too long to work in a Mauser. Also, a flyer sent with the first catalog listed a **Grade D** rifle, in .256 only, for just $37.50. It had a Model 88 action and thus incurred no royalty obligation for a flush magazine. The Grade D model didn't fit Newton's pattern of labeling costlier guns

with letters that came further along in the alphabet. Equally baffling was a listing in the same flyer of .256 **Grade C** Newtons with full-length stocks. No such rifle has been documented, so they probably were never shipped.

Newton's timing could hardly have been worse. Germany went to war on August 14, 1914, a day before the first Mauser rifles were due. Perhaps it was an omen—that Charles Newton would never keep step with the rest of the world. Apparently one shipment of Newton Mausers was received before the war cancelled further commerce.

Newton's 1914 flyer included .256 barrels "of the best Krupp steel" for Mauser and Springfield actions. These included raised and matted ribs with sight slots at a cost of $17. A stock could be ordered for $18. No shipping records exist for either item, however. Later catalogs listed a Newton loading tool and Newton bullets. The latter were patented, copper-jacketed spitzers with wire points that resisted battering in the magazine, and a paper wrap between core and jacket that insulated the core from the heat of barrel friction. These "Newton Protected Point" bullets sold for about 50 cents more per box than other bullets of their day, but some shooters thought them well worth the premium. Even Townsend Whelen, whose views on bolt-action rifles were attacked by Newton in print, liked those bullets.

. . . . Then War Got in the Way

With his supply of German rifles cut off, Charles Newton turned to the Marlin Firearms Company to produce barrels chambered in .256 Newton. These were threaded for Springfield actions and listed in catalogs throughout 1916 for $12.50 each. Newton

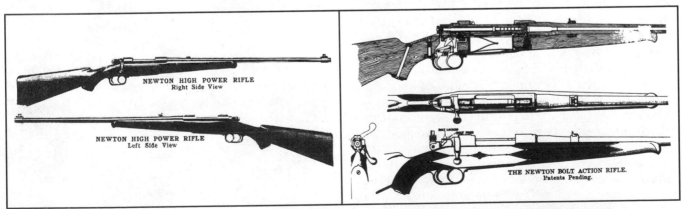

The Newton Arms Company was formed on August 4, 1914. Its first rifles were imported DWM Mausers chambered in the .256 Newton cartridge (above, left). Soon, however, Newton was building his own guns after the Mauser design (above, right).

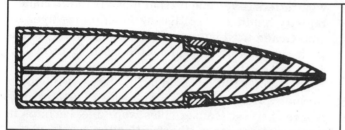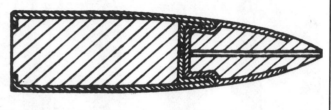

Newton's expensive Bearcat bullets (above) were designed to mushroom predictably at the high velocities (3000 fps) generated by some of Newton's cartridges.

also contracted for Springfield sporting-style stocks to be sold at the same price. But Springfields were not commercially available at that time, and Newton's components moved slowly. Plans to produce the rifle himself failed because war had by then committed nearly all available rifle-making machinery. When Newton approached major firearms firms about building his rifles, they declined. Military contracts were bigger and more lucrative—and almost risk-free.

Newton had no choice but to wait for machinery to manufacture his own rifles. He spent the time designing a better rifle, one that incorporated the best of Springfield and Mauser features along with some other Newton ideas not yet tried. In the February, 1916, issue of "Outer's Book," he pointed out that tooling shipments were not completed until February of that year and that the delays, though frustrating, had allowed him to improve substantially upon the plans he'd made for a rifle based on the 1903 Springfield. "As a result, the only part of the entire action of this rifle which has not been changed from existing models is the mainspring. . . ."

In that same article, Newton declared that: "Every part of the rifle except the barrel is built in our own factory at Buffalo. (The barrels are made for us by one of the oldest and best known rifle factories in New England)."

Late in 1916, in the 14th Newton catalog, Harry Pope is featured as superintendent of the company's barrel department. "Of course it costs us several times as much to obtain the services of the world's greatest expert in this line as a superintendent," the article stated, "yet on an output of 70 to 80 barrels per day this expense is so distributed that the increased cost is comparatively slight and every purchaser of a Newton rifle receives with it a 'Pope barrel.' . . . Heretofore any one wanting a Pope barrel had to pay from $20 to $50 for it."

The catalog also claimed Pope had helped de-

velop the segmented rifling featured in Newton barrels. The inventor had apparently experimented with oval bores but found that, while his results were good, the oval bores in some military rifles were really not oval but comprised two grooves cut with a tool whose radius was a trifle smaller than

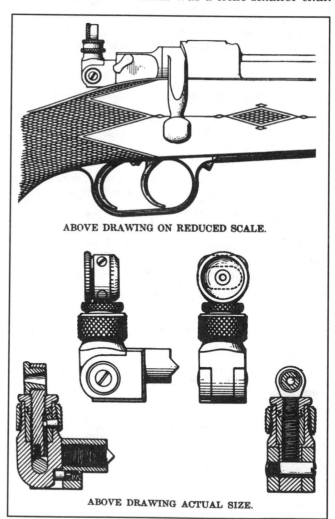

ABOVE DRAWING ON REDUCED SCALE.

ABOVE DRAWING ACTUAL SIZE.

The Newton folding peep sight was compact but adjustable—an excellent sight that, unfortunately, has no modern counterpart.

that of the bore. This segmented, or Metford-type rifling, differed from the English form only in the number and depth of grooves. Newton decided to use five-groove segmented rifling in his guns, noting further in his catalog: "The advantages claimed for this system of rifling are, in addition to far greater ease of cleaning, greater durability, increased accuracy and less strain on the bullet jackets in firing."

Newton's rifles first went to market on January 1, 1917, and received favorable reviews. But once more the timing was wrong, for on April 6 the United States entered the war and the Government took control of all domestic cartridge production. While the Newton Arms Company was building its own rifles and loading ammunition, it depended on Remington to furnish cartridge cases. Without cases there was no Newton ammunition, and without Newton ammunition there was no market for Newton rifles. And soon the Army seized the new ammunition tooling that Newton Arms had purchased but not yet set up. From a weekly production of 125 rifles, the factory lurched to a halt. On June 4, 1917, a Certificate to Increase Capital Stock was signed by Charles Newton. And by December, there were no more cartridges left in inventory.

Newton persevered. In January of 1918, the firm began tooling up to make its own ammunition from scratch, and by April it was ready to produce cartridges. With that, the banks that had carried the business immediately sent it into receivership. Bert E. Holmes acquired all assets, and Charles Newton was dropped from the board. Holmes tried to run the plant himself but soon gave it up. The machinery stopped making rifle components on August 1, 1918, but ammunition production continued for another five months.

In all, the Newton Arms Company had shipped about 2,400 rifles before it was sold by the banks. Roughly 1,600 more rifles were finished or made ready for assembly under Bert Holmes. Only a quarter of these rifles passed inspection, however, forcing Holmes to sell more than 1,000 rejected and incomplete rifles for $5 each at the time he sold the plant.

Lawsuits and Receivership

On April 3, 1919, the Newton Arms Corporation was formed by machinery dealers Lamberg, Schwartz and Land of New York. The firm's plan was to market as genuine Newton rifles the poor quality guns they'd bought from Holmes. Production facilities were moved to Brooklyn, and a sales office was opened in New York's Woolworth Building. Subsequently, the corporation raised the prices on Newton rifles, with all accessories omitted.

Charles Newton immediately brought suit on three counts: (1) an injunction prohibiting Lamberg and company from using his name or implying an association with him; (2) an injunction against using his patented bullets in their ammunition, and challenging their right to claim or imply they owned Newton patents (save for a double set trigger); and (3) an injunction preventing the corporation from using the word "Newton" as part of its name. Although the cases weren't heard until June, 1920, Charles Newton won all three. The following month, the Newton Arms Corporation declared bankruptcy.

Charles Newton had been determined to start over after his company's plunge into receivership back in 1918. Accordingly, about the time Holmes sold out to Lamberg and associates, he had formed the Chas. Newton Rifle Corporation (Newton preferred "Chas." to "Charles" in all his dealings). Incorporation papers were signed on April 29, 1919, and included a certificate (signed by Charles Newton, Arthur Dayton and Dayton Evans) declaring $20,000 in capital stock. The company plan called for a new factory, furnished with surplus equipment from the Eddystone Arsenal. But while he was securing money for that, Newton wanted to import some Mauser rifles in Newton chamberings. The company's 1919 catalog shows a Newton rifle similar in appearance to the 1917 Newtons, but with 20 improvements at a price of $66. Ammunition was listed too at $9.50 for 100 rounds of .30-06 Springfield or .256 Newton; $11 for 100 rounds of .30 Newton; and $12 for 100 rounds of .35 Newton.

The Eddystone Arsenal deal fell through. The only rifles marketed by the Chas. Newton Rifle Corporation were Mausers with butterknife bolt handles. They were well-made guns with reversed double set triggers, triple leaf sights and a Newton-style stock. Some had parabolic rifling, and some had a cloverleaf arrangement of grooves milled into the muzzle to allow gas to escape equally on all sides, thus preventing a bullet from tipping on exit. The German rifles were called "1922 Model" Newtons. Serial numbers were not consecutive and total production isn't known. Perhaps as few as 100 were shipped before production costs heated by Germany's postwar economy sabotaged the project. Meanwhile, Newton's advertising had drawn about 1,000 orders. By all accounts, the company was un-

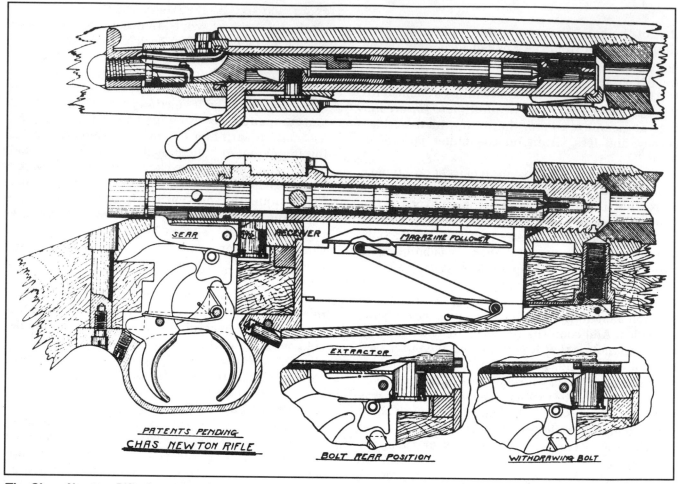

SEAR   RECEIVER   MAGAZINE FOLLOWER

PATENTS PENDING
CHAS NEWTON RIFLE

EXTRACTOR

BOLT REAR POSITION   WITHDRAWING BOLT

The Chas. Newton Rifle Corp. was formed on April 29, 1919, after the Newton Arms Company had folded. The rifle diagrammed above was its flagship product.

able to fill these; however, there is evidence that a few 1922 Models remained in stock as late as 1928.

Apparently Lamberg, Schwartz and Land, after organizing the Newton Arms Corporation, tried to stop Charles Newton from marketing his rifles while (or before) he filed charges against the Brooklyn firm for patent violations and other misdeeds. In any case, the Charles Newton Rifle Corporation did not survive. It was officially dissolved on December 31, 1932, though operations had ceased years earlier.

Buffalo Newtons—and a Turndown at Marlin

If Newton's timing was poor, his tenacity was that of a champion—for even after this last failure Charles Newton was not beaten. In 1923, with his Mauser program scuttled and no Eddystone Arsenal equipment in sight, he started a new venture. On July 23, Arthur Dayton and Dayton Evans joined him to form the Buffalo Newton Rifle Corporation.

Capitalized with $125,000 in stock, the firm was headquartered in Buffalo, New York. Soon, however, it moved to the old Fiala Arms plant in New Haven, Connecticut, where the first "Buffalo Newton" rifles were built in late 1924.

The first catalog described them as "perfected high power rifle[s] wholly designed by Charles Newton. . . ." Furnished with either single or double set trigger, the guns were available in .30-06 as well as four Newton chamberings: .256, .280, .30 and .35. Barrels were of nickel steel and receivers of chrome vanadium. The checkered walnut stocks had 1/4-inch castoff. The action incorporated all the improvements Newton had in mind to make a superlative bolt rifle. Multiple locking lugs on the bolt were of interrupted-thread design, as they had been on previous Newtons; but segmental rifling had been replaced by four-groove parabolic. The quick takedown feature listed in the first catalogs (barrel and receiver remained a unit) was retained, but the bolt stop and trigger were new. There was a cross-

This Newton lineup flanks a .30-06 cartridge (6th from left). From left: .22, .256 (100-grain), .256 (129-grain), .276, .280; then .30, .33, .35, and .40.

bolt between the magazine and trigger mortises to prevent stock splits; but, alas, it didn't help much. When he designed this bar into the stock, Newton must have thought it sufficient to absorb all the recoil, because he eliminated the recoil shoulder behind the front guard screw. Under the heavy recoil of Newton cartridges, the stock would still split. Overall, these Buffalo Newton rifles did not show as satisfactory a fit or finish as earlier Newtons.

The Western Cartridge Company, which had started producing Newton ammunition in 1921, continued to supply it. But Newton's ill luck soon found another path of attack. In October, 1924, John Meeker, who controlled the lending group for Newton's enterprise, challenged Newton for the company reins. Newton went to court and succeeded in ousting Meeker, but not before the latter had acquired parts for 260 Newton rifles. These he took to Somerville, New Jersey, and assembled them for sale under the Meeker name. Marked "Meeker Arms Co., Model 1925, New Haven, Conn.," these rifles differ from the Newtons of that era only in their safety stop and mismatched parts.

Meanwhile, Charles Newton looked around for more money. After borrowing on his life insurance, he pleaded with Marlin to produce his rifles under contract. Marlin wasn't interested. For two more years, Newton struggled, writing in a letter to a friend in 1927 that: "We are working very slowly, due to lack of money to push ahead with, [but we] could turn out almost twice the work at the same expense if we had the money to put on more men. . . . We would like to go through the winter with five or six men. . . . Working at the rate of 1,000 rifles per year they will cost us about $12 each to

build, while working at the rate of 10,000 rifles per year or 1,000 per month we can build them for $8 each." At that time, the Buffalo Newton rifles retailed for $60.

Soliciting his friend's participation, Newton described a company on the brink of success but with an urgent need for money. He pointed out that he now had a competent superintendent, one who had worked 20 years for Marlin. The lack of capable shop leadership apparently seemed to Newton a main reason for his company's 1918 failure and even the rocky start at New Haven. In the end, Newton did not get the funding he needed to save the Buffalo Newton Rifle Corporation, and in 1929 the plant was closed and the organization was officially dissolved in December of 1930. Total rifle production probably did not exceed 1,500.

The Leverbolt, Frank Kenna and Newton's Legacy

Bankrolling a new business in 1929 seems suicidal in retrospect, but Charles Newton could not know in March of that year what would happen in October. Perhaps he had a premonition; after all, his timing had failed on a grand scale before. Nonetheless, he acted aggressively and immediately to pick himself up. His project this time was a radically different gun initially called the "New Newton Straight Pull Rifle," but later simply, the "Leverbolt." It incorporated design elements of previous Newtons and the Lee Navy straight-pull rifle, with some taken from lever-actions. Charles Newton, who by this time was widely published in outdoor and shooting magazines, had often jumped into the "lever vs. bolt" debates—obviously on the side of the bolt rifle. But he knew the lever-action still commanded a big chunk of the market. His goal was to combine speed and strength, to build a quick-firing rifle that would handle powerful Newton cartridges.

Early drawings of the Leverbolt rifle show a two-lug bolt head and Springfield cocking piece, suggesting Newton's prototype was a converted Springfield. The interrupted-thread Newton bolt head might have been well intended, but the Leverbolt—Charles Newton's last firearm design—was never built. It failed despite a vigorous campaign to convince Marlin President Frank Kenna that he should make the rifles. Profits would be split 50-50. The project must have looked tempting, but Frank Kenna was shrewd. "Show me the market, and we'll make the guns," he said. So Charles Newton went to work distributing a "Special Notice" flyer that told how rifle buyers could order a new rifle with

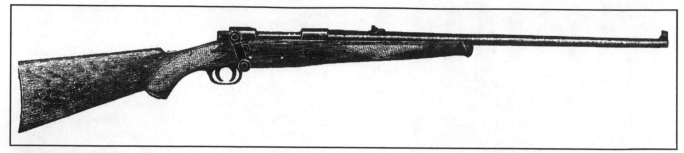

Charles Newton's LeverBolt rifle (above) was the inventor's last major gun project. Marlin agreed to manufacture the gun if it showed promise in the marketplace. Newton appealed to shooters for enough orders to start production, but too few came in.

a $25 down payment. The remaining $35 would not be due until the gun was delivered. Newton distanced himself in the text and signed the notice: "Yours Truly, Leverbolt Rifle Company, New Haven, Conn." Here is the text (in part):

> ". . . We believe, as Mr. Newton has always believed, there will be a large demand from American sportsmen for a rifle which will work as rapidly and easily as the lever action, yet handle the most powerful cartridges with all the strength and certainty of the bolt actions . . . [but] the Marlin Co., is very conservative and cannot see why anyone should want a rifle more powerful than their .30-30, Model 1893. Once they are "shown" they are ready, willing and able to build them for us to sell. You alone can show them. . . .
>
> "So it is now definitely up to you. An order now is a vote of "yes." A failure to order now is a vote of "no" regardless of the reason. . . . The question of BETTER RIFLES is in your hands. We have done what we could to make them available. . . ."

Those last words might have made a fitting epitaph for Charles Newton, who died at his home in New Haven on March 9, 1932, at the age of 62. His

Newton insulated bullets featured a thin paper wrap between core and jacket to prevent bore friction from melting the core. From left: 68-grain .22, 80-grain .22, 100-grain .256, two 172-grain .30's, and two 250-grain .35's. The sectioned .30 and .35 bullets indicate the wire core reinforcements.

Leverbolt enterprise had withered when even a 24-page catalog featuring the new rifle failed to pull the 500 orders he needed to swing Kenna's vote. Wall Street had crumbled, and few people had extra money to spend on rifles.

Charles Newton always played, it seems, with the deck stacked against him—but never with the intention of quitting. His close friends knew his genius as well as his tenacity and remarked about both after his passing. Though his rifles failed in the market and no commercial Newton cartridges have been made for some time, his products served as prototypes and his writings remain as valid texts for shooters and gun designers alike many years after his death.

To sum up, Charles Newton—lawyer, engineer, ballistician, author, entrepreneur—fell victim to the schedule of world events that played out during his time. And he was simply too early with some of his ideas. The .25-06 didn't become a popular wildcat until A.O. Neidner started chambering rifles for it in 1920, and it wasn't offered commercially until 1969. The three-position safety on Newton rifles appeared again, in modified form, on Winchester's Model 70 in 1936. It is still one of the most useful and popular safeties ever. The 70's floorplate release also looks exactly like Newton's. While bolts with multiple, interrupted-thread locking lugs are commonplace now, no commercial American riflemakers were using that design when Newton announced his. When cupro-nickel bullet jackets were fouling bores, Newton used pure copper jackets, similar to those made today. He offered (and patented) a compartmented bullet in 1915, long before Nosler announced its famous but essentially identical "Partition." In profile and ballistic performance, Newton's cartridges equal today's best short magnums. Sadly, Charles Newton and his companies just didn't last long enough to reap the rewards of his genius.

CHAPTER 14

ROY WEATHERBY: GRIT BEHIND THE GLITZ

Weatherby rifles evoke images of screen stars and black-tie banquets—Hollywood excess in rifle design and bullet speed. In photos, you'll find the Weatherby owner grinning over the corpse of a cape buffalo or peering out from his parka at a 50-inch *Ammon ammon* sheep. No pork and beans buffet at a Michigan truck stop for this nimrod—indeed, the blue-collar whitetail hunter has little in common with affluent Weatherby customers who hop from country to country in search of exotic trophies.

At least, that's the image. Actually, Weatherby rifles turn up in a lot of down-to-earth places. Hunters who drive old Chevy pickups eventually find that Roy Weatherby's Hollywood promotions are backed up by his rifles. There's grit behind that glitz. And while some hunters may buy his famous Mark V purely for prestige, that worthy model has also proven itself to woodsmen whose measure of a hunting arm is purely practical.

From Kansas to California: Bullets for the Fast Lane

Roy Weatherby's carefully cultivated market image belies his humble background. Born to a Kansas tenant farmer in 1910, Roy spent most of his childhood working in the fields. He earned his first BB gun by peddling garden seed on foot to neighboring farms. College was just a dream for most country boys in the 1930's, but Roy worked to make it come true. While employed at Southwestern Bell, he took night classes at the University of Wichita. As restless as he was ambitious, Roy left school in 1937. He and his wife Camilla headed west, to the land of opportunity called California. There Roy found work as an insurance salesman and did well. Meanwhile, he bought a lathe and a drill press from Sears and began experimenting with rifle and cartridge designs in his home shop. By September of 1945, this moonlighting venture had become a profitable sporting goods business. Roy eventually dropped his insurance job and began hiring people to help him build and promote his rifles. Cash was scarce, so he had to borrow from friends to keep going. In 1946, he sold half his business in order to obtain $10,000 in additional venture capital.

By this time, Weatherby had already developed some of the cartridges that would later bring him huge success, but still his operating budget was being sapped by repayments of old loans. Then, just in time to save the business, Camilla inherited $21,000 from the sale of her family's Kansas farm. Roy used the money to buy back the other half of his enterprise and resupply himself with rifle parts. The little firm struggled on, but Roy soon had to seek out other sources of capital. He decided to offer stock and managed to attract $75,000 from investors.

Weatherby's first rifles were built mostly from surplus military rifles—specifically, the 98 Mauser, 1903 Springfield and 1917 Enfield. He also used Model 70 Winchesters and similar bolt guns made for sportsmen. These he rebarreled or rechambered to accept his new cartridges, which he promoted as the fastest and most deadly of their caliber. Roy's first publicized wildcat round was the .220 Rocket, a blown-out .220 Swift. It was not manufactured commercially. His next endeavor—the .270 Weatherby Magnum—became the first of a line of belted cases derived from the .300 Holland & Holland. Introduced in 1943, this round could launch a 130-grain bullet at 3375 fps, which was 300 fps faster

Roy Weatherby, shown here (at right) with a company engineer, took an active part in gun design.

than the same bullet fired from a .270 Winchester. Weatherby's experiences with this potent round convinced him to pursue commercial production of a line of extra-high-velocity cartridges. His theme in marketing them was: higher speed increases killing power more effectively than does a jump in bullet weight, and it does so with little increase in recoil. In addition, he pointed out, a fast bullet offers a flat trajectory for easier hits at long range.

Promoting the Extra Punch

Contrary to what many shooters believe, Roy Weatherby did not coin the term "magnum," nor did he even bring it to the United States. Holland & Holland introduced its .375 H&H Magnum back in 1912. This round, together with the .300 H&H Magnum (or Super .30, a necked-down .375), were being marketed in the U.S. by Western Cartridge Company as early as 1925. The problem was, nobody in America made affordable rifles that could

handle them. The .30-06 was justifiably popular for North American game, and manufacturers found it much easier to build rifles for that cartridge.

In 1935, Ben Comfort used a .300 H&H to win the long-range matches at Wimbledon, and two years later Winchester listed its new Model 70 in both .300 and .375 H&H. Remington offered a 721 model chambered for the .300, and gun enthusiasts soon had surplus 1917 Enfields reworked to take these powerful rounds. Weatherby came along much later, but he did what nobody else had done— he promoted magnum cartridges for all kinds of hunting. Previously these cigar-sized cases had been marketed to hunters who went after tough, heavy animals. Since the .375 was used primarily for dangerous game, Weatherby reshaped the belted case and equipped it with light bullets that in smaller cases were traditionally used for deer. "Give those bullets a little more velocity," he predicted, "and you'll get quicker kills." Not only that, hunters wouldn't have to hold as high on long shots, and the wind wouldn't be as bothersome.

Weatherby designed his .270 Magnum for .30-06-length actions, which meant no one would have to buy an expensive magnum-length mechanism to chamber a Weatherby. His 7mm and .257 Magnums followed a year later. All three had an overall case length of 2.545 inches, only .051 inch longer than a .30-06 case. The .300 and .375 H&H hulls measured 2.850, or .356 inch longer. Weatherby reduced the body taper of the Holland & Holland case to boost its capacity, then designed the shoulder with the dual radius junctures (body-to-shoulder and shoulder-to-neck) that have remained a distinctive feature of the company's proprietary ammunition. Though the .270 Weatherby was significantly shorter than the .300 H&H, its water capacity nearly matched that of the Super 30 (roughly, 85.5 grains to 88.9). The 7mm Weatherby Magnum, with

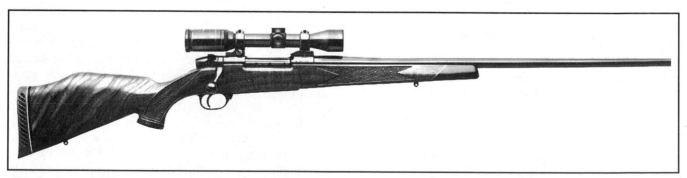

Weatherby's Mark V (above) was first produced in 1958, several years after Roy Weatherby developed his first high-velocity magnum cartridge from the .300 Holland & Holland.

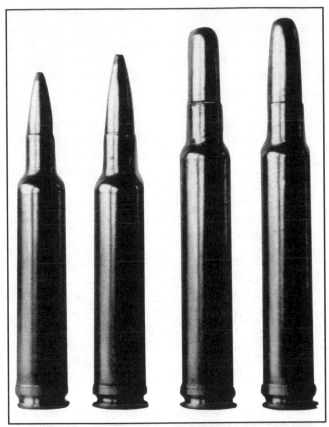

The mid-size workhorses of Weatherby's cartridge line include, from left: .257 Magnum, 7mm Magnum, .300 Magnum, and .340 Magnum.

nearly identical dimensions, preceded by 18 years the 7mm Remington Magnum, which gave about the same performance and soon became the most popular belted cartridge in America. Limiting the Weatherby version to Weatherby rifles didn't help sales; and because the company's ammunition was made in Sweden by Norma—first as empty cases, then, beginning in 1948, as Weatherby cartridges—it was significantly more expensive than domestic brands.

.300 to .460: No Game Too Big

These first Weatherby rounds met with only modest success. The .30-06 was still considered the most versatile of centerfire cartridges, and quite powerful to boot. Winchester's .270 received effusive praise from Jack O'Connor, the famous gun writer, who touted it as lightning-quick and deadly on deer-size game at long range. Lots of hunters still carried .30-30's, and scopes remained outnumbered by iron sights.

All that changed, however, when Roy Weath-

erby developed his .300 Magnum in 1946. Unlike previous Weatherby rounds, this was a full-length magnum, a .300 H&H blown out at the shoulder. The case was 2.820 inches long and held 100 grains of powder—11 more than the Holland & Holland. Its velocity with a 180-grain bullet—3245 fps—was roughly 300 fps more than that of its parent cartridge, and 650 fps more than what the .30-06 could offer.

The .300 Weatherby Magnum quickly became the cartridge of choice for globe-trotting hunters. It had plenty of energy for big bears and most African game; moreover, it shot flatter and more accurately with 180-grain bullets than the .270 Winchester with 130's and was reasonably pleasant to shoot. The .300 Weatherby proved even more versatile than the .30-06 because it gave the same wide range of bullets substantially more speed, increasing point-blank range with all of them and making the heavy ones far more effective on big-boned game, no matter the range.

Roy Weatherby's next cartridges expanded his line to reach small-game hunters and those who tracked for thick-skinned African game. The .378 Weatherby came first, in 1955, with a .582-inch rim diameter that was .050 inch greater than the standard .375 H&H case, from which previous Weatherby and other wildcat magnums had been fashioned. The .378 case was longer, too—2.91 inches compared to 2.85. Case capacity for this new monster was 138.5 grains.

The .378 upstaged Weatherby's first big-bore cartridge aimed at the safari market, the .375 Weatherby. A blown-out .375 H&H, it offered about 100 fps more velocity than the grizzled British round, not enough to make loyal Holland & Holland fans defect. Competing directly with the old .375 was tough no matter how a new cartridge was promoted, because so many rifles were chambered for

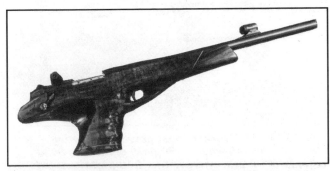

Weatherby made a limited run of this single-shot bolt-action pistol, but it was never cataloged.

the H&H case, and because ammunition was available all over the world. Since 1912, the H&H had established a reputation that no new cartridge could match, primarily because the hunting opportunities in which to prove cartridges had been drastically reduced.

So with characteristic flair, Roy Weatherby announced his .378 Magnum. It was not, he pointed out, a revamped .375. It was much bigger, with 5700 foot-pounds of muzzle energy. A 300-grain bullet left the gun at over 2900 fps—400 fps faster than the same bullet from a .375 H&H.

While full-jacketed .378 Weatherby bullets were certainly adequate for the biggest, toughest game anywhere, some African countries required that hunters who went after dangerous game must carry rifles with bore diameters of at least 40 cal-

iber. This rule might have made sense if bore diameter were an indication of stopping power, but it is not. The .378 Weatherby delivered more energy than most traditional Nitro Express cartridges of greater diameter, and with the proper bullets it could hardly be equalled for penetration. Given the rule, however, Roy Weatherby designed a new cartridge on the .378 case, calling it the .460 Weatherby Magnum. Its 500-grain bullet at 2700 fps packed more than four tons of muzzle energy, making it the most powerful sporting round in the world. The .458 Winchester, a popular short magnum for heavy game, had roughly 40 percent less muzzle energy. Even the giant .600 Nitro Express with its 900-grain bullet couldn't match the .460 on the ballistics charts.

More Magnums for the Masses

In 1962, four years after bringing out this bruiser, Weatherby announced another, more useful big-game round: the .340 Magnum. It went on to challenge the .338 Winchester Magnum, which, after its 1958 debut in the Model 70, had become popular with elk hunters in the western U.S. The .340 used the same bullets but shot them faster. Whereas Winchester's .338 was a short magnum (a necked-down .458 Magnum that adapted readily to .30-06-length actions), the .340 Weatherby was a full-length cartridge (a .300 Weatherby necked up). This limited its application but enhanced its performance. The .340 drove a 250-grain bullet at nearly 3000 fps, compared to 2700 from the .338 Winchester.

In 1963, Weatherby delighted varmint hunters with his .224 Magnum. Like the .378, its belted case had no parent. Ballistically, the petite .224 did what the .22-250 had done for years. Its only innovations were a new case shape and the Weatherby name. Once the .224 was announced, there remained no significant holes in the Weatherby cartridge line. For long-range deer and pronghorn hunting, the .257 had no peer. Its 100-grain bullet at 3550 fps beat the .25-06 by 200 fps and edged the .264 Winchester Magnum. Weatherby's .270 was perhaps the quintessential round for western deer and African plains game, with the 7mm Magnum offering a heavier bullet for hunters after elk and eland. No other .30 magnum could match the .300 Weatherby for performance or versatility; if more bullet weight was needed—say, for big bears—the .340 provided it with hardly any more bend in the bullet path. The .378 and .460 Weatherby had limited roles but filled them ably.

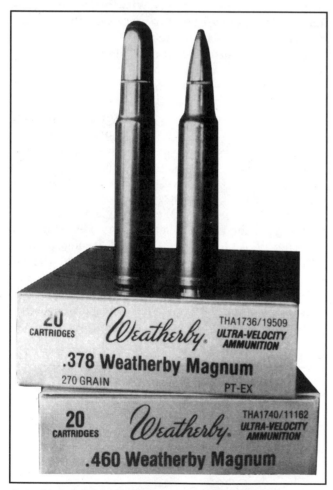

Considered the world's most powerful sporting cartridge, Weatherby's .460 (left) generates 8000 pounds of muzzle energy. The .378 (right) and .416 (not shown) are Weatherby designs based on the same oversized magnum case.

If there was a gap, it lay between the .224 and .257. Since its introduction in 1955, Winchester's .243 had done exceedingly well at market. Weatherby was without a 6mm cartridge, and there remained a big difference in case size between the .224 and .257 Magnums. So in 1968 Weatherby introduced a .240 Magnum. Like its kin, it wore a belt and had radiused shoulders. Because even the .257 Weatherby had a small bore for its case capacity, a new hull was designed for the .240. Roughly the size of a .30-06 case, it had the same rim dimensions and powered a 100-grain bullet from the muzzle at nearly 3400 fps, beating out the .243 by more than 300 fps.

It seemed after the .240 that any other Weatherby cartridge would be superfluous; but following a resurgence of interest in the .416 bore in the late 1980's, Weatherby developed its own .416 magnum on the .378 case. It bridges the gap nicely between the .378 and .416 Weatherby rounds, driving a 400-grain bullet at the same velocity (2700 fps) that the .30-06 launches a 180-grain and the .460 Weatherby a 500-grain. Muzzle energy is nearly 6500 foot-pounds.

The Mark V Rifle: Roy Weatherby's Masterpiece

Roy Weatherby's cartridges would have fared poorly without a factory rifle chambered for them. While surplus battle rifles could be overhauled, the operation was expensive, and the most useful Weatherby cartridge—the .300—mandated a long action. That meant opening magazine boxes and perhaps removing metal from the feed ramp that buttressed the lower locking lug on Mauser-type rifles. Because Weatherby cartridges generated pressures of 52,000 to 55,000 psi, early Springfields and many other military guns were unsuitable for conversion, and the conversion itself could weaken stouter actions. Winchester Model 70's and Remington 721's would have sufficed for all save .378-size rounds, but Roy Weatherby was an entrepreneur, and he knew that eventually he'd need a rifle of his own.

The first Weatherby rifles built to uniform standards came along in 1948. They featured commercial Mauser actions from Fabrique Nationale in Belgium, with crisp, single-stage triggers and low-slung bolts that accommodated scopes. In 1955, when the .378 made its debut, Weatherby chambered it in the Danish Schultz & Larsen rifle because it was too big for the standard Mauser. By then,

Norma was manufacturing Weatherby's cartridges and shipping them in Weatherby boxes.

Meanwhile, Roy Weatherby was hard at work designing an action. Fred Jennie, a bright Weatherby engineer, put Roy's ideas onto paper and then into steel, modifying them when by so doing he could improve the rifle. By 1958, the two men had developed the Mark V. It was so good that over the next 30 years only minor changes were required in its mechanism and none in its profile.

The Mark V bolt has nine lugs, set in three groups of three to allow for a 54-degree bolt lift, instead of the near-90-degree lift found on rifles with two big opposing lugs. (The .224 Varmintmaster has three sets of two lugs). This makes for quicker operation and greater scope clearance. The lugs are cut like the threads on a machine bolt for good fit. "Interrupted thread" lockup was not a new idea (Charles Newton had prototype rifles made with this feature shortly after World War I), but Roy Weatherby was the first to popularize it. Because the Mark V's lugs are the same diameter as the bolt body (.840 inch), the receiver can be economically drilled; and lug races needn't be broached. This is good news not only for the manufacturer, but also for the hunter, as the big bolt has more contact now with the receiver. This contact helps smooth bolt operation and prevents the wobble common to two-lug bolts of conventional Mauser design upon withdrawal during extraction. Weatherby's bolt is also fluted to reduce drag without compromising its snug, ball-in-a-bearing feel.

The Mark V features a fully-enclosed bolt face, plunger ejector and 3/32-inch claw extractor. Purists may prefer a big Mauser extractor and an open bolt face that permits controlled feeding, but the Weatherby's action is safer because it supports the entire case. Unsupported brass will rupture if breech pressure gets too high, spilling gas rearward. Not only does the counterbored Weatherby bolt surround the case head with steel, it is supported by a counterbored barrel, which threads into the receiver. That means three rings of steel encompass the case head. And should a case rupture, a shoulder on the firing pin will divert any back-pedaling gas safely through three ports in the bolt.

The Mark V's first safety was a thumb lever mounted on the cast alloy trigger housing. This was replaced around 1960 by a shroud-mounted safety that locked the striker instead of the sear. The trigger mechanism was improved in 1971, when Weatherby moved its Mark V production from the J.P. Sauer & Sohn plant in West Germany to the

The 100-yard test tunnel in Weatherby's South Gate, (California) plant is put to good use by a technician targeting a .257 Magnum.

Howa firm in Japan. Because high bullet speeds shorten barrel life, Roy Weatherby tried various methods to toughen his barrels, from chrome plating to using bearing-hard steel. The best results came when he hammer-forged the rifling into 4140 chrome-molybdenum blanks.

Accuracy, Not Modesty

Hammer-forging is much the same as beating cold steel around a hard mandrel with the rifling in reverse. The huge hammers, each delivering half a million pounds per blow, rain thousands of blows on the barrel blank. Actually, the hammers are cammed into the blank by a rotating shaft that spins around the mandrel. So great is the pressure that a thick-walled 20-inch barrel blank emerges a trimmer 24-inch barrel. The molecular structure of the steel is compressed, giving the bore a mirror-like finish and great resistance to erosion. Weatherby was one of the first big gun firms to use this process, which also ensures tight bore tolerances. Weatherby allows only .0005-inch variation in bore diameter from breech to muzzle in its Mark V rifles.

The Mark V barrel has been engineered to enable Weatherby cartridges to reach their potential without exceeding a 55,000 psi pressure ceiling. This is done by "free-boring"—reaming a long throat so the bullet doesn't meet the resistance of the rifling lands as soon as it pops from the case. Stiffer loads can be used—and higher velocity attained—in a free-bored rifle than in one with a short throat, given identical pressure limits. Freeboring is said to be detrimental to accuracy, and target shooters do not employ it. But Weatherby Mark V's are among the most accurate of factory-built hunting rifles, many of them grouping routinely within a minute of angle. Weatherby has traditionally offered its most powerful rifles with 26-inch barrels, but there's a choice now of 24- or 26-inch barrels on the short magnums. Barrel weight can also be specified, within limits.

Custom stockmaker Leonard Mews helped design the first Weatherby stocks. Roy wanted something distinctive, yet practical. The stock had to absorb recoil, but at the same time appeal to modern tastes and draw attention to the rifle. Before the Mark V had been perfected, Weatherby stocks had become well known for their wide-flaring grips, pronounced combs, flat forends with reverse-slanted tips, colored inlays and glossy finish. They were later labeled by shooters with more conservative tastes as "California" stocks—garish and impractical. Weatherby did not bend to the criticism and still offers that original stock design as standard issue, though the company has also developed "European" and "Classic" stocks to broaden the appeal of Mark V's. Weatherby's early commitment to

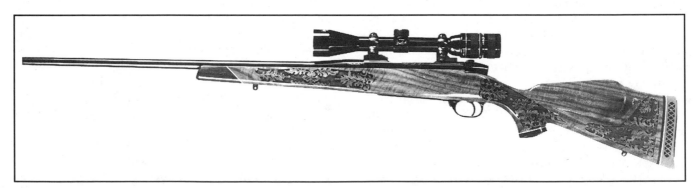

The high gloss, bold contours and extensive carving on this Mark V Lazermark rifle illustrate the flamboyant style that has become a Weatherby trademark.

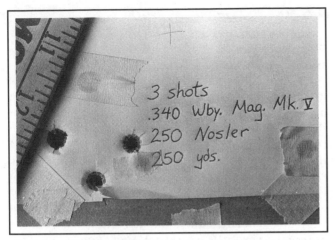

The Fibermark's synthetic stock probably helped it produce this outstanding accuracy.

highly figured Claro walnut no doubt helped sell a lot of rifles. Weatherby stocks are still among the most striking in color and grain of any found on commercial rifles.

Regardless of how it looks, the Weatherby stock is comfortable to shoot. The high, forward-sloping cheekpiece puts the shooter's eye directly behind the scope. There's lots of cheek contact to spread the upward bounce of recoil. Because the rear of the comb is higher than the front, the rifle's backward jab takes pressure off one's cheek. The grip and forend, which do not fit extra large hands well, are amply checkered and offer adequate control. All Weatherbys are furnished with rubber butt pads and sling swivel studs.

Diversity Begets Conformity—and Success

In 1970, the firm introduced its Vanguard rifle for hunters who wanted the Weatherby look without the Weatherby price. This marketing rationale was, in the Weatherby tradition, impeccable. The Vanguard does not compete directly with the Mark V because it offers no Weatherby chamberings. The only standard chamberings in the Mark V are the .30-06 and, in the Varmintmaster, the .22-250. Both the Vanguard and Mark V have since been offered with synthetic stocks and are now available in four configurations and 12 chamberings.

Weatherby also started marketing Japanese-built shotguns in 1970. That year it announced the Regency over/under, which lasted until 1982, when it was replaced by the similar Athena and Orion models. In 1972 the Centurion autoloader and Patrician pump arrived on the scene but were supplanted 10 years later by Models 82 and 92. Currently Weatherby lists only the over/under. It is made by the well-known SKB company, which has manufactured shotguns for several American firms.

Weatherby's autoloading .22 rimfire—Mark XXII—became part of the line in 1963. Offered with both tube and detachable box magazines, it had the characteristic glitzy form and finish of Weatherby bolt-action centerfires. The first Mark XXII's were made in Italy, but in 1973 production moved to Japan. Five years later, Weatherby discontinued its carriage-class .22.

In 1969, Weatherby contracted with Japanese optics firms to manufacture a scope for its centerfire rifles. At the same time it introduced a spotting scope called the "Sightmaster." For two years, Weatherby listed "Olympian" rifle scopes, changing in 1972 to the "Premier" label. This name was dropped in 1984 and a new one—"Supreme"—substituted. A short run of roof-prism binoculars, beginning in 1978 with 7x35s, ended in 1986. In recent years, production of an 8x20 model has also been listed.

Weatherby started selling hard plastic gun cases in 1966 and aluminum ones in 1974. Both are still available. Other accessories for shooters include belt buckles, tie tacks and lucite blocks show-

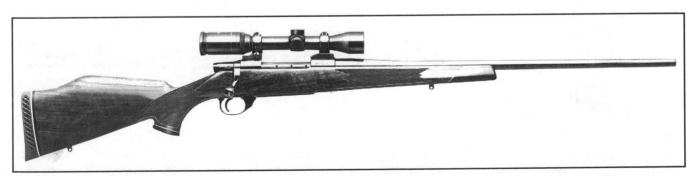

The Weatherby Vanguard (above), introduced in 1970, offered the racy Weatherby look with standard chamberings.

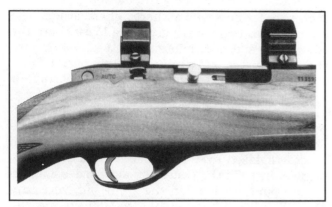

Weatherby's semiautomatic .22 rimfire rifle shown here is no longer produced.

casing a sparkling row of Weatherby cartridges. In 1990, Weatherby announced its "Supervault" gun safe. The company's ammunition is still produced in Sweden, where Norma made Roy Weatherby's first experimental cases. Now some cartridges feature Nosler Partition bullets for hunters who want premium-quality big game bullets in a factory-loaded round. Other gun companies have recently chambered limited numbers of rifles for Weatherby ammunition. The Winchester Model 70, Ruger Number One, and Remington 700 Classic have all been built for Weatherby cartridges, and Remington has assembled .300 Weatherby ammunition to be sold in its own green boxes.

A Marketing Genius at Work

More than a wildcatter and rifle designer, Roy Weatherby was a salesman. Energetic and aggressive, he nonetheless impressed people with his sincerity. He believed he had the best product, and he let others know it. He was quick to take advantage of his location, too. Southern California was an expensive place to do business, but it had a concentration of famous people who wielded great influence on the buying public. Roy Weatherby gave rifles to anyone he thought would give them a boost in the market. Some recipients—Elgin Gates, for example—were world-renowned hunters and used their Weatherby's to good advantage. But stage stars who rarely, if ever, took their guns afield also became "Weatherby people." Always the presentation was photographed and beautifully reproduced for advertising. A glossy four-color magazine, called "The Weatherby Guide," was published periodically. It featured pictures of famous people holding Weatherby rifles, of successful hunters with their game, and of opulent trophy rooms festooned with mounts of exotic game. Yes, Roy Weatherby knew how to tap powerful people for support, but when he announced the first annual Weatherby Big Game Trophy award in 1956, it wasn't meant to go to the rich and famous alone. "The Weatherby Big Game Trophy is an annual award, not for a particular record," he declared, "but for an individual who has made the greatest

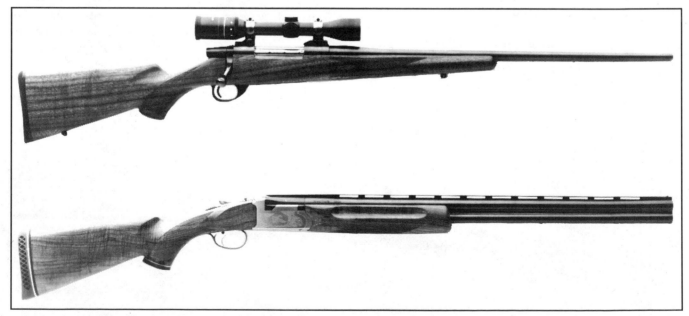

The Classic I Vanguard (top photo) features Weatherby's standard variable scope in Buehler mounts. The Orion Grade III over/under shotgun (bottom photo) is made in Japan.

Ed Weatherby, Roy's son and now company president, presents a custom-built Weatherby Athena shotgun to President George Bush.

lifetime achievements in the world of big game hunting. . . a person who has collected the greatest number of average as well as record game animals throughout the entire world . . . the difficult and rare animals . . . for the various continents hunted and the number of hunts . . . for unusual accomplishments, such as bagging all species of sheep with representative or record heads, or collecting such rare animals as the bongo . . . a person who has contributed greatly to conservation and hunting education, and one whose character and sportsmanship are beyond reproach."

The first Weatherby Big Game Trophy went to Herb Klein, and the next to Jack O'Connor. Subsequent winners included royalty and adventurers, gun writers and physicians—people of substance, intellect, and ambition. They were the kind of people Roy liked to see shooting Weatherby rifles (although several used guns from other makers).

Like other entrepreneurs, Roy Weatherby didn't consider his occupation a job. It was his life. Later he admitted that the sacrifices demanded by such a business might give him pause should he ever have to start over. The time away from his family bothered him, as did the constant concerns over money in the early years. But Roy Weatherby was not a quitter, and his work has profoundly affected the sporting arms industry, even beyond U.S. borders. He was truly "the high priest of high velocity," a man with a message who built his own pulpit.

Roy Weatherby died on April 5, 1988, following heart surgery. His only son, Ed, took over the company, which continues to market carefully crafted rifles under the enduring label: "Weatherby, Symbol of Superiority."

CHAPTER 15

THE NEW OLD GUNS OF THOMPSON/CENTER

The end of World War II brought new beginnings to people who had no alternative. For Kenneth Thompson, a New York toolmaker, it marked the birth of an adventure he elected to pursue. "Going into business for yourself can be frightening," he once reflected. "But I've not been sorry I jumped in. In fact, I feel a bit sorry for the fellows who inherit an enterprise; they miss the fun of putting it together."

From his Long Island (NY) garage, headquarters for the new K.W. Thompson Tool Company, Inc., Ken began shipping moulds and tooling for the investment casting industry. His products proved as good as his business sense, and soon demand forced a move. The new plant had its own foundry and required a staff. "Red" Ronayne, Thompson's first employee, is now a vice president of the company he helped nurture in the 1940's. Joe Behre, a high school graduate who knocked on Thompson's door for his first job, still works at the plant as vice president in charge of the Foundry Division.

By 1962, the firm was employing 25 people and generating gross sales of $180,000 annually. Robert Gustafson worked there while attending night classes to earn a degree in mechanical engineering. He is now company president, but in 1963 he helped move the Thompson machinery to Rochester, New Hampshire, where the growing firm could spread its wings. That winter proved one of the worst in memory, with frequent breakdowns making the move a grueling task.

Fortunately, Rochester proved a good place to be. Its woolen mills and shoe factories were struggling to meet payrolls at that time, so Thompson was able to hire good workers for a reasonable wage. The only hitch was a sharp seasonal fluctuation in demand for investment castings; as a result, it became increasingly difficult to keep the foundry operating year-round. One solution was to design and market a product for consumers. Since the firm was already manufacturing gun parts, a firearm seemed the next sensible step.

Warren Center and His "Contender" Pistol

In 1965, gun designer Warren Center joined the K.W. Thompson Tool Company. Like Thompson, he'd worked as a machinist and die maker. Later on, he built custom guns and worked for two highly respected armsmakers, Iver Johnson and Harrington & Richardson. In his basement shop, Center designed a new single-shot pistol he called the "Contender." Having applied for patent rights, he was looking for someone to manufacture the pistol about the same time Ken Thompson was looking for a product. Teaming up on this project meant doubling the size of Thompson's plant, to about 20,000 square feet. In true Yankee fashion, the two men plunged ahead. The first Contender pistol came off the line in 1967. The next year, to isolate their gun-building from the dust and noise of other foundry work, the partners erected a 2,500-square-foot facility nearby.

The Contender could easily have failed. Its break-action, single-shot design courted a narrow market. Priced higher than many revolvers, the gun had little aesthetic appeal and was clearly meant for serious handgunners only. To offset these liabilities, Warren Center showed his talent by devising an innovative barrel-switching system, enabling shooters to use several barrels that interchanged easily on one frame. One could buy a centerfire Contender for big game hunting and equip it with

Warren Thompson (left) points out the features of his new Contender pistol (see below) to a colleague soon after the gun appeared in 1965. It has since become the most popular single-shot pistol in the U.S.

settled on a black powder gun, made to high standards of function and finish and backed by a lifetime warranty. This, they reasoned, would compete well with the imports then being sold to shooters who wanted serviceable muzzleloading rifles. Warren Center designed the new gun, while Jim Sheridan developed a marketing campaign and wrote a detailed instruction book that enabled anyone to understand the mechanics of blackpowder shooting. The new Thompson/Center Hawken rifle soon outdistanced the imports, many of which could not match the Hawken's authentic look, sturdy action and fine finish. Since its introduction late in 1970, this gun has been chosen by more first-time black powder shooters than any other.

Two years later, with orders still piling in, Thompson/Center added 6,000 square feet of production space to its Hawken works. At the same time, it announced a muzzleloading pistol, the "Pa-

In addition to a variety of traditional black powder guns, Thompson/Center offers guns with modern butt pads and swivel studs, such as the White Mountain carbine shown here.

a .22 rimfire barrel for inexpensive practice (dual firing pins made that possible); or shooters could buy barrels of different lengths for different purposes, using iron sights or a scope.

This versatile pistol is now chambered for 20 cartridges, from the .22 Long Rifle to the .45-70 Government, including the .410 shotshell. It comes with round or octagon barrels—10, 12, 14 or 16 inches long. Adjustable sights, quick-release scope mounts, sling swivels, screw-in choke tubes and muzzle brakes are also available. In addition, the Contender Carbine model offers shoulder stocks (with Rynite as an option) and 16¼- and 21-inch barrels.

With its sound design, and seductive trappings, the Thompson-Center pistol soon eclipsed its only significant competition—Remington's XP-100 bolt-action pistol. And when metallic silhouette shooting was adapted to handguns, the Contender became a natural choice. Chamberings in 7mm T.C.U, 7-30 Waters, .30-30 Winchester and .35 Remington made .357 and .44 Magnum revolvers look anemic.

T/C: Building A Black Powder Market

By 1970, Ken Thompson and Warren Center had formed Thompson/Center Arms and were looking for other products to market. The partners

The office in front of Thompson/Center's manufacturing facility in Rochester (NH) displays both corporate names. The K.W. Thompson Tool Company was formed in 1945, and Thompson/Center began in the late 1960's.

triot,'' which received a lukewarm reception and was finally dropped. In 1973, with Hawken sales still booming, the company added a second rifle to its line—the "Seneca"—which stayed around a few years until it too was discontinued. The next new item, a rifle called the "Renegade," proved a great success, however. Introduced in 1974, this businesslike gun sported a 26-inch barrel—two inches shorter than the Hawken. Its steel, shotgun-style butt contrasted with the Hawken's hooked brass plate. Both rifles are available in .50 and .54 caliber, caplock or flintlock. The Hawken is also offered with a .45 bore, and a percussion Renegade is available with a left-hand lock.

Thompson/Center Arms produced its first catalog in 1974, and the following year the company offered a do-it-yourself Hawken kit. Adding 7,200 square feet of additional space, the firm struggled to get production capacity up to demand. In 1976, a fifth gun building was completed, and two years

later a sixth totaling 20,000 square feet. The only bad news in those days was the death of Ken Thompson in 1978.

Throughout the 1970's, plant engineers were kept busy designing, fabricating and installing the most efficient machinery with which to make metal parts as well as gunstocks. The Renegade's success prompted introduction of a Renegade kit in 1981. The next year, Thompson/Center purchased another 15 acres of property for expansion of its plant, but the new building was postponed so that the firm could buy numerically-controlled machining centers (CNC machines).

Cartridge Guns and Special Muzzleloaders

In 1983, the company announced its first centerfire rifle, the "TCR'83 Single Shot." Like the Contender, it offered interchangeable barrels. This gun was replaced later by the "TCR'87" rifle, which featured essentially the same design and was listed

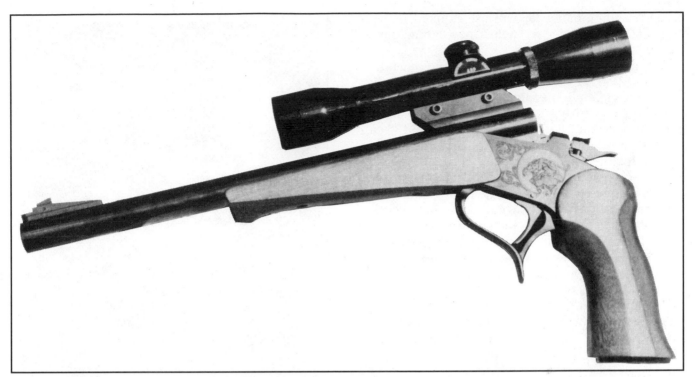

Thompson/Center's Contender (above) is one of the most practical choices for the handgun hunter. It is accurate, easily scoped, and comes in several chamberings, from .22 Long Rifle to .35 Remington.

in calibers .22 Hornet through .30-06 Springfield. Its counterpart, the TCR'87 Shotgun, offers field barrels in 10 or 12 gauge, plus a 12-gauge slug barrel with rifle sights.

While it was introducing its first cartridge rifle, Thompson/Center expanded its black powder line with the "Cherokee," a svelte cap-lock rifle in 32 and 45 calibers. The following year, an international department was added to the company, led by Jack Gillam, who quickly put together an export catalog with which to court overseas markets.

Since 1986, Thompson/Center has introduced several new black powder guns, including the "Pennsylvania Hunter," a 50-caliber rifle in cap- or flintlock. It features a barrel designed expressly for shooting round balls; and its 1-66 twist is slower than the 1-48 twist found on other barrels that take either ball or conical bullets. The Pennsylvania Hunter weighs under 8 pounds, a bit less than the Renegade and Hawken.

Thompson-Center's "New Englander" is a cap-lock rifle for which the company offers an interchangeable 12-gauge shotgun barrel. It comes in right- and left-hand versions, 50 and 54 caliber. It is the only T/C gun cataloged with an optional Rynite synthetic stock. The new Renegade single-trigger rifle, a "Plain Jane" rendition of the original, looks much like the New Englander.

For the largest thin-skinned game, Thompson/Center offers the Big Boar, a 58-caliber percussion gun. And for hunters who appreciate quick handling, the T/C catalog lists the "White Mountain Carbine," featuring .45 and .54 calibers with a one-in-48 twist (the 50-caliber is rifled 1-in-20 for use with conical bullets like the "Maxi-Ball," a company creation that has become an industry standard). The White Mountain Carbine weighs just 6½ pounds with its 21-inch barrel.

Accessories, Ammunition and Catalog Orders

Thompson/Center also builds a muzzleloading carbine and a pistol with enclosed ignition mechanisms. Called the "Scout" models, these guns come in 50 and 54 caliber and will accommodate scopes. Thompson/Center offers both rifle and pistol (extended-eye-relief) scopes for its guns, along with mounts to fit most popular centerfire rifles. The company catalog lists almost everything a black powder shooter could want in the way of accessories—tang sights, ramrods, slings and swivels, even folding knives. In addition, one can order flints, patches, shotgun wads, worms, cappers, lubers, bullet starters, nipple wrenches, powder measures, and wedge pins.

A new Maxi-Hunter bullet, looking much like the Maxi-Ball, sports a dimple in its nose for quicker and more violent expansion. Weights are about the same, with both designs available in .45, .50, .54 and .58 (the Maxi-Ball is available in 32 and 36 caliber as well). Thompson/Center also offers mold blocks for these bullets and round balls.

The investment casting operation that enabled this company to produce inexpensively the finely-shaped parts of high-quality firearms has been applied lately to other items, including outboard motor propellers. While gun parts are still its main product, a stream of work orders from outside helps keep the facility at capacity, making it more efficient and profitable.

Thompson/Center has diversified its marketing plan as well as its manufacturing. A new mail-order subsidiary, known as Fox Ridge, has been devel-

Checkering is still a hand operation at Thompson/Center's rural plant in Rochester (NH). As in most modern arms plants, skilled women comprise a large part of the work force.

This form is used for the production of brass patchbox covers on Thompson/Center's popular Hawken rifle.

oped. Initially a small division of Thompson/Center, it has become a custom shop where customers can order barrels with special chambers and the like. Gun hardware comprises less than half the merchandise available in the 850,000 Fox Ridge catalogs mailed each year. The remainder includes clothing, camping gear, outdoor novelties and items of general interest to outdoorsmen. These catalogs, however, do not offer guns available through dealers that stock the Thompson/Center line. Some guns are built only for Fox Ridge, though, and are presented as special versions of standard T/C firearms.

As a young company with only two decades in the blackpowder business behind it, Thompson/Center Arms remains the only maker of muzzleloaders that issues a lifetime guarantee. A true "Horatio Alger" among armsmakers, it gives old-fashioned guns new mechanisms, then builds them with old-fashioned care on new machines—and it deserves no apologies. A lot of shooters like that policy, along with the company's motto: "We do it all in-house."

CHAPTER 16

BILL RUGER: BUILDING GUNS THAT WORK

In 1946, William Batterman Ruger made his first try at making things to sell. His product—carpenters' tools—didn't sell well because they cost too much. And they cost too much because they were good tools and were expensive to make. As a result, the Ruger Corporation floundered, partly because Bill Ruger's heart was never in carpenters' tools. His passion lay in manufacturing, firearms, and working for himself. The tool enterprise had fed two of these interests but not the third. At the time, he simply lacked the money to establish a gunmaking firm.

About the time Bill Ruger's little tool company expired, along came Alex Sturm. A graduate of the Yale Art School, Sturm was hardly the kind of man a young industrialist might tap for help. But besides painting and writing, Alex Sturm also collected guns—and he had $50,000 to invest. Even in 1948, though, $50,000 wasn't much of a grubstake for heavy manufacturing of any type. But Sturm was willing to risk it on a gun Bill Ruger had designed, and Ruger was willing to take it.

The gun in question was a .22 autoloading pistol made out of pieces of sheet steel. Its operation offered nothing novel but its construction was revolutionary. Instead of incurring the substantial expense of machining a solid receiver, Ruger had simply joined several stamped parts together to form the shell. This allowed him to price his pistol at only $37.50, well below the competition. And yet, despite its low cost, the gun was handsome, well-finished and reliable.

The two young partners placed their first ad in *The American Rifleman* in 1949. Their pistol received good reviews by NRA technical staff member Major Julian Hatcher, who'd been Ruger's mentor.

A blizzard of orders piled in during the next few months to affirm that Sturm, Ruger & Company, Inc., had indeed taken root. Unfortunately, Alex Sturm was not able to savor fully the company's growth, for he died in 1951 while still in his 20's. To commemorate his late friend and associate, Bill Ruger ordered that the Ruger "Red Eagle" emblems appearing on the autoloading pistols be colored black. This change became permanent. Ruger's "Eagle" symbol—actually, it's the likeness of a griffin—is colored red now only in company literature, not on its guns.

Teenaged Machine Gun Engineer

Designing and manufacturing firearms had been Bill Ruger's ambition since childhood. Born in Brooklyn, New York, on June 21, 1916, he developed an early appetite for the out-of-doors. His father, Adolph Ruger, was a successful lawyer, an avid shooter, and the owner of a lodge on eastern Long Island where he often took his son duck hunting. By age 12, Bill had his own .22 rifle—a Remington pump.

One day, while carrying his .22 afield, Ruger met a man shooting a .30-06. It was an ear-ringing introduction to the world of centerfire rifles. Soon young Ruger and a pal, Bill Lett, had anted up $9.75 for a war-surplus .30-40 Krag. By the time he was in high school, Ruger had acquired several guns—not just to shoot, but to study. An avid gun collector for the rest of his life, those Colt and Luger pistols, Sharps and Springfield rifles of his teen years instilled a keen appreciation for history and fueled the young man's interest in gun design. Before he graduated from high school, Ruger had already engineered a light machine gun and built a prototype.

William B. Ruger (left) presents one of his P85 Mark II pistols to Major General Joe Engle, USAF ret.

He was a crack shot with the school rifle team as well and read voraciously to teach himself the technical aspects of gun design and manufacture.

While studying at a prep school in Salisbury, Connecticut, where guns were forbidden on campus, Ruger stored his collection nearby and spent his holidays exploring machine shops in Brooklyn (NY), learning the fundamentals of steel fabrication. He next attended the University of North Carolina, where he fashioned an autoloading rifle from a Model 99 Savage lever-action. This gun was featured in *The American Rifleman* in 1942.

Following his marriage to Mary Thompson in 1939, Bill Ruger looked around for a job designing guns. The major armsmakers didn't seem interested, so he approached Army Ordnance with a proposal for a new machine gun. It was rejected. Discouraged, Ruger finally accepted a job offer from the Springfield Armory. It paid $130 a month, enough to keep young Ruger punching in for the next 12 months.

In 1940, the Rugers and their young son moved to North Carolina, where Bill renewed his efforts to design a better machine gun. He showed his prototype to Remington, Winchester, and Smith & Wesson, but without success. His talents were obvious, however, and he got several job offers. He turned down those opportunities to start work for Auto Ordnance, maker of the Thompson submachine gun. Auto Ordnance subsequently contracted for the patent rights to Ruger's machine gun, but the end of World War II sapped government interest in the project, and the gun was never sold.

A Sheet Metal Pistol and Investment-Cast Revolvers

Ruger's three years with that company were happy ones, however. The pay was reasonable—$100 a week—but more important, he was actually allowed to design guns. It was at Auto Ordnance that he met Douglas Hammond, who gave him the idea of building a firearm from sheet metal to chop production costs. With modern factory equipment, Ruger concluded, tolerances could be held close enough to guarantee easy assembly, tight fit, and uniform finished dimensions, inside and out. The product would be handsome, functional and inexpensive to make. It could also be sold at a profit for much less than guns built on receivers that were made entirely by machine. The result was Ruger's autoloading .22 pistol.

In 1951, the year Alex Sturm died, the fledgling Sturm, Ruger gun company had offered a target version of its .22 pistol. The new Mark I, as it was called, had adjustable sights and came in three barrel lengths: 5¼, 5½ and 6⅞. The 5½-inch tube, heavier than the other two, was called a bull barrel. The standard pistol had a light 4¾-inch barrel.

Sturm, Ruger & Company planned to introduce a tip-up revolver in 1952, but this design was supplanted by another before any guns were built. The sequel—a solid frame .22 fashioned after Colt's famous Single Action Army revolver—was an immediate hit when it was announced in 1953. Called the Single Six, this gun was the first of many built by Ruger with investment-cast parts. (Investment casting is a lost-wax process that reduces the

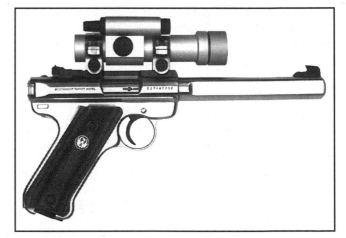

This Ruger stainless steel competition pistol derives from the very first Ruger autoloading .22 pistol, made inexpensively of stamped parts but designed to function without fail.

These Ruger Model 77 barreled actions are waiting for stocks.

amount of machining needed to shape and fit parts; it saves money without sacrificing overall quality or compromising function.) By 1956, Ruger was offering a light weight version of the Single Six, which later became available with a cylinder chambered for the .22 Winchester Magnum Rimfire. This lightweight gun sold about 200,000 copies.

Bill Ruger's success with single-action rimfires prompted work on a centerfire revolver with the same style. Thus did the now famous Ruger Blackhawk, chambered in .357 Magnum, make its debut in 1955. A year later, the .44 Magnum was added, followed in 1959 by a .44 Magnum Super Blackhawk with squared trigger guard and unfluted cylinder. The Blackhawk was subsequently offered in .41 Magnum, .30 Carbine and .45 Long Colt and remains one of Ruger's most popular guns. It now features a simpler, stronger mechanism than the early Colt's, and is offered in a stout frame with adjustable sights.

In 1959, Ruger introduced the Bearcat, a trim single-action .22 revolver with an engraved, unfluted cylinder and brass trigger guard. It had a 4-inch barrel and fixed sights, but it—along with the Ruger Hawkeye—did not last long. The Hawkeye looked like a single-action revolver but was in fact a single-shot chambered in .256 Winchester Magnum (a Hawkeye in .221 Fireball was also announced but never made).

Single-Shot Rifle to Autoloading Pistol

Ruger's entry into the long-gun field came in 1961, with the chunky .44 Magnum Carbine, an unconventional autoloading rifle that weighed just 6 pounds. Its 18½-inch barrel and factory-fitted peep sight made it ideal for close-quarter shooting at whitetail deer. Though it has since been discontinued, the Carbine was a well-designed rifle and spawned, in 1964, a rimfire look-alike, called the 10/22. This 10-shot autoloader with its rotary magazine became one of the most popular .22's of all time.

In 1968 Bill Ruger gambled on a single-shot centerfire rifle fashioned after the British Farquharson. The last single-shot big game gun marketed to any significant extent in America up to that time was Winchester's Browning-designed "High Wall," which arrived in 1885. During the early years of smokeless powders and reliable cartridge ammunition, repeating rifles had made short work of single-shots. Ruger's idea was not to promote his new "Number One" as a game-killer but as an elegant rifle that could add a sense of class to the hunt without compromising ballistic performance. Indeed, with no bolt or magazine, this drop-

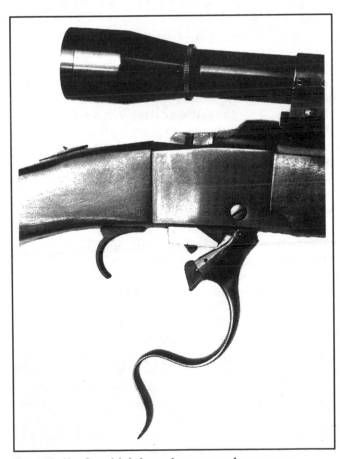

Ruger's No. 3, which is no longer made, was an austere single-shot, chambered in .22 Hornet, .223 Remington, .30-40 Krag, .375 Winchester, and .45-70 Government.

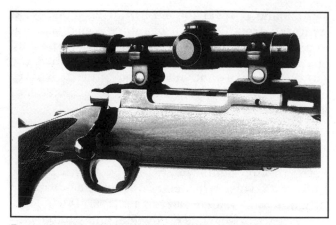

Ruger brashly challenged Remington's 700 and Winchester's 70 with its Model 77 bolt-action rifle and won a big market share. The Model 77 shown here features a 2.5× Leupold Compact scope in Ruger's cleverly engineered rings.

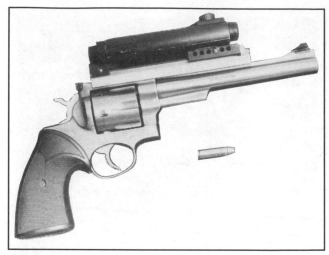

Ruger's Redhawk .44 Magnum double-action is among the most popular of hunting handguns.

ping-block rifle could wear a 26-inch barrel and slip into gun cases designed for bolt guns with 22-inch tubes. The extra 4 inches increased velocity.

Sales of the Ruger single-shot took off like an overloaded cargo plane on a soft dirt strip, but eventually shooters warmed to it. The Number One ranks among the world's best-looking modern factory rifles and is chambered for more cartridges than most bolt guns. It's available in several styles, with barrels that are long and short, light and heavy. A choice of three forend styles is available, including a full-length version. An integral quarter-rib serves as a sight mount for some models, and as a one-piece scope base for all of them. Ruger designed its own sleek, sturdy scope rings. They're cleverly engineered to clamp, with one screw apiece, in sculptured cuts on the quarter rib. They don't move, even on the Number Ones chambered to .458 Winchester.

A year after launching this venture, Bill Ruger announced a new bolt-action rifle: Model 77. While more conventional in design than the .44 Magnum Carbine or Number One, it faced competition the others had avoided, including Winchester's Model 70 and Remington's Model 700. Getting into the ring with those two well-established, state-of-the-art bolt rifles would make any good hunting rifle quiver in its scabbard.

Ruger's Model 77 not only survived, it proved itself an equal. The rifle's investment-cast receivers helped keep costs down, and a huge selection of chamberings and barrel dimensions offered shooters exactly what they wanted. Its classic-style stock, designed by crack custom rifle builders, arrived just

as many shooters were revolting against the excesses of "California-style" stocks with their wide-flaring grips, rollover cheekpieces, white spacers, and square forends with reverse-cut tips. The Ruger rifle combined versatility and classic looks with a Mauser claw extractor, tang safety, cut checkering and, on some models, a pair of machined Ruger scope rings ready to clamp on a specially-milled receiver. These and other assets proved that Ruger had done it again.

Other, more recent successes in the Sturm, Ruger & Company line include the following: an over-under shotgun, called the Red Label, which has no visible action pins; the Old Army .44 cap-

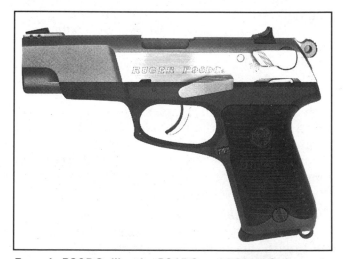

Ruger's P90DC, like the P91DC and P89DAO, is made of stainless steel at the Prescott (AZ) plant. It holds seven .45 ACP rounds.

These Ruger stocks for the Mini 14 are shaped and finished in the company's Newport (New Hampshire) woodshop.

hawk double-action revolvers in chamberings from .22 rimfire to .44 Magnum; and the Mini-14 and Mini-Thirty autoloading carbines designed after the M-14 service rifle but offered in .223 and 7.62x39 Russian. Ruger has also used stainless steel components to broaden its product line and has recently begun listing synthetic stocks for some of its rifles.

Bill Ruger's Expanding Empire

Sturm, Ruger & Company is now debt-free, with assets of about $100 million. Its home office is still in Southport, Connecticut, where the short-lived Ruger Corporation started in 1946, and where most of the early Sturm, Ruger guns were built. Ruger production, however, has moved away from Connecticut—to Newport, New Hampshire, and Prescott, Arizona. Now only the single-action revolvers and .22 autoloading pistols come from Southport. Rifles, shotguns and double-action revolvers are produced in New Hampshire, while centerfire autoloading pistols come out of the Prescott plant.

The biggest facility is in Newport, where Ruger built a huge manufacturing complex around an investment casting operation, called Pine Tree Casting. There Ruger produces gun parts, including items for other industries, using the "lost wax" process. Here, ceramic molds are fashioned over wax forms, which in turn are manufactured in master molds to look like the final product. The wax is melted and removed from the finished ceramic, and metal is poured in to replace it. The ceramic is then broken away from the hardened metal, revealing surfaces that are remarkably smooth and well within dimensional tolerances.

Most Ruger frames and receivers are investment cast, as are all but the longest revolver barrels, which come from the same barrel maker that supplies Ruger's rifle barrels. Shotgun barrels are hammer-forged in-house. Whereas Ruger button-rifles

and-ball revolver, patterned after guns of the Civil War; the Bisley single-action that combines features of the Blackhawk and Single-Six revolvers in a gun styled after the Colt Bisley, with chamberings from .22 rimfire to .45 Long Colt; the P-85, a modern 9mm, 15-shot double-action autoloading pistol for police, military and home defense use; the small-frame SP-101, medium-frame GP-100 and large-frame Red-

Ruger's Model 77 Mark II has a Model 70-type side-swing safety, which supplants the sliding tang safety of early Model 77's.

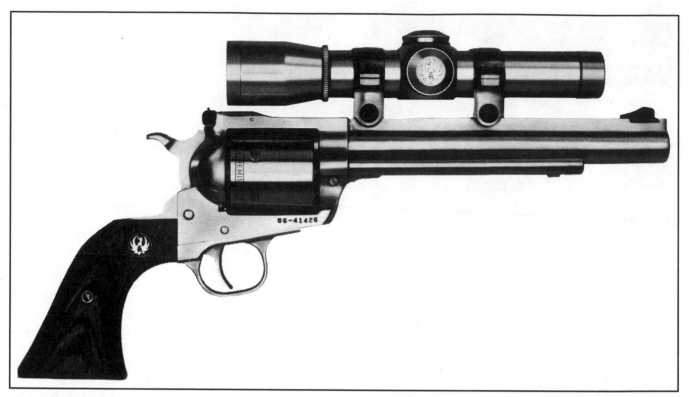

Ruger supplies one-inch scope rings and a mounting rib on its Super Blackhawk Hunter .44 Magnum revolver.

the barrel blanks that are shipped in, it uses a broach on its cast pistol barrels.

The wood shop in Newport is located directly across a driveway from Pine Tree Casting. There Ruger shapes, smooths, hand-checkers and finishes the wood that helps make its rifles and shotguns so attractive. Unlike some makers, Ruger has not substituted less expensive wood for walnut; its synthetic stocks and revolver grips come from vendors.

A machine shop connected to the casting plant includes a heat-treating facility where the metal parts, hardened from the casting process, are annealed for machining. Later, they'll be heat treated if necessary to regain some of that hardness. Even the guns built in Southport are often trucked to the New Hampshire plant for heat treating.

The biggest single building in the Newport complex is a second machine shop containing a huge assembly area, an engineering section, and an office wing. Most of the machining and fitting of Ruger

rifle, shotgun and double-action revolver components takes place here. After assembly, the guns are taken to the in-house firing range for proofing (about four million rounds go down the tunnels each year). Ruger also uses this part of the plant to hold armorer schools for police officers.

While Bill Ruger continues to hunt extensively, he is happiest when designing guns. He has also engineered automobiles and once built a car called the "Ruger Sports Tourer." Although it was never put into production, this automobile, with its 425-horsepower engine and Bentley-inspired body, has drawn high praise from the critics.

Ruger's two sons—William Jr. and James—now assume many of the company's day-to-day responsibilities, but Bill Ruger Sr. continues to work on the development of new guns. He remains the sole 20th century entrepreneur to build a successful enterprise on a scale equal to those created by the great armsmakers of the Civil War era.

CHAPTER 17

BROWN PRECISION & THE SYNTHETIC STOCK

It began with a family trip to Disneyland in the late 1960's, when Chet Brown stopped along the way to visit his old friend, Lee Six, in Fresno, California. They shot a few doves, talked about elk hunting and pondered the fate of benchrest shooters who couldn't seem to keep their rifles in tune. Brown, a relative newcomer to the benchrest game, had been frustrated by the tendency of target rifles to change their point of impact or lose their ability to cut tight groups. This happened often enough in the middle of a match that it scuttled some good scores. Bedding was almost certainly to blame—but how was one to correct it?

The Browns continued on their vacation, stopping once more to see Chet's brother, "C.K.," an aeronautical engineer. C.K. had no experience in bench shooting, but he understood the difficulty of adding strength and stability while paring weight. Chet wanted a lightweight stock without sacrificing accuracy. "Is there any rule your stocks have to be made of wood?" asked C.K. The book had no such rule. "Then why not make a stock of fiberglass? It won't absorb water, and its reaction to temperature change is about like that of steel."

Chet took the idea home and immediately set to work. There were no fiberglass stocks on the market, and no molds to make one, so he hollowed out a Model 722 Remington stock until it was a fragile shell, filled it with polyurethane foam, reshaped it and covered it with fiberglass. Because there was no solid abutment in the action well, Chet sleeved the action with a 12-inch aluminum block and used bedding compound to fit it to the wispy stock. The finished rifle was ugly; and worse, it didn't shoot well.

Subsequently, Chet found at least part of the problem lay with its barrel, and soon he started another stockmaking project. About this time, Lee Six joined him in San Jose. "My first stock mold was a plaster-of-Paris affair that failed miserably," Chet admitted later. He and Lee then decided to make the stock in two pieces that could be glued together to form a hollow shell. "Lee made the first pattern from a piece of redwood taken off the fireplace mantel in my house," Chet recalled. "We experimented with vacuum forming, using a hose hooked to the manifold of my Jeep to provide the suction. After grinding off the flanges of the raw stock halves, we glued them together."

Chet conceded the operation was pretty expensive, but he and his partner learned from their mistakes. For example, when their gun didn't shoot well they tried changing the guard screw tension. "We found that loosening the screws markedly tightened our groups," he reflected. "Tight screws led to double-grouping, a sure sign of bedding problems."

Chet pursued his vision of a practical fiberglass stock with other prototypes, built mostly on the freezer in his garage. Once, while using a cheap spray gun to build a form, he got drenched with a pint of resin when air pressure blew the pot off the gun. Another time he and Lee discovered the combination of vacuum and heat from a dryer had ballooned their fiberglass mold into the shape of a pregnant python.

But problems with molds and materials paled next to the biggest hurdle Chet Brown faced in marketing his new stock. "We had to convince the shooting public of three things: first, that my hollow fiberglass stock would improve accuracy and consistency as long as the barrel was good and the

Chet Brown, founder of Brown Precision, (left), examines a custom rifle with his son, Mark, who succeeded his father as president of the firm.

guard screws loose; second, that the shell, while light and fragile-looking, would take as much abuse as a wood stock; and third, that wood was not a requisite material, but a traditional one.

Convincing the Traditionalists

Brown knew that synthetic stocks would succeed only if he could sell these three ideas. He began with the benchrest crowd, all savvy shooters who gladly put the new stocks to a severe test. If Chet's claims did not prove true, these people would say so, and there'd be no sense in peddling the stocks to hunters. On the other hand, equipment that won the blessings of benchresters needed no apologies. Even if hunters were too tradition-bound to follow suit, a warm welcome on the bench circuit would confirm to Chet that he'd accomplished something worthwhile.

"The first stock order came from Dave Wolfe at Wolfe Publishing in Prescott, Arizona," Chet recalled. "At that time we didn't have a manufacturing facility and hadn't even settled on a pattern; we'd only built a handful of stocks for our own amusement. But I promised Dave I'd build one for him."

Wolfe's rifle, a Remington 40x in .223, arrived shortly. Chet fashioned a sleeve for the action, then stocked and bedded it and painted it robin's-egg blue (because Dave's wife liked that color). After receiving it, Wolfe fired the rifle a couple of times, then refitted it with an A & M .222 barrel. He next took it to the Speer bench match in Midland, Texas,

where he placed seventh out of 67 shooters in the Light Varmint class. A month later, he competed in the Sporter Varmint Nationals and placed second. After that, shooters began thinking seriously about the merits of this new fiberglass stock, not just its startling color.

By 1971, several benchrest competitors were using synthetic stocks. Chet Brown was surprised to see one shooter using a fiberglass stock with a wooden receiver block. He'd been using this design since 1967 himself, but hadn't promoted it because he didn't think it had a future. With most shooters now thinking of Chet Brown first when they thought of fiberglass, the business grew steadily. Even the most stubborn diehards were eventually won over by the mounting evidence in favor of synthetic stocks. One man, who once vowed he'd never switch, drilled out a NBRSA Light Varmint record in 1975 using one of Chet Brown's stocks.

The early 1970's were hectic for Chet, who continued to operate out of his garage until 1979. A magazine article or two and the display of a Brown stock (painted Chinese red) at an NRA show helped the young firm gain national publicity. As more bench shooters put fiberglass on their guns, more matches were won with them, giving Brown an additional boost. Bill Summers won the 1972 California state title with a Brown-stocked 40x in .222. And Chet, still a competitor, won the Sporter class that year with a 6×47. In 1973 and 1974, Perry Morton won the three-gun Nationals using Brown's

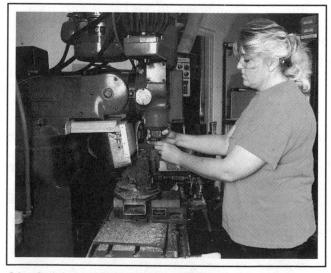

A technician sets up the automated milling machine (above) for inletting Brown Precision stocks. About 750 stocks are completed each month.

fiberglass stocks. Meanwhile, other shooters started building their own synthetic stocks, until by the mid-1970's wood stocks on benchrest guns were fast becoming obsolete.

Fiberglass Glue and Sporting Guns

Chet Brown's success with competition rifles did not derail his interest in marketing fiberglass to sportsmen as well. In 1972, he and Lee Six stocked their own hunting rifles—a .308 Remington 788 and a 7mm Magnum Winchester 70. That year, they both shot elk in Wyoming, and the following season used the same guns on moose in British Columbia. Since then Chet, an ardent hunter, has taken a great variety of big game with his synthetic-stocked rifles.

By the time Brown Precision was incorporated in 1976, competition in the business had grown. Three years earlier, Gale McMillan had come up with a stock that would take either a sleeved or unsleeved action. His brother Pat used it to shoot a .009-inch group that still stands as a world record. In 1975, Orlin Gilkerson developed a sleeve-action stock of polyester resin and fiberglass cloth over an all-foam core. His method required pillar bedding or a glue job to wed stock to action. Chet had already experimented with glued-in rifles and, while conceding that glueing was an easy way to bed and allowed the use of lighter stocks, he maintained that glue did not guarantee a more accurate rifle.

Following Brown's lead, other companies began to supply sportsmen with synthetic stocks. Light in weight, and both stable and durable, the synthetic stock had a practical edge over the admittedly more attractive wood. Some firms now offer wood-grain synthetic stocks that resemble high-grade walnut.

After Chet Brown and Lee Six split up in 1977, Chet decided to leave the Bay area and moved Brown Precision 200 miles north to Los Molinos, California. A second building was added in 1986 to house the main production facilities, which now turn out 750 stocks a month. When Chet Brown retired in January, 1991, he was succeeded as company president by his son Mark. Chet continues to promote the business, attending a dozen trade shows a year and hunting big game as avidly as ever. The biggest share of Brown Precision's business now comes from hunters, many of whom would have laughed at the idea of synthetic stocks a decade ago.

Most of Brown's stocks go out as blanks to gunsmiths, gun dealers and individuals who want to finish the stock work themselves. But some large orders have come from firearms manufacturers, who use them on cataloged guns. In recent years, all major armsmakers have added synthetic-stocked rifles to their long gun lists. Because it is more cost-efficient to buy these stocks from specialty houses, Brown Precision and its competitors have benefitted. Sportsmen who would not consider stocking their own rifle, or sending it away to be fitted with an after-market product, have responded enthusiastically to synthetic stocks on factory-built rifles.

From Components to Custom-Built Rifles

About 500 stocks a year go to Brown's custom shop, housed in the first Los Molinos building. There company gunsmiths put together special-purpose rifles for military and police units, and assemble rifles for hunters and target shooters who ask Brown to do their stock work. A typical custom gun has a Remington 700 action and a match-grade, stainless steel barrel. Chet Brown likes the 700 because it has proven accuracy potential, is inexpensive and easy to work with and comes with a fine trigger. The stainless barrels, he feels, shoot better

A Brown Precision worker finishes the inletting prior to bedding a custom rifle.

cold than chrome-molybdenum barrels, which must often be warmed up before they group well. He also likes Zeiss and Swarovski 4x scopes—especially those with 30mm tubes, because "the lightgathering capabilities are far superior to standard 1-inch tubes." According to Brown Precision, the scope should be in Conetrol rings (if there's no need for quick removal), or in Weaver rings (if quick removal is needed). Brown rifles come with the metal finished in the buyer's choice of electroless nickel or Teflon, which Chet Brown declares are much more practical on hunting guns than is the standard blued-steel finish.

Brown Precision will build a rifle to a customer's specifications and chamber it for almost any cartridge, wildcats included. The most popular hunting rounds, according to Mark Brown, are Winchester's .270 and the 7mm Remington and .375 H&H Magnums, all of which Brown recommends to uncommited customers. One of Chet Brown's favorite cartridges is the .416 Hoffman, which he has used extensively in a rifle the company calls its "Pro-Hunter." This model features a barrel-band forward swivel, iron sights and big-bore chamberings. A trimmer "High Country" series, with stock-mounted forward swivel and no sights, is more appropriate for most big game hunting. Brown redrills the receivers on its rifles to accept 8-40 screws—a great improvement over the traditional 6-48 scope mount screws. The firm also sells and installs KDF Recoil Arrestors and offers a barrel cap to protect the threads when the recoil device is removed.

A computer-operated drill inlets the trigger guardwell of a fiberglass stock.

Superior Products for the Perfectionist

As for prices, Mark Brown notes that serious hunters aren't as concerned with cost as with performance, and that modern sportsmen are "looking for top quality items they can trust." He and his father have apparently read the market correctly, because since 1975 annual company growth has stayed above 20 percent. That doesn't make the Browns feel complacent, however. They're still looking for ways to improve their products. When Kevlar came on the market, Brown Precision was among the first companies to fashion stocks from it. Though it is more expensive and harder to machine, Kevlar significantly reduces stock weight. Brown Precision's "Pound'r" classic-style hunting stock weighs about a pound, or six ounces less than a stock of the same design made of fiberglass. All told, Brown now offers 12 configurations of rifle stocks to meet the needs of hunters, benchrest shooters, and biathlon, high-power and silhouette competitors. Four more are made to fit the Remington XP-100 and Thompson/Center single-shot pistols, plus enough others to fit 35 different models of hunting and target guns—and more to come.

According to Mark Brown, "drop-in" stocks, those that require almost no fitting, represent a new market. These allow a hunter to buy an after-market synthetic stock for his factory rifle and install it with a screwdriver. Brown contends, however, that truly good bedding results only when an action is individually mated to its stock, a view shared by most experienced shooters. To accommodate hunt-

Brown Precision's chief machinist is shown here chambering a custom rifle.

ers with the urge to switch, Brown has developed "Custom Pre-Finish" and "Premium Pre-Finish" stocks. These require glass bedding but no routing or exterior finishing. Swivel studs and buttpad come installed. The Custom Pre-Finish stock has standard dimensions and a dark gray color. With the Premium option dimensions, color and even the butt pad must be specified. Brown Precision offers an assortment of fittings and finishes for do-it-yourself stockmakers.

Among the many stock-making firms that are following Chet Brown's pioneer path are McMillan, Clifton, Bell & Carlson and others. They all build good stocks because the technology is available to do so, and there's a strong market to absorb them. When Chet Brown started molding stocks in his garage, he had no examples to follow and no buyers to ensure his success. Not only did he develop practical fiberglass stocks, he built the market for them. He did the hard work the hard way, promoting a product he believed in and, in only two decades, turning the shooting world to his way of thinking.

It may be argued that Brown Precision doesn't belong in a book on American armsmakers. After all, the company does not manufacture gun mechanisms; it only provides parts and assembles custom rifles. But Brown synthetic stocks have strongly influenced the way guns are built in America. They were the first products of an industry that has grown to include many big companies servicing all major gun manufacturers. They helped draft a chapter in the history of armsmaking, and for that alone Brown Precision has earned its way into the pages of this book.

CHAPTER 18

WICHITA ARMS: PRODUCTS FOR SERIOUS SHOOTERS

Upon first hearing the name, Wichita Arms, one might think of a trail drivers' stop where single-action revolvers were once sold to cowboys. Wichita is no longer a cow town; its ribald past is now buried beneath the concrete of investment firms, aircraft plants, and suburban thoroughfares. The people who visit Wichita Arms today reflect the same air of sophistication. This small company, now 20 years old, is in the business of building high-precision rifles and pistols. As such, it caters to shooters who demand more accuracy than is available from production-line guns made by bigger firms. Many Wichita customers compete in benchrest and metallic silhouette matches; most are dedicated handloaders who do a lot of shooting.

The company was founded by Nolan Jackson, a shooter who once made parts for small aircraft—mostly Cessna—at his father's business, Wichita Engineering and Supply. The firm expanded in 1972 to manufacture gun components, such as Champlin's rifle actions. Champlin didn't market a short action, however, and Jackson's 25 years of bench shooting told him serious shooters would buy one. He decided to make a rifle that was accurate enough for competition but suitable for hunting. It would cost a lot to build, especially in small quantities, but Jackson was confident shooters would pay the extra cost.

He was right. The first Wichita actions, which were milled from bar stock, came in three weights and two lengths. They could be ordered round or octagonal in cross-section, with or without a magazine. A long stainless-steel action was also listed. Complete rifles wore stocks by Fajen and barrels were made by Wichita. Soon Jackson started buying barrels from Douglas and Hart, dedicating his shop to building actions only.

Better-Built Bolt Rifles and Pistols

Current Wichita actions look like those from the early '70s, though Jackson recently changed the bolt head design to accommodate shooters who requested coned breeches. The angled breech face smooths the feeding of .222-size rounds, which start below the bolt axis and must then jump into the bore. Wichita has not made an action specifically for the .222 group of cartridges; and in 1988 it discontinued its .30-06-length receiver, including the stainless-steel version. At one time, the firm chambered this long action for belted magnums up to the .300 Winchester in length.

Wichita now builds rifles only for .308-class cartridges, with the ejection ports admitting cartridges up to 2.80 inches long. Magazines have been discontinued too, as most Wichita customers put little stock in firepower. Stiffer, solid-bottom receivers enhance accuracy—and Wichita customers do care about accuracy! Standard receiver diameter is 1.375 inches, though a lighter model (1.200 inches in cross-section) is available. (The long action hunting rifle abandoned two years ago had a receiver measuring 1.250 inches in diameter.) Bolts are the same size. While right- and left-hand versions are still offered, the "right-hand-left-port" and "left-hand-right-port" options that were once available have been discontinued.

Wichita actions are favorites among bench shooters who appreciate their Canjar triggers, match-grade barrels and tight manufacturing tolerances. Prices start at about $475 for the right-hand action, with a complete Wichita rifle retailing for $2,200. Any reasonable chambering can be arranged. All rifles are manufactured from chrome-moly steel, but the actions are still machined from tomer there. The buyer shot it, then sent it back to Kansas, claiming it was inaccurate. Jackson benched the rifle and drilled out a one-minute group. "I didn't have a Wichita magnum sporter," he says dryly. "I figured I ought to, even if it wore German proofs." He kept the gun.

In 1978, Wichita Arms introduced its first pistol: a single-shot designed for the infant sport of handgun silhouette. Jackson used one of these guns in 1980 to topple all 120 targets at a match—the first time that had ever been done. Made with a left-hand bolt-throw for right-handed shooters, the chrome-moly "Silhouette" pistol has a hefty $7/8$-inch diameter bolt, comes with a $14\frac{7}{8}$-inch barrel, and can be ordered for any popular .308-length cartridge. A trimmer, more ornate version is the Wichita "Classic" pistol, with a $3/4$-inch bolt. It features an engraved octagon barrel and receiver, checkered bolt knob, and fancy walnut.

Silhouette Single-Shot and Accessories

To meet the needs of silhouette shooters, Jackson developed another pistol in 1982—the break-action Wichita "International." Wonderfully simple in design, it has half the working parts of Thompson/Center's popular Contender. The International was initially chambered in .357 Magnum, .357 Maximum, .30-30 WCF and 7R (on the .30-30 case). The .30 Waters and .32 H&R were added later, as were the .22 Long Rifle and .22 WMR. Barrel lengths are 10 and 14 inches. The International is available only in stainless steel. Its grips are the same as those of the 1911 Colt .45 autoloader, which Nolan Jackson considers among the most comfortable ever designed. The Wichita grips are, in fact, interchangeable with the Colt's.

Jackson recalls that the pistol was an instant success, causing production capacity to lag behind demand. The firm's sophisticated four-axis CNC machine proved a bottleneck, so Wichita added a

Nolan Jackson poses with one of Wichita's prestigious Classic Silhouette pistols.

bar stock. But Jackson isn't afraid to try new things. Wichita was one of the first companies to use bead-blasting on gun metal. "We didn't pull the industry in that direction," Jackson points out. "It just happened that way."

The company must still accommodate shooters with their own ideas. One long-action hunting rifle made in Wichita went to Germany, where it was given the necessary markings for transfer to a cus-

Wichita Arms' hand-crafted varmint rifle entices serious shooters with its accuracy.

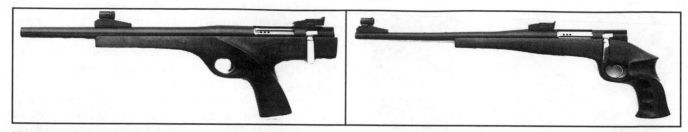

Wichita's silhouette pistol weighs 4½ pounds and comes in .308, 7mm IHMSA, and 7 × .308. It's available with center grip (above, left) and rear grip (above, right) stocks. Both feature glass bedding.

second CNC. Both machines occasionally run three shifts to keep pace with brisk orders for guns, many of which are sent overseas.

Wichita Arms makes gun accessories, too, primarily sights and recoil compensators for handguns. Its 70/80 series sight for the M1911 Colt is fully adjustable, but it crouches so low on the slide that any issue front blade can be used. The sight won't interfere with firing-pin safeties. Jackson says the company's goal is to find a vacant market niche and fill it, but not to compete with bigger firms. "Our low-profile sight for the .45 ACP resulted from stalled negotiations with Colt," Jackson says. "They'd approached us about the manufacture of a new sight, but we couldn't come to terms. Eventually we marketed our own product."

Wichita's "Insta-Comp" recoil reducer was also built for the M1911. Easily installed and removed, it replaces the recoil bushing and does not require barrel work (most such devices must be fitted to the barrel). "Slab Comp" is a similar device that attaches with a screw to the face of the ejector housing on full-lug Smith & Wesson revolvers. "It works on all the long-lug Smiths," says Jackson. "We've found only two sizes of barrels for all cal-

The Wichita International (above) is a single-shot, top-break pistol made for serious silhouette shooters. Its grips are interchangeable with those of the Colt 1911 autoloader.

ibers. The tops are machined, but the outside diameters appear to be the same diameter as forged. Once in a while we find one with different dimensions. Then we make our Slab Comp fit it."

Although Wichita does not specialize in gunsmithing, it remains a customer-conscious firm. "Our products are for serious shooters," explains Jackson. "Consequently, we offer many options. We're not a custom shop, but we take a lot of special requests." At one time, a custom stock-making shop was in the plans at Wichita, but Jackson backed off. The firm still repairs gun stocks but uses Fajen wood on its rifles and handguns.

Nolan Jackson is concerned about the future of the shooting sports. "We (shooters) haven't marketed ourselves well," he maintains. "Consequently, the public perception of shooting is neither favorable nor accurate. But public attitudes can be changed. We must convince people shooting is a safe sport. We have to show them that hunting and competitive shooting have a place in modern society. People who don't shoot must be taught that the misuse of guns by crooks and incompetents won't be corrected by denying firearms to responsible shooters."

Jackson is nonetheless optimistic that shooting—especially "fun games"—will survive. In fact, he sees a renewed interest in metallic silhouette. It has been 27 years since Jackson set a world record in the heavy varmint category with an aggregate (10 five-shot groups) of .319 inch, using a Hart-barreled Schultz and Larsen in .222½. "That wouldn't win anything now," he concedes, "but it was pretty good for its day."

At Wichita Arms, Nolan Jackson and 11 dedicated employees keep busy helping other marksmen shoot pretty good groups. Not only has the company established a good business, it has contributed to the shooting industry by pioneering better designs and products. If one looks deep enough, one can still see in this independent armsmaker the spirit of a young, vigorous cow town.

CHAPTER 19

DAKOTA: REDEFINING THE RIFLEMAN'S RIFLE

By December, 1936, Winchester Repeating Arms Company had assembled the first commercial copies of what would become its most famous modern rifle: Model 70. Combining the best features of America's Springfield and Germany's 98 Mauser service guns, Winchester's popular rifle was chambered not only for the popular .30-06, but for nine other cartridges. Only two—the .250 Savage and 7 × 57 Mauser—predated the first world war. The others were new rounds, designed for, and performing best in, strong bolt rifles.

Model 70 thus became the launching pad of choice for the .257 Roberts and .220 Swift, announced in 1934 and 1935. It was, with the retirement of its predecessor, the Winchester 54, heir to the hugely successful .270; and for hunters after the biggest game, its magnum-length action swallowed the .375 Holland & Holland and its offspring, the .300 H&H. Model 70 became the consummate centerfire rifle—"the rifleman's rifle"—having arrived just as several new and potent centerfire cartridges were looking for a home. Its practical design, handsome appearance and great durability promised to endear this Winchester to hunters for the next quarter century.

While the original Model 70 retailed for $61.25, its price soon went up as new chamberings and configurations were added. By the late 1950's, some of the Model 70's glitter had dulled. To keep the gun profitable yet affordable, Winchester looked for ways to cut production costs. Already the rifle's "cloverleaf" tang had been replaced by a spatulate extension covering the true tang. With the wood-to-metal fit hidden, tang inletting could be done much more quickly. Checkering was changed from

20 to 18 lines per inch in the 1940's, and in the late '50s the pattern size was reduced to accommodate the demands of a new checkering machine. Wood quality deteriorated through the years, and in 1959 hard rubber buttplates replaced the graceful checkered steel plates. Metal on the late guns was finished to a lesser degree as well.

The blow that really staggered the Winchester faithful, however, came in 1964 with the introduction of a new Model 70. Its basic shape was the same, but major concessions were made at the behest of company accountants. The expensive Mauser extractor was replaced by a small spring-loaded hook, and coil springs were supplanted by music wire. The stock was no longer checkered; instead, a brutish machine had left a dark, ugly scar. Winchester hoped its customers would accept this as checkering, but they did not. In fact, they rejected the gun entirely. So strong was their resistance that company engineers immediately started changing it. But there was only so much they could do—the great "pre-64 Model 70" was, alas, beyond resurrection. "It would be prohibitively expensive to build now," lamented Winchester. Meanwhile, as shooters sulked, prices for the early 70's shot through the ceiling.

That was three decades ago. Winchester's current Model 70 is comely indeed, with many of the features cherished by fans of the first Model 70's. It is competitively priced, if not cheap, and must still be considered one of the finest hunting rifles available. But purists can be finicky. To them, it doesn't matter that the new rifles work; they still aren't like the old rifles. And so early Model 70's continue to bring premium prices from collectors and hunters, as well as from gunsmiths who transfer the actions to the fine custom rifles they peddle to affluent gun fanciers.

The "Dakota 76"—an Improvement on the Original

Among the traditionalists who mourned the passing of Winchester's original Model 70 was Don Allen, a stockmaker in Northfield, Minnesota. A commercial airline pilot by profession, Don had grown up in Colorado and later flew combat missions in Vietnam. Subsequently, he and his family moved to Minnesota, close by the Minneapolis hub of Northwest Airlines. There Don's early interest in guns became a compelling hobby, leading him to build custom stocks. Soon he'd established enough ties to walnut suppliers to become a wood broker for other gunsmiths. Finally, in 1977, five years after his first commercial stock job, Don and his wife Norma incorporated their business. There Allen, an engineer as well as an artist, designed his own stock

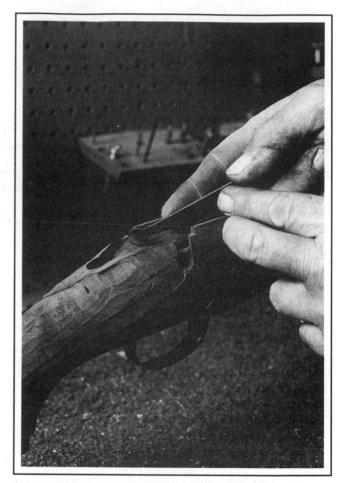

Here a Dakota technician shows his skill at inletting, the precise fitting of metal to wood.

Don Allen displays a walnut stock blank individually selected to a customer's specifications.

duplicating machine, along with the tooling to make it. This, combined with a heavy work load in the custom shop, kept him busy whenever he wasn't flying. All the while, he nursed along the idea that a limited but solid market existed for a rifle like the pre-1964 Model 70—a well-built rifle that would be priced right and at the same time please the most discriminating big game hunter.

By the early 1980's, Don's idea for a classic-style hunting rifle had become an all-consuming goal. Producing one in Minnesota, however, seemed untenable. "The business climate there was not good for us," Norma Allen explained, hinting that gunmaking had less appeal to some locals than did other industries. So the Allens moved to Sturgis, South Dakota, and there, in 1984, they founded Dakota Arms. Two years later, Don was joined by Pete Grisel, a crack metalsmith from Oregon who'd already made and marketed his own Mauser-type actions. The two men collaborated on a redesign of Winchester's Model 70, calling it the "Dakota Model 76."

The Dakota action had several refinements lacking in the old Model 70. Its trigger, safety and extractor were similar, but a Mauser-style breeching had replaced the Model 70's coned breech. This design provided a more effective block for escaping powder gases in the event of a ruptured case. A clever side-swing bolt stop and one-piece triggerguard assembly also distinguished the Dakota rifle, as did a sculptured tang with a blind guard screw hole. Left-handed Model 70's are a rarity, but a southpaw shooter can easily find a Dakota with a left-hand bolt at the standard price.

The first Dakotas retailed for $1750, perhaps four times the cost of a new Model 70. But Don Allen's shop didn't spew out rifles like so many bottles of pop. Getting things right—surpassing the fit, finish and overall quality of early Model 70 Winchesters—took time. And time, as everyone knows, is

money. Each Dakota rifle featured stock wood and checkering rivaling that found in many custom guns costing two or three times as much.

"We wanted to delight shooters who missed the Model 70," Allen pointed out. "We offered classic, elegant styling, top-drawer workmanship and first-rate materials at a sensible price. We're not competing with big armsmakers and retailers. We sell to a clearly defined group of people. We must be doing it right, too, because our business is growing. We're now shipping 700 to 800 guns a year."

The .416 Rigby: Positioned for the 1990's

The Model 76, a production-line gun with the features and finish of a custom rifle, is offered in four action lengths: short, standard (short magnum), long magnum, and ".416 Rigby." The Rigby action is ½-inch longer than that for the .375 and other long magnums. It is wider, too, so as to digest the fat, rimless Rigby cases.

A Dakota worker adjusts the controls on a sophisticated milling machine before inletting the bottom metal on a Dakota 76 rifle.

Dakota Arms will chamber a client's rifle for almost any factory-listed round. "We don't like to fool with wildcats," Allen declares. "Liability is on everyone's mind now, and we're no exception." The company lists 25 chamberings as standard, with the most popular being the .270 and .375—that is, until the advent of the .416 Rigby.

Barrels for Dakota's 76, with a standard length of 23 inches, come from Shilen and Douglas. "We also make a lightweight 'Alpine' rifle with a 21-inch barrel," Allen explains. "This short-action gun has a blind magazine, an extra-trim stock, and weighs only 6½ pounds."

A customer can special-order a barrel of any reasonable length for his Dakota. In fact, many of the standard features on this rifle can be tailored to suit the buyer. "Try asking Winchester to substitute Bastogne for Claro, or add a quarter-rib or forend tip, or change the checkering pattern," declares Don. "We do it all at Dakota."

The Dakota Model 76 hasn't changed a great deal since its introduction in 1986, and Don admits his company is conservative. "Just like the rifles," he points out. "We didn't set out to design a new gun; rather, we wanted to refine the Model 70, make it better than Winchester could ever afford to, then offer it to people who know about rifles and are willing to spend a little more for a superior product."

The only other rifle to emerge from Allen's shop is a dropping-block single-shot that resembles an artfully trimmed Ruger Number One. Weighing only 6 pounds with a 23-inch barrel, it comes in most standard chamberings (rimmed and rimless) and

Each walnut stock at Dakota receives a hand-rubbed oil finish.

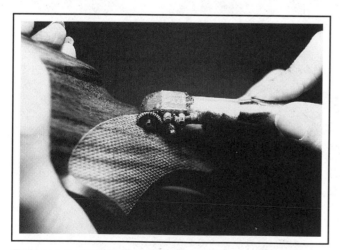

Dakota stocks are checkered by hand, making them look more like custom stocks than those turned out by an arms company.

sells for around $2000. Actions and barreled actions are available. Allen has also designed a top-grade .22 rimfire to replace—and outshine—Winchester's legendary Model 52 Sporter, which costs too much, according to Don, for those who are most interested in using it. "We'd like to provide a rimfire rifle anyone would be proud to claim as a hunting rifle," he explains. "Most .22's that are meant to be used are turned out like cookies. They may work, but so do production-grade centerfires. Some shooters want better quality."

An amateur ballistician, Don has been working on at least two new cartridges for his Dakota 76. They are based on the .404 Jeffery, a rimless British round slightly larger at the head than a belted magnum. Allen's shop has developed a .416 (which is essentially a .404 necked up) and a .330 Dakota necked to .338. The latter holds 15 grains more powder than the .338 Winchester and should match the .340 Weatherby in performance.

Dakota Arms also offers components to the gunsmithing trade and any customer who wants someone to build a custom gun. From actions to sling swivel studs and stock blanks, Allen can supply it. He even offers guard assemblies for Winchester, Remington and Mauser rifles.

Don Allen remains owner and president of Dakota Arms, which now includes 12 machinists, eight polishers, four stockmakers and three checkerers. The company's stock duplicator is also manufactured at the 21,000-square-foot facility in Sturgis. "We're also among the largest importers and exporters of high-quality stock wood," Allen states proudly. "We sold blanks to Browning when it was building guns in Liege (Belgium). We've supplied Winchester and Remington, too. And a few Ruger .416's wear our walnut, which we import from Turkey, France, Morocco, Australia and New Zealand. Hard, highly-figured walnut is becoming scarce, so our job is getting tougher. Of course, the rising prices reflect that, but we've not seen a significant dip in demand."

Between transcontinental trips for walnut, the establishment of a gunmaking plant, and Don's commercial flight obligations, the Allens' family life has been hectic at times. Fortunately, their married daughter lives close by; and their son flies F16's from a distant Air Force base.

Dakota Arms owes part of its success to

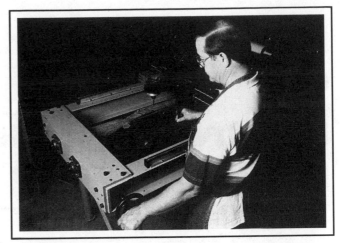

Don Allen works on his 5-Axis precision duplicating machine.

Winchester for conceiving its Model 70, and another part to that same company for eviscerating the gun in 1964. But Dakota's success derives mostly from vision and hard work, the kind of stuff that gritty American frontiersmen needed to plant themselves in a new land. No doubt those frontiersmen, who depended so heavily on their rifles, would have appreciated the high quality and uncompromising attention to fit and function that characterize a modern Dakota rifle.

CHAPTER 20

KENNY JARRETT: SIMPLY, RIFLES THAT HIT

It's hard to tell how old he is, because the full red beard and brawny build disguise his years. He may be 40, but what is certain about James Kenneth Jarrett is that he builds what some shooters claim are the most accurate rifles in the world.

A fourth-generation farmer from Jackson, South Carolina, Jarrett grew up on his Uncle J.M. Brown's 10,000-acre Cowden Plantation. There he hunted whitetails and started tinkering with rifles, discovering in a hurry that most of them weren't accurate enough for the long shooting he liked to do across the broad soybean fields. What he wanted was a hunting rifle that would keep all its bullets in a tennis ball—which is about the same size as a crow's chest—at 300 yards. To guarantee hits at that distance, a rifle would have to shoot into about $3/4$-inch at 100.

After high school, Jarrett worked full time for his uncle before opening his own gunshop in the late 1970's. "It was a part-time job for me at the time," he explains. "I didn't know how to build rifles, mind you. I just bought a lathe and went to work, figuring I could do as well as anybody and might just come up with an accurate rifle."

Jarrett's concept of accuracy had already been molded by a few trips to benchrest matches, where group sizes were smaller than any he'd ever seen from a hunting rifle. Building a rifle that consistently shot competitive groups, he found, proved frustrating. Things turned around, though, when Jarrett accepted an invitation by Texas gunmaker Harold Broughton to see how it was done. After a time at Broughton's shop, Jarrett returned to South Carolina. He still credits Broughton for a substantial part of his training. "Hal was a bench shooter and knew what he wanted. He knew how to build accurate rifles. I came back with my head crammed full of ideas."

A gunmaker needed barrels, so Jarrett next visited Jerry Hart, whose barrels had built a good reputation on the target range. Soon he was "accurizing" bench guns and hunting rifles—and liking it. In 1979, Jarrett gave up farming completely, managing to gross $17,000 in his first year in the gun business. Despite Ken's country-boy image, he was sharp enough in business to have realized early on that not many people shot benchrest matches, and those who did would probably be using the same gun for a long time. He wanted to build guns, not just tune and repair them. The big market, he concluded, lay with hunters, whom Jarrett thought were poorly served by the major arms companies. "If you shoot close up and just want meat," he observed, "you can get by with two-minute accuracy. But I figured I wasn't the only deer hunter who shot across beanfields and wanted to hit right where I aimed, not just nearby."

Accuracy is More Important Than Price

The hitch was that hunters might not be willing to pay for the kind of superior rifle Jarrett had in mind building. Benchrest shooters were accustomed to the premiums charged for topflight materials and workmanship. After all, they needed the best gun to be competitive; but a hunter didn't need the best gun to kill a deer. Lots of people told Kenny Jarrett that, until he decided to prove them wrong.

From a one-man operation in 1979, the Jarrett Rifles company grew to 13 people, with gross sales reaching $520,000 (1990). The original 2,200-square-foot shop, built of cypress lumber sawn on the farm and roofed with cedar shakes, has had

The modest front of this cedar-boarded shop in Aiken County, South Carolina, belies its 6,000-square-foot interior filled with sophisticated machinery.

four additions put on. The facility, which comprises 6,000 square feet, houses five lathes and a full complement of milling machines, surface grinders, belt sanders and other necessary paraphernalia.

To be sure, Kenny Jarrett's rifles aren't for everyone. His least expensive model, the Standard Hunter, sold for $2850 in 1991, while the Ultimate Hunter, which offers more options, listed at $3495. A Jarrett rifle can be built on almost any bolt action, but unless specified otherwise buyers will get a Remington 700 or, if the cartridge chosen has an extra large body, Weatherby's Mark V. After first truing the lugs by surface grinding and hand fitting, Jarrett chases the action threads, so that the barrel will screw in perfectly straight.

Hart barrels are supplied in calibers .30 and under; for bigger bores, Jarrett will fit a Schneider to the buyer's action. Currently, the company lists 68 different reamers in its inventory, including wildcat rounds, which are specified by 70 percent of Jarrett's customers. Ken has developed several wildcats himself, including the .220 Jaybird (a fast varmint round) and the .338 Kubla-Kahn (a blown-out .378 Weatherby case necked to .338). The Kubla-Kahn swallows 100 grains of powder and reportedly launches a 250-grain bullet at 3385 fps.

The most popular wildcat is really an "improved" cartridge—the .280 Ackley Improved, made by blowing out the shoulder on a .280 Remington case. Ballistically, this round nearly matches the 7mm Remington Magnum. Jarrett's choice of a factory cartridge is Winchester's .300 Magnum, which, predictably, is a best-seller in the commercial category. "We've supplied 75 chamberings so far," Jarrett confirms, "from the .17 Remington to the .50 Belted Machine Gun. You get your choice of barrel length, weight and taper, and rate of twist. We'll cheerfully tell you what we think works best."

Since Jarrett prefers stainless steel barrels, these come standard on all his rifles. Buyers can choose a polished or bead-blasted surface finish for both barrel and receiver. Receivers are usually blued, but the company also offers electroless nickel plating, NP3 nickel-Teflon and a black matte finish. These work on stainless barrels too; standard bluing doesn't.

The company has added versatility to its rifles with what it calls a "switch-barrel" system. This feature can be specified for any Jarrett rifle with a

Kenny Jarrett, shown here at work in his shop, confesses he didn't know how to build a rifle in the beginning—he just bought a lathe and went to work.

Because wood "walks," thereby compromising accuracy, Jarrett uses synthetic stocks. Here he inspects a batch of rifle stocks provided by McMillan.

Remington action; buyers can then select barrels in different chamberings to augment whatever ones are installed on their guns. A simple wrench and five minutes at the bench are enough to change barrels, as long as the two rounds have the same head dimensions and thus fit the same bolt face.

Little Groups and How They Got That Way

Jarrett lists only synthetic stocks, because wood "walks" as moisture and temperature fluctuate, changing pressure against the barrel and action and compromising a rifle's accuracy. McMillan provides the stocks in several styles and finishes for almost all of Jarrett's rifles. The company drew up its own design for the Ultimate Hunter stock, however. It has a classic form with straight comb and understated cheekpiece, with fine molded checkering.

Proper bedding is a requisite for top accuracy, and Jarrett gunsmiths use the same methods and care for hunting rifles—which comprise 85 percent of their business—as they do for target guns. That means using pillars around the guard screws to control the degree and isolate the placement of pressure on the action. Then they adjust the Remington trigger down to a crisp two pounds (or, if one prefers, install a Shilen or Jewell trigger).

The next step is to develop a load that meets Jarrett's accuracy standards. And the standards are tough—three-shot groups of 1/2 inch or less from rifles of 25 caliber or smaller; and 3/4-inch groups for rifles with bigger bores. Jarrett and his chief stockmaker, John Lewis, have developed accurate

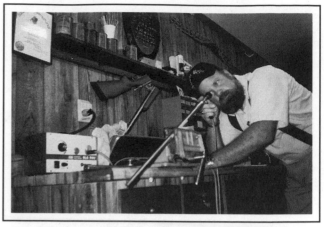

A Jarrett-made rifle must shoot within stringent specifications: ½-inch three-shot groups for rifles through 25 caliber, and ¾-inch for rifles of bigger bore; otherwise they are pulled apart and each component is carefully examined, as Jarrett demonstrates here.

loads for every cartridge they offer; and if a rifle won't shoot well with one of several good loads, it's taken apart and rebuilt. "I've scrapped as many as three barrels on one rifle," Jarrett recalls, "and I've even had to discard actions. That's expensive for me, but the customer is paying a lot for a rifle that shoots better than other rifles, so it's my job to give him one."

This fanatical dedication to accuracy has charmed serious shooters who've been disappointed by the mediocre performance of factory rifles. And yet, despite some excellent publicity in such leading magazines as *Field & Stream, Outdoor Life* and *Sports Afield,* not every shooter knows about Jarrett guns. Because rifles don't wear out quickly, Jarrett is understandably eager to lure new customers. His mailing list now contains more than 5,000 names, and he's working to add more.

Who buys a Jarrett rifle? "Most of our customers are well-read and reasonably well off," Ken Jarrett comments. "In fact, some are very well off. One fellow has bought $46,000 worth of rifles here. But we don't just cater to the wealthy. I know a local youngster who saved his summer hay money for three years to buy a Jarrett rifle. I threw in a Leupold variable scope on that deal."

Leupolds and Schmidt & Benders are the scopes of choice in Jarrett's part of the country. He approves of few other brands. A new rifle, called the "Professional Hunter" and chambered for big-bore cartridges, made its debut in 1991. The package included two Leupold 1.5-5x scopes (both zeroed),

Bench shooters know that clean rifles shoot better. Here Jarrett inspects a gun with a black matte finish that works on either chrome-moly or stainless barrels. Electroless nickel and NP3 nickel-Teflon finishes are also used.

plus a quarter rib with express sights. This gun, built on a Super Grade Winchester Model 70 action and stocked in classic Griffin & Howe style, is, according to Jarrett, "the last word" in African rifles. It comes with 60 rounds each of custom-tailored soft-nose and solid ammunition.

His firm's steady growth has helped Jarrett forget about the seasonal ebb and flow of orders, which have always made scheduling difficult. But there are still plenty of things to troubleshoot. The staff is a constant concern—not because they aren't good at what they do; rather, it's because they are almost too good. Jarrett keeps all new hires on trial for 30 days to make sure they'll fit in with the group. Skills are important, but so is ambition and a willingness to work with other members of the crew. The people who work in his shop, all of them trained by Jarrett, are young. They spend their off-hours together and cook one meal in the shop each week as a "community event."

Lots of Options; One Ambition

"Most of my people probably wouldn't do well in a big firm." observes Jarrett, "and neither would I. Some folks have said I'd make lots more money if I moved to a large city. They say I could boost my production and retire in a few years. They're wrong. You can only make accurate rifles the way we're making them—slowly, with great care. We use the best of modern machinery and we all work hard to build 125 rifles a year. To double production, I'd have to double my staff and the size of my shop, no matter where I lived. That would be ex-

Kenny Jarrett has a benchrest shooter's uncompromising attitude, and a range (above) that lets him test each rifle thoroughly.

pensive. Besides, I'm not in this business for the money. I like being independent. I like to shoot. My best times have been when I drilled out (six) world-record groups with guns that I'd made. My goal in life is to be the man that builds the most accurate rifles that you can buy anywhere in the world, for any amount of money."

More than 1,000 Jarrett rifles have now been sold to sportsmen who don't mind paying a surcharge for accuracy. Ken's future plans include marketing gun parts and tools to shooters who care enough about small groups to work for them. The company already offers scopes, cleaning supplies, ammunition, loading tools and specialty items ranging from T-shirts to muzzle brakes to barrel vises. It also lists a shotgun (on a Remington 870 action) and can fix up a customer with just about any handgun worth having. The company now offers action and barrel work on single- and double-action revolvers, Colt 1911 autoloaders, and single-shot pistols like the Remington XP-100. Jarrett lists "competition packages" for the Colt, which include the following: Caspian slide and frame; Clark barrel with compensator; BoMar sights; Brown grip safety; Swenson ambidextrous thumb safety; Ahrends exotic wood grips; Smith and Alexander mainspring housing and magazine funnel; full-length recoil spring guide; McCormick trigger and hammer; lowered and fluted ejection port; extended magazine release; two fitted magazines; checkered front strap and trigger guard; and matte-black or chrome finish. The price for all this in 1991 came to $2195.

Jarrett also tantalizes pistol shooters with his

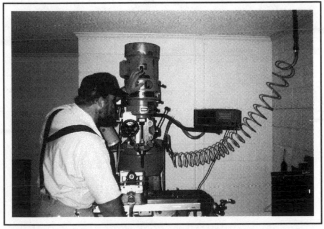

Jarrett insists that precise machining, as evidenced by this photo, is essential to building accurate rifles. His rifles are expensive because they are made with great care and are guaranteed to shoot well.

"Ultimate Redhawk" package for Ruger's big single-action, and a custom XP-100 that's built in the rifle shop in a variety of chamberings. All the trimmings make these guns expensive, but then Ken Jarrett isn't marketing low price. He's giving his customers the smoothest-functioning, most accurate gun he can make, and charging just enough to keep the business going.

Before Jarrett Rifles, Inc., arrived on the scene, the only armsmakers who could get $2,000 for a rifle or pistol were those who loaded them with embellishments—fancy wood, complex checkering patterns, intricate engraving, and the like. Some of these guns performed well and some didn't. The customer wasn't paying for accuracy; he was buying prestige. Whether Ken Jarrett has tapped a market nobody else has mined, or has created one nobody else could envision, remains a moot question. Certainly, the people at his cypress-board shop in Aiken County, South Carolina, don't have time to ponder this matter—they're too busy filling orders.

EPILOGUE

Guns have been called weapons, tools and works of art. They are all three, depending on what the maker and user have in mind. Their evolution and proliferation have accelerated in wartime because people have chosen them over screwdrivers and tablecloths as offensive and defensive weapons. Guns have enabled people to seize what is not their own as well as to protect what is. The bullet has no brain.

Like a stool or platform, a gun extends a person's reach. It expands his capabilities, increases his stature. A platform will accommodate without judgment demagogues and statesmen. Removing his platform gives scant pause to someone committed to a speech. Nor does it change the message.

Gunmaking used to be an accepted industry in the U.S. Your neighbor may have been a gunsmith, your son his apprentice. The mercantile store carried Winchesters and Colts along with garden seed, groceries and dry goods. People used guns to kill game animals for food, protect their crops and livestock and ensure the safety of their homes. Almost every man had a gun; few boys grew up without learning to shoot. By the time Americans turned their guns on each other in 1861, the gun industry had vacated its backwoods forges, moving to cities in the Northeast where it matured in great factories that employed thousands of workers.

Those factories remain; but some are skeletal in their hollow silence. The gun industry has fallen on hard times because Americans have long been without war. Since 1945, only limited military action has been sanctioned for U.S. troops; and an all-out war would now make limited use of the small arms we commonly think of as guns.

Sportsmen still use guns; but a gun lasts a long time, and hunting opportunities are dwindling. No longer does everyone see utility in a sporting gun. As opposition to blood sports mounts, guns become implements of cruelty, if not the cause of cruelty. Distinctions between barbarism and sportsmanship become blurred. An urban upbringing breeds little knowledge of or tolerance for a winter's venison or well-shot brace of partridge.

The genius of John Browning and his contemporaries, in an era when gun and cartridge design advanced at dizzying speed, is not lost to people who condemn guns now. "But that was another time," they say. "We no longer need guns." They point to hoodlums who brandish guns, children who shoot themselves. "Modern America is better off without guns." They'll not concede that a hoodlum is by profession a lawbreaker and would have guns even if gun ownership was banned. They'll not concede that harsh penalties for violent crime and conscientious gun handling in the home would prevent many assaults and accidents. They're quite willing to deny second-amendment rights to people who use guns for target shooting and hunting on the premise that such a sacrifice is necessary. They do not consider necessary the abolition of automobiles, though these are, statistically, the more deadly machines. Such logic hinges on the ownership of the gored ox.

The old men with files who chiseled art out of gun steel in the 19th century have been supplanted by young men with keyboards who make images dash about on computer screens. Could they meet, neither of these artisans would understand, quite, the motivation of the other. But understanding is not a requisite for change.

Gunmaking is moving out of the big factories now. Shooters look to specialists to sell them just what they want—not a gun to use for gathering meat as you might an ax for splitting wood, but a gun that offers the craftsmanship of another time. Major firms accommodate this trend with limited runs of firearms built for a special purpose or exceptionally well finished or designed after an obsolete model.

The resiliency and enterprise of America's gun industry has never been more severely tested. To the credit of its leadership and workers, it perseveres. Shooters cannot ensure its vitality as they once did; economic tides and people who don't shoot have great influence now. But the entrepreneurship and tenacity that built industrial empires in the 19th century are still available to sustain America's great gunmakers.

INDEX